BUSINESS ETHICS
TODAY

STEALING

WESTMINSTER
THEOLOGICAL SEMINARY

Center For Christian
BUSINESS ETHICS
Today

Business Ethics Today: Foundations
Copyright © 2011 Center for Christian Business Ethics Today, LLC.

ISBN 978-1-936927-00-5

BUSINESS ETHICS TODAY: STEALING was Published by the Center for Christian Business Ethics Today, 2424 E York St. Suite 226, Philadelphia, PA 19125, in association with Westminster Theological Seminary, P.O. Box 27009, Philadelphia, PA 19118.

Scripture quotations marked NIV are from HOLY BIBLE: NEW INTERNATIONAL VERSION®. © 1973, 1978, 1984 by International Bible Society. Used by permission of Zondervan Publishing House. All rights reserved.

Scripture quotations marked NASB are from NEW AMERICAN STANDARD BIBLE®, © The Lockman Foundation 1960, 1962, 1963, 1968, 1971, 1972, 1973, 1975, 1977, 1995. Used by permission.

Scripture quotations marked ESV are from THE ENGLISH STANDARD VERSION. © 2001 by Crossway Bibles, a division of Good News Publishers.

Scripture quotations marked KJV are from KING JAMES VERSION, AUTHORIZED STANDARD VERSION.

Scripture quotations marked NLT are from *Holy Bible*, New Living Translation. © 1996. Used by permission of Tyndale House Publishers, Inc., Wheaton, Illinois 60189. All rights reserved.

Scripture quotations marked NRSV are from NEW REVISED STANDARD VERSION of the Bible. © 1989 by the Division of Christian Education of the National Council of the Churches of Christ in the U.S.A. All rights reserved.

Additional Services in the publishing of the *Business Ethics Today: Conference Papers:*
Publishing services by KLO Publishing Service, LLC (www.KLOPublishing.com).
Cover design by Roark Creative Group (www.RoarkCreative.com).
Interior design by Katherine Lloyd (www.TheDESKonline.com).

THE CENTER FOR CHRISTIAN BUSINESS ETHICS TODAY

The Center for Christian Busienss Ethics Today was established in 2009 to address the need for the application of Christian principles to strengthen business operations. The Center's research shows that Christianity, as found in the Westminster Confession of Faith, laid the foundations for the commercial world, as we know it today. The current movement of society across the world risks the abandonment of these business practices. To reinvigorate the study of founding business principles, the Center challenges those sharing God's calling to business, to use God's Word and His principles to shape their engagement in business.

Visit us at www.cfcbe.com.

FORWARD AND ACKNOWLEDGEMENTS

This anthology is the result of the vision of John (Jack) Templeton, Jr., in seeing the need to look into the contribution of Christianity to our communities. In 2003, Templeton challenged Philip J. Clements, a fellow board member of the National Bible Association, to consider the contribution of Christianity to commerce. That challenge led to six years of research and analysis based upon both Clements' experience in business and his connection with Christianity personally and through his obtaining a Masters in Theological Studies at the Reformed Theological Seminary. The conclusion was that Templeton was right – Christianity that came out of the Reformation did create much of the commercial environment we experience today.

As part of their work on the National Bible Association, both Templeton and Clements connected with Peter A. Lillback, president of Westminster Theological Seminary (WTS). Clements and Lillback explored the possibility of a business ethics conference to begin the process of creating a business, seminary and church discourse on this important topic. That possibility bore fruit into an annual conference co-hosted by the Center for Christian Business Ethics Today, and the Westminster Theological Seminary. Many of the papers in this text were developed and presented for the 2011 conference, Business Ethics Today: Business and the Eighth Commandment.

The conversion of conference papers into a text requires extensive efforts by many people. Acknowledgement goes to Jon Cooper, the Center's director. Jon and the Center's staff tirelessly worked to organize the conference and to oversee the conversion to this text. Next, special thanks goes to the many encouragers for both this text and the work of the Center, particularly Wayne Grudem who helped solidify my thinking on the blessing of business, and the stealing that takes place in robbing the blessings of business. Additionally many thanks goes to all of the speakers and moderators who traveled from around the country and around the world to be at the conference and gave encouragement after the conference. Finally, I thank Julie Clements, my wife, who encouraged, supported, patiently endured the normal distractions of these kinds of projects and aided through many a reread.

Philip J. Clements, September 15, 2011

AUTHORS

Arranged by Chapter with Page Number

CONTENTS

BUSINESS ETHICS TODAY:
STEALING

INTRODUCTION: READER START HERE!

PHILIP J. CLEMENTS

*Two things have I required of thee; deny me not before I die: Remove far from me
vanity and lies:
Give me neither poverty nor riches: feed me with food convenient for me: Lest I be
full, and deny thee, and say, Who is the Lord? Or lest I be poor, and steal, and take
the name of my God in vain. Proverbs 30:7-9* [1]

The reader is encouraged to start with this introduction to better understand the purpose of the material in this text and the layout of the text. This text is an anthology of the papers developed for and presented at the Business Ethics Today: Business and the Eighth Commandment Conference (Conference) of June 10 and 11, 2011. To the Conference papers have been added two papers that add further richness to the topic being covered. The papers endeavor to address how the Eighth Commandment [2] affects the way we should engage in commerce.

This text is designed to be readable by those wanting to better understand the Eighth Commandment and business, to be a study tool for those wishing to delve deeper in this topic and a resource tool for those doing research. The Editorial Comments at the beginning of each Section are to assist the reader in understanding the messages in the Section's papers. The Appendix and the Indexes are to assist the researcher in finding material within the text.

Text Structure

The text has an Introduction, five Sections and an Appendix with supplemental material. The **Introduction** presents the overall framework for contemplating the Eighth Commandment in God's world. **Section 1 Theological Framework** presents the theological framework of the Decalogue and the Eighth Commandment as found in the Bible and in the *Westminster Larger Catechism,* [3] *(Catechism).* The Editor Comments summarize the various perspectives found in the papers on both the Decalogue and the Eighth Commandment. Two papers frame the theology for this Section. Peter A. Lillback covers the Decalogue and the Eighth Commandment. Philip Ryken, Robert Doll and Ron Ferner discuss a world without stealing. **Section 2 Property Rights and Human Flourishing** papers present the case for the Eighth Commandment as foundational for human flourishing. When God's precepts for His world are followed, mankind prospers. **Section 3 Social Structures and the Eighth Commandment** reviews modern issues of government, capitalism and socialism, and business profits against the mandate of the Eighth Commandment. The five papers present different perspectives on the shifting landscape of political-economic thought. **Section 4 Application of the Eighth Commandment to Business** has six papers. These papers give the reader a series of specific business settings and the violations of the Eighth Commandment. The reader will find a good illustration of how to use the Bible to answer business ethics questions. **Section 5 Church Leaders Helping the Business Person Keep the Eighth Commandment** papers endeavor to aid the Church Leader in understanding how to better minister to the business person in the congregation. At the beginning of each Section, Editor Comments provide a subject matter briefing and review the flow of the papers in the Section. The **Appendix** has two tables that the reader may find useful in applying the Eighth Commandment to business situations. The first is a "Chart on the Eighth Commandment and Business Practices" and the second is "List of Business Cases and Examples" used in the text's papers.

The Joy of Conference Papers

Papers prepared for Conference presentation are often viewed by editors with mixed emotions. Each paper has its own style, the paper explores the topic with its own perspective, and often, when the conference has a narrow topic, such as the Eighth Commandment, there appear to be overlaps. As the editor of this text, I have been blessed with knowing the authors of these papers and in listening to their presentations of the material. The richness that comes from papers on a topic that is as seemingly narrow as "Thou shalt not steal" testifies to the depth and breadth of God and His Creation.

The reader should take the time to consider the variety of ways the papers describe the Eighth Commandment, its setting, its richness in scope, and the importance to our world. The scale of theological thinking is extraordinary. For those of the business persuasion, that thinking should put us in awe of our God, His wonder and majesty, and humble us to pray a fervent prayer of thanks for His salvation, because we see how far our business practices are from His Holy standards. A single author cannot capture the sweep of this material as wonderfully as the many authors of these papers. Let us express our thanks for each person who has worked so hard and contributed so much. Please enjoy the papers as much as I have.

The need for the Introduction

This Introduction's title recommends to the reader - start here. Why? Since this book is an anthology, the papers address specific topics. The Introduction puts the papers into overall context and fills in the voids not covered by the papers. This text covers very rich subject matter, needing substantial contextualization. The Introduction provides this context and gives guidance where needed to better appreciate the material in the text.

The Introduction is not intended to be a presentation of the editor's views. As much as possible, the Introduction material will summarize paper material, with the paper's author being credited, or bring in other material, with credit given. If the editor feels that the material has migrated into a personal perspective, then a comment such as "in the editor's view" will be used. General knowledge or information will not be given a reference. To make this Introduction and the Editor Comments more readable general information will be used as much as possible rather than quotations from outside of this text.

Introduction topics

The topics covered in the Introduction set the context for the remainder of the text. Human Flourishing is a central theme for the first part of the Introduction. Then the Problem of Ethics is reviewed to better understand why mankind does not agree on what is right or how to do what is right. The problem of Stealing In Today's World presents the problem we face today.

The Christian Faith as found in the Bible and framed in the *West-*

minster Confession of Faith,[4] *(Confession)* underlies the principles to be discussed in this text and its papers. Throughout the editorial comments, the belief that Christianity directly impacts every aspect of a person's life, including our business conduct, and that Christianity creates a distinctive response to the events of life, will be assumed. The discussion on The Problem of Ethics explores why Christianity makes such a difference.

Human Flourishing

In Genesis chapters 1 and 2, God creates the heavens and earth and all that is in them. In this creation, God makes man in His own image and places man in the Garden of Eden to tend and keep it. When man is created and placed in the Garden, he is directed to be fruitful and multiply; fill the earth and subdue it; have dominion over it.[5] God gives man the abundance of the Garden for food.[6] God completes creation on the sixth day and declares that creation is very good.[7]

The picture painted by these simple statements is of God creating mankind to flourish on the earth. Part of that flourishing is to be reproduction; part is to have needs and wants fulfilled; part is to be able to exercise the creative "image of God" component of our nature in our dwelling upon the earth; and part is to be in fellowship with our Creator God. Flourishing is the term used for mankind's development and blessing. Before we consider why man has not achieved the flourishing envisioned in these statements, let us explore the world order that God had intended to create such flourishing.[8]

God, as Creator, owns all, including us. He gives what He wishes to whom He wishes. The receiver is not the owner relative to God, because it and the receiver belong to God. Vern Poythress and John Coors say in their paper,[9] "God is the owner of the whole world, and he gives as gifts whatever we have. So God calls on us to respect human ownership, which is derivative from and reflective of God's original divine ownership." Calvin Chin and William Goligher in their paper describe it this way

> In His Providence, God gives people property so in the Old Testament we find each family in Israel given a portion of land in Canaan (Exod. 33:1-3; Lev.25:10-55) while, in the New Testament, believers own houses and lands (Acts 12:12; 16:14; 21:8). Abraham makes a business deal with the Hittites to buy a burial plot for his wife Sarah, while Paul ply's his trade as a

tentmaker to support his gospel work. And His generosity is not confined only to his own people, but He shows common grace to the family of unbelieving Cain so that they become innovators in the areas of agriculture and metallurgy for Jabal 'was the father of all those who dwell in tents and have livestock,' while Tubal-Cain 'was the forger of all instruments of bronze and iron' (Gen. 4:20-22). Common grace would bring forth the argument that there is no sacred and secular divide. We are to be God's instruments and work with all people, in our communities, to bring glory to the King. [10]

Chin and Goligher's description helps frame the fullness of what God gives to each person. God gives a person time on earth, talents and skill, and property interests. Therefore, all that a person has comes from God and belongs to God.

An additional point in Chin and Goligher's paper is the concept of common grace. Human flourishing applies to all mankind. God designed the world to be a place for humans to flourish. This condition is called common grace. In Gen 8:22, God describes a measure of common grace where He promises that there will be seasons or predictability on the earth. Jesus describes common grace as the sun shining on the good and the bad.[11] Common grace is fundamental to understanding how the world works. But we must remember that common grace is an extension of God's providence. The *Confession* Chapter 5 "Of Providence" states the richness of God's providence that makes the world work. Providence is a term understudied today, but which we all count upon for our daily lives.

Other people are to respect God's choice of what and to whom He has given what is His. Therefore, one person cannot take what God has given to another. These simple statements are the foundation of property ownership as framed in the Bible and the Eighth Commandment. "God's will defines its scope and purpose. We do not have the right to re-interpret and re-define it according to our own desires. This principle is relevant for business, where each party is tempted to define moral standards in his own favor."[12]

God owns everything and has charged mankind with tending and keeping it. Mankind is charged with stewardship of that which God has given. Stewardship is not consumption or preservation. Luke 19:11-27 is a parable of Jesus' that makes it very clear that God expects us to employ what He has given to us and to create more. God gave mankind part of His image which includes His creativity. God expects us to use this creativity in exercising our stewardship responsibilities.

God did not design the world to be a "zero-sum" game. "Zero-sum" is more fully explored in Section 2. In a "zero-sum" situation, nothing gets added to the available resources. Instead God makes it clear that He is not limited as to resources. We are limited as to what He has given to us to utilize for His purposes, but we are also told to look to Him for more. Therefore, mankind can create more. The business environment is a critical component of creating more. For example, if there is one blueberry pie, a "zero-sum" approach to its division between those who wish some is to cut smaller pieces. What this means is that a person who desires a larger piece, will feel the need to take someone else's piece. In God's world, the answer is to make another pie or two so all can have as much as they want.

Adding the modern economist to this mix, we would get the suggestion of raising prices to the point where supply, one pie, meets demand; only those with enough funds can buy the piece that can be afforded. Such a world causes the rich to flourish, where those with less go without. In God's world, the rich are not the only people blessed. Because more pie can be made, prices can be driven down. Many more can share in the abundance. This blessing of creating more directly relates to property ownership, the creativity given by God to humans, and the stewardship function of using what God has given to further bless God's creation.

So we see that the outcome of a proper perspective on property ownership is another series of principles. The world can be viewed as a place of abundance and opportunity. Some are given the ability to see needs and the resources to meet these needs and the talent to create increase in this process. The community benefits from the needs being met. Those who create increase with what God has given, keep the increase as part of God's further blessing. And the circle continues since those who have been blessed use the blessing to meet more needs of the community, while creating further increase. The community is blessed by having more resources available to meet its member's needs and wants.

This short summary is how God's providence in giving resources to individual humans in His earth create human flourishing.

Role of capitalism in human flourishing
People struggle with the definition of capitalism. The editor's preference is the following three principles: (1) Privately owned enterprises responding

to a need seen in God's world decide what and how much to produce and at what price to sell in order to be profitable. (2) Labor is free to develop and sell its skills and services to enterprises. (3) As God's stewards, owners, including laborers, reinvest profits in their enterprises rather than using them for personal consumption.[13] Let us consider each briefly, because the natural outcome of respect for property in God's world is generally referred to as capitalism.

The first principle describes business's core activity. Business sees or anticipates a need in the community. Then business determines how to meet the need at a cost and price which the community can afford, while the business makes a profit. Business is fundamentally about meeting needs in the community.

The second principle recognizes that God gives to each person individual capacities. Some people are to lead companies; some are to work in them. Before God all people are of equal worth. But God-given talents, including both skill and energy, should be respected. A laborer is charged with the same stewardship responsibilities for his skills and skill development as is the land owner. Therefore, the laborer cannot waste the available time or energy God has given to him, but is to seek diligently to use it for God's blessing.

The result of the first two principles is that there is increase, or gain, or profit. Simply put there is more value in the world because of the activities of the business and the worker. What should be done with this increase? Because it belongs to God and in turn to those whom God has entrusted the increase, the increase should be reinvested into God's world. What should not happen is that the increase is completely consumed by the individual entrusted for the individual's pleasure. Please note that not addressed here is the dynamics of how a person decides on what is appropriate for their consumption levels. Section 3 has some important observations on respecting God's determination of who gets the increase and what the person is to do with the increase.

That capitalism is part of God's creation for human flourishing is very clear. Capitalism is a natural outcome of the way God would have the world function, not a human created institution. Where capitalism has functioned properly, the communities have been blessed beyond all other times in human history. This is well documented in *The Protestant Ethics and the Spirit of Capitalism*[14] and *Culture Matters*.[15]

Free markets and capitalism

Larry Kudlow, a CNBC evening TV show host, declares that "free market capitalism is the best path to prosperity." Kudlow links free market with capitalism, as do most people. Instead it is better to understand that markets and capitalism are actually two separate and distinct concepts that affect the business world. The definition of capitalism, above, does not require free markets. Rather it does require respect for ownership of property, i.e., time, talent, and treasure.

But what about markets and the need for markets to be free for human flourishing? Markets are about the buying and selling of goods and services. Markets are settings where individuals can come together to get their needs and wants satisfied by those who can meet them. In the market an individual with a product can offer it to one who has a need or desire for the product. The two agree on the price and the exchange is made. This is how markets work.

Free markets allow buyers and sellers to come together without oversight or restraint. The freedom to negotiate the terms of the exchange is the second component of a free market. The seller needs to have a price that gives him a profit. The buyer needs the price to be within his available resources for meeting this particular need. A third component of a free market is the sharing of risk, but alas this is beyond the scope of this paper.

Efficient markets improve the exchange of goods and services between those who have needs and wants and those who have the capacity to supply such needs and wants. This exchange is fundamental to human flourishing. Therefore, efficiency in markets can be said to be fundamental to human flourishing.

In conclusion, the principles of capitalism and markets are fundamental to the way God created the world. Respect for ownership of property, i.e., time, talent, and treasure, as set forth in the Eighth Commandment, is a further fundamental component of the world God would see. These principles are as fundamental to God's world's design as scientific components such as gravity and time. Business has principles such as revenue less expenses equals profits. For the physical scientist, gravity is studied as a given; so, for the commercial enterprise business principles are a given. However, commercial enterprises tend to have a strong human element. This human element obscures the principles and thus determining proper behavior becomes a blending of principle and ethics. An analogy would be the use of gravity to drop an atom bomb. Is gravity bad? Similarly, the making of profits is fundamental to business. When we say that profits are bad, it is the same as if we were to say that gravity is bad.

The Fall of Man

If capitalism and markets are fundamental to the way God made the world, then why have they not been standard in the world's history? The Christian faith holds the answer to both why these two components have not been part of the history of mankind and why in the past 400 years, their presence has arisen.

The Old Testament describes the fall of man in Genesis chapter 3. Simply put, man rejected God's requirement and decided he wanted what he was not to have. The implications to man's thinking strike directly at the Eighth Commandment. God told Adam that Adam was not to eat of the tree of knowledge of good and evil. But Adam disobeyed and took it for himself. Stealing. The papers in this text articulate these implications well, because this act of stealing happens today.

Change in character

For the purpose of this text it is important to see that mankind continues to reject God's requirements. In the fall, mankind's very character was changed such that man fundatmentally does not want to do what God requires. Man knows what he should do, but does not do it. Similarly, man knows what he should not do, and does it.[16]

Genesis 9:6 says that mankind retains a measure of God's image even after the fall. Therefore, the creativity and knowledge of God's framework for the world remain. Romans 1:18ff says that man continues to reject this knowledge. The principle of common grace says that God's providence and goodness abound such that even when mankind rejects God's principles a measure of blessing still flows to man.

Satan's role in the Universe

To this discussion of human character and the effect of the fall needs to be added a brief introduction to the spiritual dimension of the universe. In Genesis chapter 3 Satan is introduced as the serpent that successfully tempted Adam and Eve to eat of the forbidden fruit, thereby rejecting God's order. Satan is said to be a liar and destroyer;[17] a being who desires to be God;[18] and a usurper. Satan is active in the affairs of mankind as shown in the book of Job. God gives Satan permission to test Job, whereupon Satan destroys Job's business, family and health. Yet, Job remains faithful to God. For this discussion, we need to see that in addition to mankind and mankind's character, there is an additional spiritual dimension to the world. In Ephesians 6, Paul says that we do not struggle only in the physical world, but we also struggle against principalities and powers in the spiritual world.

Much more needs to be said on these matters, but space does not allow for more than this brief introduction to these important foundations to the world in which we do business.

Implications to commerce
What does this mean to commerce? This means that people will have a propensity to do bad things, but can do good. Since the basics of commerce are like gravity, they can be learned and followed and will produce success, even success defined as profits.

Christianity's explanation of why the world is as it is should help explain why business and commerce are rejected. The misrepresentation of capitalism should be seen as a continuation of man's rejection of God's order for the world. Labeling profits bad, or the rich as evil, are all part of this rejection. Placing restrictions on markets or limitations on business serve to destroy the human flourishing that God intended.

At the same time, the Christian understands that people engaged in business will abuse their customers and engage in evil actions, because of the fall. The propensity to maximize profits, to create wealth for personal gain, the entrapment of customers, the overreaching in transactions, and such business actions all relate to man's fallen nature.

The book *Culture Matters* touches on the fact that it is clear that mankind has indeed systematically undermined its capacity to flourish. At the Business Ethics Today: Eighth Commandment conference, Wayne Grudem handed out a photograph of Phoenix and the surrounding tribal lands as a comparison of flourishing and non-flourishing environments. Phoenix area had neat houses where people lived wonderful air-conditioned lives. The tribal lands appeared as abandoned wastelands. But a little research would show that the tribe was very wealthy.

Man knows that these behaviors are not the way things should be. Thus we have the current discussions on business ethics.

The Problem of Ethics
What are ethics? The terms ethics, morals, and values tend to get mixed in common usage. The editor recommends using ethics as the standards by which behavior is judged and morals as the individual's values that lead to

actions. Values are based on an individual's faith or beliefs, with upbringing forming a significant component of that faith.

How do ethics fit into the discussion of capitalism and commerce and the Eighth Commandment? The Eighth Commandment is one of God's standards for behavior.[19] Because it is God's world, not stealing is proper ethical behavior. This means that all humans are to respect each other's property, including time, talent and treasure. But because mankind has fallen and rejects God's standards, we should not be surprised to see mankind systematically undermining the respect for property ownership.

Humanistic philosophy
Worse is that mankind makes up other ethical frameworks to justify his behavior. Section 3 is a partial discussion about how the modern man has rethought property ownership and the concepts of profits. But a quick exploration here of some mankind level concepts of ethics is useful. Peter Lillback covers these in his papers. Mankind's perspectives on ethics are generally found in the social science called philosophy.

The first observation about philosophy is that like all science it is an outsider perspective on what is happening. Like all social sciences, the philosopher is trying to explain what is happening to mankind through observation and to set out some parameters that will enhance mankind's world. The perspective is not grounded in an independently defined standard, but on the philosopher's views of proper behavior. This is one of the clearest things about philosophy, that there is not agreement on a standard for evaluating behavior. Once there is a diversity of views, then mankind is left with relativism, which in turn leads to anarchy.

The second observation about philosophy is that the Christian knows that in man's fallen state, he rejects God's truth. The philosopher may know of God's standards for behavior, but will reject them. The rejection may be overt or covert. Therefore, it is to be expected that man's ethics will undermine God's standards, including God's blessing. Undermining God's standards for behavior is often troubling, because mankind claims to know how to be good and claims that on balance it is pretty good. However, the facts in history show man does not do good and he undermines the blessings God would have for his fellow man. Modern social treatment of business is an example of stealing the blessings that God would have for a community while claiming to be doing good for mankind. Cowan's paper specifically addresses this problem.

A further problem with man's views of proper behavior standards is man's notions of self interest. Many social scientists believe that man does what is in his best interest. Cowen addresses this point in his paper when he reviews the notion of self-interest and selfishness. Mankind acts selfishly, rather than in his self-interest. History shows this to be the case as well.

A final observation goes to mankind's efforts to rationalize away the difference in behaviors and to develop a uniform approach to the question of what are the right standards for mankind. It should not surprise a Christian that philosophy does not hold an answer for where to find standards for behavior. In *Business Ethics Today: Foundations*,[20] this topic is explored more fully. Here we note that philosophy cannot find uniform standards, and what standards may be articulated, simply are not followed. The reason is that man is fallen and in his selfishness cannot follow standards. The answer remains that the Bible is God's standard for mankind's behavior and Jesus is the answer to how we fulfill these standards now and forever.

Why Christian ethics are different

For the Christian, the Bible declares the ethical standards for behavior are found in the law of God, which is found in the Bible. Jesus made it clear that the standards apply to the individual's heart not just his actions.[21]

Giving God all of the glory and honor

What is the core purpose for the actions of man against which he is to be evaluated? The *Catechism* in its first question asks what is the chief end of man? And the answer is to glorify God and enjoy Him forever. All of our actions should be motivated to glorify God or to enjoy Him. Jesus in the Pastoral prayer in John 17 articulated this well when He said,

> "I have glorified You on the earth. I have finished the work which You have given Me to do. And now, O Father, glorify Me together with Yourself, with the glory which I had with You before the world was." John 17:4-5.

> "Father, I desire that they also whom You gave Me may be with Me where I am, that they may behold My glory which You have given Me; for You loved Me before the foundation of the world. O righteous Father! The world has not known You, but I have known You; and these have known that You sent Me. And I have declared to them Your name, and will declare it,

that the love with which You loved Me may be in them, and I
in them." John 17:24-26.

In this picture is the wonder of our salvation – that we might be filled with
the love of God, even as Jesus shared that love.

Why does mankind not have this love naturally? Genesis 3 describes man placing himself first, ahead of God. In effect, man became selfish. Satan said that man could become like gods, rather than being as God
had designed us. And so it began, man ate the forbidden fruit, fell from a
state of goodness and now has a propensity to be selfish. As we consider
why mankind does not respect property ownership, we need to see this
selfishness as one of the causes. In Section 1 some of the other causes will
be explored. But for now, let us consider the contrast of Jesus' prayer and
these concepts of self-interest and selfishness.

There is a difference between self-interest and selfishness. Jesus
shows that balance in His pastoral prayer in John 17.

Jesus' self-interest is shown by Jesus requesting, "O Father, glorify
Me together with Yourself, with the glory which I had with You before the
world was." Having faithfully completed the work God requested, Jesus
asks for God to reinstate Him. Reading the passage, the balance between
being given glory and giving glory to God, the Father, is powerfully clear.
Jesus asks for His glory to be such that the Father is glorified. Similarly,
when Jesus prays for the disciples it is that the Father might be glorified.

Similarly, the work that Jesus did was to fulfill the Father's request.
It was to give honor to the Father. A quick study of the Gospels shows
that Jesus faced the same issues and needs as we do today.[22] Sometimes He
met needs, even of those who did not ask. Sometimes He had to chastise.
Sometimes He just had to work. Sometimes He was tired and needed to
retire to seek physical, spiritual and personal strengthening. All of these
things Jesus did to honor and glorify God. It was then for God to give
Jesus honor and glory.

For Christians in business, this model applies. We are given a calling, a business, by God. We may or may not have asked for this calling,
but we are to do it faithfully. In exercising our calling, we will encounter
all of the trials, tribulations and blessing that Jesus encountered. Yet, in
all, we need to keep our perspective that it is God whom we serve and to
whom all of the glory and honor need to go.

Enjoying God forever – Living in God's presence today
What about enjoying God forever? This passage in John 17 finds Jesus praying about the wondrous love that He shared with God, "You loved Me before the foundation of the world." As we listen to this prayer in the words of John, we hear the depth of a love from eternity. It is a love of fellowship. A love of oneness. Jesus then prays that we will share this same love, "And I have declared to them Your name, and will declare it, that the love with which You loved Me may be in them, and I in them." It is our relationship with Jesus that enables us to experience this love.

So the Christian is in Christ and experiencing the loving oneness with the Father. This unique relationship exists only in the Bible and it was the Reformation that created the fuller awareness of this wondrous position that comes from placing our trust in the finished work of Jesus on the cross. The Reformation added a number of theological points to this understanding, one of which is noted here – assurance. The Christian, who truly believes and places his trust in Christ, is saved. The Reformers noted that even before the foundations of the world, God knew who would be saved. Jesus noted this same point in John 17, when He indicated that He did not come for the whole world, but for those whom the Father gave to Him. Because of this assurance of salvation, the Christian knows that when he dies, he will be immediately in the presence of God. Further the Christian knows that he is indwelt by God through the Holy Spirit adding to that assurance. Therefore, the Christian should live everyday as if he were walking in God's very presence, enjoying God forever – starting now. [23]

What is interesting is that assurance was the distinction seen by Max Weber and written in his work *The Protestant Ethic and the Spirit of Capitalism*.[24] The Protestant ethic is a behavior pattern grounded in and coming out of this faith. Weber was not a Christian and did not understand the implications of assurance and tried to rationalize it away as a works based effort. However, Weber did see Protestant assurance of salvation as the distinctive and that this distinctive created a different conduct. That conduct changed the way commerce was and is done.

Enjoying God forever – Enjoying fulfillment
For the business person, we get enjoyment out of exercising our God given time, talent, and treasure for the glory of God. Enjoyment is also fulfillment. For God created us for a purpose, which purpose was to be part of His world. In being in His world we contribute to it in our individual

fashion because He made us who we are. Therefore, He expects us to meet our God given needs and desires. Some are natural, like needing food to sustain ourselves, and some are personal, like preferring beets to potatoes. But all are to be exercised so that we can bring God glory, even as Jesus brought God glory when He turned water into wine so that a wedding party could go on without embarrassment. This first miracle of Jesus is one of the great testimonies that God does love us and made us and His world for blessings. We need to enjoy Him in His world.

When we exercise the God-given time, talents, and treasure as business people, we become a blessing to our communities. We see needs and wants of others in the community and develop businesses that can meet those needs profitably. The result is there is more blessing in the world, in God's world. The world is enjoying God through His blessing, which may be coming from the people He has created and empowered to do business.

Enjoying God forever – Experiencing God's love
The Christian's answer to why assurance makes the behavior change, is that we do indeed experience the loving oneness with God through Jesus Christ by the power of the Holy Spirit within us. Therefore, the Christian will go into the world enjoying God forever, living in the presence of God's love. A number of the papers in this text emphasize this concept of God's love and that it is love which creates proper behavior. Jesus' prayer in John 17 does point us in this direction.

The problem of continued sin
The problem the Christian has and the world points to, is that while we are here on earth, we are saved but not perfect. Therefore, the Christian will still engage in sinful acts.[25] The Christian still violates the Eighth Commandment. The Christian is perfected only in glory, in heaven after this life.

Even with this drawback on the Christian life, it is clear that the Christian business person will be different. We are God's witnesses to the power of His salvation.[26] The Christian is to be prepared to give an answer to those who ask about the hope that is within us.[27] The Christian business person goes through his days operating with a different perspective, because he has the hope of eternity with God, starting this very day.

Recognizing that God makes people different
Further, in evaluating ethics and behavior of Christians, it is helpful to

see that God creates people different. Just as birds are different, so people are different. We accept this in stature and gender. But we struggle with needs, wants, desires, capabilities, and achievements. The Declaration of Independence says that we are all created equal. The Bible makes it clear that we are all equal before God, but we are also all individuals before God. Modern man has perverted the notion of equality to mean that we are all the same. Yet, the God that can create such a variety of birds, of fishes, of dogs, of cats, and the list can go on, must be a God that loves diversity. It is clear that each individual is different. The love of God is such that He enjoys our differences, He made us this way.

In the business world these differences are very real. One aspect of differences is the ability to see actions and consequences. Some people just go blindly along, whereas others are able to anticipate issues and outcomes. Discipline is another attribute. Some are more disciplined than others and the results are clear. Social conscience is something that some individuals have far more than others. What is clear as well is that an individual can develop himself. An undisciplined individual cannot claim to be created as undisciplined, blaming his poor performance on God. Proverbs over and again instructs the undisciplined to develop discipline. But we do need to recognize that individuals are gifted and that these gifts become part of God's blessings to the community.

Stealing In Today's World

The question often raised is whether ethics in business have declined over the decades. The general sense is that yesterday was a better time; today, society is on the brink of disaster. But stealing is an increasing problem in commerce today. Let us consider two reasons for this increase: (1) the cultural foundations of commerce have shifted and (2) the capacity to steal has increased.

Alas, the culture of the world is shifting. In *Foundations* Chuck Colson[28] and K. Scott Oliphint[29] each have papers that note the relativism that is sweeping the world. They explain that a relativistic world has no authority for ethics. Instead, each person's view is equal to another's view. Respect for property rights falls directly into this view. One person declares that all property should be owned by the community, allowing property to be taken away by community leaders and given to another. On the other hand, someone says that what they create belongs to them as creator. Which is correct? In the relativistic world we are living in, both are viewed as correct. The answer of which view will govern behavior goes to the person or people with the power or authority to enforce their view. This makes ethics "Might Makes Right." But most people would agree that such a conclusion is completely unsatisfactory. In this text, Sections 2 and 3 explore this problem of shifting views in society. Even the Church today is not free from the subtle influence of the siren song of equality of outcomes.

Reinforcing the idea that there is a change in culture, are the books *Clash of Civilizations*,[30] *Culture Matters*,[31] and *Who are we?*,[32] where Samuel Huntington makes his case that religions create the culture in a society. Since the fall of the iron curtain in 1989, faith has increased in the world. With increasing diversity of faith has come increasingly faith-based cultural structures. Huntington's point is that various world faiths do not have or create the same values. Therefore, the world will be increasingly diverse in its value systems. Business has to understand the scope of these differences. An example of the difference can be found by Centenary College closing it campuses in China and Taiwan in July, 2010.

> The cheating was so extensive that the Hackettstown [New Jersey] college is withholding degrees from all 400 Chinese-speaking students in its master's of business administration programs in Beijing, Shanghai and Taiwan, said Debra Albanese, Centenary's vice president for strategic advancement.[33]

The war on terror has created an environment where religious extremism is acknowledged. Those in the mainstay of any religion are viewed to hold the same core values as people in every other part of the world. This is a particularly American idea. However, Centenary was dealing with the culture embodied in the students from the community and found that community's values inconsistent with American values. Huntington is correct; different faiths create different cultures with different values.

The Center for Christian Business Ethics Today's [34] (Center) research points to the fact that Christianity, as articulated in the *Confession*, created a change in commerce ethics that is not found in any other religion. This means that as the cultures of the world become more separate, the faith values underlying these cultures will become more prevalent in commerce. The principles of the Eighth Commandment are unique to the Judeo-Christian community. Therefore, it is to be expected that the world will see more stealing, even as Centenary experienced cheating on its campuses.

At this point, it should be acknowledged that many people, including Christian theologians, will disagree with the above statements. *Foundations* is recommended to the reader who wishes to obtain a better understanding of some of these foundational principles. Suffice it to say that this disagreement in modern Christianity and the shifts in global culture for commerce are the underlying reasons for the formation of the Center. Failure to study, understand, apply and train on the foundational principles that were articulated 400 years ago, means that these principles will be lost. Even as Israel lost its knowledge of God's work and fell away,[35] so we too can lose the blessings of commerce by not following and training the next generation in the principles that have been part of God's blessing to the world from the Reformation.

The second observation on whether there is more stealing today in commerce goes to the notion that there are more opportunities to steal. In the Appendix: List of Business Cases and Examples, the papers' cases and examples of stealing in commerce are listed. It is a useful overview of the variety of stealing activities. The Appendix: Chart on the Eighth Commandment and Business Practices contains a chart of the *Catechism's* list of stealing situations as applied to business.

Let us consider some of the ways stealing occurs today through situations that could not exist even decades ago. Two examples are cited here: identity theft and public place security. While the *Catechism's* list in the Appendix suggests that stealing was always prevalent, these two examples point to a basic change in culture and its effect on commerce.

Identity theft is a hot topic today. When identity theft happens, the following have been stolen: (a) the actual identity, (b) the funds and credit taken with the identity, (c) the freedom of use of our identity, because of the need for passwords and other passive security, (d) our funds, because all of the security systems cost money, (e) the freedom to engage in business without the burden of the liability for the threat of someone taking the entrusted identity, (f) the time that it takes to log in and keep security current, and (g) the freedom from worry about our identities as we conduct our daily lives. Laws have been passed making it a crime to take an identity. Laws have been passed making those entrusted with an identity liable, if they allow a theft of the identity. Numerous new businesses provide services to protect our identities.

Airport, transport and office security are other areas to consider. In many cultures streets are lined with walls, and behind the walls are where people do business or live their lives. The United States has a uniquely open society, where a rolling lawn joins a house to a street or a white picket fence is the wall. What is the difference? Walled streets arose in a time when stealing was so prevalent that safety of person and property required enclosure. A visit to the leadership of Nigeria in 2006 showed the walled environment. A visit to Guatemala in 2009 showed the same environment. Both the Nigerian and Guatemalan areas visited were constructed in the past decade. Culture? Yes. Need? Yes. The razor wire that was prevalent in both countries testifies to the need for protection of person and property. The editor's observation to the leadership of African countries meeting in Nigeria, was that in the United States, razor wire is used predominately to keep bad people in, rather than people out.

Let us journey back to the United States today. You cannot get into an office building without a security clearance. Twenty years ago this was an exception, generally for government offices where secrets existed or military bases. In addition, many buildings have pilings to prevent a vehicle from driving up to or into the building. Why is this? The events of 9/11/2001 and the follow-on events caused the United States to have to implement protections of person and property. What about walled and gated communities? Indeed, over the decades the U.S. has seen an increasing amount of walled or gated communities. Many were for status, but today many are for safety of person and property. Finally, we can consider travel security. Due to 9/11/2001 and its progeny, the U.S. has implemented an increasing amount of security to try to prevent another attack. While the list is long, the most notable is airport screening, especially the newer full body scan, and related body pat-downs. What has been stolen by these actions? (a) Our presumed innocence, which is little discussed today. All people are now presumed to be terrorists or people with evil intent, until the scan or I.D. proves them innocent; (b) Our freedom of movement; (c) Our money because of the costs to install and maintain these systems; and (d) Our dignity when we have to subject our person to pat-downs.

The list of increased opportunities for stealing can go on, but the point is made. Today we not only see more stealing, we have to invest an increasing amount of our time, talent and treasure in our security. Clearly the Eighth Commandment was given to point to a world which was much better than what we are seeing evolve before our very eyes.

Notes

1. King James Version, approved in 1611 by King James of England for use by the Churches of England, is the text quoted, unless otherwise noted.
2. The Eighth Commandment is found in Exodus 20:15 and Deuteronomy 5:19. Some Christian communities interpret the Decalogue such that the Commandment, Thou shall not steal, is the Seventh Commandment. For the purposes of this text, the Protestant numbering for the Commandments is used.
3. *Westminster Larger Catechism*, Approved 1648, Free Presbyterian Publications, 1958.
4. *Westminster Confession of Faith*, first published 1646, reprinted Glasgow: Free Presbyterian Publications, 2001.
5. Genesis 1:28.
6. Genesis 1:29, 30; 2:15-17.
7. Genesis 1:31.
8. The world order for human flourishing begs to be properly answered based on the fullness of the Bible. Human flourishing is used to frame a positive perspective for the world. Alas, that world does not exist. The Decalogue and the Eighth Commandment were given to point man in the direction of this world. Paul tells us that God gave the law so that sin may grow. Rom 5:20. The law is to point out our sins and our need for a savior. Gal 3:24. Paul also says that where sin grows, God provides the needed salvation. Rom 5:21. In short, God is in the soul saving business and gave the Decalogue and the Eighth Commandment so that we could see our need for His savior, Jesus Christ.
9. Vern Poythress, John Coors, "Contracts and the Destructive Effects of Unfaithfulness."
10. Calvin Chin, William Goligher, "The Eighth Commandment and Respect for Capital."
11. Matthew 5:45.
12. Poythress.
13. See footnote 27, "Introduction," *Business Ethics Today:Foundations*, Philip J. Clements ed. (Philadelphia: Westminster Seminary Press, 2011) p. 23 for a fuller review of the definition of capitalism.
14. Max Weber, *The Protestant Ethic and the Spirit of Capitalism*, 1904, Translated, Talcott Parsons, rept. New York: Scribner's, 1958.
15. Lawrence E. Harrison and Samuel P. Huntington, ed.s, *Culture Matters: How Values Shape Human Progress*, New York: Basic, 2000.
16. In Romans 7 and 8 Paul describes that he does what he knows he should not do, and does not do what he knows he should do. Chapter 8 is the declaration that even still the Christian remains assured of his salvation.
17. John 8:44, 1 Peter 5:8
18. Isaiah 14:12-17.
19. In Matthew 5:17-20, Jesus says he came to fulfill the law, God's law, not to abolish it. Jesus goes on in the Sermon on the Mount to clarify the depth of the challenge of God's laws and to make it clear that all of God's laws are the standard for human behavior.
20. *Business Ethics Today:Foundations*, Philip J. Clements ed., Philadelphia: Westminster Seminary Press, 2011.
21. Man attempts a similar kind of evaluation in the criminal action standard, where it is not just the action but also criminal intent that is required.
22. Hebrews 4:15
23. In "Introduction," *Foundations*, p17, a more detailed discussion of why the Christian with assur-

ance lives differently is presented. A key factor is the awareness of the presence of God and that we live under His watchful care. Another factor listed in this Introduction is the Christian's love for God for providing such a wondrous redemption at such a high cost.

24. Weber, note 15.
25. Romans 7.
26. Acts 1:8.
27. 1 Peter 3:15.
28. Chuck Colson, "The Problem of Ethics," *Business Ethics Today: Foundations*, Westminster Seminary Press, 2011, p. 35-52.
29. K. Scott oliphint, "Prolegomena to the Practice of Ethics in Business," *Business Ethics Today: Foundations*, Westminster Seminary Press, 2011, p. 53-76.
30. Samuel P. Huntington, *Clash of Civilizations and the Remaking of World Order*, New York: Touchstone, 1996.
31. Harrison.
32. Samuel P. Huntington, *Who are we? The Challenges to America's National Identity*, New York: Simon, 2004
33. http://www.nj.com/news/index.ssf/2010/07/centenary_college_closes_satel.html
34. The Center for Christian Business Ethics Today, LLC was formed in 2009 to develop material to help the Christian business person operate his business with biblical business principles based on Protestant Christianity. The Center co-hosted the conference that is the source of the papers for this text.
35. Judges 2:10-11, "And also all that generation were gathered unto their fathers: and there arose another generation after them, which knew not the LORD, nor yet the works which he had done for Israel. And the children of Israel did evil in the sight of the LORD, and served Baalim."

SECTION 1

THEOLOGICAL FRAMEWORK

FOR THE DECALOGUE AND THE EIGHTH COMMANDMENT

SECTION 1: THEOLOGICAL FRAMEWORK

FOR THE DECALOGUE AND THE EIGHTH COMMANDMENT

PHILIP J. CLEMENTS

The Editor Comment for Section 1, Theological Framework for the Decalogue and the Eighth Commandment, reviews the theology surrounding the Decalogue and the Eighth Commandment. Then the specific duties and sins of the Eighth Commandment are explored as these relate to business. Many of the papers in this text have comments on the Decalogue and the Eighth Commandment. This comment endeavors to capture and synthesize these observations.

Section 1 has two papers. Peter A. Lillback provides an overview of the Decalogue and the Eighth Commandment in order to provide a framework for the rest of the text. Philip Ryken, Robert Doll, and Ron Ferner in "An Optimistic Look at the 8th Commandment" provide a look at the world if the Commandment were followed. The development of this paper is very challenging because we live in a fallen world where it is hard to fully envision how it would function if everyone followed something as simple as "Thou shalt not steal."

Section 1 Editor Comment is not intended to be a presentation of the editor's views. As much as possible, the comments present material found within this text, with the paper's author(s) being credited, or bring in other material, with credit given. If the editor feels that the material has migrated into a personal perspective, then a comment such as "in the editor's view" will be used. General knowledge or information will not be given a reference. To make the Editor Comment more readable, general information will be used as much as possible rather than quotations from outside of this text.

Before jumping into the specifics of the Decalogue or Eighth Commandment, we need to pause and consider the sources of the material to guide our discussion. The *Westminster Confession of Faith* [1] Chapter 1 "Of the Holy Scripture" articulates the Reformers' fundamental concept that the Bible is the authorative document for understanding God and His will. *Sola Scriptura*, Scripture alone, was the principle. The Center for Christian Business Ethics Today [2] (Center) adopts this perspective. Therefore, principles discussed need to be referenced, where possible, to passages in the Bible. Church documents are secondary material and need to be used as such. The *Confession* and *Westminster Larger Catechism* [3] (Catechism) are used to frame the discussion of business ethics, because these documents express the foundation, with Biblical references, of Protestant Christianity. The Center's research shows that Protestant Christianity created commerce as we know it today. Another advantage of using the *Confession* and the *Catechism* is that it allows for a discussion on a given set of interpretations and applications, rather than on differing views of what the Bible may or may not say or mean. Within Christianity there is a broad spectrum of interpretations of the same material. President Lincoln articulated this dilemma well in his second inaugural address.[4] Within this text the Protestant interpretations of Scripture are used because of the Center's findings with regard to the Protestant ethic's effect on commerce.

THE DECALOGUE

Exodus 20:2-17 and Deuteronomy 5:6-21 record what is commonly referred to as the Decalogue or the Ten Commandments. Who is the author of The Ten Commandments? It is the God of Abraham, Isaac, and Jacob; the God and Father of our Lord Jesus Christ. These are the ten sets of words that out of the whole Bible were spoken and then inscribed by God Himself.[5] The books of Moses, the Pentateuch, contain the Decalogue. The Pentateuch was written about 3,500 years ago.

This raises the question of whether these rules are for mankind, the Israelites alone, or an expression of God's character. Christians interpret the Decalogue as a set of rules to be observed. Certainly they are this. The Decalogue was given by God as a framework for the more specific laws that man is to follow. Jesus affirms that every part of the law is to be complied with in Matthew 5:17-20. This principle that God is oriented to the "jot and tittle" speaks to the level of detail and discipline we need as Christians in our business lives.

Galatians 3 and Romans 5:20 declare that the law cannot be complied with, but is designed to reveal to us our sins and to point us to Christ's redemptive work. In Matthew 5 – 7 and Luke 6, in the Sermon on the Mount, Jesus similarly raises the bar of ethical behavior from just actions to intent – to the heart.

Ryken, Doll, and Ferner in their paper presented a set of four principles for understanding the Decalogue. The following is but a brief recap of this wonderful framework of thinking. The first is the *theological principle* highlights that each of the Commandments is an articulation of God's character. Such a perspective changes the way to consider the Commandments. If a Commandment is an extension of God, then it is not just a set of rules, but a aspect of being. God does not steal; God does not commit adultery; God does not lie; and so on, because it is who God is. It is what He is. It is not possible for Him to do these acts. So when we read the Commandment, "Thou Shalt not steal," we are faced with the concept that this is not an option. It is not that we "should not," it is that our essential being is not designed to permit us to steal. In the Sermon on the Mount, Jesus was articulating this principle when He brought in the heart, not just the actions. For the editor, this creates a new understanding of the Christian notion of a "new creation." When we have been saved, we are born again, a new creation. This new creation is to be conformed to the likeness of God, no longer to have the capacity to violate the Commandments.[6]

Sadly, we know that Romans 7 has Paul reciting that we are not glorified here on earth, but our hope remains that we will be so in heaven. Perhaps this is part of the hope articulated in Hebrews 11:1 about the blessing of faith. That hope leads to a different life as described in 1 Peter 3:15.

The second principle is the *two-sided principle* wherein "each commandment has both a positive and a negative side. Where a sin is forbidden, the corresponding duty is required, where a duty is required, the corresponding sin is forbidden." The *Westminster Larger Catechism*[7] adopts this two-sided approach. The result is a far more robust set of principles than just the "do not steal" that so many adopt as the standard from a commandment. The third principle is the *categorical principle* wherein "each of the Ten Commandments covers a wide scope of sin and obedience, not just one narrow area of obedience." Where the second principle covered duties, this principle says that a commandment is not narrow, but sweeping, bringing in all of the related Bible passages that contain related material. It is this third principle that explains how all of the law fit within the Decalogue. The paper properly notes that the lesser sins are just as forbidden. The fourth principle is the *Christological principle* wherein each commandment is related to the person and work of Jesus Christ. "Jesus claimed to be the perfect and personal fulfillment of the law of God." Therefore obedience to Christ means obedience to the law of God. "If we trust in Jesus Christ, then we are connected to the Commandment-Keeper."

Julias J. Kim and John R. Mescher in their paper, "Thou shall Not Steal – From Your Customers: The Eighth Commandment and Antitrust Legislation" add further thoughts to how to think about the Decalogue with

1. The concept of duties:

In the *Westminster Larger Catechism* the commandments have at least three questions: 1) what is the commandment; 2) What duties does the commandment require; and 3) what sins does the commandment prohibit. This structure raises the important concept of duties and sins. Man having been created for a purpose has duties to fulfill. Failure in man's duties is just as much as sin and an action proscribed. A fuller understanding of the duties of a man and its application to business would be most useful.

It would be nice to say that the duties are the active items in a commandment and that the sins are a prohibition component. Yet, the Catechism suggests that there is more to it than just do not do an act.

2. The concept of sins:

In the *Westminster Larger Catechism* there are a list of sins related to each commandment. The breadth of these sins raises the framework noted above. At the same time there are specific sins that must be addressed as well. Most of the specific sins are what are discussed relative to a commandment. It is the broader set of sins we need to explore based upon the higher standards that arise when we fully understand that we live in God's world and that He has given us certain duties and responsibilities.

A contemporary of the Puritan period with some useful insights on the Decalogue can be found in Thomas Watson's *The Ten Commandments*. [8]

The division of the Decalogue

Kim and Mescher's paper provides "The Ten Commandments have traditionally been divided into two categories, or "Tables". The First Table spells out the duties we are to render God himself in the first four commandments: honor God only, worship God only, revere His name, and keep the Sabbath. The Second Table outlines the remaining duties we have toward our neighbors: honor our father and mother, do not murder, commit adultery, steal, lie, and covet. What Jesus does in the New Testament, however, is reveal that these duties to God and neighbor are essentially two sides of the same coin. In summarizing the Decalogue, Jesus states,

> "You shall love the Lord your God with all your heart and with all your soul and with all your mind. This is the great and first commandment. And a second is like it: You shall love your neighbor as yourself. On these two commandments depend all the Law and the Prophets" (Matthew 22:37-40)." [9] [10]

As one evaluates the breadth of each commandment and how Jesus references these two parts in the New Testament passages, the whole becomes critical, rather than the separation by groups or individually. [11] In the business world today, many have moved away from the two halves concept into a Golden Rule concept. The worry for Christian business leaders is that the core messages of the Decalogue will be lost and what will be taught will be legalism or just a set of "thou shalt nots."

The Golden Rule as an ethical standard for business

John Maxwell's book *There Is No Such Thing As Business Ethics* [12] starts with the Golden Rule – do unto others as you would have them do unto you – as the guiding principle. [13] The Golden Rule presents a good practice, a right way to function, a best practice for operating a business. However, the Golden Rule is a single summary statement among many ethical and spiritual principles stated in the Sermon on the Mount contained in Matthew 5-7 and Luke 6.

The Golden rule is similar to the second great commandment, love your neighbor as yourself.[14] Adopting the Golden Rule as the guideline based on the second six commandments, does allow the fulfilling of the commandments to be set in a non-spiritual context. In the business world today, we see regularly the Golden Rule put forth as a workable humanistic standard for behavior. This text is concerned that modern man is not learning the details of God's requirements contained in all of the Ten Commandments. Like Jesus did with the leaders of His day in the Sermon on the Mount, business leaders need to be challenged as to the specific principles that underlie these broader summary statements.

Two issues arise when adopting the Golden Rule rather than the full Decalogue. The first is the necessary interplay between the first four commandments and the second set of six commandments. The second issue arises when one considers the fullness of each commandment that leads to the conviction that this commandment is set into a larger framework.

Let's consider the second issue first, that the Decalogue forms a larger or complete framework, which must be reflected in the analysis of each commandment. This larger framework can be simply stated as "it is God's world." Adopting the first of the Ryken, Doll, Ferner principles, all Ten Commandments are needed to gain the perspective of God's character in His world. God gave the Decalogue to the people of Israel so that they had guideposts for living and functioning in God's world. In giving the Decalogue, God acted in His positional role of Creator, Sovereign, and Lord. God created the universe, the earth, everything in the earth, and each man. God did this creation with a purpose and that purpose is to be followed so that He, alone, should receive glory and honor. Therefore, man lives and functions in service to God, for this was man's created purpose. Each aspect of a man's life is governed by this relationship. When each commandment is considered within this framework, the richness and implications for daily living are much clearer. As a result, use of a single phrase, such as the Golden Rule, as the full principle to represent the implications of the need for discipline in life is shown to be weak and incomplete.

Understanding the necessary interplay between the first four commandments and the second set of six commandments helps explain why man simply does not function well with his fellow humans. There are places where the Golden Rule is stated in the Bible. Only one time does the Golden Rule stand alone. All of the other places start with man's relationship to God, then look to man's relationship to man. In other words, man should start by getting his relationship to God correct. This means man must address his own sins and his failure to relate to God with a proper perspective. Necessarily this means that the salvation of Jesus Christ will become the starting point for keeping the Golden Rule; then man can walk in the strength of the Holy Spirit.

When man has his relationship to God correct and is walking in the power of the Holy Spirit, man can fulfill the commandments in treating his fellow man. Without the power of the Holy Spirit, man cannot consistently walk in God's ways.[15] Therefore, the opening discussion on business ethics needs to address this broader perspective of the Decalogue.

THE EIGHTH COMMANDMENT

The *Catechism* has three questions related to the eighth commandment.

Question 140: Which is the eighth commandment?
Answer: The eighth commandment is, Thou shalt not steal.

Question 141: What are the duties required in the eighth commandment?

> Answer: The duties required in the eighth commandment are, truth, faithfulness, and justice in contracts and commerce between man and man; rendering to everyone his due; restitution of goods unlawfully detained from the right owners thereof; giving and lending freely, according to our abilities, and the necessities of others; moderation of our judgments, wills, and affections concerning worldly goods; a provident care and study to get, keep, use, and dispose these things which are necessary and convenient for the sustentation of our nature, and suitable to our condition; a lawful calling, and diligence in it; frugality; avoiding unnecessary lawsuits and suretyship, or other like engagements; and an endeavor, by all just and lawful means, to procure, preserve, and further the wealth and outward estate of others, as well as our own.

Question 142: What are the sins forbidden in the eighth commandment?

> Answer: The sins forbidden in the eighth commandment, besides the neglect of the duties required, are, theft, robbery, man stealing, and receiving anything that is stolen; fraudulent dealing, false weights and measures, removing landmarks, injustice and unfaithfulness in contracts between man and man, or in matters of trust; oppression, extortion, usury, bribery, vexatious lawsuits, unjust enclosures and depopulations; engrossing commodities to enhance the price; unlawful callings, and all other unjust or sinful ways of taking or withholding from our neighbor: What belongs to him, or of enriching ourselves; covetousness; inordinate prizing and affecting worldly goods; distrustful and distracting cares and studies in getting, keeping, and using them; envying at the prosperity of others; as likewise idleness, prodigality, wasteful gaming; and all other ways whereby we do unduly prejudice our own outward estate, and defrauding ourselves of the due use and comfort of that estate which God has given us.

The questions and answers show that the Westminster divines framed a commandment as having both duties and sins. In addition, the passive and active nature of sin contributes to the evaluation of the listed items in the answers to questions 141 and 142.

"The Heidelberg Catechism (Answer to question 110) offers a shorter list, which nonetheless includes some forms of theft that other definitions leave out: "God forbids not only outright theft and robbery, but also such wicked schemes and devices as false weights and measures, deceptive merchandising, counterfeit money, and usury; we must not defraud our neighbor in any way, whether by force or by show of right. In addition God forbids all greed and all abuse or squandering of his gifts."[16]

"It is worth noting that many of the sins that fall under the category of "theft" relate specifically to the world of business. This would not surprise the humorist Scott Adams, who has defined "the Weasel Zone" as that "gigantic gray area between good moral behavior and outright felonious activities." The Eighth Commandment tells us what we should call the morally questionable deeds that fall under this category: we should call them all "stealing." [17]

Some framing concepts for the Eighth Commandment

As seen above, God is the owner of all the earth. Everything created is to give Him glory. God gives to those whom He pleases, that which He pleases. The Eighth Commandment states what is proper in God's world. Let us explore this further.

What does God give to individuals? Time, talent and treasure work reasonably well as a summary of what God grants to each person. Jonathan Edwards captures that God alone gives a person each day in his paper, *Sinners in the Hands of an Angry God*,[18] "There is nothing that keeps wicked men at any one moment out of hell, but the mere pleasure of God." Jesus in Matthew 6:27 said that we cannot add a single day to our life. Time is our lifespan here on earth. Passages in the Bible suggest that our time is short[19] and its length is not known to us.[20]

Talent is the skills and experiences God has given to us. We are all unique and it is the wonder of God that He relates to us in our uniqueness. This uniqueness equips us to fulfill His purpose and calling here in His world.[21] It is for us to use these talents to contribute to God's kingdom here on earth.[22] Throughout the Bible, people with talent are called to and provided for God's purpose. An interesting example is the master craft person supplied by the King of Tyre to King Solomon for the building of the temple.[23] The unanswered question was whether Hiram, king of Tyre, was a believer in the God of Israel or a respecter of God and Israel. Many Christian business people are challenged by the notion that they can associate with unbelievers or those who do not fully share the same spectrum of Christianity. Yet, here Solomon reaches out to a neighbor for the talent needed to build the temple that will be the central place of worship for God.

Treasure tends to be the easiest aspect to understand of what God gives to each person that falls under the Commandment. Treasure is the possessions God gives to us. Naked we came into the world and naked we leave.[24] Yet, while we are here God gives to us material substance.[25] God warns us not strive for material things,[26] not to become dependent upon material things;[27] rather we are to store our treasure in heaven.[28]

We can add to time, talent, and treasure, the idea that God brings us opportunities both to help in the development of these three and our character[29] and to allow us to utilize them for His glory.[30] The Bible is replete with descriptions of God's giving to both the deserving and the undeserving.

Therefore, the Commandment requires that we respect what and to whom all is given.

Some papers go a step further than just a Commandment not to steal. These papers point to the fact that humans have been created as God's image bearers.[31] Therefore, the honoring of God directly relates to loving our neighbors, who bear God's image.

Kim and Mesher's paper points out that what has been given can be seen as an inheritance. As His children, we can see that the not stealing directly relates to loving God. Further, as His children, that which has been given, can be seen as an inheritance. An inheritance, because God is our Father and knows what we need. In Matthew 7:9-12 Jesus makes clear the blessing of having God as our Father and that this fact should lead us to treat others as He treats us.

God grants to individuals rather than mankind. This is a fundamental distinction between the Christian perspective and the modern socialist perspective. Sections 2 and 3 cover this in detail and the implications can be seen in this principle.

The grant of property, i.e., time, talent and treasure, create individual responsibility to use them to honor God. Section 2 develops the blessing that come to God's world from those who comply with this requirement.

What is stealing?

"The thing forbidden in this commandment, is meddling with another man's property. The civil lawyers define *futum*, stealth or theft to be 'the laying hands unjustly on that which is another's;' the invading another's right."[32] *Webster's Third New International Dictionary* has the following definitions for steal:

> 1. To practice theft: take property of another. 1a. To take and carry away feloniously, unobserved: take aor appropriate without right or leave and with intent to keep or make use of wrongfully. 1b. To appropriate (as another's conception or invention) and use as one's own. 1c. To take away by force or unjust or underhand means: deprive one of. 1d. abduct, kidnap. 1e. to take secretly or without permission [a kiss]. 1f. to take over: adopt, borrow [the various gyrations have been stolen from boxing, basket ball] 1g. To appropriate entirely to

oneself or beyond one's proper share. 2a. To move, convey or introduce secretly. 2b. To aim furtively: direct secretly [stole several glances at him] 2c. To accomplish in a concealed or unobserved manner. 3.To use for an irregular, unscheduled or secret purpose. 4a. To win away by persuasion or deception: entice. 4b.To take possession gradually or imperceptibly. 5. To seize, gain or win by trickery, skill or daring. 6b. To make use of [the nest] of another hen.[33]

The internet definition by MerriamWebster is

-intransitive verb
1: to take the <u>PROPERTY</u> of another wrongfully and especially as a habitual or regular practice
2: to come or go secretly, unobtrusively, gradually, or unexpectedly
3: to steal or attempt to steal a base

-transitive verb
1a : to take or appropriate without right or leave and with intent to keep or make use of wrongfully <*stole* a <u>CAR</u>> b : to take away by force or unjust means <they've *stolen* our liberty> c : to take surreptitiously or without permission <*steal* a kiss> d : to appropriate to oneself or beyond one's proper share : make oneself the focus of <*steal* the show>
2a : to move, convey, or introduce secretly : SMUGGLE b : to accomplish in a concealed or unobserved manner <*steal* a visit> 3a : to seize, gain, or win by trickery, skill, or daring <a <u>BASKETBALL</u> player adept at *stealing* the ball> <*stole* the election> b *of a base runner* : to reach (a base) safely solely by running and usually catching the opposing team off guard[34]

These definitions are given to aid us in seeing the richness of this term throughout the ages. Mankind has developed many ways to take what belongs to another. Some very subtle; some more overt; all, except some of the sports uses, violate the Eighth Commandment. Is it any wonder that there are so many notes in the *Catechism*?

What can be stolen?

In this text the cases give a good example of what can be stolen. To the basic property concepts of time, talent and treasure, need to be added honor, worship, position, personal traits, such as innocence. In short all that is a person can be, and is, stolen.

For this point, we need to see God as a being where these apply. For example, failing to give God worship is stealing the worship that is due to Him. Failing to recognize His providence in providing for us, is stealing His glory for ourselves. Putting our trust in government or social security to supply our needs is stealing His character as a loving Father and His providence as our provider.

From whom is something stolen?

As noted above stealing started with taking and misappropriating what was God's in the Garden of Eden. From whom is something stolen, needs to be answered as "from God," who owns all and gives to whom He pleases. Cowan highlights this in his paper as renegotiating the deal with God. God gives us what we are to have, but we are unsatisfied and decide to change the deal – we steal what God has for another.

In business we can steal from our customers [contract terms, pricing], the government [taxes], our employees and suppliers [failure to pay on time] and from our company [opportunities misappropriated to another organization including ourselves]. In business, we need to see that often when we steal we are creating "self-help" in violation of trusting God's provision. So we deprive the company of the blessing that is received when God meets our company's needs by providing what we cannot otherwise provide for ourselves. James 4:13-15 is an example of this principle that our businesses operate in God's world and receive the blessing that God gives.

But we also steal from ourselves. In the passage in the Introduction discussion of Jesus' pastoral prayer, we see the blessed state that mankind was meant to have with God. When we break our relationship with God by stealing in any of its forms, we lose that relationship. We steal from ourselves the blessings God desires for us. The Catechism adds several additional examples of stealing from ourselves:

> (A.143) "as likewise idleness, prodigality, wasteful gaming; and all other ways whereby we do unduly prejudice our own outward estate, and defrauding ourselves of the due use and com-

fort of that estate which God has given us."

These passages apply to companies as well as to individuals. Many a company suffers from the management team that is tired, lacking diligence in the pursuit of the business entrusted to it. Or the CEO is extravagant as cited in the Krzeswhy, Peterson and Austin paper about Tyco's CEO. Or the company takes on risks that are inappropriate, leading to undue failure. Examples are Lehman Brothers and AIG in the 2008 financial crisis where the derivative risks were beyond what the companies could bear. The editor's favorite example of the CEO not allowing undue risks is a personal experience with the CEO of Unilever, the maker of Dove soap, who hired the editor, while at a former firm, to lead a review of an acquisition target where there were some potential tax risks among other concerns. The editor briefed the CEO on the findings of the review explaining that indeed the tax risk was there and was as large as was thought, but that there was a potential to manage the risk. The management of the risk could not bring assurance that the tax exposure would not become due. At this point the CEO looked at this editor and said something to the effect of "I have been entrusted this company and I will leave it stronger. This trust precludes this company from ever taking on such an exposure as this. Meeting over." And we all went home. To this day the depth of understanding that in business, leaders of companies are entrusted the company, remains a key lesson that is under-taught in our business schools. But this is exactly what the *Catechism* calls unduly prejudicing our estate.

Why do people steal?
Why do people steal? The text papers contain a number of answers. The following is a summary of the reasons people steal.

The fallen nature of man is the number one reason. Too often Christians and non-Christians look for answers in other places than this fundamental aspect of human nature. In Genesis 3 the Bible makes clear that man rejected God's provision and became selfish, stealing the forbidden fruit. Mankind continues to reject God's provision.

Failure to trust God to provide one's needs, which can also be described as unbelief. "Man has a high distrust of God's providence. 'Can God furnish a table in the wilderness?'"[35]

Covetousness: Man wishing to renegotiate the deal that God has granted him is another reason that is cited by Cowan in his paper. Similar to the first reason, a person is not happy with what God has provided so he takes more from another. In essence, the individual is renegotiating the deal God has given to him. The individual is telling God what He has provided is not good enough; I am taking more.

Love: Man breaks the relationship of love with God. As noted in several papers, man bears the image of God, therefore each person deserves the love of God that we individually experience. When a person steals from another, the person violates the other and does not show the love of God towards the other.

Poverty and trust: Man steals because his situation causes him not to trust God. In Proverb 30:7-9 the individual asks not to be made poor, lest he steal. Poverty is a cause of stealing, but underlying this cause is the failure to trust God to provide.

Greed, selfishness and envy are also factors that cause stealing. Each of these can be traced back to the fall of man in Genesis 3. 1 Timothy 6:10 says that the love of money is the root of all sorts of evil. Stealing is just one of the evils that arise from the love of money. Jesus warned in Matthew 6:19—34 not to serve material goods. Jesus said that God can provide for us. But we want more, we store our treasure here on earth. We serve mammon.

Satan: "the external cause of theft is Satan's solicitation."[36] Judas was a thief because Satan entered into him.[36] "The devil is the great master-thief, he robbed us of our coat of innocence, and he persuades men to take up his trade; he tells men how bravely they shall live by thieving, how they shall catch an estate."[38] In the presentations at the 2011 Business Ethics Today conference, the speakers discussed that in many cultures thieving was more honorable than work, because thieving required taking on risks and danger, where working was laborious and tedious. A thief gains quickly, where the worker gains slowly, if at all.

Summary of the implications of the Eighth Commandment

Each person needs to see God in His role as Creator, Sovereign and Lord. All that we have, including ourselves, belongs to Him. All that we do is to give glory and honor to Him. Even in our enjoyment of His provisions, we honor Him.

Each person needs to trust God for all needed provisions. The Bible makes it clear that God provides for our needs. The provision is both specific and general. General provision would be God's providence found in the common grace that is the wondrous world in which we live. As noted in the Introduction, the world is designed for human flourishing. God deserves our honor in recognizing that our needs are supplied by His providence. Specific provision is the direct meeting of our individual situation. Jesus spoke of the attentiveness of God in meeting our needs in Matthew 6:31-34. Failure to fully trust God is to steal the glory and honor He deserves.

The individual is not to trust in anything other than God to meet his needs. He is not to trust in wealth, in community or his own strength. God may use all of these to meet our needs, but our trust remains with Him. Placing our trust in anything other than God for our needs, places another god before Him, which is a First Commandment violation.

At the same time, the individual is to use what God has given to him, i.e., time, talent and treasure, diligently to God's honor and glory. Failure to be diligent in the use of resources given to God's glory is stealing from God the glory He deserves. Some examples are warranted here: (a) The individual failing to use his time on earth well, being lazy. (b) The individual failing to develop his talents and apply them to useful situations, steals blessings God wishes both for the individual and the community. (c) The individual failing to productively employ the treasures entrusted to him, steals the increase that God deserves. (d) The individual failing to develop the opportunities God presents him to apply the time, talent, or treasure entrusted, steals the increase God deserves. In all of these the individual is also stealing from himself the blessing that comes from being a blessing to God and to his community.

The individual steals from others in a vast array of situations. (a) When the individual takes the time, talent or treasure, that God has granted to another without compensation or permissions. (b) When the individual takes the opportunity God has presented to another to apply his time, talent or treasure so that the other can generate increase in God's world. (c) When the individual takes or wastes another's time. (d) When an individual distracts another from God's purpose. (e) When an individual depletes another's energy. This can be done by depressing conversations, usually that do not acknowledge God's providence. (f) When the individual fails to aid the other with the time, talent or treasure God has given the individual to meet the other's needs, including aiding the other in being successful.

Notes

1. *Westminster Confession of Faith*, first published 1646, reprinted Glasgow: Free Presbyterian Publications, 2001.

2. The Center for Christian Business Ethics Today, LLC was formed in 2009 to develop material to help the Christian business person operate his business with biblical business principles based on Protestant Christianity. The Center co-hosted the Conference that is the source of the papers for this text.

3. *Westminster Larger Catechism*, Approved 1648, Free Presbyterian Publications, 1958.

4. Abraham Lincoln's second inaugural address on March 4, 1865, contains the following, "Both read the same Bible and pray to the same God, and each invokes His aid against the other. It may seem strange that any men should dare to ask a just God's assistance in wringing their bread from the sweat of other men's faces, but let us judge not, that we be not judged. The prayers of both could not be answered. That of neither has been answered fully. The Almighty has His own purposes." A powerful reminder that the same Bible passage can be used for different purposes and interpretations.

5. From the paper in this text by Calvin Chin and William Goligher, "The Eighth Commandment and Respect for Capital."

6. The term ontology could apply here. What is being described is a position of being. The Christian was one being before salvation and now is born into another being. The new being has a different position relative to sin. While this is a brief introduction, the power of understanding this change in relationship to God as part of who we are as Christians directly affects how we act.

7. *Westminster Larger Catechism* Glasgow: Bell and Bain, first published in 1648, rep. 2001.

8. Thomas Watson, *The Ten Commandments*, 1692, rept. Carlisle: Banner of Truth, 1995, p 43 – 49.

9. English Standard Version.

10. Jesus in Matt 22:35-40, Mark 12:2-34, and Luke 10:25-29 references this two-part structure. Jesus does not specifically address His comments to the Decalogue, but the overall teaching found in the laws and prophets. However, the settings and general theological understanding fit nicely with the Decalogue and is often so used.

11. In Matt 19:16-12, Mark 10:17-22, Luke 18:18-23, Jesus talks to the rich ruler, sometimes referred to as the rich young ruler, and lists each of the second set of commandments, with an addition of "love your neighbor as yourself." Then Jesus instructs him to sell all that he has and give it to the poor and follow Jesus, but the ruler is rich and thus very sad. What was the problem? The ruler had failed the first commandment in that his wealth held higher priority than God. The parable illustrates that all of the commandments go together.

12. John Maxwell, *There Is No Such Thing As Business Ethics*, New York: Warner, 2003, wherein he articulates that the Golden Rule works as the foundation for business ethics.

13. Matt 7:12; Luke 6:31.

14. Lev 19:18b "… you shall love your neighbor as yourself…" More fully "You shall not take vengeance, nor bear any grudge against the children of your people, but you shall love your neighbor as yourself: I am the Lord." (NKJV) John MacArthur, *The John MacArthur Study Bible*, Nashville: Word ,1997, footnote on Lev 19:18, "This, called the second great commandment, is the most often quoted OT test in the NT (Matt. 5:43; 19:19; 22:39; Mark 12:31, 33; Luke 10:27; Rom. 13:9; Gal. 5:14; James 2:8)."

15. The editor would remind the reader that Christians may be assured of heaven, but are subject to error while here on earth. See Romans 7 and 8 for this challenging aspect of the Christian life.

16. See Rykin, Doll, Ferner paper.

17. *Ibid*

18. Jonathan Edwards, *Sinners in the Hand of an Angry God*, 1741, http://www.religionfacts.com/christianity/library/edwards_sinners.htm.

19. James 4:14.

20. Matt 24:44, 50 and Matt 6:27.

21. Rom 8:28, 9:17-24.

22. Eph 4:7-16, 1 Cor 12:12-30.

23. 1 Chronicles 2:1-16.

24. Job 1:21.

25. Job, Abraham and many others are great examples of God's blessing while on earth.

26. Pv 28:20.

27. Deut 28 is the great warning to Israel that when the come into the land and receive the blessings that are there, they will forget God and turn away. Pv 30:7-9 contain the same as a prayer. In Matt 6:24 Jesus warns you cannot serve both God and material things.

28. Matt 6:19-21.

29. James 1:2-4.

30. Esther 4:14.

31. Kim and Mesher, Chin and Goligher, Poythress and Coors.

32. Watson, p. 164.

33. *Webster's Third New International Dictionary*, Springfield: Merriam, 1966. p. 2232.

34. http://www.merriam-webster.com/dictionary/steal

35. Watson, p. 164.

36. Watson, p. 164.

37. Ibid. John 13:27.

38. Ibid.

A SUMMARY OF THE TEN COMMANDMENTS

THE LAW OF GOD

PETER LILLBACK

EDITED BY PHILIP CLEMENTS

PETER LILLBACK

Doctor Peter A. Lillback is President and Professor of Historical Theology at Westminster Theological Seminary located in Philadelphia and the senior pastor of Proclamation Presbyterian Church in Bryn Mawr, Pennsylvania. Lillback also serves as the President of The Providence Forum, the nonprofit organization that is committed to preserving and promoting America's spiritual roots of religious and civil liberties.

Living between Philadelphia and Valley Forge for many years, Dr. Lillback has pursued an avid interest in the history of the Judeo-Christian heritage of the United States. He has done much research and study on the founding and Founders of our nation through examination of original source documents in numerous libraries and archives. His books Freedom's Holy Light *and* Proclaim Liberty *are outgrowths of his research. In 2006, Dr. Lillback's bestseller on the Christian faith of George Washington was released.* George Washington's Sacred Fire *represents the culmination of over twenty years of original research and scholarship. In May 2010, the paperback reached #1 on Amazon.com.*

Lillback is a frequent lecturer on many worldview issues and has debated Barry Lynn, president of Americans United for the Separation of Church and State and appeared on panels broadcast by C-Span. He is the voice of Proclaiming the Word, *a fifteen-minute Bible teaching radio and television program, which airs weekdays across the country.*

His primary passion in life is serving the Lord wherever he is called. As a result of being in ministry, he has enjoyed the privilege to teach and preach in numerous missions, popular and scholarly contexts. These experiences have only increased his love for travel.

He has an avid interest in all things historical—especially theology and American history—and enjoys researching original sources. For fun, he plays a Liberty Tree Guitar. He loves to hike when possible, both locally and on vacations, and has hiked up mountainsides around the globe.

In addition to Greek and Hebrew, he reads French for fun and continues to improve his speaking ability, aiding in his role with the Huguenot Fellowship.

Dr. Lillback considers himself a "generalist." Those who work with him see him as a "servant leader" who seeks to do any job that is required, including taking out the trash, moving boxes, cleaning floors, etc. He is known for his gifts as a teacher, preacher, and mediator. He is a visionary who can see potentials and connections which are not always obvious to others and, thus, has been successful at starting many new ministries and initiatives.

Doctor Lillback grew up in Painesville, Ohio, the middle of three boys. He lives in Wayne, Pennsylvania, with his wife, Debbie. They have two grown daughters.

Here we shall seek to see the relevance and value of conducting business in God's world according to the law of God as summarized in the moral law of the Ten Commandments.[1] In the process, the wisdom and importance of the morality of profits as taught in the *Westminster Larger Catechism* questions #140-142 will be considered. This *Catechism* identifies the duties required in the 8th commandment (Thou Shalt not Steal), to include "trust, faithfulness and justice; ..[and] by all just and lawful means, to procure, preserve, and further the wealth and outward estate of others, as well as our own."

Because of the vastness of this topic, the endnotes contain outlines to aid the reader in understanding the material touched upon in this paper.

I. A Summary of the Ten Commandments [2]

In today's crisis over values, schools are required to present "values clarification" rather than moral values. In 1980 the Supreme Court ruled that the Ten Commandments could not be placed in a public school building. Courts continue to deliver verdicts that require public places to remove the Ten Commandments, as if to scour every vestige of religion and morality from the goals and activities conducted in the public square. We are facing an ethical crisis that in many ways is self-imposed. In this context it is necessary to rediscover and to review the teaching of Scripture in regard to God's moral law that is summarized in the Ten Commandments. The following are the Ten Commandments grouped into two tables.

The First Table of the Law-- Commandments 1-4 teach us how to Love God, Ex. 20:1-11

> **#1 God is first** –Ex. 20:3 -- *You shall have no other gods before me.*

> **#2 Worship God's Way** – Ex. 20:4-6 -- *You shall not make for yourself an idol in the form of anything in heaven above or on the earth beneath or in the waters below. 5You shall not bow down to them or worship them; for I, the LORD your God, am a jealous God, punishing the children for the sin of the fathers to the third and fourth generation of those who hate me, 6but showing love to a thousand [generations] of those who love me and keep my commandments.*

> **#3 God's Name is Holy** – Ex. 20:7 -- *You shall not misuse the name of the LORD your God, for the LORD will not hold anyone guiltless who misuses his name.*

> **#4 A Day for Worship** -- Ex. 20:8-11 -- *Remember the Sabbath day by keeping it holy. 9Six days you shall labor and do all your work, 10but the seventh day is a Sabbath to the LORD your God. On it you shall not do any work, neither you, nor your son or daughter, nor your manservant or maidservant, nor your animals, nor the alien within your gates. 11For in six days the LORD made the heavens and the earth, the sea, and all that is in them, but he rested on the seventh day. Therefore the LORD blessed the Sabbath day and made it holy.*

The Second Table of the Law—Commandments 5-10 teach us how to Love our Neighbors

#5 There is Legitimate Authority – Ex. 20:12 -- *Honor your father and your mother, so that you may live long in the land the LORD your God is giving you.*

#6 Life is Sacred – Ex. 20:13 -- *You shall not murder.*

#7 Marriage and the Family are to be Protected and Preserved -- Ex. 20:14 -- *You shall not commit adultery.*

#8 The Right to Personal Property – Ex. 20:15 -- *You shall not steal.*

#9 Truth must be Preserved in the Courts and Beyond – Ex. 20:16 -- *You shall not give false testimony against your neighbor.*

#10 Contentment with our Personal Circumstances – Ex. 20:17 -- *You shall not covet your neighbor's house. You shall not covet your neighbor's wife, or his manservant or maidservant, his ox or donkey, or anything that belongs to your neighbor.*

There appears to be a direct connection between our moral plunge in ethics and our rejection of the moral law of God. Even many Christians do not know the Ten Commandments. But we must not only know the Ten Commandments, we must understand them as well. [3]

II. The Three Uses of the Law

Psalm 1:1-3 says that the righteous man delights in the study of the Law. Here we explore the three uses of God's law: The mirror use, the master use, and the map use.

The First Use of the Law (The Gospel's use of the Law). The law is a **mirror** to show us our sin and our need for salvation in Christ. (Galatians 3:23, 24; 1 John 3:4, 5.) As a jailer it holds us under condemnation. As a rehabilitator it leads us to Christ, who is the "end" of the law (Romans 10:4.) John Bunyan illustrates the work of the law as a sweeping of a dry dusty floor in a dark room. The room looks clean until the light shines in revealing the dust in the air and the dirt swirls on the floor.. Such is the use of the law in calling us to the Gospel--it shows us our sin. [4] "The

Moral Law tells us the tune we have to play: our instincts are merely the keys…." "There is nothing indulgent about the Moral Law. It is as hard as nails…If God is like the Moral Law then He is not soft." (*Mere Christianity* by C. S. Lewis). The Scriptures emphasize mankind's inability to keep God's law.

> Ecclesiastes 7:20; "There is not a righteous man on earth who does what is right and never sins."

> Romans 3:10; "As it is written, 'There is no one righteous, not even one.' "

> Romans 3:23; "For all have sinned and fall short of the glory of God."

But it's even worse than that. For "All men alike stand condemned, not by alien codes of ethics, but by their own, and all men therefore are conscious of guilt." *(The Problem of Pain)* Indeed, "The road to the promised land runs past Sinai." *(The Problem of Pain)*

The Second Use of the Law (The Civil, social, or cultural use of the Law). The Law is a **master** to show us our duty, our sin, and our freedom. (James 1:22-25; Romans 13:1-5.)

The Law points us to true Freedom in God's grace and to civil and moral freedom through self-government. Even as roads restrict automobiles but give them freedom to go anywhere, so the moral restraints of the law bring freedom to all who follow its dictates. There is no accident that historically a Christian culture placed the Ten Commandments on the walls of the Court House.

The Third Use of the Law (The Christian's Use of the Law as the Standard of Loving God). The Law is also a **map** to guide us in our love toward God (Psalm 119:9-16; 1 John 5:3.) To love God truly without a guide is not possible for fallen man, any more than it is possible for a man to find his way through a large city without a map.

Our failure to keep God's law because of our fallen nature underscores our need for grace.

III. The Grace of the Gospel in the Preface of the 10 Commandments [5]

The Ten Commandments are found in Ex. 20 and Deut. 5. But these classic words point us directly to the good news of Jesus Christ as our Redeemer. Ex. 20:1-2 declares, "And God spoke all these words: 'I am the LORD your God, who brought you out of Egypt, out of the land of slavery.'" God rescued Israel, His covenant people, by grace from slavery. Similarly, God rescues His covenant people today from the slavery in sin by grace. Thus God did not give His Law as a mere list of moralistic "dos" and "don'ts". Instead, He gave His Law to us as a way in which we could say thank you to Him for His gracious salvation and our liberation from the slavery of sin.

We all need this gospel. The seeds of sin are in the heart of every man, even every Christian. We need the Redeemer who takes us out of the bondage of sin if we are to be righteous before God. P. T. Forsyth said it well, "'God is Love' is not the whole gospel. Love is not evangelical till it has dealt with holy law. In the midst of the rainbow is a throne." This is the whole point of the Gospel of redemption from slavery that is contained in the Preface to the Ten Commandments in Exodus 20:2.

While there is not a righteous man on the earth. There is a righteous man sent from God to rescue sinners: Jesus Christ the righteous (I John 2:1). He did what is righteous. He fulfilled all of the law (Matt. 3:15). He never sinned (Heb. 4:15; II Cor. 5:21). He has the glory of God. He finished God's work, and asked to be glorified by the Father (John 17: 4-5). He has provided the greatest transaction of history: while Adam's sin was credited to all of his posterity (Rom. 5:12 ff), all our guilt was placed upon Christ on the cross (II Cor. 5:21). Christ's perfect righteousness is imputed or credited to the account of believers (Phil. 3:9; II Cor. 5). Is the Redeemer yours by a saving trust in the Passover Lamb, the Lord Jesus Christ, who takes away the sins of the world? [6]

Thus to love God, we must know our need of the Savior. J. C. Ryle declares,

> But how shall we obtain this love towards God? It is no natural feeling. We are "born in sin," and as sinners, are afraid of Him. How then can we love Him? We can never really love Him till we are at peace with Him through Christ. When we feel our sins forgiven, and ourselves reconciled to our holy Maker,

then, and not till then, we shall love Him and have the Spirit of adoption. Faith in Christ is the true spring of love to God: they love most who feel most forgiven. "We love Him because He first loved us.". . .We cannot have fruits and flowers without roots: we cannot have love to God and man without faith in Christ, and without regeneration. (*Expository Thoughts on Matthew*, p. 294.)

So to Love God, we must know our sin. When we understand our sin, we can have only one true response:

> We have not loved thee as we ought,
> Nor cared that we are loved by thee;
> Thy presence we have coldly sought,
> And feebly longed thy face to see.
> Lord, give a pure and loving heart
> To feel and own the love thou art.

Truly, a life of loving God is necessarily to live a life of daily repentance.

IV. The Ten Commandments are about Love.

Christians have been often confused about the Law of God. Doesn't Paul say, "You are not under law, but under grace." (Romans 6:14.) Are we not "justified by faith apart from observing the law"? (Romans 3:28.) But Paul also explains that Christ's death was to "condemn sin in sinful man, in order that the righteous requirements of the law might be fully met in us, who do not live according to the sinful nature but according to the Spirit." (Romans 8:3, 4.)

As we consider the question of the Law of God, or the Ten Commandments [7], and their significance for the believer, there is not a more remarkable statement in this regard than that found in the *Westminster Confession of Faith*, (XIX.7),

> Neither are the forementioned uses of the law contrary to the grace of the Gospel, but do sweetly comply with it; the Spirit of Christ subduing and enabling the will of man to do that

freely, and cheerfully, which the will of God, revealed in the law, requires to be done.

In Matthew 22:34-40, Jesus teaches that love is the nail upon which the Ten Commandments hang. The first four commandments teach love to God. The last six commandments teach love to one's neighbor. They are based upon God's redeeming love for His people found in the Preface. They create a society where one is to love and to be loved. [8] We have the dignity of God's Law because we have the dignity of being made in God's image (Genesis 1:26-27).

Hence we must never exalt material things or materialist philosophies over human beings. C. S. Lewis wrote, "You have never talked to a mere mortal. Nations, cultures, arts, civilizations—these are mortal, and their life is to ours as the life of a gnat. But it is immortals whom we joke with, work, marry, snub, and exploit—immortal horrors or everlasting splendours." (*The Weight of Glory and Other Addresses*). In *Prince Caspian*, Lewis writes, "You come of the Lord Adam and the Lady Eve,' said Aslan. 'And that is both honour enough to erect the head of the poorest beggar, and shame enough to bow the shoulders of the greatest emperor in earth.'"

V. The Great Commandments Show That Love Is The Motive of the Law

Love and law are not antithetical, but are intimately related. Both call upon us to honor God and our neighbors who are made in God's image and likeness. Romans 13:8-10 teaches,

> 8Let no debt remain outstanding, except the continuing debt to love one another, for he who loves his fellowman has fulfilled the law. 9The commandments, "Do not commit adultery," "Do not murder," "Do not steal," "Do not covet," and whatever other commandment there may be, are summed up in this one rule: "Love your neighbor as yourself." 10Love does no harm to its neighbor. Therefore love is the fulfillment of the law.

The two great commandments and The Golden Rule summarize the Law of God:

Mt. 22:37-40 -- 37Jesus replied: "'Love the Lord your God with all your heart and with all your soul and with all your mind.' 38This is the first and greatest commandment. 39And the second is like it: 'Love your neighbor as yourself.' 40 All the Law and the Prophets hang on these two commandments."

Mt. 7:12 -- So in everything, do to others what you would have them do to you, for this sums up the Law and the Prophets.

The first great commandment is an **Explicit** command for love which touches our affections, our attitudes and our actions. This is not an option, it is obligation. It is **Extensive** in that it impacts our heart, soul, mind, strength. It is to be **Exhaustive** in that it repeatedly calls forth our "all. . .all. . .all. . .all."

MacClaren put it well: "God is one and all. . .To love such an object with half a heart is not to love. True, our weakness leads astray, but the only real love corresponding to the natures of the lover and the loved is whole-hearted, whole-souled, whole-minded. It must be 'all in all, or not at all.'"

Note the connection of love and keeping God's commandments in Scripture: Ex. 20:6; Dt. 5:10; Jn 14:21; 1 Jn. 2:3-6. In fact, when we truly love God, it is a joy, not a burden to keep his commandments. Consider 1 John 5:3 teaches, "This is love for God: to obey his commands. And his commands are not burdensome, . . ." Gen. 29:20 says, "So Jacob worked seven years for Rachel, and they seemed like a few days because he love her."

J. C. Ryle explains, "Love is the grand secret of true obedience to God. When we feel towards Him as children feel towards a dear father, we shall delight to do His will: we shall not find His commandments grievous, or work for Him like slaves under fear of the lash; we shall take pleasure in trying to keep His laws, and mourn when we transgress them. None work so well as they who work for love: the fear of punishment, or the desire of reward, are principles of far less power. They do the will of God best who do it from the heart." (*Expository Thoughts on Matthew*, p. 293.)

Do you desire to know if you really love God?; then ask yourself if you delight to obey His word. Your answer to the second question is also the answer to the first! One of the great benefits of the New Covenant is the work of the Holy Spirit. By the grace of the Spirit, the law of the Ten

Commandments is written on believers' hearts.
(See Jer. 31:31-34; 2Cor. 3:1-6; Rom. 8:1-17; Gal. 5:16-25.)

> I have always been humbled by the staggering love that the per-
> secuted Christians in Russia have shown for Christ. Richard
> Wurmbrand writes in *Tortured for Christ* (p. 43), It was strictly
> forbidden to preach to other prisoners. It was understood that
> whoever was caught doing this received a severe beating. A
> number of us decided to pay the price for the privilege of preach-
> ing, so we accepted their terms. It was a deal; *we preached and*
> *they beat us.* We were happy preaching. They were happy beat-
> ing us, so everyone was happy. The following scene happened
> more times than I can remember: A brother was preaching to
> the other prisoners when the guards suddenly burst in, surpris-
> ing him half way through a phrase. They hauled him down the
> corridor to their 'beating room'. After what seemed an endless
> beating, they brought him back and threw him--bloody and
> bruised--on the prison floor. Slowly, he picked his battered
> body up, painfully straightened his clothing and said, 'Now,
> brethren, where did I leave off when I was interrupted?' He
> continued his Gospel message! I have seen beautiful things."

In the face of such love for God, we can feel that we will never measure up
to a love that will ever be worth bringing to God. But that it is not so. G.
Campbell Morgan has written,

> Yet hear again the great commandments and mark how reason-
> able they are. 'With all *thy* heart, and with all *thy* soul, and
> with all *thy* mind'; not with thy neighbor's heart or soul or
> mind. If indeed it be true that your heart is a small thing, that
> your life is a weak thing, that your mind is a feeble thing, yet
> God is asking for that small heart, weak life, feeble mind. Only
> I pray you, remember this, your heart is not so small as you
> have imagined, your life is not so weak as men have thought,
> your mind is not so feeble as you yourself have dreamed. If
> you will but love with all that you are, you will find enlarge-
> ment of heart and life and mind in the power of love. Do not

sigh through the days because you do not love God as someone else does. He does not ask you to love Him as someone else does. He asks you to love with all your heart. Just as I am, weak, poor, unworthy, I come in answer to the love of God, and begin to love, and that is all He asks. (*The Westminster Pulpit*, VII:126.)

To love God means that we must know God through Scripture. Therein we find Him to be the eternal Spirit who loves with a holy love. He is the Jealous God who demands all of our love. And thus to love God means we know ourselves to be sinners and those who need the loving work of the Savior to forgive our unloving souls. It is then and only then that we can begin to love God. We do so, then, by joyful obedience to His commandments giving him all of our hearts, even if what we offer seems so small in comparison to what others can bring.

And when we learn to so love God, perhaps we will be able to offer the daring prayer that St. Augustine expressed over 1500 years ago, "Lord, hast thou declared that no man shall see Thy face and live?--then let me die, that I may see Thee."

VI. The Eighth Commandment

All of the Ten Commandments apply to business. For this paper we will look at the Eighth Commandment. We start with an exposition, then consider some of the implications.

The exposition of the Eighth Commandment of the *Larger Catechism* is found in Questions #140-142. The answers to these questions are extensive and detailed and appeal to many Scriptural texts. Below is an outline that presents the supporting biblical texts.

Q. 140 Which is the eighth commandment?
A. 140 The eighth commandment is, *Thou shalt not steal.*

Q. 141 What are the duties required in the eighth commandment?
The **duties** required in the eighth commandment are,

    1.   In regard to **business dealings**:
        a.   truth,
        b.   faithfulness,

      c.   and justice in
- i.   contracts
- ii.   and commerce between man and man; (Psalm 15:2,4; Zech. 8:16-17.)
- iii.   restitution of goods unlawfully detained from the right owners thereof; (Lev. 6:2-5; Luke 19:8.)

2.   In regard to **generosity**:
- a.   giving and lending freely,
- b.   according to
  - i.   our abilities,
  - ii.   and the necessities of others; (Luke 6:30, 38; 1 John 3:17; Eph 4:28, Gal. 6:10.)

3.   In regard to **one's own financial condition**:
- a.   moderation of our:
  - i.   judgments,
  - ii.   wills,
  - iii.   and affections
  - iv.   concerning worldly goods; (1 Tim. 6:6-9; Gal. 6:14.)
- b.   a provident care and study to :
  - i.   get, (1 Tim. 5:8.)
  - ii.   keep,
  - iii.   use,
  - iv.   and dispose
  - v.   these things which are necessary and conve nient for
    - 1) the sustentation of our nature,
    - 2) and suitable to our condition; (Prov. 27:23-27; Eccl. 2:24; Eccl. 3:12-13; 1 Tim. 6:17-18; Isa. 38:1; Matt. 11:8.)

4.   In regard to a **lawful calling**, (1 Cor. 7:20; Gen. 2:15; Gen. 3:19.) and diligence in it; (Eph. 4:28; Prov. 10:4.)

5.   In regard to **frugality**; (John 6:12; Prov. 21:20.)

6.   In regard to **legal matters**:
- a.   Avoiding unnecessary law-suits, (1 Cor. 6:1-9.)
- b.   and suretiship,
- c.   or other like engagements; (Prov. 6:1-6;

Prov.11:15.)
7. In regard to **wealth**:
   a. and an endeavor, by all just and lawful means,
   b. to procure, preserve, and further
      i. the wealth and outward estate of others,
      ii. as well as our own. (Lev. 25:35; Deut. 22:1-4; Exod. 23:4-5; Gen. 47:14,20; Phil. 2:4; Matt. 22:39.)

Q. 142 What are the sins forbidden in the eighth commandment?
The **sins** forbidden in the eighth commandment are the neglect of the duties required: (James 2:15-16; 1 John 3:17.)
   1. In regard to **property or persons**:
      a. theft, (Eph. 4:28.)
      b. robbery, (Psalm 62:10.)
      c. man-stealing, (1 Tim. 1:10.)
      d. and receiving any thing that is stolen; (Prov. 29:24; Ps. 50:18.)
   2. In regard to **business dealings**:
      a. fraudulent dealing, (1 Thess. 4:6.)
      b. false weights and measures, (Prov. 11:1; Prov.20:10.)
      c. removing landmarks, (Deut. 19:14; Prov. 23:10.)
      d. injustice and unfaithfulness
         i. in contracts between man and man (Amos 8:5; Ps. 37:21.)
         ii. or in matters of trust; (Luke 16:10-12.)
   3. In regard to **unjust ways to take or withhold a neighbor's property**:
      a. oppression, (Ezek. 22:29; Lev. 25:17.)
      b. extortion, (Matt. 23:25; Ezek. 22:12.)
      c. usury, (Ps. 15:5.)
      d. bribery, (Job 15:34.)
      e. vexatious law-suits, (1 Cor. 6:6-8; Prov. 3:29-30.)
      f. unjust enclosures and depopulations, (Isa. 5:8; Micah 2:2.)
      g. ingrossing commodities to enhance the price; (Prov. 11:26.)
      h. unlawful callings, (Acts 19:19, 24-25.)

    i.   and all other unjust or sinful ways of

          i.   taking

          ii.   or withholding

          iii.   from our neighbor what belongs to him,

          iv.   or of enriching ourselves; (Job 20:19; James 5:4; Prov. 21:6.)

4.   In regard to **inappropriate desires for worldly goods**:

    a.   covetousness; (Luke 12:15.)

    b.   inordinate prizing and affecting worldly goods; (1 Tim. 6:5; Col. 3:2; Prov. 23:5; Ps. 62:10.)

    c.   distrustful and distracting cares and studies in

          i.   getting,

          ii.   keeping,

          iii.   and using them; (Matt. 6:25, 31, 34; Eccl. 5:12.)

5.   In regard to **envying at the prosperity of others**; (Ps. 73:3; Ps. 37:1, 7.)

6.   In regard to **harming one's own financial estate**:

    a.   as likewise idleness, 2 Thess. 3:11; Prov. 18:9.)

    b.   prodigality,

    c.   wasteful gaming;

    d.   and all other ways whereby

          i.   we do unduly prejudice our own outward estate, (Prov. 21:17; Prov. 23:20-21; Prov. 28:19.)

          ii.   and defrauding ourselves

               1)   of the due use

               2)   and comfort of that estate which God hath given us. (Eccl. 4:8; Eccl. 6:2 1 Tim. 5:8.)

Consider the following summary of the Biblical teaching on the legitimacy of business and personal financial activities, most of which are included in the *Larger Catechism* proof texts cited above.

The following biblical texts[9] speak in regard to **one's own financial condition**:

> 1 Tim. 6:6-10, "Now there is great gain in godliness with contentment, for we brought nothing into the world, and we can-

not take anything out of the world. But if we have food and clothing, with these we will be content. But those who desire to be rich fall into temptation, into a snare, into many senseless and harmful desires that plunge people into ruin and destruction. For the love of money is a root of all kinds of evils. It is through this craving that some have wandered away from the faith and pierced themselves with many pangs."

Gal. 6:14, "But far be it from me to boast except in the cross of our Lord Jesus Christ, by which the world has been crucified to me, and I to the world."

Prov. 27:23-27, "Know well the condition of your flocks, and give attention to your herds, for riches do not last forever; and does a crown endure to all generations? When the grass is gone and the new growth appears and the vegetation of the mountains is gathered, the lambs will provide your clothing, and the goats the price of a field. There will be enough goats' milk for your food, for the food of your household and maintenance for your girls."

Eccl. 2:24-26, "There is nothing better for a person than that he should eat and drink and find enjoyment in his toil. This also, I saw, is from the hand of God, for apart from him who can eat or who can have enjoyment? For to the one who pleases him God has given wisdom and knowledge and joy, but to the sinner he has given the business of gathering and collecting, only to give to one who pleases God. This also is vanity and a striving after wind"

Eccl. 3:9-13, "What gain has the worker from his toil? I have seen the business that God has given to the children of man to be busy with. He has made everything beautiful in its time. Also, he has put eternity into man's heart, yet so that he cannot find out what God has done from the beginning to the end. I perceived that there is nothing better for them than to be joyful and to do good as long as they live; also that everyone should eat and drink and take pleasure in all his toil—this is God's gift to man."

1 Tim. 6:17-19, "As for the rich in this present age, charge them not to be haughty, nor to set their hopes on the uncertainty of riches, but on God, who richly provides us with everything to enjoy. They are to do good, to be rich in good works, to be generous and ready to share, thus storing up treasure for themselves as a good foundation for the future, so that they may take hold of that which is truly life."

Isa. 38:1, "In those days Hezekiah became sick and was at the point of death. And Isaiah the prophet the son of Amoz came to him, and said to him, 'Thus says the Lord: Set your house in order , for you shall die, you shall not recover.'"

Matt. 11:8, "What did you go out to see? A man dressed in soft clothing? Behold, those who wear soft clothing are in kings' houses."

The next passages address **wealth** and the endeavor, by all just and lawful means, to procure, preserve, and further the wealth and outward estate of others, as well as our own.

Lev. 25:35-38, "If your brother becomes poor and cannot maintain himself with you, you shall support him as though he were a stranger and a sojourner, and he shall live with you. Take no interest from him or profit, but fear your God, that your brother may live beside you. You shall not lend him your money at interest, nor give him your food for profit. I am the Lord your God, who brought you out of the land of Egypt to give you the land of Canaan, and to be your God."

Deut. 22:1-4, "You shall not see your brother's ox or his sheep going astray and ignore them. You shall take them back to your brother. And if he does not live near you and you do not know who he is, you shall bring it home to your house, and it shall stay with you until your brother seeks it. Then you shall restore it to him. And you shall do the same with his donkey or with his garment, or with any lost thing of your brother's which he loses and you find; you may not ignore it. You shall not see your brother's donkey or his ox fallen down by the way and ignore them. You shall help him to lift them up again."

Exod. 23:4-8, "If you meet your enemy's ox or his donkey going astray, you shall bring it back to him. If you see the donkey of one who hates you lying down under its burden, you shall refrain from leaving him with it; you shall rescue it with him. You shall not pervert the justice due to your poor in his lawsuit. Keep far from a false charge, and do not kill the innocent and righteous, for I will not acquit the wicked. And you shall take no bribe, for a bribe blinds the clear-sighted and subverts the cause of those who are in the right. You shall not oppress a sojourner. You know the heart of a sojourner, for you were sojourners in the land of Egypt."

Gen. 47:14-21, "Now there was no food in all the land, for the famine was very severe, so that the land of Egypt and the land of Canaan languished by reason of the famine. And Joseph gathered up all the money that was found in the land of Egypt and in the land of Canaan, in exchange for the grain that they bought. And Joseph brought the money into Pharaoh's house. And when the money was all spent in the land of Egypt and in the land of Canaan, all the Egyptians came to Joseph and said, 'Give us food. Why should we die before your eyes? For our money is gone.' And Joseph answered, 'Give your livestock and I will give you food in exchange for your livestock, if your money is gone.' So they brought their livestock to Joseph, and Joseph gave them food in exchange for the horses, the flocks, the herds, and the donkeys. He supplied them with food in exchange for all their livestock that year. And when that year was ended, they came to him the following year and said to him, 'We will not hide from my lord that our money is all spent. The herds of livestock are my lord's. There is nothing left in the sight of my lord but our bodies and our land. Why should we die before your eyes, both we and our land? Buy us and our land for food, and we with our land will be servants to Pharaoh. And give us seed that we may live and not die, and that the land may not be desolate.' So Joseph bought all the land of Egypt for Pharaoh, for all the Egyptians sold their fields, because the famine was severe on them. The land became Pharaoh's. As for the people, he made servants of them from one end of Egypt to the other."

Phil. 2:3-4, "Do nothing from rivalry or conceit, but in humility count others more significant than yourselves. Let each of you look not only to his own interests, but also to the interests of others."

Matt. 22:36-40, "'Teacher, which is the great commandment in the Law?' And he said to him, 'You shall love the Lord your God with all your heart and with all your soul and with all your mind. This is the great and first commandment. And a second is like it: You shall love your neighbor as yourself. On these two commandments depend all the Law and the Prophets.'"

It is clear that the believer is to avoid **inappropriate desires for worldly goods**: such as covetousness; (Luke 12:15.), the inordinate prizing and affecting worldly goods; (1 Tim. 6:5; Col. 3:2; Prov. 23:5; Ps. 62:10.); the distrustful and distracting cares and studies in getting, keeping, and using them; (Matt. 6:25, 31, 34; Eccl. 5:12.) as well as **envying at the prosperity of others**; (Ps. 73:3; Ps. 37:1, 7.). Still, lest **he harm his own financial estate**, he is to avoid idleness, (2 Thess. 3:11; Prov. 18:9.), prodigality, wasteful gaming; and all other ways whereby we do unduly prejudice our own outward estate, (Prov. 21:17; Prov. 23:20-21; Prov. 28:19.) and defrauding ourselves of the due use and comfort of that estate which God hath given us. (Eccl. 4:8; Eccl. 6:2 1 Tim. 5:8.)

Several of these last biblical texts are worthy of quoting in this context of one's duty to avoid **harming one's own outward estate**.

Prov. 21:17, "Whoever loves pleasure will be a poor man; he who loves wine and oil will not be rich."

Prov. 23:19-21, "Hear, my son, and be wise, and direct your heart in the way. Be not among drunkards or among gluttonous eaters of meant, for the drunkard and the glutton will come to poverty, and slumber will clothe them with rags."

Prov. 28:18-20, 22, 24-27, "Whoever walks in integrity will be delivered, but he who is crooked in his ways will suddenly fall. Whoever works his land will have plenty of bread, but he who follows worthless pursuits will have plenty of poverty. A faithful man will abound with blessings, but whoever hastens to be rich will not go unpunished....A stingy man hastens after wealth and does not know that poverty will come upon him....Whoever robs his father or his mother and says, 'That is no transgression,' is a companion to a man who destroys. A greedy man stirs up strife, but the one who trusts in the Lord will be enriched. Whoever trusts in his own mind is a fool, but he who walks in wisdom will be delivered. Whoever gives to the poor will not want, but he who hides his eye s will get many a curse."

Eccl. 4:4-14, "Then I saw that all toil and all skill in work come from a man's envy of his neighbor. This also is vanity and a striving after wind. The fool folds his hands and eats his own flesh. Better is a handful of quietness than two hands full of toil and a striving after wind. Again, I saw vanity under the sun: one person who has no other, either son or brother, yet there is no end to all his toil, and his eyes are never satisfied with riches, so that he never asks, 'For whom am I toiling and depriving myself of pleasure?' This also is vanity and an unhappy business. Two are better than one, because they have a good reward for their toil. For if they fall, one will lift up his fellow. But woe to him who is alone when he falls and has not another to lift him up! Again, if two lie together, they keep warm, but how can one keep warm alone? And though a man might prevail against one who is alone, two will withstand him—a threefold cord is not quickly broken. Better was a poor and wise youth than an old and foolish king who no longer knew how to take advice. For he went from prison to the throne, though in his own kingdom he had been born poor."

Eccl. 6:1-2, "There is an evil that I have seen under the sun, and it lies heavy on mankind: a man to whom God gives wealth, possessions, and honor, so that he lacks nothing of all that he desires, yet God does not give him power to enjoy them, but a stranger enjoys them. This is vanity; it is a grievous evil."

1 Tim. 5:8, "But if anyone does not provide for his relatives, and especially for members of his household, he has denied the faith and is worse than an unbeliever."

Matthew 25:19-29, "Now after a long time the master of those servants came and settled accounts with them. And he who had received the five talents came forward; bringing five talents more, saying, 'Master, you delivered to me five talents; here I have made five talents more.' His master said to him, 'Well done, good and faithful servant. You have been faithful over a little; I will set you over much. Enter into the joy of your master.' And he also who had the two talents came forward, saying, 'Master, you delivered to me two talents; here I have made two talents more.' His master said to him, 'Well done, good and faithful servant. You have been faithful over a little; I will set you over much. Enter into the joy of your master.' He also who had received the one talent came forward, saying, 'Master, I knew you to be a hard man, reaping where you did not sow, and gathering where you scattered no seed, so I was afraid, and I went and hid your talent in the ground. Here you have what is yours.' But his master answered him, 'You wicked and slothful servant! You knew that I reap where I have not sowed and gather where I scattered no seed? Then you ought to have invested my money with the bankers ,and at my coming I should have received what was my own with interest. So take the talent from him and give it to him who has the ten talents. For to everyone who has will more be given, and he will have an abundance But from one who has not, even what he has will be taken away."

VII. Conclusion

If we are going to be in relationship with God, we need to have a relationship with the law as a **mirror** (to show our sin and our need for the gospel), as a **master** (to provide true justice for our society), and as a **map** (to show us how to love God wherever we go, including in our business pursuits). The law requires us to act in justice and in conformity to the second table of God's law. It calls on us to see that we come to this law with mercy and love as the heart of our motivation to please God and to serve our neighbor. We are to pursue our business activities on our neighbors' behalf as well as on our own behalf as legitimate business interests. The Law gives us the sweet demand of walking in covenant with our God as seen especially in the first table of the Law. Thus the business person is to learn the joy of walking in whole-hearted covenant fellowship with God as he or she lives out the full implications of the Eighth Commandment.

Truly, a moral reformation will only begin if we as believers strive to live our ethics. A non-Christian cannot live Christian ethics although he is impacted and influenced by them. So let us remember that we evangelize by our gospel proclamation and by our business integrity done to the glory of God. We are called to show the great benefit of living Christian ethics in the business market and in the public policy arena.

We are called to obey even when it is not easy or evidently pleasant. Cross-bearing is expressed in our decisions in the ethical arena. Indeed, "If Jesus had loved the way we love, He would have lived to a ripe old age." So in conclusion, do you know the Ten Commandments? Have you ever read and studied the *Larger Westminster Catechisms* with its great insights into godly Christian business ethics?

Notes

[1] Below is an Outline of the Westminster Confession of Faith, Chapter XIX, "Of the Law of God"

Of the Law of God (XIX)
I. *The Law of Creation*: God gave to Adam a law,
   A. as a covenant of works,
   B. by which He bound
      1. him and all his posterity,
      2. to obedience,
         a. personal,

b. entire,

c. exact,

d. and perpetual

3. promised life upon the fulfilling,

4. and threatened death upon the breach of it,

5. and endued him with power and ability to keep it.

II. *The Law After the Fall:* This law, after his fall,

A. continued to be a perfect rule of righteousness;

B. and, as such, was delivered by God upon Mount Sinai, (see Further Reading, *A Summary of the Ten Commandments*)

1. in ten commandments, (see Further Reading, *Ten Suggestions?*)

2. and written in two tables: (see Further Reading, *The Nail the 10 Commandments Hang Upon*)

a. the first four commandments containing our duty towards God;

b. and the other six, our duty to man. (see Further Reading, *The Greatest Commandment and Loving God*)

III. *Ceremonial Laws:* God was pleased to give to the people of Israel Ceremonial laws, as a church under age,

A. These were in addition to the law of the ten commandments, commonly called moral.

B. These Ceremonial Law contain:

1. several typical ordinances:

a. partly of worship,

1) prefiguring Christ,

2) His graces,

3) actions,

4) sufferings,

5) and benefits;

b. and partly, holding forth divers instructions of moral duties.

2. All which ceremonial laws are now abrogated, under the new testament.

IV. *Judicial Laws:* God also gave sundry judicial laws,

A. To Israel, as a political body

B. These judicial laws expired together with the state of that people;

C. not obliging any other now,

D. further than the general equity thereof may require.

V. *The Moral Law:*

A. It forever binds:

1. all,

a. justified persons

b. as well as others,

2. to the obedience thereof;

3. and that,

a. not only in regard of the matter contained in it,

b. but also in respect of the authority of God the Creator, who gave it.

4. Neither does Christ, in the Gospel,

    a. Any way dissolve,

    b. but much strengthen this obligation.

VI. *True Believers & the Moral Law.*

  A. Although true believers, are not under the law as a covenant of works,

    1. to be thereby justified,

    2. or condemned;

  B. yet it is of great use

    1. to them, as well as to others;

    2. in that,

      a. as a rule of life (see Further Reading, *Christian Ethics: The Law of the City of God*)

        1) informing them of the will of God,

        2) and their duty,

      b. it directs and binds them

        1) to walk accordingly;

        2) discovering also the sinful pollutions

          a) of their nature,

          b) hearts,

          c) and lives;

    3. so as, examining themselves thereby

      a. they may come to

        1) further conviction of,

        2) humiliation for,

        3) and hatred against sin,

      b. together with

        1) a clearer sight of the need they have of Christ,

        2) and the perfection of His obedience.

  C. It is likewise of use to the regenerate,

    1. to restrain their corruptions,

      a. in that it forbids sin:

      b. and the threatenings of it serve to show what even their sins deserve;

      c. and what afflictions,

        1) in this life, they may expect for them,

        2) although freed from the curse thereof threatened in the law.

    2. The promises of it, in like manner, show them

      a. God's approbation of obedience,

      b. and what blessings they may expect upon the performance thereof:

        1) although not as due to them

        2) by the law as a covenant of works.

  D. So as, a man's doing good, and refraining from evil,

    1. because the law encourages to the one,

    2. and deters from the other,

    3. is no evidence of his being under the law;

    4. and not under grace.

VII.   *The agreement of the Law and Gospel: These previously mentioned uses of the law*

A. are not contrary to the grace of the Gospel,

B. but do sweetly comply with it;

   1. the Spirit of Christ

      a. subduing

      b. and enabling

   2. the will of man

      a. to do that freely,

      b. and cheerfully,

   3. which the will of God,

      a. revealed in the law,

      b. requires to be done.

[2] Below is an outline of the introductory portion of the Westminster Larger Catechism's teaching on the Ten Commandments.

HAVING SEEN WHAT THE SCRIPTURES PRINCIPALLY TEACH US TO BELIEVE CONCERNING GOD (Questions #6 to #90), IT FOLLOWS TO CONSIDER WHAT THEY REQUIRE AS THE DUTY OF MAN

The Larger Catechism teaches that the rule of Man's duty of obedience to God is the Moral Law, which is summarized in the Ten Commandments. This is the focus of Questions #91-148. Questions #91-98 prepare for the study of the Ten Commandments by considering the concept of the Moral Law. Questions #99-148 deal with the Ten Commandments specifically.

A. Man's Duty to God.

   Q. 91   What is the duty which God requires of man?

   A. 91   The duty which God requires of man, is obedience to his revealed will.

B. The Rule of Man's Obedience to God.

   Q. 92   What did God at first reveal unto man as the rule of his obedience?

   A. 92   The rule of obedience revealed to Adam

          1. in the estate of innocence,

          2. and to all mankind in him,

          3. besides a special command not to eat of the fruit of the tree of the knowledge of good and evil,

          4. was the moral law.

C. The Moral Law.

  1. The Moral Law Defined.

   Q. 93   What is the moral law?

   A. 93   The moral law is

          1. the declaration of the will of God to mankind,

          2. directing and binding every one to

              a. personal,

              b. perfect,

              c. and perpetual

              d. conformity

              e. and obedience thereunto,

          3. in the frame and disposition

a. of the whole man,

b. soul and body,

4. and in performance of all those

a. duties of

1) holiness

2) and righteousness

b. which he owes to

1) God

2) and man:

5. promising life upon the fulfilling,

6. and threatening death upon the breach of it.

2. The Use of the Moral Law.

a. Since the Fall.

Q. 94   Is there any use of the moral law to man since the fall?

A. 94

1. Although no man, since the fall, can attain to righteousness and life by the moral law;

2. yet there is great use thereof,

3. as well common to all men,

a) as peculiar either to the unregenerate,

b) or the regenerate.

b. The Use of the Moral Law to all Men.

Q. 95 Of what use is the moral law to all men?

A. 95

1. The moral law is of use to all men,

a) to inform them

1) of the holy nature and the will of God,

2) and of their duty,

3) binding them to walk accordingly;

b) to convince them

1)of their disability to keep it,

2)and of the sinful pollution of

a)their nature,

b) hearts,

c) and lives:

c) to humble them

1) in the sense of

a) their sin

b) and misery,

2) and thereby help them to a clearer sight of the need they have

a) of Christ,

b) and of the perfection of his obedience.

c. The Particular Use of the Moral Law to Unregenerate Men.

Q. 96   What particular use is there of the moral law to unregenerate men?

A.96

1.The moral law is of use to unregenerate men,

a) to awaken their consciences to flee from wrath to come,

b) and to drive them to Christ;

c) or, inexcusable, and under the curse thereof.

d. The Special Use of the Moral Law to the Regenerate.

Q. 97   What special use is there of the moral law to the regenerate?

A. 97

1. Although they that are regenerate, and believe in Christ,

a) be delivered from the moral law as a covenant of works,

b) so as thereby they are neither justified nor condemned,

2. yet, besides the general uses thereof common to them with all men, it is of special use,

a) to show them how much they are bound to Christ

1) for his fulfilling it,

2) and enduring the curse thereof in their stead,

3) and for their good;

b) and thereby

1) to provoke them to more thankfulness,

2) and to express the same

a) in their greater care to conform themselves thereunto

b) as the rule to their obedience.

3. The Summary of the Moral Law.

Q. 98   Where is the moral law summarily comprehended?

1. The moral law is summarily comprehended in the ten commandments,

a) which were delivered by the voice of God upon Mount Sinai,

b) and written by him in two tables of stone;

c) and are recorded in the twentieth chapter of Exodus.

2. The four first commandments containing our duty to God,

3. and the other six our duty to man.

The Three Special Considerations in the Study of the Ten Commandments.

Q. 100   What special things are we to consider in the ten commandments?

A. 100   We are to consider in the ten commandments,

1. the preface,

2. the substance of the commandments themselves,

3. and several reasons annexed to some of them, the more to enforce them.

The Four Commandments Containing Man's Duty to God. (Questions 102-121.)

A. The Sum of the Four commandments containing man's duty to God.

Q. 102   What is the sum of the four commandments which contain our duty to God?

A. 102   The sum of the four commandments containing our duty to God is,

1. to love the Lord our God

2. with all our heart,

3. and with all our soul,

4. and with all our strength,

5. and with all our mind.

The Six commandments that Contain Our Duty to Our Neighbors. (Questions #122-148.)

A. The Sum of the six commandments which contain our duty to man.

Q. 122   What is the sum of the six commandments which contain our duty to man?

A. 122

1. The sum of the six commandments which contain our duty to man, is,

a. to love our neighbor as ourselves,

b. and to do to others what we would have them to do to us

[3] How Does One Interpret the Ten Commandments? According to the *Westminster Larger Catechism* Question #99 there are eight rules for interpreting the Ten Commandments.

The Eight Rules for Interpreting the Ten Commandments. (Questions #99-100.)

Q. 99   What rules are to be observed for the right understanding of the ten commandments?

A. 99   For the right understanding of the ten commandments, these rules are to be observed:

1. *The Law's Perfection:* That the law is perfect, and binds every one
   a. to full conformity
      1) in the whole man
      2) unto the righteousness thereof,
   b. and unto entire obedience for ever;
   c. so as
      1) to require the utmost perfection of every duty,
      2) and to forbid the least degree of every sin.

2.   *The Inward Spirituality of the Law:*
   a. That the Law is spiritual, and so reaches
   b. the understanding,
   c. will,
   d. affections,
   e. and all other powers of the soul;
   f. as well as
      1) words,
      2) works,
      3) and gestures.

3. *The Same Duty Is Implied in Different Commandments:*
   a. That one and the same thing,
   b. in divers respects,
   c. is required
   d. or forbidden
   e. in several commandments.

4. *The Law of Contraries:*
   a. That as, where a duty is commanded, the contrary sin is forbidden;
   b. and, where a sin is forbidden, the contrary duty is commanded;
   c. so, where a promise is annexed, the contrary threatening is included;
   d. and, where a threatening is annexed, the contrary promise is included.

5. *Time and the Law:*
   a. That what God forbids, is at no time to be done;
   b. what he commands, is always our duty;

      c. and yet every particular duty is not to be done at all times.

    6. *The Synechdochal Character of the Law:*
      a. That under one sin or duty,
          1) all of the same kind are forbidden
          2) or commanded;
      b. together with all
          1) the causes,
          2) means,
          3) occasions,
          4) and appearances thereof,
          5) and provocations thereunto.

    7. *My obedience requires that I seek in an appropriate way the same obedience from my neighbor:*
      a. That what is forbidden or commanded to ourselves,
      b. we are bound, according to our places
          1) to endeavor that it may be avoided
          2) or performed by others,
          3) according to the duty of their places.

    8. *My Neighbor's du ty to obey requires that I assist him in an appropriate way to obey:*
      a. That in what is commanded to others,
      b. we are bound, according to our places and callings,
          1) to be helpful to them;
          2) and to take heed of partaking with others in what is for bidden to them.

[4] Why No One Keeps God's Law Perfectly.

There are none who can withstand God's biblical scrutiny and declare themselves "sinlessly perfect" before the perfect requirements of His Law.

I. The Heavenly Standard: The Absolute Moral Perfection of God's Holy Nature.
    A. Scriptural references
      1. "There is no one who does what is right and never sins"; Ecc. 7:20.
      2. "All fall short of the glory of God"; Romans 3:23.
      3. "Be ye perfect even as your Father in Heaven is perfect";
         Matthew 5:48.

    B. The standard of our sinfulness is not in comparison to someone else on earth, but in relation to God in His holiness in Heaven.

II. The Earthly Standard: The Perfect Requirements of God's Law
    A. The Three Uses of God's Law:
      1. *Conviction* (a **Mirror** to show us the reality of our sin before the Holiness of God and to

draw us to the grace of the Gospel of Christ.)

2. *Civil* (a **Master** to restrain a community's sinfulness by true justice.)
3. *Christian* (a **Map** to guide us in our love for God.)

B. When measured by this law we all fall short.
   1. Sins of commission; Doing what is prohibited in the Ten Commandments in deed, word, thought.
   2. Sins of omission; Not doing the positive duties required by the Ten Commandments in deed, word, thought.

[5] The Gospel in the Ten Commandments.

The Preface of the Ten Commandments Presents God's Redemption. (Question #101.)

Q. 101   What is the preface to the ten commandments?

A. The preface to the ten commandments is contained in these words, *I am the Lord thy God, which have brought thee out of the land of Egypt, out of the house of bondage.*

    1. Wherein God manifests his sovereignty,

        a. as being,

            1) JEHOVAH,

            2) the eternal,

            3) immutable,

            4) and almighty God;

        b. having his being in and of himself,

        c. and giving being to all his words and works:

    2. and that he is a God in covenant,

        a. as with Israel of old,

        b. so with all his people;

    3. who,

        a. as he brought them out of their bondage in Egypt,

        b. so he delivers us from our spiritual thraldom;

    4. and that therefore we are bound to take him for our God alone, and to keep all his commandments.

[6] Consider Luther's experience of the Gospel.

I hated that word "righteousness of God," which, according to the use and custom of all the teachers, I had been taught to understand philosophically regarding the formal or active righteousness, as they called it, with which God is righteous and punishes the unrighteous sinner.

Though I lived as a monk without reproach, I felt that I was a sinner before God with an extremely disturbed conscience. I could not believe that he was placated by my satisfaction. I did not love, yes, I hated the righteous God who punishes sinners, and secretly, if not blasphemously, certainly murmuring greatly, I was angry with God, and said, "As if, indeed, it is not enough, that miser able sinners, eternally lost through original sin, are crushed by every kind of calamity by the law of the decalogue, without having God add pain to pain by the gospel and also by the gospel threatening us with his righteousness and wrath!" Thus I raged with a fierce and troubled conscience. Nevertheless, I beat importunately upon Paul at that place, most ardently desiring to know what St. Paul wanted.

At last, by the mercy of God, meditating day and night, I gave heed to the context of the words, namely, "In it the righteousness of God is revealed, as it is written, 'He who through faith is righteous shall live.'" There I began to understand that the righteousness of God is that by which the righteous lives by a gift of God, namely by faith. And this is the meaning: the righteousness of God is revealed by the gospel, namely, the passive righteousness with which merciful God justifies us by faith, as it is written, "He who through faith is righteous shall live." Here I felt that I was altogether born again and had entered paradise itself through open gates. (*Preface to Latin Writings*, 1545.)

7 Two Types of Reformed Ethics

"Philonomy" or the love of God's law, the view taken in this paper, teaches that we are to love the law of God (Ps. 19:7-10; 119:47, 48, 97, 127, 163, 165). This view seeks to apply the "general equity" of God's law of the OT to the NT situation. This is the view of the *Westminster Confession of Faith*. A Biblical example of General Equity is found in 1 Tim. 5:17-18; 1 Cor. 9:9-10. Paul applies the principle of letting the threshing oxen eat unmuzzled to the issue of compensation for Pastors! (Pastors work like oxen and eat like oxen!)

"Theonomy" literally meaning "God's Law" asserts that an exact application of OT law is required by Christians in the NT age, even in the case of its penal sanctions (all the death penalties of the OT are still required in the NT age). "Reconstruction" is often seen as a view in harmony with Theonomy. But it is usually applied with a post-millennial perspective and its attendant optimism for the future of human civilization prior to the return of Christ.

[8] Love is central to the Bible--Mt. 22:40. The whole OT Scriptures (Law & Prophets) hang on these commands to love. Eternal life requires either man's perfect love to God (Luke 10:25-28), or else God's perfect love to man (John 3:16; Romans 8:28-39).

Love isn't simply an emotion, or else it could not be commanded. It is not a self-guiding principle, otherwise, God would not have needed to give us His law. Love is not our standard. The word of God is. Rather, love is our motive to keep the standard.

Consider St. Paul's teaching on love in 1 Corinthians 13:1-8, 13.

     1. Great actions without love are ultimately nothing before God. Vv. 1-3.
     2. What love is: patient, kind. Vv. 4-7.
     3. What love doesn't do: envy, boast.
     4. What love is not: proud, rude, self-seeking, easily angered.
     5. What love doesn't do: keep records of wrongs, delight in evil.
     6. What love does: rejoices with the truth.
     7. What love always does: protects, trusts, hopes, perseveres.
     8. What love never does: fails because it is the greatest. Vv. 8, 13.

[9] **These references are taken from the ESV.**

An Optimistic Look at the 8th Commandment

ROBERT DOLL, PHILIP RYKEN
AND RON FERNER

ROBERT DOLL

Bob Doll is Chief Equity Strategist and Senior Portfolio Manager at BlackRock, the world's largest asset management firm. Mr. Doll's service with BlackRock dates back to 1999, including his years with Merrill Lynch Investment Managers (MLIM), which merged with BlackRock in 2006. At MLIM, he served as the President and Chief Investment Officer and Senior Portfolio Manager of the Merrill Lynch Large Cap Series Funds. Prior to joining MLIM, Mr. Doll served as the Chief Investment Officer of Oppenheimer Funds, Inc. He received a BS in Accounting and a BA in Economics from Lehigh University and an MBA from the Wharton School of the University of Pennsylvania. Mr. Doll is both a Certified Public Accountant and a Chartered Financial Analyst. Bob appears regularly in the national financial press discussing economic developments and markets. Bob and his wife Leslie live in Princeton, New Jersey and have three children. He is also choir director at his local church. Bob serves on a number of boards including the Alliance of Confessing Evangelicals, Word of Life Fellowship, New Canaan Society, Kingdom Advisors, and the Wharton Graduate Executive Board.

PHILIP RYKEN

Philip Graham Ryken is President-Elect of Wheaton College. Through July he continues to serve as Senior Minister of Tenth Presbyterian Church in Philadelphia, where he has preached since 1995. He is Bible Teacher for the Alliance of Confessing Evangelicals, speaking nationally on the radio program Every Last Word.

Doctor Ryken was educated at Wheaton College (IL), Westminster Theological Seminary (PA), and the University of Oxford (UK), from which he received his doctorate in historical theology. When he is not preaching or playing with his five children, he likes to read books, shoot baskets, and ponder the relationship between Christian faith and American culture. He has written or edited more than thirty books, including Written in Stone: The Ten Commandments and Today's Moral Crisis.

Dr. Ryken is adjunct faculty for Beeson Divinity School and Westminster Seminary California. He is a board member for Westminster Theological Seminary in Philadelphia and Wheaton College. Dr. Ryken is a council member of Alliance of Confessing Evangelicals and a member of the Evangelical Theological Society and the Union League of Philadelphia.

RON FERNER

Ron joined Philadelphia Biblical University in 1997 after retiring from Campbell Soup Company. He presently serves as Dean of the School of Business and Leadership, and Chair of the Undergraduate Business Administration program.

Ron developed the Bachelor of Science–Business Administration degree program for Philadelphia Biblical University (PBU). He has created a program that allows students to apply their classroom knowledge in real-world situations through a faculty-mentored internship program and community service projects. Ron is currently in the process of developing an MBA Program for Philadelphia Biblical University. The planned start date for this program is the fall of 2010, and it is set to have a positive influence in the development of leaders in the business and non-profit sectors.

During his career at Campbell's, he held plant manager positions at several Campbell plants including Fremont, Nebraska; Worthington, Minnesota; and Chicago, Illinois. Ron also held management assignments at Campbell's World Headquarters in Camden, New Jersey, including Vice President–Operations/Logistics Strategy. He was transferred to Sacramento, California, as Vice President–Manufacturing, Western Region. His last assignment was at Campbell's World Headquarters in Camden, New Jersey, as Vice President–Low Cost Business Systems, responsible for improving manufacturing and customer service processes throughout the company.

Ron received a Bachelor of Science degree in Food Engineering from the Illinois Institute of Technology and an MBA from the University of Chicago.

The famous Bible teacher Harry Ironside liked to tell about the spiritual life lessons he learned as a young boy working for an old Scottish shoemaker named Dan Mackay—a fine Christian businessman who often spoke to his customers about the saving necessity of faith in Jesus Christ. Ironside's responsibility was to pound the leather to make the soles of the shoes. He would soak cowhide in water and then place it on a piece of iron, where he pounded the leather until it was hard and dry. This time-consuming process toughened the leather to produce long-lasting soles.

One day Ironside walked by the shop of another cobbler and saw—to his surprise—that the owner did not pound his leather at all. He simply took the cowhide out of the water and nailed it to the upper section of the shoe, with the water splashing out as he drove the nails in. Ironside went inside and asked the man why he made shoes that way. The cobbler gave him a naughty wink and answered, "They come back all the quicker this way, my boy!"

Young Ironside thought he had learned an important principle for profitable business, so he went back to his boss and told him that pounding the shoe leather was a waste of time. Mr. Mackay stopped his work and opened his Bible to Colossians 3:23-24, where he read, "Whatever you do, work at it with all your heart, as working for the Lord, not for men, since you know that you will receive an inheritance from the Lord as a reward." Then the shoemaker said, "Harry, I don't cobble shoes just for the money I get from my customers. I am doing this for the glory of God. I expect to see every shoe I have ever repaired in a big pile at the judgment seat of Christ, and I do not want the Lord to say to me in that day, 'Dan, this was a poor job. You did not do your best here.' I want him to be able to say, 'Well done, good and faithful servant'."[1]

This true-life story illustrates the difference between two entirely different ways of doing business in God's world. One shoemaker wanted to make a dishonest profit. In effect, he was stealing from his customers by giving them an inferior product with a built-in flaw. The other shoemaker refused to steal from his customers at all, but honored God by making them a durable pair of shoes.

It is sad to say, but not everyone runs a business with the integrity of Dan Mackay. Still, it is inspiring to imagine what the world would be like if people did. How would business be practiced in a world without sin? More specifically, how would the economy prosper—and how would our personal relationships flourish—in a world without any theft?

In this paper we take an optimistic look at the law of God, trying to imagine what the world would be like if people actually kept the Eighth Commandment. First we will analyze the Bible's prohibition against stealing, unfolding the comprehensive implications of the Eighth Commandment. Then we will show the difference it makes for business and society when people actually do what the commandment says and respect other people's property.

UNDERSTANDING THE EIGHTH COMMANDMENT

It is generally acknowledged that people do not know the Ten Commandments as well as they ought to. Most people—including many Christians—would be hard pressed to name all ten of them. But even people who do know the Ten Commandments may not fully understand what they mean. What principles can help us interpret and apply the law of God, specifically the Eighth Commandment?

FIRST PRINCIPLE: THE EIGHTH COMMANDMENT AND THE CHARACTER OF GOD

First, there is the *theological principle* of the Eighth Commandment. According to this principle, each commandment is grounded in the character of God. Every law reveals something about the lawgiver, so every one of the Ten Commandments is stamped with the attributes of Almighty God. For example, the Sixth Commandment—which tells us not to commit murder—shows that God is the Life-Giver who claims absolute sovereignty over life and death. Similarly, the Ninth Commandment—which tells us not to bear false witness against our neighbor—reminds that God is true in everything he is, everything he says, and everything he does. The Ten Commandments are theological as well as ethical: they help to teach us the doctrine of God.

When we see how God has put himself into his law, it becomes obvious that he could not have given us any other commandments than the ones he gave. The Ten Commandments express God's eternal will for our lives because they flow from his character. This helps to answer an ancient dilemma that Plato posed in one of his famous dialogues: Does God command the law because the law is good, or is the law good because God commands it?[2] The answer is both! The law, with all its goodness, springs from the goodness of God's character. The law is good because God is good, and his goodness permeates every aspect of his law.

What, then, does the Eighth Commandment teach us about the good character of God? It tells us that he is our Creator and Provider. The reason God tells us not to steal is because he has promised to give us everything we need. To steal, therefore, is to mistrust his promise to provide. It is also to deny God's provision for someone else—whoever is the victim of our crime. That person, too, has a right to the stewardship of his own property—a right that is grounded in God's ownership of everything there is and in his prerogative to give it to whomever he pleases.

Keeping the Eighth Commandment is a practical way to honor the generous providence of God, both in our own life and in the lives of others. Whenever we take something that does not belong to us, we deny that God has given us everything we need. But when we keep the Eight Commandment, we acknowledge that everything belongs to God, and therefore we do not have the right to take what he has given to someone else. The entire commandment is grounded in the providence of God.

SECOND PRINCIPLE: THE POSITIVES AND THE NEGATIVES

Second, there is the *two-sided principle* of the Eight Commandment. According to this principle, each commandment has both a positive and a negative side. Where a sin is forbidden, the corresponding duty is required, and where a duty is required, the corresponding sin is forbidden.

People usually think of the Ten Commandments as a list of "don'ts": don't make other gods, don't work on Sunday, don't commit adultery, and so forth. Admittedly, most of the commandments are worded as "don'ts" rather than "dos." In fact, the only completely positive commandment is the fifth: "Honor your father and your mother" (Exod. 20:12).

All of these "thou shalt nots" may sound rather negative. When we interpret the Ten Commandments properly, however, we find that they are positive as well as negative in their intention. There is a "flip-side" to every commandment. Each one condemns a particular vice, while at the same time commanding a particular virtue. For example, the Third Commandment forbids the misuse of God's name. Yet by sheer force of logic, this command also requires us to use God's name honorably and reverently. To give another example, the commandment that forbids murder simultaneously requires the preservation of life. The true intent of each commandment is to tell us what *to* do as well as what *not* to do.

The two-sided principle makes the Ten Commandments at least twice as hard to keep as most people think. It also helps keep us from following the letter of the law while avoiding its full application. We cannot just say, "Well, at least I don't shoplift," while failing to give what we can to the poor, and still think that we are really keeping the Eighth Commandment. We must do everything God commands us to do and not simply avoid a handful of specific and obvious sins.

The *Westminster Larger Catechism* (Q. and A. 141) gives one of the most comprehensive statements of what the Eighth Commandment demands— the positive side of the law. In response to the question "What are the duties required in the eighth commandment?" the catechism replies:

> The duties required in the eighth commandment are, truth, faithfulness, and justice in contracts and commerce between man and man; rendering to everyone his due; restitution of goods unlawfully detained from the right owners thereof; giving and lending freely, according to our abilities, and the necessities of others; moderation of our judgments, wills, and affections concerning worldly goods; a provident care and study to get, keep, use, and dispose these things which are necessary and convenient for the sustentation of our nature, and suitable to our condition; a lawful calling, and diligence in it; frugality; avoiding unnecessary law-suits, and suretiship, or other like engagements; and an endeavor, by all just and lawful means, to procure, preserve, and further the wealth and outward estate of others, as well as our own.

Even if some of the catechism's language sounds archaic, the overall thrust of its answer is unmistakable: the Eighth Commandment requires us to do everything we can to protect the property and advance the material welfare of ourselves and our neighbors, especially through honest business. This law is not simply about not stealing, therefore; it is also about faithful stewardship. A clear example of this way of thinking comes from Ephesians, where the apostle Paul tells burglars to become benefactors: "Let the thief no longer steal, but rather let him labor, doing honest work with his own hands, so that he may have something to share with anyone in need" (Eph. 4:28).

Keeping the Eighth Commandment means acknowledging that everything belongs to God and then fulfilling our sacred trust to use it for his glory. It also means giving away what God has given to us so that other people will have what they need. Jerry Bridges has observed that there are three basic attitudes we can take towards possessions. The first says, "What's yours is mine; I'll take it." This is the attitude of the thief. The second says "What's mine is mine; I'll keep it." Since we are selfish by nature, this is the attitude that most of us have most of the time. The third attitude—the godly attitude—says, "What's mine is God's; I'll share it."[3] This is the positive side of keeping God's commandment not to steal.

THIRD PRINCIPLE: THE EIGHTH COMMANDMENT IN FULL

Third, there is the *categorical principle* of the Eighth Commandment. According to this principle, each of the Ten Commandments covers a wide scope of sin and obedience, not just one narrow area of obedience. Put more simply, each commandment stands for a whole category of sins. It governs not only the specific sin that is mentioned, but all the sins that lead up to it, and all the supposedly lesser sins of the same kind. The *Westminster Larger Catechism* states this rule formally: "That under one sin or duty, all of the same kind are forbidden or commanded; together with all the causes, means, occasions, and appearances thereof, and provocations thereunto" (A. 99.6).

Perhaps the easiest way to explain what this means is to give an example. Consider the Sixth Commandment: "Thou shalt not murder." Taken literally, this is a commandment that relatively few people break (although, as Jesus explained, since the law is spiritual, it also condemns very common yet sinful attitudes like hatred; see Matthew 5:21-22). But in addition to outright murder, the Sixth Commandment forbids any form of physical violence, including fist-fighting, bodily injury, and domestic violence. It also condemns the willful neglect of our personal health. Further, it includes everything that leads up to these sins, such as fits of anger, reckless driving, or even playing violent video games. What God forbids is not simply murder, but everything that harms the body, threatens our physical well being, or inures us to the dangers of violence.

This example helps us understand that the Ten Commandments generally forbid the most extreme form of a particular kind of sin. Murder is the most harmful act of violence. But listing the worst sin in each category of transgression is not intended to make us think that the big sins are the only ones that matter. On the contrary, this approach shows that God considers every sin in any category to be as unrighteous as the most heinous form of that particular sin. What the Eighth Commandment tells us, therefore, is that every form of poor stewardship is as culpable as stealing.

The rule of categories warns us not to commit lesser sins that by their very nature are bound to lead us into greater sins. People generally do not start out with grand larceny; they start with petty theft. But God rules out the little sins in order to help prevent the big ones. The Swiss Reformer Francis Turretin explained the principle like this: "What are most base and capital in each species of sin are forbidden, under which all the others are included, either because they flow thence or because they lead at length to it; or because what appear the smallest to men are in the most accurate judgment of God rated more severely. This is not done, therefore, to excuse or exclude lesser sins, but that a greater detestation of sin may be impressed upon our minds."[4] Rather than telling us that big sins are the only ones that matter, the Ten Commandments are intended to show us that God hates every type of sin, and so should we.

The range of sins forbidden by the Eighth Commandment is impressive, and sobering. In its simplest form, to steal is "to appropriate someone else's property unlawfully." But here is a more complete summary of the sins that fall under this category:

> *Ganaf*—stealing—covers all conventional types of theft: burglary (breaking into a home or building to commit theft); robbery (taking property directly from another using violence or intimidation); larceny (taking something without permission and not returning it); hijacking (using force to take goods in transit or seizing control of a bus, truck, plane, etc.); shoplifting (taking items from a store during business hours without paying for them); and pick-pocketing and purse-snatching. The term *ganaf* also covers a wide range of exotic and complex thefts... [such as] embezzlement (the fraudulent taking of money or other goods entrusted to one's care). There is extortion (getting money from someone by means of threats or misuses of authority), and racketeering (obtaining money by any illegal means).[5]

The wide variety of words we have to describe different kinds of theft is a sad testament to human depravity. Yet even this list, as impressive as it seems, is only partial. The *Westminster Larger Catechism* (A. 142) employs some of the same vocabulary, but it also expands our understanding of everything this commandment truly condemns:

> The sins forbidden in the eighth commandment, besides the neglect of the duties required are, theft, robbery, man-stealing, and receiving any thing that is stolen; fraudulent dealing, false weights and measures, removing land-marks, injustice and unfaithfulness in contracts between man and man, or in matters of trust; oppression, extortion, usury, bribery, vexatious lawsuits, unjust enclosures and depopulations; engrossing commodities to enhance the price; unlawful callings, and all other unjust or sinful ways of taking or withholding from our neighbor what belongs to him, or of enriching ourselves; covetousness; inordinate prizing and affecting worldly goods; distrustful and distracting cares and studies in getting, keeping, and using them; envying at the prosperity of others; as likewise idleness, prodigality, wasteful gaming; and all other ways whereby we do unduly prejudice our own outward estate, and defrauding ourselves of the due use and comfort of that estate which God hath given us.

The Heidelberg Catechism (A. 110) offers a shorter list, which nonetheless includes some forms of theft that other definitions leave out: "God forbids not only outright theft and robbery, but also such wicked schemes and devices as false weights and measures, deceptive merchandising, counterfeit money, and usury; we must not defraud our neighbor in any way, whether by force or by show of right. In addition God forbids all greed and all abuse or squandering of his gifts."

It is worth noting that many of the sins that fall under the category of "theft" relate specifically to the world of business. This would not surprise the humorist Scott Adams, who has defined "the Weasel Zone" as that "gigantic gray area between good moral behavior and outright felonious activities."[6] The Eighth Commandment tells us what we should call the morally questionable deeds that fall under this category: we should call them all "stealing."

FOURTH PRINCIPLE: THE COMMANDMENT-KEEPER

The fourth—and for our purposes, final—principle for interpreting and applying the Eighth Commandment is the *Christological principle*. We have already seen how the Bible's prohibition against theft reveals the character of God as a wise and generous provider. But we also need to relate each commandment to the person and work of Jesus Christ, whom the Scriptures identify as "the end"—meaning the goal or true purpose—"of the law" (Rom. 10:4).

In a move that must have astonished the people who heard him preach, Jesus claimed to be the perfect and personal fulfillment of the law of God. "Do not think that I have come to abolish the Law or the Prophets," he said. "I have not come to abolish them but to fulfill them" (Matt. 5:17). The personal connection between God's Son and God's law makes sense when we remember that the law reveals the character of God, and when we know further that the Father and the Son are one. The character of God is the character of his Son, Jesus Christ, for as the Scripture says, "The Son is the radiance God's glory and the exact representation of his being" (Heb. 1:3). If Jesus is one and the same as the God who revealed his law to Moses, then the law expresses the character of the Son as well as the Father.

What does the moral law, as summarized in the Ten Commandments, reveal about the person and work of Jesus Christ? Rightly interpreted, the law reveals the full extent of his perfect obedience. The Bible assures us that although Jesus was "born under the law" (Gal. 4:4), he "fulfilled all righteousness" (Matt. 3:15) and "committed no sin" (1 Pet. 2:22). This was no small accomplishment! As we have seen, the law of God searches to the very soul. It is utterly exhaustive in the obedience it requires. We are not capable of keeping even a single commandment with perfect integrity. But Jesus kept all the commandments, down to the last detail, and he did it on our behalf.

The obedience of Christ includes the Eighth Commandment. Has anyone ever exercised better stewardship of what God had given him than Jesus did? Has anyone ever lived with less greed, or done more to promote the welfare of others? The Scripture thus invites us to remember "the grace of our Lord Jesus Christ, that though he was rich, yet for your sake he became poor, so that you by his poverty might become rich" (2 Cor.8:9).

If we trust in Jesus Christ, then we are connected to the Commandment-Keeper. Since we are joined to Jesus by faith, God regards us as having kept the whole law perfectly. Christ accomplished his saving work "in order that the righteous requirements of the law might be fully met in us" (Rom. 8:4). Thus law thus reveals what perfect righteousness we have in Christ.

The moral law also reveals the full extent of Christ's atonement. The Bible teaches that Jesus died on the cross for our sins. If we have a narrow understanding of God's law, then we might imagine that we did not have very many sins to pay for. But a full interpretation of the Ten Commandments reveals the true scope of our sin, and thus it reveals the wide breadth of our Savior's atoning work. Christ died for all the sins we commit in every category of God's commandments, suffering the full penalty that our guilt deserves. He died for our sins of thought as well as deed, for our sins of omission as well as commission. He died for all the times we break the Eighth Commandment (which, as we are starting to see, is a lot more times than we ever realized). The more thoroughly we understand the total implications of God's law, the more truly grateful we are for the grace that God has shown us in the atoning death of his Son. The more clearly we understand what the law requires, the more we completely we understand the cross.

Finally, for those who have put their faith in Jesus Christ, the moral law reveals the full duty of the Christian life. Theologians sometimes speak of "the third use of the law." The law's first use is governmental: to restrain sin in society. Its second use is to lead us to salvation by showing us our sin. But the law's third use is to show us how to live. The moral law expresses God's perfect and righteous will for our lives. Thus the Ten Commandments remain binding for us today, not as a means of salvation by moral performance, but as an expression of God's purpose for our existence; they express what Calvin called the "true and eternal rule of righteousness."[7] God wants us to live in a way that brings glory to his name. So Jesus commands us to keep the law that he has fulfilled. We do not do this as a way of getting right with God, but as a way of pleasing the God who has made us right with him.

Pleasing God by keeping his law includes full obedience to the Eighth Commandment. This particular law shows redeemed people how to live for God's glory, by the power of the Holy Spirit, with respect to property. When we give this law its full interpretation, we gain a better grasp of God's perfect standard for stewardship, and get a better idea how to please him with our business.

KEEPING THE EIGHTH COMMANDMENT

One good way to expand our understanding of righteous business is to take an optimistic view of the Eighth Commandment and imagine what the world would be like if everyone kept it. To keep God's law is to receive God's blessing, as Moses promised: "And if you faithfully obey the voice of the LORD your God, being careful to do all his commandments that I command you today, the LORD your God will set you high above all the nations of the earth" (Deut. 28:1).

How much more productive would the economy be if people and organizations kept the Eighth Commandment? God's world was designed to provide rich opportunities for personal and social benefit when people follow God's law. It seems so simple: just follow a few simple rules and we can have it all. But something gets in the way . . . our sin nature, and sin always has its costs. Yet as we consider the cost of theft, we are also able to calculate the potential productivity gains we could enjoy by bringing our business under obedience to God.

THE VALUE OF NOT STEALING CALCULATED FROM CRIMINAL ACTIVITY

So what does stealing cost the economy? Theft involves the loss of trust, and leaves a feeling of violation. In our free enterprise society, trust is essential for our economy to function efficiently and effectively. So theft becomes a burden in terms of economic loss, productivity loss, and social costs.

One way to calculate the high cost of breaking the Eighth Commandments to categorize the types of stealing that are tracked by law enforcement as criminal activity:

Robbery (taking of property by violence or intimidation)
Larceny (taking of property)
Burglary (breaking into a building)
Embezzlement (stealing things entrusted to one's care)
Shoplifting (stealing from a store during normal business hours)
Low productivity (stealing time from employers)

Examining these categories can provide us with a list of opportunities for improving the productivity of our economy through keeping the Eighth Commandment. Losses in the United States for robbery,[8] larceny,[9] and burglary[10] totaled over $11 billion in 2008. The Human Resource Executive Online reports that employee theft has been estimated by the United States Chamber of Commerce to cost American businesses as much as $50 billion on an annual basis.[11] The Chamber goes on to say that as many as 30% of small business failure can be attributed to employee theft and estimates that 75% of all employees steal once, and one-half of those steal a second time. Hayes International estimates that between $10 and $13 billion is lost annually to shoplifters.[12] These thefts add up to approximately $72 billion, or more than the combined 2010 profits of Wal*Mart, Exxon-Mobil, Chevron, General Electric, Bank of America, and ConocoPhillips. When looked at from another perspective, theses losses add up to opportunities for economic growth. If everyone kept the Eighth Commandment, the United States economy would be astonishingly more productive.

For employers, the bottom line is crucial. Most businesses must make a profit to survive, and employee costs are a major portion of business costs. A business owner must consider: am I getting 100% of the employee time that I am paying for, or are extra breaks, long lunches, and fantasy football reducing my organization's productivity? What about the work time that employees spend writing personal emails, doing online shopping, or even looking for a new job on the Internet? Are employees coming in late and leaving early, or do they waste an inordinate amount of time around the water cooler?

By way of example, suppose that an employer pays workers $15 an hour or $120 for an 8 hour day (taxes and benefits not included). Let us say that the employees spend 10% of their work time on activities unrelated to business. The result is a loss of $12 in productivity for the day. Over the course of a year, the loss would amount to nearly $3,000. Multiply this by ten or by one hundred, depending on the size of the business. The point is that productivity losses add up quickly. It may be too much to expect to engage an employee for every minute of every day, but reductions in time-stealing would lead to substantial savings—the benefits of keeping the Eighth Commandment.

THE VALUE OF NOT STEALING CALCULATED FROM WHITE COLLAR CRIME

Modern civilization offers more ways to steal than were ever imagined in biblical times. We have yet to consider categories of stealing that are sometimes referred to as "white collar crime," such as fraud, identity theft, intellectual property theft, and cyber-crime.

Fraud is by far the largest category of loss, and includes such acts as cheating on income tax, credit card fraud, insurance fraud (reporting false claims or inflating claims), and occupational fraud (using one's occupation for personal enrichment through deliberate misuse of special knowledge, or misapplication of resources or assets).

Insurance fraud is a growing epidemic. The nonprofit Coalition Against Insurance Fraud (CAIF) reports that insurance fraud costs upwards of $80 billion in the United States alone.[13] This number is larger than the combined profits of America's top eight companies. About 16% of this fraud is related to car insurance. Who pays for this fraud? Fraud is never a victimless crime. We all bear the cost for insurance fraud by paying increased premiums, which in the case of car insurance can amount to almost $1000 per family per year. Similarly, Medicare fraud is paid for with higher taxes.

In their "2010 Global Fraud Study: Report to the Nations on Occupational Fraud and Abuse," the Association of Certified Fraud Examiners (ACFE) estimate a potential worldwide fraud loss of more than $2.9 trillion.[14] ACFE also estimates that smaller organizations are more heavily affected by fraud as they typically lack sophisticated anti-fraud controls that are commonplace at larger organizations. These types of fraud range from a local mechanic overcharging for a car part to the major frauds committed by corporations such as Enron and WorldCom.

In April 2001, Fortune magazine ranked Enron as the seventh largest company in America. In December of that same year, Enron filed for bankruptcy. Enron's $63.4 billion in assets made it the largest bankruptcy up until that time. Enron executives told the world that their company was achieving unprecedented success, with more to come, even as they knew that the corporation was collapsing around them. They sold their stock, reaping millions in profits. But those who listened to the Enron executives and held on to their stock saw the price of Enron's stock plunge from $90 in mid-2000 to below $1 per share in November 2001. The employees and investors lost billions of dollars. The bottom line is that the Enron executives stole in a variety of ways. They inflated their stock price by telling lies. Then they sold their stock, enjoying a windfall. The fallout from the demise of Enron included the virtual destruction of its auditing firm, Arthur Andersen. Auditing and accounting firms must have a reputation based on trust and honesty. Arthur Andersen, one of the "big five" accounting firms, could not survive the damage to its reputation caused by the demise of Enron. The failure of Enron, and Arthur Andersen was one of the driving factors behind the creation of the Sarbanes-Oxley Act of 2002.

Not to be outdone by the corporate scandals of the beginning of the 21st century, Bernie Madoff pulled off the largest Ponzi scheme in history.

The cost of this fraud is estimated at about $50 billion.[15] There was a cost to Mr. Madoff, too: on June 29, 2009 he was sentenced to 150 years in prison.

What lessons can be learned from the collapse of Enron, Arthur Anderson, and Bernie Madoff? Did these companies and their managers deliberately set out to defraud or was it a case of "the frog in the kettle"? Place a frog in boiling water, the frog will jump out of the pot. But place the frog in cool water, gradually increase the temperature, and the frog will be cooked. In their book, *The Ethical Executive*, Hoyk and Hersey show how a similar progression in the business world leads to moral failure: "Often, unethical behavior happens little by little, in *small steps*, and progressively becomes more and more severe. After awhile, one is able to tolerate a certain severity of one's own unethical behavior. One would not, however, tolerate this level if it occurred all at once in a large dose at the very beginning."[16]

The Bible warns us to avoid this type of psychological trap. God has told us to be aware of what is going on around us. Examples of these warnings can be found in 1 Corinthians 16:13 ("Be watchful, stand firm in the faith") and 1 Peter 5:8-9 ("Be sober-minded; be watchful. Your adversary the devil prowls around like a roaring lion, seeking someone to devour").

The City of Philadelphia has taken vigilance to a new level, in a desperate attempt to deal with yet another area of white collar crime. Philadelphia recently announced a new weapon in the fight against fraud and corruption in city government: a new app, called "Philly Watchdog," that will make it easier for citizens—at least those with iPhones—to report instances of fraud. City Controller Alan Butkovitz said,

> This is a free app that lets citizens instantly report incidents of fraud, waste or abuse directly to my Fraud Unit. When it comes to reporting fraud and waste in Philadelphia, I'm proud to say that "we now have an app for that." Like any investigative unit of government, we oftentimes rely on the public to help us identify waste and fraud in city government. It is critically important for government to be on the same technological page as our citizens.[17]

The point of sharing these examples is not simply to lament our losses, but also to see the possibilities. Keeping the Eighth Commandment would provide a massive boost to the economy, strengthen family finances, build trust in human relationships, provide investors with a better return on their investments, promote more efficient government, and generally improve everyone's prosperity.

THE VALUE OF NOT STEALING CALCULATED FROM INTELLECTUAL CRIME

We can apply the same cost/benefit analysis to intellectual property, which *The Business Dictionary.com* defines as "knowledge, creative ideas, or expressions of human mind that have commercial value and are protectable under copyright, patent, servicemark, trademark, or trade secret laws from imitation, infringement, and dilution. Intellectual property includes brand names, discoveries, formulas, inventions, knowledge, registered designs, software, and works of artistic, literary, or musical nature."[18]

The misuse of protected ideas, music, movies, writings, inventions, and proprietary products is stealing, and has been facilitated by the popularity of the Internet. In the United States, the Federal Bureau of Investigation has created a cyber program to "focus on the theft of trade secrets and infringements on products that can impact consumers' health and safety."[19]

Identity *theft* occurs when personal information is taken by another person without explicit permission. Identity *fraud* is the actual misuse of this personal information for unlawful financial gain. Such fraud has been growing rapidly due to the popularity of Internet shopping. It is estimated that 8.1 million adults in the United States are victims of identity theft annually, with an estimated financial loss of $37 billion.[20] Add to this the $59 billion that "The 10th Trends in Propriety Information Loss Survey" reported that U.S. companies lost in a given year.[21] Similarly, a study entitled "The Cost of Cyber Crime" reported that cyber theft is costing Great Britain at least $44.5 billion a year, mostly through the theft of industrial secrets and intellectual property.[22]

One unintended consequence of the violation of intellectual property rights is that it tends to stifle creativity and innovation. It does this by misappropriating the creator's right to earn from his or her creative product. One of the laws of economics is that people respond to incentives. If ownership and other incentives for the creation of new work are eliminated, innovation and creativity are diminished.

Another form of copyright infringement—namely, plagiarism—has been simplified by the growth of the Internet. Students can now easily copy or buy papers and submit them as their own work. Ironically, in one case at a Christian university, a student plagiarized a paper on ethics! Teachers who detect that a paper is beyond the abilities of a given student can simply type in the suspected portion into Google to find the original source of the material. So here is another benefit of keeping the Eighth Commandment: in a theft-free world, teachers could simply grade their students' papers without worrying about the possibility of plagiarism.

An excellent summary of the full opportunity cost embedded in the category of stealing is provided in David A. Anderson's paper, "The Aggregate Burden of Crime":

> Beyond the expenses of the legal system, victim losses, and crime prevention agencies, the burden of crime encompasses the opportunity costs of victims', criminals', and prisoners' time; the fear of being victimized; and the cost of private deterrence. More accurate information on the repercussions of crime could guide our legal, political, and cultural stance toward crime and allow informed prioritization of programs that curtail criminal activity. The net annual burden of crime is found to exceed $1 trillion.[23]

Keeping God's law with respect to stealing and stewardship would significantly reduce costs on society and result in improved productivity. This includes reducing the time and money spent for theft prevention, protection, prosecution, and restoration. The annual revenues for the top ten companies in the United States total $1.7 trillion. If Crime, Inc. existed as a company, it would be over three times the size of Wal*Mart and listed as number one by *Fortune* magazine. As these figures show, the economic implications of keeping the Eighth Commandment—instead of breaking it the way we do—are massive.

FURTHER BENEFITS OF KEEPING THE EIGHTH COMMANDMENT

Although the implications of obedience are society-wide, God's law must be kept one individual at a time, one commandment at a time. In the case of the Eighth Commandment, keeping God's law includes paying fair wages and salaries, and setting fair and reasonable prices. It also means giving your best to your employer whenever you are "on the clock." What a blessing it would be to work where there is a reasonable quality of work life in an atmosphere of mutual commitment and trust, and where coworkers use their talents for the lawful attainment of wealth for themselves and others. This was the apostle Paul's vision for the workplace when he said, "And whatever you do, in word or deed, do everything in the name of the Lord Jesus, giving thanks to God the Father through him" (Colossians 3:17).

Keeping the Eighth Commandment means keeping one's word (contract faithfulness). It means telling the truth about a product or service . . . both the risks and the benefits. It includes not only "truth in advertising" from the standpoint of the letter of the law, but also in keeping with the spirit of the law (full disclosure—the good news and the bad news).

What about the area of competition? Business competition can be fierce. Is this wrong? Not if it is done according to the broad interpretation of the rules given in the Ten Commandments. Godly business owners might even find new ways to compete. Consider the local mechanic who services his neighbor's automobile. If he does his work fairly and honestly, his neighbor will not hesitate to recommend the mechanic. The trust he builds with his customers enables him to compete on the basis of his honesty and skill.

In a world without theft, we could live without locks, computer firewalls, online passwords, or home security systems. We could live with a reduced police force and judicial system—even if we needed judges and police officers at all. In their book, *Business for the Common Good,* authors Kenman L. Wong and Scott B. Rae explain that the biblical word *shalom* signifies wholesomeness, health, peace, welfare, prosperity, rest, harmony, and the absence of agitation or discord.[24] These synonyms for *shalom* are apt descriptions of doing business within the bounds of the Eighth Commandment. Everything would be right with the world.

The problem, of course, is that currently we live in a world broken by sin. Yet we also wait in hope for the day described in the hymn *Blest Be the Tie That Binds*—a day when the Eighth Commandment will be kept in perfect integrity and everyone will prosper:

> From sorrow, toil and pain,
> And sin we shall be free;
> And perfect love and friendship reign
> Through all eternity.

BETWEEN TWO THIEVES

In this paper we have tried to take an optimistic view of the Eighth Commandment. The sad reality, of course, is that this commandment gets broken as often as all the rest of them. A familiar example comes from a well-known painting by the American illustrator Norman Rockwell. The painting, which first appeared on the cover of *The Saturday Evening Post*, shows a woman buying a turkey for Thanksgiving dinner. The turkey is being weighed on a scale for price. Behind the counter is a jolly butcher, with his apron stretched tightly over his ample belly and his pencil tucked neatly behind one ear. His customer is a respectable looking woman of perhaps sixty, looking as pleased as the butcher.

The shopkeeper and the customer exchange a knowing smile, almost as if they are sharing a joke, but the joke is really on them because the painting shows what they are secretly doing. The butcher is pressing the scale down with his big fat thumb, so as to raise the price. At the same time, the woman is trying to get a better deal by pushing the scale up with her forefinger. The reason both of them look pleased is that neither is aware what the other is doing!

In Rockwell's typical style, the painting is a charming scene from American life that makes us laugh at our own foibles. But what the butcher and his customer really were violating the Eighth Commandment! According to Cecil Myers, "Both the butcher and the lovely lady would resent being called thieves. The lovely lady would never rob a bank or steal a car. The butcher would be indignant if anyone accused him of stealing; and if a customer gave him a bad check, he would call the police, but neither saw anything wrong with a little deception that would make a few cents for one or save a few cents for the other."[25] To put it bluntly, these fine, upstanding citizens were both thieves.

They are not the only ones. Martin Luther went so far as to say, "If we look at mankind in all its conditions, it is nothing but a vast, wide stable full of great thieves."[26] Luther also speculated what would happen if all of us were brought to justice and given the legal penalty that was customary in the 16th century. "It is the smallest part of the thieves that are hung," Luther said. "If we're to hang them all, where shall we get rope enough? We must make all our belts and straps into halters!"[27]

This may seem like an overly pessimistic perspective on the human condition. But Luther found optimism in the cross where Christ died in the place of sinners—specifically, in the place of thieves. The Bible says that when Jesus was crucified, "Two robbers were crucified with him, one on his right and one on his left" (Matt. 27:38), thus fulfilling the prophecy that the Savior would be "numbered with the transgressors" (Isa. 53:12). In effect, by being crucified with these men, Jesus was considered a thief. Luther explained it like this:

> Christ is innocent so far as His own Person is concerned; therefore He should not have been hanged from the tree. But because, according to the Law, every thief should have been

hanged, therefore, according to the Law of Moses, Christ Himself should have been hanged; for He bore the person of a sinner and a thief—and not of one but of all sinners and thieves.
For we are sinners and thieves, and therefore we are worthy
of death and eternal damnation. But Christ took all our sins
upon Himself, and for them He died on the cross. Therefore it
was appropriate for Him to become a thief and, as Isaiah says
(53:12), to be "numbered among the thieves."[28]

It is well known that Christ was crucified between two thieves. But as far as
God's justice was concerned, there were really *three* thieves on the cross that
day: two who died for their own crimes and one who took our sins upon
himself. Luther demonstrated this truth by using an analogy:

A magistrate regards someone as a criminal and punishes him if
he catches him among thieves, even though the man has never
committed anything evil or worthy of death. Christ was not
only found among sinners; but of His own free will and by the
will of the Father He wanted to be an associate of sinners, having assumed the flesh and blood of those who were sinners and
thieves and who were immersed in all sorts of sin. Therefore
when the Law found Him among thieves, it condemned and
executed Him as a thief.[29]

The condemnation of Christ is a great comfort to everyone who has ever
broken the Eighth Commandment. When Jesus died on the cross, he died
for thieves, so that every thief who trusts in him will be forgiven. The very
first thief to be saved was the one hanging next to him on the cross, the one
who said, "Jesus, remember me when you come into your kingdom" (Luke
23:42). Jesus gave that man the answer he gives to every lawbreaker who
turns to him in repentance and faith: "You will be with me in paradise"
(Luke 23:43).

The promise of paradise is for us, too. Although we are guilty of breaking the commandments of God, all our sins are forgiven and atoned for
through the cross where Jesus died. Therefore, we live in the hope of the
paradise he has promised to everyone who trusts in him for salvation. In
the meantime, whenever we resist the temptation to steal, and whenever we
protect other people's property, we bring a little bit of heaven to earth.

Notes

1. H. A. Ironside, *Illustrations of Bible Truth* (Chicago: Moody Press, 1945), 37-39.

2. The dilemma is posed in *Euthyphro*, where Plato has Socrates ask, "Do the gods love an act because it is pious, or is it pious because the gods love it?" See Samuel Enoch Stumpf, *Socrates to Sartre: A History of Philosophy*, 3rd edn. (New York: McGraw-Hill, 1982), 38.

3. Jerry Bridges, *The Discipline of Grace: God's Role and Our Role in the Pursuit of Holiness* (Colorado Springs, CO: NavPress, 1994), 88.

4. Francis Turretin, *Institutes of Elenctic Theology*, trans. George Musgrave Giger, ed. James T. Dennison, Jr., 3 vols. (Phillipsburg, NU: P&R, 1992-1997), XI.VI.3.

5. Rob Schenck, *The Ten Words That Will Change a Nation: The Ten Commandments* (Tulsa, OK: Albury, 1999), 155.

6. See Scott Adams, *Dilbert and the Way of the Weasel* (New York: HarperBusiness, 2002).

7. John Calvin, *John Calvin's Sermons on the Ten Commandments*, ed. and trans. by Benjamin W. Farley (Grand Rapids, MI: Baker, 1980), 24.

8. Federal Bureau of Investigation, "Crime in the United States 2008: Robbery" (Washington, DC: GPO, 2009)

9. Federal Bureau of Investigation, "Crime in the United States 2008: Larceny-Theft" (Washington, DC: GPO, 2009)

10. Federal Bureau of Investigation, "Crime in the United States 2008: Burglary" (Washington, DC:GPO, 2009)

11. www.hreonline.com/HRE/story.jsp?storyId=250192419.

12. www.hayesinternational.com/thft-surveys.html.

13. www.insurancefraud.org/80_billion.htm.

14. www.acfe.com/rttn/rttn-2010.pdf.

15. Lenzner, Robert, "Bernie Madoff's $50 Billion Ponzi Scheme", *Forbes* (December 12, 2008).

16. Robert Hoyk and Paul Hersey, *The Ethical Executive* (Palo Alto, CA: Stanford Business Books, 2008).

17. www.philadelphiacontroller.org/page.asp?id=669.

18. www.businessdictionary.com.

19. www.fbi.gov.

20. www.javelinstrategy.com/research/brochure-209.

21. ASIS International, PricewaterhouseCoopers, and U.S. Chamber of Commerce, "The 10th Trends in Proprietary Information Loss Survey" (2002).

22. www.detica.com/uploads/press-releases.

23. David A. Anderson, "The Aggregate Burden of Crime," *Journal of Law and Economics* (The University of Chicago: October, 1999), Vol. XLII.

24. Kenman L. Wong and Scott B. Rae, *Business for the Common Good* (Downers Grove, IL: InterVarsity, 2011), 71.

25. T. Cecil Myers, *Thunder on the Mountain* (Nashville: Abingdon Press, 1965), 119-20, quoted in Maxie D. Dunnam, *Exodus*, The Communicator's Commentary (Waco, TX: Word, 1987), 251.

26. Martin Luther, quoted in Michael S. Horton, *The Law of Perfect Freedom* (Chicago: Moody, 1993), 206.

27. Martin Luther, quoted in Dunnam, *Exodus*, 265.

28. Martin Luther, *Luther's Works: Lectures on Galatians*, 1535, Chapters 1-4, ed. by Jaroslav Pelikan (Saint Louis: Concordia, 1963), 26:277.

29. Luther, *Galatians*, 26:277-78.

SECTION 2

THE ROLE OF PROPERTY RIGHTS IN GOD'S WORLD

Section 2: The Role of Property Rights in God's World

PHILIP J. CLEMENTS

In this Section, the emphasis is on human flourishing. The short summary is that God created a world where humans can flourish. But to flourish humans need to follow His commandments; His plan for the way the world is designs to operate. The Eighth Commandment uniquely affects the potential for human flourishing. The past several centuries have been a unique period in mankind's prosperity, and this Section's papers explain how this uniqueness is attributed to the implementation of the Eighth Commandment.

The Introduction frames that the Christian worldview holds that God, as Creator, owns everything and gives it to whom He pleases. The individual recipient has responsibility to God for the stewardship, employment and enjoyment of what God has given to him. Section 1 covers the theology underlying the commandment not to steal, including that what can be stolen is more than property; stealing includes time, and talent and opportunity. These framing thoughts are not repeated here. Rather the principles here go to the effect on an individual and the individual's community when these basic principles are respected.

Barry Asmus and Wayne Grudem's paper, "Property Rights Inherent in the Eighth Commandment: Are Necessary for Human Flourishing," shows how God's providence in the commercial aspect of His world can create human flourishing. *Flourishing* is a wonderful word to describe how God would like to see mankind in His world. In Genesis 1:26-31, the Bible describes man's creation. God created man in His image; [1] God commanded man to be fruitful, multiply, to fill the earth; God gave man dominion over every living thing, and God commanded man to subdue the earth. After the six days of creation, God looked upon creation, including man, and declared that creation was very good. This brief passage paints a picture of man in God's creation that connotes flourishing.

Asmus and Grudem look at the positive side of the Eighth Commandment. As noted in Section 1, the Decalogue represents God's Character. Therefore, the Eighth Commandment represents the world the way God designed it to be. Property rights are a foundational part of God's world. The authors set the stage by reviewing the Decalogue and the role of the Eighth Commandment in it.

> The Eighth Commandment is unique. It protects property and possessions. By implication, we are also right to think it protects another person's time, talent and opportunities – everything over which people have been given stewardship. We are not to steal someone else's property or time or talents or opportunities.

> Without the Eighth Commandment ... the Ten Commandments would not cover all aspects of life. We would have God's instructions protecting worship, life, marriage, family, and truth. But where would the Ten Commandments tell us what we should do with our possessions and our talents and opportunities? ... Would we be expected to achieve anything beyond mere subsistence living? Would we be expected just to act as the animal kingdom does: eat, sleep, bear offspring, and die, with no other achievements to show the excellence of the human race created in the image of God?

These questions posed by the authors capture the sentiment in the Genesis creation account. Mankind is a bearer of God's image and is charged to use it while here on earth. We are not animals, we are humans. We were not created to live and die, but to give glory to God and enjoy Him forever. Part of giving God glory is using what He has given us to purpose. As Asmus and Grudem note, private property implies stewardship, and stewardship implies an expectation of human achievement.

The immense challenge of the Eighth Commandment arises from the nature of stewardship that "requires use of immense wisdom and mature judgment in the complex balancing of multiple factors such as love of neighbor, care for one's family, wise planning for the future, fear of God, desire to advance God's Kingdom, and a desire to subdue the earth to the glory of God."

On the broader community level another result of the Eighth Commandment is the creation of *free markets*. Free markets are one of the concepts most of us do not put into the Decalogue, let alone the Eighth Commandment. But it is clear that respect for each person's property allows for free exchange. When free exchange is combined with a proper understanding of proper self-interest, a free market is a natural outcome.

But to the free market needs to be added the concept of needs and wants, which David Cowan's paper, "Covenant and the Eighth Command-ment," nicely adds to this section. While Cowan's paper addresses some of the negatives of community violations of the Eighth Commandment, it also answers the problem of self-interest. The Decalogue has two parts, with the second part being summarized as "Love thy neighbor as thy self." This commandment implies a love of self. So self-interest is a natural extension of a love of self. In Section 3 the issue of self-interest and greed is more fully explored. But here we need to see that mankind was created with the capacity to have a wide variety of needs and desires. The free mar-ket and its underlying property rights allow man to exercise his God-given creativity to invent, design, create and then deliver to others items to meet these needs and wants.

Mankind, in undertaking this kind of regular commercial activ-ity, adds more value to God's world. There is a concept of zero-sum game, which is inconsistent with both the Eighth Commandment and God's providence in creating the world. The notion of zero-sum defines the world as finite. Therefore, for me to have more, you must give up some of what you have. Zero-sum is often illustrated by a pie, where if I want a large piece, then others must divide up a smaller remainder. What is miss-ing is God, and God designed the world and man so that man can actually create more. The pie is not finite, but infinite! If we want more pie, we can make another. Jesus modeled this in the feeding of the 5,000. Thank goodness Jesus did not have fixed pie thinking when he shared the loaves and fishes![2] Today many people would say there are only five loaves and two fish, so everyone can only get a tiny piece of each. This fundamental principle of God's providence is critical to human flourishing. I do not need yours in order to have enough. Therefore, I can and should respect what is yours.

Cowan further explores the problem of happiness and zero-sum as a basis for evaluating flourishing:

There is a common fundamental error shared by peoples in Capitalist, Socialist and Communist economies, and this is the error that the economy can make us happy. The Capitalist assumes that wealth (for the richer) and consumption (for the poorer) makes us happy. The Socialist assumes that education and sharing resources, which they regard as scarce, will make us happy. The Communist assumes the loss of property ownership makes us happy. The point is, happiness has another source, which can find expression in the economy, but economy does not create it. The economy is a means, not an end. Happiness only happens when God is at the center.

In Section 3 the social structure side will be more fully explored, but here we see how mankind's fallen thinking leads to misplaced understanding of how God's world works. The errors in thinking start with excluding an infinite loving God, making the world finite; then making equality in outcomes the standard for happiness; then making mankind the enabler of all activity resulting in centralized economic controls.

But flourishing goes even further. At the 2011 Business Ethics Today conference, [3] Dinesh D'Souza presented the idea that the free market arising from the Eighth Commandment created an environment where humans would create things they believe would be useful even before there was a demand. Rather than commerce being reactive, it becomes proactive. D'Souza reached into his pocket and pulled out an iPhone. Holding it up, he noted that Apple, Inc. had created the iPhone before he, D'Souza, even knew he wanted or needed an iPhone.

This point is enormous when put into the context of human flourishing. The image of God empowers mankind to be able to invent things to better man's existence even before the user will be aware of the benefits. This is flourishing, this is exercising dominion, and this is bringing glory to God who created a world where we could share such blessings.

Let us pause for a moment to remember that one of the things God asks is that He be honored in all we do. His providence and love for mankind gave us the ability and created the world with the resources to allow mankind to flourish.

We must now ask some questions: Why has man not flourished over all of human history as man has in the past 400 years, especially that over past 50 years? Why has man not adopted the concepts for social and economic thinking that match these presentations? Why has human flourishing not been even across the globe over the past 50 years?

The Center for Christian Business Ethics Today's [4] research holds some measure of answer to these important questions. The reader is referred to the material in *Business Ethics Today: Foundations* and the Introduction, Section 1 of this text as a starting place for the answers. The short summary is that the Reformation revealed truths in the Bible that changed the way commerce was done because the Reformation Protestants conducted their lives differently. The fundamental difference in Protestant Christianity is the assurance of being in heaven such that the Protestant practices living in the presence of God here on earth, while looking with expectation to being with Him in heaven. This blessing to mankind started in the period 1550 to 1750 in the Protestant countries and is generally referred to as the Industrial Revolution. After World War II, there were only two fundamental social structures in the world, the free West and Communism. The free West was based on the Protestant ethic as described for commerce by Max Weber in 1904. [5] After the fall of the Berlin Wall in 1989, many declared that the free West had won both the Cold War and the social-economic ideology war. The flourishing of the West was very clear and it was because of the Protestant ethic that underlay the West's culture. The bankruptcy of socialism/communism was equally as clear, because these were based on humanism. It is faith that creates cultures and not social-economic models. *Clash of Civilizations* [6] and *Culture Matters* [7] capture this important principle. Therefore, the world now is returning to the pre-Reformation cultures, and commerce will return as the faith structures of the world create country cultures in their own image. The implications on human flourishing, property rights, and social thinking are clear.

Mankind can be said to have seen God's blessing in the Eighth Commandment and now rejects God and His provision, even as man rejected God's command in the Garden of Eden.

Notes

1. Genesis 9:6 confirms that even after the fall man bears God's image.
2. Mark 6:32-44.
3. Business Ethics Today: Business and the 8th Commandment: You Shall Not Steal Conference, Philadelphia, June 10-11, 2011; co-hosted by Center for Christian Business Ethics Today, LLC and Westminster Theological Seminary.
4. The Center for Christian Business Ethics Today, LLC was formed in 2009 to develop material to help the Christian business person operate his business with biblical business principles based on Protestant Christianity. The Center co-hosted the conference that is the source of the papers for this text.
5. Max Weber, *The Protestant Ethic and the Spirit of Capitalism,* 1904, Translated, Talcott Parsons, rept. New York: Scribner's, 1958.
6. Samuel P. Huntington, *Clash of Civilizations and the Remaking of the World Order,* New York: Touchstone, 1996.
7. Lawrence E. Harrison and Samuel P. Huntington, ed.s, *Culture Maters: How Values Shape Human Progress,* New York: Basic, 2000.

PROPERTY RIGHTS INHERENT IN THE EIGHTH COMMANDMENT

ARE NECESARRY FOR HUMAN FLOURISHING

BARRY ASMUS & WAYNE GRUDEM

BARRY ASMUS

Doctor Peter A. Lillback Barry Asmus is a Senior Economist with the prestigious National Center for Policy Analysis. Doctor Asmus has been named by USA Today *as one of the five most requested speakers in the United States. He has spoken to thirty world bankers at the home of Harvard's President, three thousand farmers in Des Moines, and seven thousand members of the Million Dollar Round Table at Radio City Music Hall.*

He has testified before the House Ways and Means Committee regarding our income tax system; was a featured speaker in a privatizing Social Security conference for Western European leaders; and has addressed the faculty of the Young Presidents Organization in Cape Town, South Africa. His appearance at the Forbes Chateau de Balleroy in France with former Czech Prime Minister Vaclav Klaus, members of British Parliament, and other Western European leaders focused on the importance of public policy decision in Europe.

Recent trips to Romania and Albania have encouraged government leaders to pass free-market, low tax, and pro-trade policies. Doctor Asmus is the author of nine books. His latest is Bulls Don't Blush, Bears Don't Die (2006), which explores the limitless opportunities emerging from a borderless and knowledge-driven society, sharing the international economic and political trends shaping business and investment strategy in today's global economy. As a Professor of Economics, he was twice voted University Professor of the Year and was honored with the Freedom Foundation Award at Valley Forge for Private Enterprise Education. Doctor Asmus has a client list that reads like a who's who in corporate America.

WAYNE GRUDEM

Wayne Grudem is Research Professor of Theology and Biblical Studies at Phoenix Seminary in Phoenix, Arizona. Prior to Phoenix Seminary he taught for twenty years at Trinity Evangelical Divinity School, Deerfield, Illinois, where he was chairman of the department of Biblical and Systematic Theology. He received a BA from Harvard University, an MDiv from Westminster Seminary, Philadelphia, and a PhD (in New Testament) from the University of Cambridge, England. He has published sixteen books, including Systematic Theology, Recovering Biblical Manhood and Womanhood *(co-edited with John Piper),* The TNIV and the Gender-Neutral Bible Controversy *(co-authored with Vern Poythress),* The First Epistle of Peter *(Tyndale NT commentary), and* Business for the Glory of God. *He was also the General Editor for the* ESV Study Bible *(published October 2008).*

He is a past president of the Evangelical Theological Society, a co-founder and past president of the Council on Biblical Manhood and Womanhood, and a member of the Translation Oversight Committee for the English Standard Version of the Bible. He and his wife, Margaret, have been married since 1969 and have three adult sons.

Extended reflection on the words of the Bible will often yield deeper insight than what is evident on a first reading. This should not be surprising. If we believe that the Bible is the product of the infinite wisdom of God, we will naturally expect that the Bible contains more wisdom than human minds will ever fully understand.

This is certainly true with regard to the 8th Commandment, "You shall not steal (Ex. 20:15)." [1] Our first impression is that the commandment is quite simple. It tells us not to steal, which tells us we should not take something that does not belong to us. It is a simple command, consisting of only four words in English, and only two words in Hebrew: *lo' tignob*, "You shall not steal." What part of that do we not understand?

On deeper reflection, however, we will discover that this commandment provides the necessary foundation for all human flourishing on the face of the earth. Governments and cultural traditions violate the 8th Commandment at their peril, for wherever this commandment is ignored, entire nations remain trapped in poverty forever. When that happens, they tragically fail to achieve God's purposes for them on the earth.

A. Not stealing implies private property

The command, "You shall not steal," assumes that *there is something to steal* —something that belongs to someone else and not to me. I should not steal your ox or your donkey – or your car or your cell phone or your iPad – because it belongs to you and not to me.

Therefore, the command, "You shall not steal," assumes private ownership of property. Other passages in the Old Testament show that God was concerned to protect the private ownership of property. Property was to be owned by individuals, not by the government or by society as a whole. For instance, God told the people of Israel that when the Year of Jubilee came, "It shall be a jubilee for you when *each of you shall return to his property* and each of you shall return to his clan (Lev. 25:10)."

There were many other laws that defined punishments for stealing and appropriate restitution for damage of another person's farm animals or agricultural fields (see, for example, Ex. 21:28-36; 22:1-15; Deut. 22:1-4; 23:24-25). These were the property that belonged to someone else, and the Jewish people were to honor such property rights. Another commandment guaranteed that property boundaries would be protected: "You shall not move your neighbor's landmark, which the men of old have set, in the inheritance that you will hold in the land that the Lord your God is giving you to possess" (Deut. 19:14). To move the landmark was to move the boundaries of the land and thus to steal land that belonged to one's neighbor (compare Prov. 22:28; 23:10) [2]

The Old Testament also shows an awareness that governments could wrongly use their immense power to disregard property rights and steal what they should not have. At the urging of wicked Queen Jezebel, King Ahab wrongfully stole Naboth's vineyard, and had Naboth killed in the process (1 Kings 21). And the prophet Samuel warned the people of Israel of the evils of a king who would "take" and "take" and "take":

> So Samuel told all the words of the Lord to the people who were asking for a king from him. He said, "These will be the ways of the king who will reign over you: he will *take* your sons and appoint them to his chariots and to be his horsemen and to run before his chariots. And he will appoint for himself com-

manders of thousands and commanders of fifties, and some
to plow his ground and to reap his harvest, and to make his
implements of war and the equipment of his chariots. He will
take your daughters to be perfumers and cooks and bakers. He
will *take* the best of your fields and vineyards and olive orchards
and give them to his servants. He will take the tenth of your
grain and of your vineyards and give it to his officers and to his
servants. He will *take* your male servants and female servants
and the best of your young men and your donkeys, and put
them to his work. He will *take* the tenth of your flocks, *and you
shall be his slaves.* And in that day you will cry out because of
your king, whom you have chosen for yourselves, but the Lord
will not answer you in that day" (1 Sam. 8:10–18).

Sometimes people claim that the early church practiced a form of "early
communism" because it says in Acts, "All who believed were together and
had all things in common" (Acts 2:44). But this situation was far different from communism, because (1) the giving was voluntary and not
compelled by the government, and (2) people still had personal possessions
and owned property, because they still met in "their homes" (Acts 2:46),
and many other Christians after this time still owned homes (see Acts
12:12; 17:5; 18:7; 20:20; 21:8; 21:16; Rom. 16:5; 1 Cor.16:19; Col. 4:15;
Philem 2; 2 John 10). Peter even told Ananias and Sapphira that they did
not have to feel any obligation to sell their house and give away the money
(see Acts 5:4). [3]

 If the 8th Commandment implies private ownership of property,
then the focus of the 8th Commandment is different from the other nine
commandments. The 8th Commandment covers an entire range of human activity that is not the purpose of these other commandments.

 Commandments 1-4 (Ex. 20:3-11) focus primarily on our relationship to God and the duties we owe to God. (The 4th Commandment does
require us to labor, but it does not specify what we should labor for).

 Commandment 5 protects family ("Honor your father and your
mother," Ex. 20:12).

 Commandment 6 protects life ("You shall not murder," Ex. 20:13).
Commandment 7 protects marriage ("You shall not commit adultery," Ex.
20:14).

 Commandment 9 protects truth ("You shall not bear false witness
against your neighbor," Ex. 20:16).

Commandment 10 requires purity of heart ("You shall not covet your neighbor's house; you shall not covet your neighbor's wife . . . or anything that is your neighbors," Ex.20:17). By implication, Commandment 10 also requires purity of heart regarding all the other commandments, but it adds no unique area of life as an additional focus that was not already treated in the previous commandments.

Therefore the 8th Commandment is unique. It protects property and possessions. By implication, we are also right to think it protects another person's time and talents and opportunities ¬¬– everything over which people have been given stewardship. We are not to steal someone else's property, or time, or talents, or opportunities.

Without the 8th Commandment, therefore, the Ten Commandments would not cover all aspects of life. We would have God's instructions protecting worship, life, marriage, family and truth. But where would the Ten Commandments tell us what we should *do* with our possessions and our talents and opportunities? Yes, the first four commandments would instruct us in the worship of God, but beyond such worship, would we be expected to achieve anything beyond mere subsistence living? Would we be expected just to act as the animal kingdom does: eat, sleep, bear offspring, and die, with no other achievements to show the excellence of the human race created in the image of God?

But the 8th Commandment implies that we have property to care for. Therefore it is the 8th Commandment that sets us apart from the animal kingdom as property owners and those who have been given stewardship of possessions. In that way the 8th Commandment relates to most of our work activity for most of our earthly lifetimes.

B. Private property implies stewardship

If human beings were all alone in the universe, without any accountability to any God, then people might assume that private ownership of property carried no obligations with it. Or, conversely, people might assume that "society" or government should take the property away, lest people use it for their own selfish purposes. This is the view of Communist societies.

But if *God himself* has commanded, "You shall not steal," and if in that commandment *God himself* establishes a system of private property, then it immediately follows that we are accountable to him for how we use that property. This is certainly the Bible's perspective: Our ownership of property is not absolute, but we are stewards who will have to give an account of our stewardship. This is because, ultimately, "The earth is the Lord's and the fullness thereof, the world and all those who dwell therein" (Ps. 24:1).

We now have greater insight into the wisdom of God in the 8th Commandment. The command "You shall not steal" implies private ownership of property. And private ownership of property which is given by God implies responsible stewardship and accountability for the use of that property. Once I realize that God commands others not to steal my land or my ox or my donkey, or my car or my laptop, then I realize that I have an individual responsibility for how those things are used. I have been *entrusted* with these things by the God who created the universe, and I must act as a faithful "steward" to manage what he has entrusted to me.

This idea of stewardship also broadens our idea of what God has given to us as stewards. We have been entrusted with much more than merely physical possessions and land. God has also entrusted us with time, talents and opportunities. We have these things as a stewardship from God as well. We are accountable to him for how we use them.

But what if a government takes away this right to own property? Then I am no longer free to act as a steward in deciding how that property is to be used, for I can no longer control the use of that property. Or if a government places burdensome restrictions on how I can use my property, then my ability to exercise stewardship is also diminished.

C. Stewardship implies an expectation of human achievement

There is still more to this idea of stewardship of private property. If God *entrusts* me with something, then he expects me to do something with it, something worthwhile, something that he finds valuable. This is evident from the very beginning when God placed Adam and Eve on the earth. He said:

> Let us make man in our image, after our likeness. And *let them have dominion* over the fish of the sea and over the birds of the heavens and over the livestock and *over all the earth* and over every creeping thing that creeps on the earth.

> So God created man in his own image,
> in the image of God he created him;
> male and female he created them.

> And God blessed them. And God said to them, "Be fruitful and multiply and fill the earth and *subdue it* and have dominion . . . over every living thing that moves on the earth" (Genesis 1:26-28).

The Hebrew word translated "subdue" in verse 28 (Hebrew *kabash*) means to make the earth useful for human beings' benefit and enjoyment. In this way, God was entrusting Adam and Eve, and by implication the entire human race, with stewardship over the earth. And God wanted them to create useful products from the earth, for their benefit and enjoyment and benefit.

This implies that God wanted Adam and Eve to discover and create and invent products from the earth – at first, perhaps, simple structures in which to live and store food, and later, more complex forms of transportation such as carts and wagons, then eventually modern homes and office buildings and factories, as well as cars and airplanes – the entire range of useful products that could be made from the earth.

Stewardship implies the expectation of expectation of *human achievement*. When God entrusts us with something, he expects us to *do* something worthwhile with it.

Therefore the 8th Commandment gives both the *opportunity* for human achievement (by entrusting property to us), and *the expectation* of human achievement (by making us accountable stewards).

What do we mean by human achievement? The range of human activity is vast: It includes the arts, the physical sciences, technology, industry, commerce, and all of the social sciences and the relationships that we find in family, community, nation and church. Human activity also includes bearing and raising children with all the challenges unique to each child. All of these are areas of human activity for which we have been entrusted with a stewardship.

In addition, the human drive to understand and to create from the world is *unlimited*. Rabbits and squirrels, birds and deer, are content to live in the same kinds of homes and eat the same kinds of food for thousands of generations. But human beings have an innate desire to explore, to discover, to understand, to invent, to create, to produce – and then to enjoy the products that can be made from the earth. This innate human drive to subdue the earth has never been satisfied throughout the entire history of mankind. This is because *God created us not merely to survive on the earth but to flourish.*

God has created us with very limited needs (food, clothing, shelter) for our physical survival, but he has also created us with unlimited wants. For many centuries, human beings did not know that they wanted cell phones, because such things did not exist. (In fact I lived quite happily without a cell phone for about 40 years of my life, but now I've realized that I want one and I'm willing to spend money to buy one.) When I was growing up as a child in Wisconsin, I didn't realize that I wanted Cherry Garcia ice cream, or pomegranate raspberry frozen yogurt, because those products did not exist. The only ice cream store in my childhood town sold vanilla, chocolate, and strawberry, and what a treat they were! Now we want dozens of varieties.

The same is true of electric light bulbs, plastic water bottles, gas furnaces, air conditioners, automobiles, computers and airplane travel. For thousands of years, human beings did not know they wanted these things, because nobody knew they could be made. In these and thousands of other areas, human achievement continues to progress and thereby human beings give more and more evidence of the glory of our creation in the image of God. With such inventions we demonstrate creativity, wisdom, knowledge, skill in use of resources, care for others who are distant (through use of a telephone or by email), and many other other God-like qualities.

Plants and animals show a measure of God's glory by merely surviving and repeating the same activities for thousands of years, while human beings glorify God by *achieving* much more than mere survival. We glorify God by understanding and ruling over the creation and then producing more and more wonderful goods from it, for our enjoyment, and with thanksgiving to God. God is the one who "richly provides us with everything to enjoy" (1Tim. 6:17). And "everything created by God is good, and nothing is to be rejected if it is received with thanksgiving, for it is made holy by the word of God and prayer (1Tim. 4:4). The command "You shall not steal," when viewed in the context of the entire Bible's teachings on stewardship, implies that God created us not merely *survive* but to *achieve much* and to *flourish* on the earth.

God gives us these various stewardship responsibilities so that through them we will have unlimited potential for glorifying him through discovery, creation, production, distribution, and use of potentially unlimited material and intellectual resources.

D. Therefore the 8th Commandment is God's wonderful gift that leads to human flourishing

The ownership of property which is implied by the 8th Commandment gives people the freedom they need to try to be faithful stewards of what God entrusts to them. In addition, ownership of property motivates people to create, invent, and produce, because they have hope of keeping and enjoying what they earn.

Therefore the ownership of property which is implied by the 8th Commandment is *essential for human flourishing.* God in his wisdom gave a command that laid the foundation for human flourishing throughout all ages of human existence on the earth.

E. The immense challenge of the 8th Commandment

Obeying the 8th Commandment rightly is immensely challenging. Only someone made in the image of God can obey it, and even those redeemed by Christ never obey it perfectly in this age.

Now someone might think "I'm not a shoplifter, or an embezzler or a thief. I don't cheat on my taxes. I think I have been obeying the commandment, 'You shall not steal.'"
But have you been a faithful steward? Faithful stewardship of what God entrusts to us requires wise use of *all* of our possessions and time and talents and opportunities.

Faithful stewardship requires use of immense wisdom and mature judgment in the complex balancing of multiple factors such as love of neighbor, care for one's family, wise planning for the future, fear of God, desire to advance God's Kingdom, and a desire to subdue the earth to the glory of God.

Grateful stewardship in obedience to the 8th Commandment also requires avoiding the temptations and sins connected with possessions, such as gluttony, greed, selfishness, materialism, and waste. It also requires that we avoid laziness, apathy and false asceticism. While *self interest* is acceptable in biblical ethics, selfishness and greed are not acceptable, but are distortions of rightful self interest. [4] The stewardship requirements implied by the 8th Commandment are life-long. They begin in childhood, with the responsibility to care for one's toys and small responsibilities, and they continue until the day of one's death, when we must make wise choices regarding the disposition of any goods that we leaves behind.

Therefore who among us can say from his heart, "I know that I have always made right stewardship decisions. I know that God is pleased with how I've managed my resources. I've made wise investments and judicious allocation of funds between giving to others, investing, saving, and using for my own present enjoyment. I have been a wise steward of all the intellectual, creative, artistic, and managerial opportunities and abilities that God entrusted to me. My talent has made ten talents more"? I doubt any living person could honestly say that today, for, "If we say we have no sin, we deceive ourselves, and the truth is not in us" (1 John 1:8).

Therefore the challenge of the 8th Commandment is immense. Hidden within the simple words, "You shall not steal," we discover the infinite wisdom of God. Through these words, God laid the foundation for a system of private ownership of property, of stewardship and accountability, and of an expectation that we would achieve much and flourish as we lived on the face of the earth.

The immensity of this challenge should not discourage us, however. It should excite us that God has entrusted such a great challenge to us. It should excite us to know that God fills us with joy and delight as we seek to accomplish these tasks. In seeking to fulfill the 8th Commandment rightly, we will find opportunities to use *every capacity* with which he has richly endowed us. We will discover the joy of using all of our God-given abilities to express love to fellow human beings through creating business products and services that truly bring good to other people, and (for those who know Christ) also produce much thanksgiving to God.

Therefore the opportunities provided by the 8th Commandment show us God's pathway to human flourishing on the earth, for the glory of God.

F. Governments break the 8th Commandment when they steal private property

We must acknowledge at the outset that governments have a proper authority to collect taxes for legitimate government functions. Paul says that because the civil authority is "God's servant for your good" (Rom. 13:4), "you also pay taxes, for the authorities are ministers of God attending to this very thing. Pay to all what is owed to them: taxes to whom taxes are owed . . ." (Rom. 13:7). Governments have a moral right to collect taxes for the legitimate functions of government, to reward good and punish evil and establish order in society, for Peter says that governors are sent "to punish those who do evil and to praise those who do good" (1 Peter 2:14).

However, too often in history governments have gone far beyond these legitimate functions. We cannot here define in detail the exact limits of legitimate or illegitimate use of government's power of taxation, but we can point to several examples of governments that have so diminished or abolished private property that they have destroyed human flourishing in their nations. This is because, if people are to exercise stewardship fully, they must have freedom to use their property as they think best. But if government owns or controls all the property, people no longer have freedom to use their property as they think best, and to be rewarded for their effort. Human achievement is thereby stifled and true human excellence will occur rarely, if ever.

Some examples of governments that have broken the 8th Commandment by wrongfully stealing property from their people are as follows:

(1) Communist countries prohibit private ownership of land. Karl Marx said "The theory of the Communists may be summed up in the single sentence: abolition of private property."[5] Communist countries such as North Korea, Cuba and the former Soviet Union prohibited all private ownership of property such as land and buildings. In doing this, these governments trapped their people in a depressing cycle of poverty.

(2) Socialism is a form of government where individuals can own private homes and have other possessions, but the government owns all of the businesses and factories (what are called the "means of production"). This ultimately restricts and diminishes human flourishing, but it does not destroy it completely.

(3) Some nations prevent private ownership of property because private property is owned by the tribe, not by individuals. This is the system found on most American Indian reservations. It is also the system found in many nations in sub-Saharan Africa. Every nation that has tribal ownership of property is poor, and will always remain poor. This is because tribal ownership of property prevents private property and thus prevents human

flourishing.

(4) Economic historian David Landes, in his book, *The Wealth and Poverty of Nations* [6] points out some other examples of nations in past history that prevented private ownership of property. In India prior to the advent of British rule in 1757, local mogul princes had unquestioned regional authority and essentially took from the people whatever they wanted. This system effectively prevented private ownership of property, and thus greatly hindered human flourishing for centuries.

Landes also points out that in China, for many centuries, the Emperor had absolute rule and took whatever he wanted from the people. Once again this system prevented a workable system of private ownership of property, and thus hindered human flourishing for the vast majority of the Chinese population.

Similarly, in Eastern Europe for several centuries the feudal system meant that a few wealthy lords would own all the property and the vast majority of the population were therefore trapped in poverty. The lack of an easily accessible means to acquire private ownership of property meant that human flourishing was effectively prevented for centuries.

(5) Peruvian economist Hernando de Soto, in his landmark book *The Mystery of Capital,* points out that documented ownership of private property in many Latin American countries, as well as in other poor countries such as Haiti and Egypt, is made nearly impossible by excessive government procedures and bureaucracy that are designed to keep property ownership in the hands of a wealthy few, and to prevent ordinary people from owning their own property.

In all of these situations, these governments are really "stealing" property from individuals who should have been able to acquire and own their own property. In preventing private ownership of property, these governments removed most of the incentives for people to strive for greater economic achievement and to flourish as human beings on the earth.

H. Private property and individual stewardship naturally create a free market

When only one individual owns property, there can be no market for buying and selling. But as soon as several individuals in a community each have some property, it leads naturally to trading, and then to buying and selling with what a person owns. This is because individuals naturally seek to better their own situations. When a man who has some bread and no eggs can voluntarily trade with a man who has some eggs but no bread, they find that they both can make an egg sandwich and they both are better off than before. And soon after that, an entrepreneur will arise and realize that he can buy supplies from both of them and sell egg sandwiches to everyone in town. Therefore out of *private ownership of property in a community* there naturally will emerge the amazing mechanism of a free market, with all the benefits of commerce that flow from the market.

I. Conclusion: The 8th Commandment lays the foundation for human flourishing on the earth

When the 8th Commandment establishes the ideas of property rights, stewardship, the expectation of human achievement, and the foundation for a free market, it puts in place the necessary components for human economic flourishing on the earth. Therefore the 8th Commandment provides the moral basis for an economic system that will best lead to the fulfillment of God's command to Adam and Eve that they should "fill the earth and subdue it and have dominion" over it (Gen. 1:28). Therefore the 8th Commandment lays the foundation for human flourishing on the earth.

J. The attack on property rights and markets from modern political liberalism

The view we have presented above is always under attack, particularly so from those with leftist political convictions. For whatever reason, they continue to glorify the state and strongly favor the politicization of human affairs. Invariably, government is their solution to human problems. But the more that is controlled by government, the less that is controlled by individual stewardship of property. The profound crossroad facing every generation, then, is to turn either to the collectivist vision which worships the state and political solutions, or to turn to those who lean towards America's great experiment in private ownership of property, and with it individual liberty and "we the people" individual dignity.

The Left's endgame strategy is straightforward. First, generate as much provocative class warfare rhetoric as you can. A good example is the recent Congressional election in New York's District 26. The candidate that won ran endless video clips of a mean man pushing an old lady in a wheelchair off a cliff. The Republican plan for saving Medicare could hurt or even kill old people! Emotionalism and fear still seem to work. Visual stories usually trump written persuasion. Robin Hood stealing from the rich and giving to the poor; the rich not paying their fair share; spread the wealth around; always pitting white vs. black, male vs. female. Wherever there is class, there is room for dividing people.

Next comes the vast assumption that *government* could better control the economy then the *market*. Education, health care, transportation, electric, gas, and water utilities are usually the first to be collectivized.

Clarence Carson in his series of articles entitled "World in the Grip of an Idea," said, "If the twentieth century were a play, it would long since have driven the audience mad. The incongruity between the words spoken by the actors and the action on the stage would be too great to be borne. The actors speak of peace, prosperity, progress, freedom, brotherly love and a forthcoming end to the age-old ills of mankind. The action on the stage has been world wars, dictatorships, class and racial animosities, terrorism and a more general coarsening of human behavior." Carson goes on: "It is possible to grasp what has been happening on a world wide scale by ignoring all the political promises and keeping your eyes fixed on the action and the ideas that are producing it."

Neglecting the Biblical truth of the sinfulness of man is a common, even frequent mistake. Then comes a state promising minimum wage laws, rent controls, price controls, tariffs, subsidized rents, interest rate ceilings, agricultural price supports, federal loan guarantees, passenger rail service subsidies, fixing public utility rates, protecting the right of labor to strike, affordable housing, and even free health care. The never-ending list of entitlements becomes a never-ending list of promises, all of course provided by the state and higher taxes.

But what happens when the *takers* exceed the *makers* and producers are overwhelmed by government planners and economic progressives? Debt, deficits and economic unsustainability could become reality. Unfortunately, a bigger government also means a smaller individual and a smaller citizen; a government big enough to give you all you want is big enough to take everything you have; a helping hand almost always turns into a controlling hand.

Human liberty, by contrast, with its foundation resting on the eighth commandment and the institution of private property, titles, deeds, and a free market economic system, has enormously beneficial consequences. The invisible hand of the market that Adam Smith describes in his *Wealth of Nations* produces order, harmony, coordination, and diversity.

The market is a miraculous instrument of communication and a stupendous transmitter of opinions, while determining value. Producing a singular price resulting from millions and billions of interacting suppliers and consumers, the market becomes a spontaneous and productive social order that is truly a gift from God. The more complex the economy becomes the less amenable it is to human design and conscious direction. But the market continues to function well, ever adjusting, ever adapting to meet human wants with human supplies in seemingly infinite variety.

The market is a self-adapting process, a transcendent galactic bathroom scale producing prices that can meaningfully cause humans to act. It is one of God's common graces that is little understood, but in it lies one key to human progress and freedom.

Without the 8th commandment, we would have protection for none of this. Liberty would be lost and the possibility of human flourishing would be destroyed. To the extent that governments steal property from individuals, they steal the opportunity for human flourishing, and, to that extent, they steal glory from God.

Notes

1. This is the 7th Commandment according to the numbering system used in the Lutheran and Roman Catholic traditions. We have used here the numbering system found in the rest of Protestant tradition and in the *Westminster Confession of Faith*. The wording of the commandment itself is of course the same, no matter which number is assigned to it.

2. The previous two paragraphs have been adapted from Wayne Grudem, *Politics-According to the Bible* (Grand Rapids: Zondervan, 2010, p. 262).

3. The previous paragraph was adopted from the *ESV Study Bible*, Wayne Grudem, general editor, (Wheaton: Crossway, 2009), note on Acts 2:44; p. 2085.

4. See the excellent discussion of the difference between selfishness and self interest in Jay Richards, *Money, Greed and God: Why Capitalism is the Solution and not the Problem* New York: HarperOne, 2009), pages 115-123.

5. Karl Marx, *Communist Manifesto* (New York: International Publishers, 1948), page 23.

6. David Landes, *The Wealth and Poverty of Nations* (New York: W.W. Norton, 1999).

COVENANT AND THE EIGHTH COMMANDMENT

DAVID COWAN

DAVID COWAN

David Cowan is an expert on Religion and International Relations, including economics. He holds a Bachelor of Theology and Master of Theology, both from the University of Oxford, and a Master of Letters from the University of St Andrews, where he is currently a PhD researcher on the influence of the "Religious Right" on American Foreign Policy from Nixon to the present day. He is author of "Economic Parables: The Monetary Teachings of Jesus Christ" (Paternoster USA, 2007, 2nd Edition 2009). He has contributed essays on "Christianity and Economics" to the Encyclopedia of Christian Civilization (Blackwell) and on "Religious Minorities" to the International Encyclopedia of Political Science (CQ Press USA), both published this year.

He previously worked as a journalist, editor, and as an executive in banking and industry in Europe and North America for over twenty years, including Financial Times, Euromoney, and the World Bank Group in Washington DC. He has written for the Washington Times, Financial Times, The Times of London, The Middle East and has been interviewed by major print, television and radio media, including CNBC, Bloomberg TV, Wall Street Journal, Financial Times, and BBC Radio.

I. Covenant and Theft

There is a common fundamental error shared by peoples in Capitalist, Socialist and Communist economies, and this is the error that the economy can make us happy. The Capitalist assumes that wealth (for the richer) and consumption (for the poorer) makes us happy. The Socialist assumes that education and sharing resources, which they regard as scarce, will make us happy. The Communist assumes the loss of property ownership makes us happy. The point is, happiness has another source, which can find expression in the economy, but economy does not create it. The economy is a means, not an end. Happiness only happens when God is at the center.

There is another fundamental human error, and this is the idea that theft can make us happy, by giving us what we do not have, or cannot have, by unfair means. Naturally, all economies – feudal, communism, capitalist - experience theft, because theft is a human act. The problem of theft operates on many levels, and so this paper offers a contextual study of the subject on these main levels, from the global down to the individual. I will seek to highlight the business issues involved, and connect these to specific theological ideas.

The fundamental point to make is that we are to seek to please God. This is what our faith points us to; it is what I call the instinct of faith. The question to consider is this: can we do this in business?

We are all in business to make money. The symbol of Capitalism is the Dollar sign. It is about money, which consists of coins and notes, and in America it bears the legend "In God We Trust". It is electronic, whizzing round the world 24 hours a day, nonstop and restless. It is also scorned as the object of greed. Just mention money is involved in something and people change their attitude. Money can make something desirable when we have enough, or think we can earn enough to acquire the objects of our desires. Money can also taint something because it has to be paid for, or it is being used corruptly. Money can be stolen, and things can be stolen and changed into money. What horrible stuff it is! Or, is it?

We can think of money from the level of an individual right up to global levels. A nation is the Lender of last resort in the world, because a nation is thought to be too big to fail. Companies can fail, but nations cannot, is the theory. With the level of debt in America spiralling, the theory is under test. With a recession still hanging over the nation, many are now questioning the role of Capitalism in America and the world. We are in difficult times right now, and money, it seems to some, is the cause of the problem. It is not. The sickliness of the economy is down to people, not inanimate money.

To address this biblically, we can recall what Paul tells us about the love of money. Many misquote this as "money is the root of all evil", so let's remind ourselves of what Paul in fact writes in 1 Timothy 6:10, "For the love of money is a root of all kinds of evil. Some people, eager for money, have wandered from the faith and pierced themselves with many griefs." It is not money itself then that is the problem, but the love of money. Money is not the root of all evil, we know who that is! It is, however, at the root of all kinds of evil. The outcome of this is simple, many griefs ranging from resentment of what others have to theft of another's property.

Theft is a problem because it is forbidden by the eighth commandment. The reason for making a commandment out of this, rather than just leaving as a minor rule is that it is to do with broken relationship. It is not the money but the love of money that is the root of all evil, and this is because it substitutes the love of God. Martin Luther divided the Ten Commandments in two: You shall Love the Lord your God, and then all the rest. What he was telling us is this: if we love the Lord then we won't want to break the other Commandments. We can only act right when we love God. This is what makes us happy.

I want to look at Capitalism, money and theft at four descending levels:

1. Global
2. National
3. Organizational
4. Individual

First, let me suggest some principles about God and relationship. First, God. All that is in the world is God's, and God provides all that is necessary in the world. Theft is a fundamental presumption that God neither owns all nor provides all. If all is God's then I deny God by stealing what is ultimately His. If God provides all then I ultimately deny God because I say He is not providing for me. Because all things come from God does not, however, mean that all things belong to everyone. God has His purposes and gives us what we need to achieve His ends.

Second, relationship. Our innovation in the world is really a process of us discovering what God has already offered. We work in relationship with each other to advance our society, on family and organizational levels. Our seeking to bypass or abuse norms of relationship is a denial of God, in whom our relationships are ultimately rooted – whether we accept Christ or not. I will refer to these principles from time to time, but please keep it in the back of your mind as I work my way through the various levels.

II: GLOBAL LEVEL - THE THEFT OF AN IDEA

We live in a globalized world, where Capitalism is the sole organizing economic system. To varying degrees, this system is socialized. This is essentially the "mixed economy", which in Europe is socialized to a higher degree than America, though America is moving in the same direction. The fall of the Soviet Union and the end of Communism may have ended systemic Socialism and Communism, but many of the Marxist and Socialist ideas have remained and imbued much economic thinking in Capitalist societies, giving rise to zip code socialists. These are people who still love the idea of Socialism, so long as it applies to a group like "the poor" or "the working class," but don't want it in their zip code, which is usually at the desirable end of the social scale. The prevalence of socialist ideas in Capitalist societies leads some of us to suggest we should in fact try Capitalism!

The reality is that caution about Capitalism exists because the global assumption made, not just by anti-Capitalists but also others, is that Capitalism is a zero-sum game. In other words, there are only winners and losers. We hear about the rich/poor divide, and those on the margins of society compared to "fat cats." This is underpinned by a suspicion that Capitalism is inherently selfish and greedy; indeed, in this view, Capitalism needs these in order to thrive.

It is important to debunk such false criticisms of Capitalism as a selfish, greedy, zero-sum game; at least, no more so than any other area of human activity in a fallen world. Yes, in Capitalism we act in our self-interest, the point made by Adam Smith. However, what is in our self-interest is not inherently something selfish, though it often is; a trite example will suffice. A gambler is acting selfishly, but hardly in his economic self-interest, unless he is actually successful at it; the result being the loss of job, home, family and more.

To act in our self-interest often demands that we act in a nonselfish way. In providing for my family or my church, I can be unselfish, though it is self-interested. It may be in my self-interest to promote someone in a job, even though selfishly I might want the job to go to someone else (perhaps it is a woman I am interested in), because the issue is what will make the business, and me, successful in the long run.

My reason for offering this argument is that anti-capitalism and anti-business sentiments on both a global and intellectual level promotes envy and theft. In terms of envy, people are provoked into resentment of what others have, and to ponder why they have less. Critics may mock individuals for trying to "keep up with the Jones's", but their pitch is "resent the Jones's". In terms of theft, this is often seen as victimless, and stealing justifiable because business is inherently bad in the first place. There is also a global view that business is a form of theft: all property is theft, said Marx. It is a short leap from theft to redistribution of wealth.

Related to this, is the idea that resource allocation is inherently unfair, leading to "fixed-pie thinking." This is the idea that there is a finite range of resources to share amongst us all, and this needs to be redistributed to bring a new balance. If I get a piece of the pie then that is one less piece for someone else. This underpins socialist and welfare thinking, which believes we all need to share in a piece of the pie. Yet, Capitalism is not just a zero-sum game. Capitalism says, if there is not enough pie you go and make another one! Thank goodness Jesus did not have fixed pie thinking when he shared the loaves and fishes! Of course Socialism would say there are only five loaves and two fish, so everyone can only get a tiny piece each. However, since the loaves and fishes would quickly run out many would simply go would have to go without, for the good of the cause. As Margaret Thatcher once observed, the problem with Socialism is you eventually run out of other people's money.

In Capitalism, the focus is on creating alternatives, by moving forward in exploration and seeking new ways of innovation. This is what expands the pie. We can believe in a humanity that uses investment and innovation to solve practical problems. For instance, one hundred years ago people couldn't "see" past coal, they thought the world was running out of coal and spelled the end of energy. Who worries about coal today? The point is technological innovation, in this case nuclear energy, allows resource utilization that was not possible before.

Let us then reflect on some theological aspects. Can it not be that God has given us some economic rules to govern our use of resources? I don't mean here a prosperity gospel, but a set of rules to govern the left-handed kingdom.

We believe in a God who isn't confined by a set number of resources. However, God, as we have known since our banishment from Eden, does not give us everything on a plate. He expects us to exercise wise stewardship. God does not want us to be complacent. This principle has found expression, in some quarters, in modern-day social planning and environmentalism. However, what God expects, I propose, differs from social engineering and environmentalist religion and the assumptions used in their models. I propose the model to follow is one of covenant. Let me explain, by going back to the beginning rather than to Marx and other 19th Century optimists.

The big picture, the global context for our discussion, is that God is source of all and we are in a covenant relationship with Him. Therefore, any economy that is solely based on human relationship as its goal is bound to fail. Capitalism is a free system of relationships, which may be sourced from many places and formed for many reasons. The attack often made on Capitalism is directed primarily at America as the Capitalist nation par excellence, except they do not except its excellence. The insidious infiltration of Socialistic thinking into current economic decision-making is the theft of an idea, and ultimately undermine the thinking and direction of a nation. It is to the level of nation I now turn.

III: NATIONAL LEVEL – IDENTITY THEFT

In the beginning, God makes a covenant with a nation, the nation of Israel, not just an individual or a small community. This covenant coincides with wealth. In the book of Genesis, wealth is first mentioned in the form of gold and silver 13:2, where we read Abram is rich with silver and gold, livestock and possessions, after Abram had left Egypt to go up north to Palestine. God had blessed him with great wealth. From this first mention of wealth we learn that because it is from God then it is not something evil. In other words, we can think of wealth as a good thing, but only because it comes from God, not for its own sake, not as an end for its own sake as it is in Socialism and Marxism.

The first mention of "money" occurs in the Bible at Genesis 17:12. It is set in the context of Genesis 17:1-14, the covenant made by God to Abraham. When God makes this covenant it is with the solemn divine institution of circumcision. The covenant God makes does include specific provisions, including money. But before we go into that, let us think about some major economic things which have been going on in the world since the creation up to this point.

First, we read that God had created humanity, and humanity had fallen. As a result of his sin, Man was told to work the land from which he was taken, to use his labor to get at the rich resources God had created to sustain His creature (Gen 3:23). We learn from this that we have natural resources and God has provided these resources for our use. However, the responsibility lies with us individually to access and use these resources. Nothing is given to us on a plate! Adam and Eve did not have these worries before the Fall, but all this has changed. We have to work for it!

Next we read, after God had cleansed the earth with the flood and Noah sets his foot on dry land, he becomes a man of the soil and plants a vineyard (9:20). The Covenant promised Noah (Gen 6:18) comes into effect (Gen 9:8f). God makes the covenant and freely binds Himself to His creature. A rainbow in the cloud is a sign to remind Noah of the covenant, borne out of the flood, as the sun dried the earth and made it habitable once more. Noah has a new covenant from God, but Noah still has to work at it!

So, we know we need to work! We could understand work as a result of sin, a separation from God. It can stand between us and service. However, the point that we work the land from where we have been taken means that it is good, for God created the earth from which he took us. Man is now bound to the soil, which he was in the first instance privileged to control. God has determined there is a relationship between Him and us, and work and money are part of this relationship.

When we talk of God blessing a nation, it is the people He blesses. If the rules of Capitalism work akin to the rules of nature, then America is blessed because the American people have played by the rules. Fixed pie thinking, as we learn from the history of Manifest Destiny in America, was never part of the thinking. The spread westwards was not just geographic, it was economic. It took hard labor and innovation, to take the nation shore to shore. This is the nature of Capitalism. We saw this in Eden, and see this in the birth of a nation.

Out of this economy grew a self-reliant nation, which is currently paving a path to dependency based on international ideas, which sadly draw from a different source of economic ideas. This has given rise to the notion that the economy, and business, should perform a social function. Many churches have bought into this, and sacralised the notion. All of this comes under the titles of "Corporate Social Responsibility" and "sustainability."

My point is somewhat out of fashion with the direction of current social ethics, but sustainable business is business that will be around at the end of year and decade. Yet, corporate social responsibility is a recent phenomenon that businesses have grown to accept; to the ironic extent that it is a business in itself. CSR is about social ethics and the "green" agenda. In other words, businesses are increasingly coming under social control through rules, regulations and finger-wagging. The assumed "guilt" of Capitalism makes the charge easy to stick, and leads to businessmen assuming they are essentially wrong and need to do the right thing.

However, this is a political agenda, one which means businesses are increasingly under secular ethical demands. What we are seeing in the environmental and social demands being placed on business is the promotion of a particular political agenda. The difficulties here include increased environmental costs and increases in taxes and wages. This extends beyond just "complaints" about individual companies or unscrupulous business operators. It leads to a systemic emphasis on heavier regulations and constraints on doing business. We do not, in this schema, rely on God or the hard work and conscience of the individual, but on those who seem to know what is best for us all. It is a shift from self-reliance, rooted in God, to dependency on humanitarian goals. It is little wonder that environmental projects have names like "The Eden Project," for they have replaced God in their secular universe.

American capitalism, in this way, is being attacked by international rules. The pressure comes externally from the international community, and internally from those who buy into the international approach (arguably this applies elsewhere politically, not just in economic terms). Notions of corporate Social Responsibility is a political construct which places demands on American businesses to be good citizens according to international norms, which has been gradually imposed in the same way that high temperatures are imposed on a frog and leads to its demise.

I could be harsh and call this approach by another name: theft.

The reality is that ethics are rooted in a different place from business demands. The problem of this approach is that it lends itself to Legalism. It says "I'm ok because I haven't broken any laws." In this approach, theft becomes defined by staying within the rules, rather than being rejected in a state of mind. This is theologically backward, an Old Testament view of the issue, yet it is supported by many church groups and Christian advocates. Christ came to free us from the law, and modern society has become legalistic. The nation has become a legalistic construct based on an ever-growing set of regulations and rules, which ultimately lead to a lack of scope for innovation, a dependency culture and a diminished sense of individual responsibility.

IV: ORGANIZATIONAL LEVEL – THEFT OF RELATIONSHIP

Now turning to the organizational level, we can look at what binds businesses together. Businesses are not just about the hard numbers. They comprise a complex range of inter-relationships, which are measured by price and terms. They do not operate efficiently on greed. The word "greed" is emotive, and has become the *mot du jour* for condemning business leadership. While many suffer in the economy generally, the Socialist points to the greed. When many suffer in a particular economy then the general public join in the chorus. Yet, greed occurs in all areas of human society. There is greed for power, for success in business, politics, the universities, and even in the churches.

In the parable of the unjust manager, Jesus appears to be praising the astute manager. The teaching here is that wealth is of the world, and may be acquired in ungodly ways, but it can also be used in godly ways. The issue here, for Jesus and I contend for the economy today, is not the intrinsic value of wealth, but our relationship to wealth. Socialistic thinking may appear superficially to be saying the same thing, but in fact creates dependency and resentment. Part of our relationship with wealth is not to put it before God. Resenting others, becoming dependent unnecessarily on others, or, stealing from those who have, are ways of putting wealth before God. Jesus also explains that if we cannot be trusted with this little thing called wealth, for wealth is a little thing because it passes into dust, then we cannot be trusted with the big things, which are the things of God.

We see this in business. We can detect from little things that people do whether we can trust them with the big things. Ask any compliance officer in a business and they will tell you they look for little tell-tale signs which point them to a fraud or embezzlement in the company. In reverse, if we have our eye on the big things this will be reflected in the little things. If an individual believes in the company mission, it will show in the respect they show customers or the care they take of their work environment. The two work off each other like an infinity sign. For a Christian in business, the big thing is God and this will show in the care they take in all they do. The Christian business manager can use worldly wealth wisely, precisely because he or she uses it standing in the light of the Gospel. When he or she does wrong it is not the compliance officer or the auditor they fear, it is God Himself they fear.

This plays nicely into the self-interest discussion. We are told by critics of Capitalism that business relies on playing on people's selfishness. However, selfishness is actually very destructive and counter-productive. Because we have a sinful nature, our actions when selfish are self-destructive as well. When they are self-interested, rooted in a self-interest that resides in pleasing God, then we will act in our self-interest and defeat the selfish acts we might do.

If I am right so far, then this is not a zero-sum game. For a start, God would not be behind a system that is zero sum, expect when it comes to evil. In economic terms, it is not zero sum, so let's look at what happens in a business. I provide a service, you provide funding. I may use that funding to buy a service from someone else, and you may use my service to gain funding from another party. Everyone wins, where is the zero sum? If I conduct my business relationship in order, excuse the terminology but it seems to capture the point, to "screw you", then ultimately we do not maintain a good working relationship. At the first opportunity the "screwee" will go elsewhere. You can only abuse business relationships for so long. On a more positive note, in a healthy business relationship we will also find that by working well together in an organization, we receive benefits from this good relationship. Again, it is to early Marxist and socialist critique we owe the notion that business relationships are all about advancing the cause of the rich capitalist. Naturally, bad business relationships do exist, but as a corruption of good business. It leads to squandering of resources and talent. It needs to be better monitored. It also leads to loss of capital and assets, both human and financial. Every morning you go into your business, you hope for two things. First, your employees will come to work and your customers will buy your product or service; the better the business, the happier the workforce and the customer.

Capitalism is not a zero sum, because it is based most fundamentally on agreement. In other words, contract. Business relationships are established and governed by contract. We make contracts every day. The business we do is defined by terms of contract. This is a concept rooted in covenant, and so we can easily draw some important theological lessons from this. In business, an organization operates on the basis of a covenant with customers, employees, suppliers, government, and consumers. We have obligations to provide a product or service, pay and support our employees, and many other routine matters. In faith, we are the covenanted people of the Lord, which means we have obligations: to worship, pray, serve Him, be Christ to others. Let me explain these further. First, let us think about contracts.

If we buy a tank of gas or a rail ticket, we are making a contract. I pay; the pump dispenses gas. I pay; the train takes me to my destination. When we get to work, we have another contract. I work; my company pays me at the end of the week or the end of the month. I serve a customer, and there is another contract, one I manage on behalf of my employer. When I use my mobile phone to say I will be home later than usual, I use a contract I have with my mobile service provider. Contracts, contracts and more contracts!

Every day we could add up how many contracts we make that day, each governing different relationships. They are personal and professional. They are short term like a train ride, or long term like an employment contract. You can see from this that some contracts are minor, like a train ticket, while others are central to our life, like our work contract. Of course, the definition of Communism is "We pretend to pay you, you pretend to work." In Capitalism, we compete, we work and we have freedom to do as little or as much as we want. Contracts also change over time. Maybe we change jobs and don't need to take a train. Maybe we decide to work for ourselves. Our life moves on, and the contract comes to an end.

Can we say the same of covenants? Let us then explore this idea of covenant.

In Genesis 17:1-14, we learn that the covenant with Abraham and God's people is for all time. Imagine if you were forced to have the same work contract your whole life? It's okay to have the same job your whole life, but along the way you like to know you can change it if you want. You also know you get to retire! Here is where it gets interesting, though. The covenant God makes is with His people as a group. The text tells us, we can choose not to enter into the covenant. Verse 14 reads "Any uncircumcised male, who has not been circumcised in the flesh, will be cut off from his people; he has broken my covenant." We can break away individually, like resigning or changing our travel plans, but the covenant between God and His people continues. The result of breaking away is to be cut off, losing our relationship with God, not sharing in the community of the covenant, and, not receiving the benefits of the covenant. This is different from contracts, so let's dig deeper.

There are ways in which we can think about covenant in our economy, and we can see how the model of covenant might be employed to understand business and work dealings. God is stronger than Abraham, but he does not set arduous terms on us, it is our rebellious nature which takes care of this. We can reflect here on how a more covenantal relationship can successfully work in the case of a big business, and for us individually. These are just a few reflections to help you think of your own examples, at your work and in your life.

A bigger business can be generous in attitudes towards employees, customers and smaller suppliers. For instance, we can look at how business contracts are honored. Big companies should pay small suppliers and individuals on time when they get a bill. All too often big companies can damage the cash flow of smaller organizations by holding up paying their bill. Again, big companies have resources to help their smaller suppliers, and can offer technical support and advice to help them grow. Big companies can offer longer-term contracts, rather than have their smaller suppliers wondering year-to-year if they have a contract beyond the current one. These are just some ways big companies can help build relationships with their small suppliers. While God is powerful, He does expect we are faithful to the covenant. Likewise, if big companies are going to covenant with smaller suppliers, then the smaller companies cannot abuse the relationship either. It is easy to get a nice contract and offer poorer work in return while saving best efforts for new customers. To covenant successfully the relationship has to work in both directions.

We can look more specifically at the Old Testament covenant established with Abram, who is renamed Abraham. Right away, we learn about the promise of this covenant. "I am God Almighty; walk before me faithfully and be blameless", God tells Abram. In other words, good conduct is a sign of being a true servant of God, by walking with God. We know from 17:3 Abram fell on his face, because he realizes how unworthy he is of this literally God-given opportunity. The man falls down before God because he knows where he is relative to God. In recognition of this development in relationship, the name of Abram is changed to Abraham. This covenant is with him and with all nations, and all those who will be faithful children. This is why he is to be called Abraham (17:4).

God appears to Abram, not the other way round. All too often, people understand the relationship the wrong way round! Abram is being called and God shows him a nation, for God covenants with His people. This emphasizes that this is not simply an agreement between God and one man called Abram - it is a covenant with the people who God calls His own. However, this is not a mutual agreement between equal partners. It is a covenant which comes solely from God towards Abram and God's people. In the spirit of this covenant, with his new name, Abraham can both reflect the goodness that comes from following God, and is warned against doing those things that will harm the covenant. This is not a new covenant - it is a realization of the blessings of the covenant foretold in Genesis 15:18.

We also learn this is not just for His people at that time, but for future generations as well. In Verse 12, we read every male 8 days old must be circumcised, including those "born in your household or bought with money from a foreigner—those who are not your offspring". The rite is described in the text, and we need not go into detail here. What we want to get to is the fact that this circumcision is a "sign" of the covenant. The Gentiles mocked the Jews for this practice, but they only see superficially what it means. We can understand more than this. Abraham and the people of God are already in the faith by virtue of birth, not because of circumcision. The circumcision is a reminder of the obligation under God, a sign, and foreshadows baptism. There are a set of conditions attached to this covenant, and it is in this context we find the mention of money. Money is more than an impersonal trade or substitution; it sets things right with God. Those bought with money are acceptable as full members of the household. This is not about slavery, but about our status before God.

In the text, gold and silver are mentioned (Gen 13:2) in terms of blessing, but here money is mentioned in terms of an obligation. An obligation is established in this covenant. The people are required to keep this covenant, and as a sign the males must be circumcised. The terms of this covenant are set. We can compare and contrast this covenant to contract in our modern economy. In a contract there are two or more parties. Something is given in return, what lawyers call "good consideration". There is a transaction, as goods or services are exchanged for money. Both sides of the contract are thus advantaged: one side has money and the other has the goods or services. We exchange our time and labor for a wage. There is no zero sum, there is no systemic apparatus of greed, there is relationship between individuals and there is covenant with God. This Which brings me to the individual level.

V: Individual level – Theft by Renegotiating the Deal

As individuals, we all rely on relationship. In business, we need to work together to create and generate business. We don't just work in business, however, we have social lives, live in communities and have family. This is where we search for a work/life balance, because work so often gets in the way of other areas of our life. We get tired, get tied into a major project, work weekends or work overtime. This can lead to resentment, a sense that work and business is theft of time we should be devoting to others. The working time eats into time we could be helping with the Lord's work and our church! These are times we could be out doing good in our community! Well, no actually. Without wealth there is no church building or Bibles for distribution. Without wealth in the community there is no real community. The tremendous advances in science and technology are not achieved by holding hands and singing kumbaya. They are achieved by hard work and smart investing. This is life, this is reality.

Picking up on where we left the discussion on the organizational level, we can also think about covenant between individuals. When we make contracts, do we question the consequences? When we plan our contracts, do we build our covenant relationship with God into our plans? Some of us could, for instance, take a train instead of driving to work and use that time productively to read about our faith. We could plan our schedule to build a weekday Church activity into our schedule. How often do we say on a Sunday morning "sorry, can't make that, I have a work thing to do"? Perhaps if we planned our work differently, we might free up some time to make the activity. It is easy to try and organize our faith to fit into our work, but it is difficult to do it the other way round, right? Yet, we know from Jesus that this doesn't feel right. Jesus generously gave Himself for us, but still we squeeze him into maybe an hour or so at church as week, and maybe a few other times. There are doubtless many ways in which we can more effectively to build covenant thinking into our work schedule.

When we make contracts and the contract negotiations are realistic, we do not deprive the other party, rather we recognize the contribution of the other party. What works best in a contract is a relationship arising out of mutual benefit. This is how we sustain long-term relationships in business. Violation of a contract can lead to many corruptions; including services being held to ransom and a mercenary approach to delivery of a product or service. A violation can also be instigated as much by an employee or a customer as it can the "big, bad" organization. In this respect, the whole area of Torts is a can of worms I'm not going to open, but is well worth thinking about. Torts are important, and damages are often deserved. However, tort claims often leads to rising insurance costs for the pool of insured, and is often selfish and exhibits the worst of our behaviors. Tort is what happens when relationship breaks down.

From tort, it can be a short step to theft. Theft is a breakdown in relationship. It is contrary to covenant; transgressing the contractual and personal commitments we have given. In business, this may appear obvious and I don't need to go into all the effects and ramifications of theft in business. What I want to focus on is this: the violation of the Eighth commandment is ultimately breaking the relationship with God. It is a way of "renegotiating" our deal with God. What we are saying to God is that in the economy "I'm not getting my due, I'm not getting enough." People steal because they want more. They want what they can't get easily by normal means. The covenant we have we God, and in business, is not giving us what we want and so we resort to the means of theft to get what we believe we are due. It is the end of relationship, because we have selfishly dictated the terms for how we will find our reward, in the hope that other parties to the relationship do not find out. The point is to get away with it. The problem, ultimately, is that God knows. We transgress our relationship with Him, and so our relationship to wealth has shifted from God to another idolatrous place. Wealth and theft are both measured by money, and so money becomes the idol to replace God. This is a lifeless idol; it is only the idolatrous individual who gives this money life as an idol. It is Marxist and Socialist thinking that builds a case against wealth and money as the cause of wrong, it is only the measure of the wrong we do.

VI: CONCLUSION – FOR LOVE NOR MONEY

Theft is the love of money. It is a sign, along with many other actions, which show the exact opposite of Covenant. These are signs of the last days, as Paul writes in 2 Tim 3:1-3, "There will be terrible times in the last days. People will be lovers of themselves, lovers of money, boastful, proud, abusive, disobedient to their parents, ungrateful, unholy, without love, unforgiving, slanderous, without self-control, brutal, not lovers of the good." To love money, and to make it the core of being and reason, is something which lacks true meaning. As Paul explains in Ecclesiastes 5:10, "Whoever loves money never has enough; whoever loves wealth is never satisfied with their income. This too is meaningless." We end up with a shallow existence, because we are far from the one whom we should love, namely Jesus. As Jesus warns us (Mt 6:24, Lk 16:13), "No one can serve two masters. Either you will hate the one and love the other, or you will be devoted to the one and despise the other. You cannot serve both God and money."

At base, money is not really about physical nickels and dimes or dollar bills. It is about relationship. It is about how we center our relationships. Are we friends because of the money another has, and the status it buys them? Or, are we friends because we share union in Christ?

Money reflects our relationships, and so it also measures what we think is important. If I pay hundreds of dollars for a football season ticket yet only put $5 a week into the collection plate at church, then the football is more important to me than the work of the church. I put my money where my mouth is, as the saying goes. If money appears wicked, it is only playing its role of showing in cents and dollars what we most care about.

If we see money as a means, then it can be used positively. It can be used to invest to be self-sufficient. It can be used to invest in others, to enable them to be self-sufficient. Money, like property, is more important when it is ours, rather than a handout from the State. "In God We Trust" is what a dollar bill says, not "In Government We Trust". What we need is a Godly relationship. We need to trust more in God, that He will provide us with all we want.

Remember Paul? "Whoever loves money never has enough; whoever loves wealth is never satisfied with their income." We know from this that money cannot replace God, we can only be satisfied with God. When we realize this is what relationship means, we find that what we always thought we wanted to buy with money is in fact happiness, and we can't buy that, because our true happiness can only come from God.

Why do people steal? It is the love of money, or rather the love of other people's money. Money is a measure of what we have and what we want. To understand this biblically, we need to understand money as a sign of something greater that we desire. Our modern Bible translations say you cannot serve both God and money. However, this is not really a helpful translation, because it suggests only money as the problem. It ignores the fullness of what Jesus is telling us here. I prefer the older biblical translations which say you cannot serve both God and "Mammon". This word "Mammon" is a biblical term of Syrian origin. It refers to all material wealth or corporeal substance. It is a reference to your possessions, property and equity, but most significantly it points us toward our spiritual attitude toward all the things we own.

Jesus sets before us this contrast, God and Mammon, so what do we value most? The reality is that we do try to serve two masters. As we pursue our work and home security, there are many occasions when our desire to please God, to serve Him, comes into conflict with our earthly pursuits. Jesus knows this. Does he condemn us in this reading? No. He doesn't tell us that we cannot serve both masters, and then go on to tell us the consequences of getting it wrong. Though, we do know the consequences of sin, the cause of this conflict. Instead Jesus seeks to guide us. He tells us not to worry about things.9

It is a question of trust that Jesus is getting at here. As we pursue earthly things we are feeling self-reliant, as if it is truly we who make everything happen. We are fearful of letting God in to ensure we get what we need, which may not always be want we want! Our selfish desires are often very short-term in their goals, whereas God knows what is in our long-term interest.

Let us think for a moment about what it means to serve Mammon as our master. Augustine put it very bluntly, when he wrote, "he that serves mammon sustains a hard and pernicious master; for, led captive by his lust, he is a slave of the devil, though he love him not. Is there anyone who loves the devil? Yet there are those who sustain him." It is not that we are thus despising God, we are abusing His goodness. The things we pursue all came from God, and we are His creature. In our captivity we push Him away, like a drowning man lashing out at his rescuer.

As Jesus, tells us, we are rejecting what is truly valuable. We worry about our money all the time, but Jesus challenges us on this as well. He asks "can any one of you by worrying add a single hour to your life?" He tell us we can overcome worry by trusting in God. Easier said than done! Jesus knows this, which is why his words are encouraging and soothing. There are two horizons to this worry. The first horizon is before problems and worries occur. We need to have to a trusting relationship with God, and by listening to Him we will avoid many of the difficulties on our road through life. There are many problems we face which if we look more closely are self-inflicted. Debts, for instance, are often caused by our desires or greed for something. The second horizon is when we face problems, often which are not of our own making. Then we need to have trust in God that we will get us through the difficulties we face.

When we try to serve two masters, we diminish one. If we serve the devil then we diminish God. If we serve God then we diminish the devil. It is an easy choice to make if we trust in God, because God sustains us, but as Augustine warns it is we who sustain the devil.

Theft is also lust. Jesus specifically talks about treasures, and what we treasure most is stored in our heart. He knows how difficult it is for anyone to live in this world according to the Gospel. We still cling to the things of this world, and what greater things than treasures? Yet, Jesus shows us a contrast between the treasures of this world and the treasure that is God, from all whom all things in the world originate. All too often we are chasing treasures and prizes which are mere trinkets when the hour comes that we leave this earth. We are risking the greatest treasure of all when we fix our minds on piling up earthly treasures.

Jesus sets this in the context of service. How can we serve two masters? Wealth is not really a master, because it is inanimate. Money and objectives are lifeless things, and it is only the world and ourselves that put value into them. Ultimately, it is each individual who decides what is valuable and what is not. If you look around your home or workplace, you will see things you value, but they do not get up and walk away from you. They are things you want, not things you need. When we say the Lord's Prayer, we ask for our daily bread, in other words what we need to sustain us. We do not ask for our daily treasures. Jesus did not teach us to pray for wealth beyond our wildest dreams. We are to pray for those things we need to sustain us in order to serve God. Does this mean we should ideally give up what we have? No, it means we need to change our relationship to the things we have. We need to see them as subordinate to our relationship with God.

We can reflect on some brute facts about our world. First, we should know that money, property and things are necessary things in this world. What is the use if we are all beggars? We need to support our loved ones, our family, so poverty is not the answer. Second, we cannot idealize the poor. As Luther said "There is many a beggar getting bread at our door more arrogant and wicked than any rich man, and many a miserly, stingy peasant who is harder to get along with than any lord or prince." Third, we cannot place our values in temporal goods. We cannot think that either having such goods, or lacking such goods, is the key to our entry into the kingdom.

A rich individual like David is a good example here. David gained riches and power, yet before God he stood in spiritual poverty. In Psalm 39:12 he sings: "Hear my prayer, LORD, listen to my cry for help; do not be deaf to my weeping. I dwell with you as a foreigner, a stranger, as all my ancestors were." David realized what we must realize, that when it comes to the things we have and own, we are like guests in a strange place. Such is the temporary nature of our goods before the timeless God. Instead of idolizing, lusting after or stealing things, we are to value the things in the world on the basis of the heart. We should be capable of giving up all we have for God's sake, if we are called upon to do so. We should not be held captive by the things of the world, however much or little we have. It is possible for a rich man, like David, take on spiritual poverty, by understanding this teaching. All of us, rich and poor, are to use all we have, what God gives us, to live, as Luther puts it, by our "labor in faith".

SECTION 3

SOCIAL STRUCTURES AND THE EIGHTH COMMANDMENT

Section 3: Social Structures and the Eighth Commandment

PHILIP J. CLEMENTS

The Introduction frames that the Christian worldview holds that God, as Creator, owns everything and gives it to whom He pleases. The individual recipient has responsibility to God for the stewardship, employment and enjoyment of what God has given him. Section 1 covers the theology underlying the commandment not to steal, including that what can be stolen is more than property; stealing includes time, and talent and opportunity. These framing thoughts are not repeated here. Rather the principles here go to the effect on an individual and the individual's community when these basic principles are respected. Section 2 presents the role of property rights as an essential element of human flourishing.

Now we come to the challenges of social structures and the Eighth Commandment. Social structures necessarily lead to contemplations on the role of government and its actions. Underlying governments are the community itself and the differing views on how a community should be structured. The four papers in this Section explore these elements as they relate to the Eighth Commandment.

The papers illustrate the complexities of discussing social policies and the resulting social structures. By definition social structures are institutions for human governance. Whether the structure is founded on a constitution, such as the United States, or on unwritten customs, such as tribal communities, underlying each is a set of philosophies on how people relate to each other and their community's resources. Here we can summarize the two core structures: (a) Individual rights predominate and (b) community rights are dominate. While it can be argued that some community structures are balanced between these two perspectives, these communities will tend to lean towards one or the other. Thus the West has traditionally been viewed as leaning towards the individual. The individual's rights predominate over the community. A core task of the government is to protect the individual's rights. The concept of "rule of law" underlies the principle of a government's role in protecting the rights of the individual. Contracts are to be enforced, property rights protected and individual sanctity secured.

Community rights are dominant in the socialist or communist community. Tribal communities have the individual subsumed into the tribe. Property and individual resources are viewed as part of the tribe or community. Therefore, the individual is prepared to share all with the community and the community is comfortable with reallocating resources to create fairness and equality amongst the members of the community. In the past one hundred years, socialistic communities have abounded on the earth, whether tribal groups or socialistic/communistic countries.

The contrast in human flourishing between these two core structures cannot be clearer. The papers in *Culture Matters* [1] place faith at the base of these two core structures. The Reformation-based Christian heritage, often referred to as the Protestant Ethic, clearly leads to the highest human flourishing. Other faiths lead to various levels of economic flourishing in a community. However, the papers do note that the closer the faith structure is to the Protestant Ethic, the more robust the economy. Therefore, Western Europe shows the blessing of having at one time been a Reformation-based faith community. Today these same countries are much more socialistic. The editor's forecast is for economic decline without God's intervention. Further analysis on this subject can be found in *Clash of Civilizations* [2] and *Who Are We?* [3]

Underlying the Protestant ethic is the view that the Bible forms the primary text for understanding the principles for this world, because this world is God's world. The Eighth Commandment is one of the key principles. As discussed in the prior Sections, the Eighth Commandment sets forth that the individual and the individual's time, talent and treasure are all given to him by God. The community is to respect God's granting and to protect the individual in his exercise of ownership over what God has given to him.

But man is a fallen creature and has rejected God's principles as mankind's foundation for his behavior. Therefore, it cannot be a surprise that mankind in its wisdom as represented by Renaissance thinking would reject individual rights for community preeminence. Arguing the doctrine of fairness [4] between members of a community, causes the members to feel that what has been articulated is "right." Unfortunately, the doctrine of fairness has many faults, starting with the problem of who defines what is fair. Defining fairness quickly degrades to relativism, which then leads to anarchy. Anarchy opens the door to the totalitarian where might makes right. In short, throughout human history, starting in Genesis 4, social structures set by human hands have always ended up as "Might Makes Right." Those with more power impose their wishes on those with less power. No community has survived long periods without degrading to this fallen state of mankind.

Culture Matters highlights the shocking blessing that the United States and other Protestant ethic based countries have experienced. In these countries the Eighth Commandment has been a foundation of the culture and social structure. Section 2 discusses human flourishing. We need to see that God built the world for human flourishing. Respecting God's allocation of time, talent, and treasure creates an amazingly blessed community. The prosperity of the last 400 years is astounding.

It is this editor's belief that the key distinctive of the period between 1500AD to today as compared to all of the millennia before is the Reformation. It is that under the enabling power of the Holy Spirit, those who trusted in the finished work of Jesus on the cross for their sins, in other words are "born again," had an effect on their community. Central to this effect was the respect for the principles in the Decalogue. The outcome of adopting the Decalogue principles was the acceptance of the Eighth Commandment's message that to whom much is given, it belongs. It is then between that individual and God as to what he does with what has been given. The Church will engage in instruction through preaching and teaching such that the blessed individual knows his duty and responsibility to God for God's blessing.

While these comments that follow describe community behavior, similar principles are becoming part of our business structure design. Therefore, the business person needs to be aware of this difference. Jesus tells the parable of the day laborers in Matthew 20:1-16. A key aspect of this parable is the challenge of property ownership in a business setting as opposed to a group's sense of fairness. See footnote 4 above. Our business community needs to devote significant time and effort understanding the distinctions between God's structure and man's as it is being taught in business schools and modern business books.

Because business in America is increasingly regulated and governments have the power to take from their constituents, the Center for Christian Business Ethics Today [5] (Center) asked Bret Schundler and William Edgar to address the implications of the 8th Commandment on government regulations. Edgar, in "Eighth Commandment and Public Policy," looks at the paradox of the globalizing world. Culture on one hand "is increasingly universal." Yet, "there are strong counter-trends." As an example, "India is trying to succeed as a democracy and promote freedom for religion, while at the same time there are aggressive groups such as the Hindu nationalist Bharatiya Janata Party doing great damage." "... Neither offers much hope for meaning and human flourishing to its citizens." Edgar is wrestling with hard concepts that the global business person is interacting with and needs to have a clearer perspective on how to respond from a biblical worldview.

The Asmus and Grudem paper in Section 2 and Edgar complement each other well. Edgar goes on to consider the importance of the breadth of the Eighth Commandment in reestablishing meaning in public life. Then Edgar uses the examples of Abraham Kuyper's *sphere sovereignty* and the *subsidiarity* principle from Roman Catholic community to illustrate the limitations on government. Considering stewardship and the Eighth Commandment, the paper highlights several important aspects of the *Catechism's* duties that are viewed as arising from it. In conclusion, Edgar observes "it has become clear that globalization and rapid change cannot in themselves bring about a sense of meaning and human flourishing." Next comes the vast assumption that *government* could better control the economy then the *market*. Education, health care, transportation, electric, gas, and water utilities are usually the first to be collectivized.

Edgar explains,

> "Often, then, our social institutions are unable to provide meaning and human flourishing. Generally, they need to guide societies, which are moving from fate to choice, one of the principal dynamics of modernization. So far, though, the two major social institutions on the global stage, markets and gov-

ernments, do not seem to be moving ahead with the proper moral and theological frameworks needed. Markets tend to be transactional. Governments are often procedural and managerial. Those are fine, as long as they are operating within a proper framework. Religions, for their part, often serve the purposes of theocracy rather than the prophetic purpose of guiding people into the higher purpose for which they were created."

Asmus and Grudem would add,

"Neglecting the Biblical truth of the sinfulness of man is a common, even frequent mistake. Then comes a state promising minimum wage laws, rent controls, price controls, tariffs, subsidized rents, interest rate ceilings, agricultural price supports, federal loan guarantees, passenger rail service subsidies, fixing public utility rates, protecting the right of labor to strike, affordable housing, and even free health care. The never-ending list of entitlements becomes a never-ending list of promises, all of course provided by the state and higher taxes.

But what happens when the *takers* exceed the *makers* and producers are overwhelmed by government planners and economic progressives? Debt, deficits and economic unsustainability could become reality. Unfortunately, a bigger government also means a smaller individual and a smaller citizen; a government big enough to give you all you want is big enough to take everything you have; a helping hand almost always turns into a controlling hand.

Human liberty, by contrast, with its foundation resting on the eighth commandment and the institution of private property, titles, deeds, and a free market economic system, has enormously beneficial consequences. The invisible hand of the market that Adam Smith describes in his *Wealth of Nations* produces order, harmony, coordination, and diversity."

In "The Eighth Commandment and Civil Law: Biblical Faith and Engagement in the Shaping of Public Policy," Schundler endeavors to present "what the Commandment suggests Christians should seek to have *government* do, require, or encourage, and what Christians should seek to have *government* not do, prohibit, or discourage in regard to business practice." A key principle for this point is "Bible-believing Christians... do not cede to popular majorities the authority to determine what is right or wrong, just or unjust. They hold that God is the ultimate authority in such matters." Schundler addresses some critical social policies against the Eighth Commandment understanding as outlined in the *Westminster Larger Catechism*. Schundler then explores stealing from God and stealing from ourselves and what, if any, governmental intervention should be desired. While it would be easy to summarize Schundler's approach as one of limited government, the more important point is the underlying reasoning and biblical based rationales for his conclusions.

The next two papers explore the shifts in the world's thinking about business and property rights. In "Are Profits Moral: Answers from a Comparison of Adam Smith, Max Weber, Karl Marx, and the Westminster Larger Catechism," the change in perspectives and discourse of the world is dramatically shown by the citation of the texts from a series of widely read and accepted materials. Starting with quotes from the *Westminster Larger Catechism* [7] which was written in 1647, the paper quotes Adam Smith's *Wealth of Nations*, [8] written in 1776, then goes on to quote Max Weber's *The Protestant Ethic and the Spirit of Capitalism*, [9] written in 1904, and closes with Karl Marx's *Communist Manifesto*. [10] Just reading these passages with the editorial introductions helps the reader see how far our social thinking has shifted. In their day, each of these writings reasonably reflected the thinking of that time.

In "For Love or Money? The Ethics of Profits in God's World," Peter A. Lillback delves into the current state of our social thinking and its implications on business ethics. Lillback starts by noting the decay of the foundational ethics principle that doing right is the first rule. This paper shows that unfortunately today the idea that the end justifies the means has become a part of mainstream thinking. The business community is not immune from this shift. Worse still, the paper recounts the continuing problem in our business schools with teaching proper business ethics. Looking at Harvard Business School, the challenge of including ethics in the curriculum has been there and has been under addressed from its beginning. The good news is this paper then takes us to a clearer understanding of the role of self-interest and profits in both the business community and God's world.

In summary, Cowan in Section 2 notes,

> "The big picture, the global context for our discussion, is that God is source of all and we are in a covenant relationship with Him. Therefore, any economy that is solely based on human relationship as its goal is bound to fail. Capitalism is a free system of relationships, which may be sourced from many places and formed for many reasons. The attack often made on Capitalism is directed primarily at America as the Capitalist nation par excellence, except they do not except its excellence. The insidious infiltration of Socialistic thinking into current economic decision-making is the **theft of an idea**, and ultimately undermines the thinking and direction of a nation."

> American capitalism, in this way, is being attacked by international rules. The pressure comes externally from the international community, and internally from those who buy into the international approach (arguably this applies elsewhere politically, not just in economic terms). Notions of corporate Social Responsibility are a political construct which places demands on American businesses to be good citizens according to international norms, which has been gradually imposed in the same way that high temperatures are imposed on a frog and leads to its demise.

> I could be harsh and call this approach by another name: theft."

Notes

1. Lawrence E. Harrison and Samuel P. Huntington, ed.s, *Culture Maters: How Values Shape Human Progress*, New York: Basic, 2000.
2. Samuel P. Huntington, *Clash of Civilizations and the Remaking of the World Order*, New York: Touchstone, 1996.
3. Samuel P. Huntington, *Who Are We?: The Challenges to America's National Identity*, New York: Simon & Schuster, 2004.
4. Fairness principles as used in social structure design is very relevant to the business person. Jesus'

parable in Matthew 20:1-16 shows that the issues are not new. Here the complaint is that the pay was not fair, even if the land owner fulfilled the agreements. Fairness for these purposes can be summarized as an outcomes based concept where whether the activity is fair is an evaluation on the equality in the outcomes. The other perspective on fair is equality of opportunity. The problem of equality of opportunity is that the individual is responsible for the outcome. Some individuals have more talent, given by God, some work harder, personal choice, some have more opportunity, given by God, and some simply achieve more, usually a blessing given by God. In this we see that God controls the outcome; therefore making fairness an outcome standard is a direct rejection of God's will. What man can do is create as much equality in opportunity or respond to the outcome. Charity is an example of responding to an outcome.

5. The Center for Christian Business Ethics Today, LLC was formed in 2009 to develop material to help the Christian business person operate his business with biblical business principles based on Protestant Christianity. The Center co-hosted the conference that is the source of the papers for this text.

6. Philip J. Clements, et. al., "Are Profits Moral: Answers from a Comparison of Adam Smith, Max Weber, Karl Marx, and the Westminster Larger Catechism," was first printed in *Business Ethics Today: Foundations Philadelphia*, Westminster Seminary Press, 2011.

7. *Westminster Larger Catechism* Glasgow: Bell and Bain, first published in 1648, rep. 2001.

8. Adam Smith, *The Wealth of Nations* (New York: Bantam Classic, first published 1776, rept. 2003).

9. Max Weber, *The Protestant Ethic and the Spirit of Capitalism* New York: Scribner, 1958. The Protestant Ethic and the Spirit of Capitalism was first published in German in 1904.

10. Karl Marx and Friedrich Engels, *Communist Manifesto*, public domain, first published in German in 1848.

EIGHTH
COMMANDMENT AND
PUBLIC POLICY

WILLIAM EDGAR

WILLIAM EDGAR

Bill Edgar was born in Wilmington, North Carolina, in 1944 and grew up in Paris, France. He studied at St. George's School (secondary), Harvard University (Honors, BA in Music), Westminster Theological Seminary (MDiv), and the University of Geneva (DTh). He has taught at the Brunswick School in Greenwich, Connecticut, and at the Faculté Libre de Théologie Réformée, in Aix-en-Provence, France, where he continues as Professeur Associé. He has been at Westminster since 1989 and is currently Professor of Apologetics, Coordinator of the Apologetics Department, and Chairman of the Faculty.

Doctor Edgar belongs to a number of learned societies, including the American Musicological Society, the Evangelical Theological Society, the American Historical Association, and the Society for Ethnomusicology. He serves on several boards, including the Huguenot Fellowship (President). He is on the editorial committee of La Revue Réformée. He regularly takes part as a speaker in the Veritas Forum programs. He also serves on the Institutional Review Board and the Medical Ethics Committee of The Chestnut Hill Hospital.

Edgar is an ordained minister in the Presbyterian Church in America and has served on several denominational committees. His books include Taking Note of Music (London: SPCK, 1986), Reasons of the Heart (Baker/Hourglass, 1996; P & R, 2003), La carte protestante (Labor et Fides, 1997), The Face of Truth: Lifting the Veil (P & R, 2001), and Truth in All Its Glory: Commending the Reformed Faith (P & R, 2004). He has written numerous articles on such subjects as cultural apologetics, the music of Brahms, the French Huguenots, and African-American aesthetics. His favorite avocations are soccer and jazz piano. He plays regularly with a professional jazz band.

INTRODUCTION

Increasingly, economic trends in one country affect trends in other countries, often far removed. The earthquake and tsunami in Japan has had repercussions on markets around the world. Political decisions in Latin America mean the United States must adjust its trade policies in order not to aid and abet the drug trade. Everyone is discussing the rise of market capitalism in China. In a recent issue of The Economist China's extraordinary entrepreneurial ventures are described. The article discusses the amazing growth of business, industry and construction in China, and highlights the way extraordinary amounts of capital have been procured, and opportunities have been advanced, by means "fair and foul." [1]

Is there any place for the law of God in such a scenario? Does the Decalogue have any bearing on the growth of business in China, and in many parts of the world, including our own, or is this an arcane set of tablets handed down from Mount Sinai by the Hebrew leader, Moses, over 4,000 years ago, with limited application to the ancient world?

We strongly believe God's law is of everlasting significance. In particular, the eighth commandment, "Thou shalt not steal," is of enormous relevance for business life today even as it always has been. Having said that, the question is, how exactly do we move from the law of God to public policy issues? Here are a few thoughts from a theologian-apologist with a strong interest in ethics.

I. GLOBALIZATION AND THE THREAT TO MEANING

Why begin with globalization? So much has been said. The reason is that globalization has a massive impact on business. While globalization has much to commend it from a biblical point of view, it carries many dangers as well, especially the loss of meaning. Both in the East as well as the West, the threat to losing the very reason for human existence is great.

Simply stated, globalization is the increasing interconnectedness of people, goods and ideas throughout the world. Increasing interconnectedness means change, rapid change. Someone has said that the rate of change is itself changing. Among the catalysts for globalization we would have to include both rapid transportation and rapid communication. There have been many episodes in history which have witnessed advanced transportation and communication. But the contemporary phenomena are perhaps without equal for their intensive and extensive dynamics. One can think of the astonishing way in which it is possible to travel from one continent to another in a matter of hours, and cross most borders with relative ease of access. And all of us have been greatly influenced by such communications devices as broadcasting, emails, smart phones and the internet.

One of the momentous events in world history which has affected globalization is the end of the Cold War. 1989 has rightly been dubbed the *miracle year*. Not only did Communism fall in country after country, but borders became porous and capital was able to flow far more easily across the globe than ever before.

Globalization brings a great paradox. On the one hand, global systems define our lives more and more. Economic markets are interconnected in an unprecedented way. A rebellion against a ruthless ruler in Lybia poses major threats in the world's oil markets. The global interconnectedness of trends throughout the world reinforced by the presence of institutions such as the World Trade Organization, and the thousands of NGOs throughout the globe. Perhaps we do not exactly have a one world economy, but it seems that some version of neo-liberal capitalism can be found just about anywhere, even in places formally defined by planned economies.

Furthermore, cultural trends are increasingly widespread. For example, Hip-Hop and Rap culture originated on the streets of New York and Los Angeles, particularly among the unemployed. But now we find Rap artists in Marseille and Hong Kong. Baggy pants have replaced short shorts in virtually every sport around the world. Faced with this kind of cross-pollenisation certain institutions are unable to weild the power they formerly did, while others are taking their place. National governments are less and less able to control the flow of money in and out of their countries. Nor are they able to control what people are learning over the internet. Yet local "authorities' such as radio and TV programming can affect radical change. Consider this: in Romania, the communist government sought to eradicate the cultural distinctives of its Hungarian ethnic minority, but was unable to do so. However, in a very short time Western capitalism and Western popular culture have succeeded very well. In other cases there are blends of Western consumer culture with Buddhism or Islam or Roman Catholicism.

The city is increasingly becoming the center for power and decision-making. Cities are becoming the "brains" of the global economic system. Perhaps it is more accurate to talk of greater metropolitan regions rather than the classical city. Decisions such as what to market, what to program on TV, leadership strategies and the like are decided in world-class cities. Missionaries know that if you want to reach a particular people group it is better to go to their neighborhoods in these great cities than to go away to the countries where they are from. Africans and Asians are as present in places like New York and Brussels as they are in Gabon and Malaysia. Missions are now thinking about "city growth" rather than "church growth."

At the same time, and this is the other part of the paradox, there are strong counter-trends. Sometimes they are simply reactions to the steamroller of modernity. We used to live in southern France. The traditional language there is *Provençal*, a derivative of Latin and other Romance languages. The French government at one point tried to enforce a French-only policy. You can guess what happened. There are more Provençal societies and writers guilds today than ever before. Somewhat comically, José Bové has led a movement against American fast foods, including the destruction of drive-in restaurants.

Less amusing is what Benjamin Barber has called *Jihad vs. McWorld*. Even though on one level our planet is coming together, through music, computers, and the rest, at the same time, there is a Balkanization of tribal rivalries wherein culture is pitted against culture. Religion is on the rise, and that can be good news. But all depends on the way in which religions assert themselves. For example, India is trying to succeed as a democracy and promote freedom for religion, while there are at the same time there are aggressive groups such as the Hindu nationalist Bharatiya Janata Party doing great damage.

Do these opposites have anything in common? One sad thing is that neither in themselves offer much hope for meaning and human flourishing to its citizens. As one pundit puts it, it is the "centrifugal whirlwind" of Jihad against the "centripetal black hole" of McWorld.[2] Not much of a bargain between a whirlwind and a black hole. When both are concerned for mere survival, or for mere economic growth, then meaning and human flourishing take a back seat.

Often, then, our social institutions are unable to provide meaning and human flourishing. Generally, they need to guide societies which are moving from fate to choice, one of the principal dynamics of modernization. So far, though, the two major social institutions on the global stage, markets and governments, do not seem to be moving ahead with the proper moral and theological frameworks needed. Markets tend to be transactional. Governments are often procedural and managerial. Those are fine, as long as they are operating within a proper framework. Religions, for their part, often serve the purposes of theocracy rather than the prophetic purpose of guiding people into the higher purpose for which they were created.

As Jonathan Sacks puts it, "Something happens when change is so rapid that nothing confers meaning – when lives become lifestyles, commitments become experiments, relationships become provisional, careers turn into contracts, and life itself ceases to have the character of a narrative and becomes instead a series of episodes with no connecting thread."[3]

II. THE RECOVERY OF MEANING IN PUBLIC LIFE

Is it possible to recover meaning and human flourishing in public life? So much seems to lean against it. Even the more modest goal of conscientizing people on the importance of the eighth commandment appears naïve at best, hopeless at worst. Here is the place to remember our basic commitments. As the Apostle Paul puts it, the gospel is "the power of God for salvation for everyone who believes" (Rom. 1:16). That this salvation is comprehensive, not simply the guaranty of the passage of souls into Heaven, is clear from the entire Bible. Paul elsewhere states that Jesus Christ, by whom all things were created, rules over every human institution, and is busy reconciling all things to himself (Col. 1:15-20).

The Bible does not relegate human institutions to "the world," as though they were of secondary significance, next to the human soul. Rather, it gives us a rich theology of these institutions and their significance for human life. The church, the family, the civil government, the workplace, markets, and many more, constitute such institutions. They are what the Apostle names thrones, dominions, rulers, authorities and families in his letters (Col. 1:15; Eph 1:21; 3:15).

Thus, when the Bible tells us to respect the government, pay taxes, etc., this is not simply a grudging necessity of life. Mark Twain talked of the two certainties, death and taxes, as though both were wet blankets. Though surely meant to be limited, there is a place for governing authorities, and they are due not only our taxes but our respect. For they are God's instrument for promoting good conduct, human flourishing, as well as ensuring social justice (Rom. 13:1-7; 1 Pet. 2:13-17). Indeed, the new Testament provides for basic principles to inform all of our institutions, not just government.

Our Puritan forefathers got it right when they explained the eighth commandment as applying across life. Explaining the eighth commandment's reach, the Larger Catechism contains much wisdom for business and economics. The duties enjoined include "truth, faithfulness, and justice in contracts and commerce between man and man; rendering everyone his due; restitution of goods unlawfully detained… giving and lending freely… moderation; a lawful calling…," and even furthering wealth, our neighbor's and our own. The sins forbidden include theft, robbery, manstealing, fraud, false weights and measures, breaking contracts, and so forth.

Neither the Westminster Standards nor the New Testament itself give us a blueprint for the exact ways to implement these duties. Many thinkers and theologians have made attempts as applying these principles to the actual institutions we deal with every day. Two examples will suffice.

The first is Abraham Kuyper (1837-1920), who famously developed the principle of "sphere sovereignty." The basic idea is that God has placed a proper differentiation in the created order. Thus, societal communities exist to provide the basic dynamics of human life, including education, family, government, worship, agriculture, and so on. While overlapping, these spheres have boundaries, and apply the norms of revelational authority differently according to their purpose. Thus, the family is not basically a corporation, the church is not a coercive authority, the school is not a business, etc. As the Kingdom of God is extended, there ought to be more clarity about these callings. Because of the fall, there is confusion, all too often. In the gospel we can work to see the effects of the fall pushed back.

The implications of sphere sovereignty for business are manifold. Peter Heslam, working out of the University of Cambridge, England, directs the group, Transforming Business, which attempts to provide Kuyperian principles to he conduct of business. He studies such areas as profit-sharing, teaching social entrepreneurship to the poor, reducing structural deficits, balancing governmental with NGO agencies, and the like. At the heart of his work, it appears to me, is the broad application of the eighth commandment taught by the Puritans, combined with Kuyper's concern for integrity within each sphere of society.

A second example comes mainly from the Roman Catholic community. Called *subsidiarity*, the idea is that authority should always serve the whole. Where possible, immediate authorities should be fully empowered to carry out their tasks. This means that central authorities such as government should perform only those duties which cannot be performed by more local organizations.

Subsidiarity is not a version of libertarianism, although some have taken it that way. The European Union applied subsidiarity to its form of government in the Maastricht Treaty of 1992, then in the Treaty of Lisbon, in force since 2009. It holds that member states must carry out all of their responsibilities, and only when that is not possible would the Union intervene.

The implication for business is that the central power of the Union (or any central government) should rarely be invoked in order to ensure regulation and fair trade. One of the major contributions of subsidiarity is the criticism of the welfare state. Naturally, there is variety here. But in general, subsidiarity tries to clarify where there is a proper need for state intervention and where issues such as unemployment, health-care, retirement insurance, and regulation of business, are better handled at the local level. In the 19th century Alexis de Toqueville praised the nascent America for its display of local initiative and the lack of over-dependence upon central government. We need to be cautious here. Many Americans have a knee-jerk reaction to "socialism" which sometimes imagines that if only we did not have a central government things would go well. Doctrinaire socialism has, of course, been a great evil, justifying Stalinism and Hitlerian oppression. But measured, just and normed government is a gift of God, and not to be resisted, following Paul's counsel.

III. STEWARDSHIP AND THE ENTREPRENEURIAL SPIRIT

One of the major theological underpinnings for business practice is the idea of stewardship. The basic idea of stewardship is that we human beings have been called to care for the earth, and develop its possibilities in a godly manner. As image-bearers we are the Lord's vice-gerents, and as such charged with overseeing the earth's undeveloped features. For business the implications are clear. Again, according to the eighth commandment, as interpreted by the framers of the *Westminster Larger Catechism*, this includes, "giving and lending freely, according to our abilities, and the necessities of others, and... a provident care and study to get, keep, use, and dispose these things which are necessary and convenient for the sustentation of our nature, and suitable to our condition."

The idea of stewardship has come under scrutiny of late. In his very helpful book on *The Bible and Ecology* Richard Bauckham warns against an over-zealous notion of stewardship which results in giving license for a careless approach to the environment.[4] Having said that, we also must avoid the extreme of pantheism, which sees humankind as basically on the same level as the entire universe. The biblical idea of human Lordship helps keep the balance.

Among other corollaries we can think of property rights. The Bible certainly allows for the ownership of property. But only if we hold it, as it were, with a light hand, can we truly be proprietors. First, because the earth is the Lords and the fullness thereof, including mankind itself (Ps. 24:1). Second, because the reason to own property is to glorify God, and to benefit not only ourselves but our neighbors. Third, every believer is meant to be generous with his or her goods, and benefit the needy.

Finally, we might say a word about the Weber Thesis. Max Weber (1864-1920) published a landmark study, entitled, *The Protestant Ethic and the Spirit of Capitalism* (1912), in which he argued that there were several connections between the Reformation mentality and the principles of economic growth in the capitalist system. First, because the Reformation saw every profession as worthy before God, from the cobbler to the lawyer. Second, because work itself was considered noble, and not only a means to personal security. So, for example, he argues that in pre-capitalist times laborers higher wages were offered during times of harvest, hoping to motivate laborers to come and work toward this crucial season. However, the opposite happened, as laborers simply came to work less time for the same money, and became more and more attracted to leisure. But when they are taught to see their craft as an end in itself, the general level of society is considerably bolstered.

Weber did not always get the theological details right. He quotes Benjamin Franklin at length, putting him in the same camp as the Puritans. He also understands Reformed theology to insist on divine election in such a way that hard work becomes a means of making God's blessings more visible. Still, when one compares countries which have a Roman Catholic substratum to the more Protestant ones, his arguments generally hold. One of the great recent best-sellers in France is *Le mal français* (French evil) by Alain Peyrefitte, who held a number of high-level government positions, including Minister of Justice.[5] His argument (and he is Roman Catholic) is that France's biggest mistake was to persecute the Huguenots, the fledgling Protestant group. In his own version of the Weber Thesis he says France missed out on an enormous opportunity to achieve prosperity because it was hemmed-in by the inertia of the Catholic subculture.

CONCLUSION

We hope to have convinced our kind audience that a proper application of the eighth commandment to business will not only bear much fruit, but will raise the general level of prosperity in those societies where the commandment can be applied. But we hope, more deeply, that it has become clear that globalization and rapid change cannot in themselves bring about a sense of meaning and human flourishing. Unless tempered by the proper practices of moral institutions, stewardship and subsidiarity, growth will be unchecked and will lead to decadence rather than to good things.

Notes

1. "Let a Million Flowers Bloom," *The Economist* 398/8724 (March 12-18, 201), 179-81
2. See Benjamin Barber's own comments [http://www.theatlantic.com/magazine/archive/1992/03/jihad-vs-mcworld/3882/]
3. Jonathan Sacks, *The Dignity of Difference*, London: Continuum, 2002, 75.
4. Richard Bauckham, *The Bible and Ecology*, Waco: Baylor University Press, 2010
5. Alain Peyrefitte, *Le mal français*, Paris: Fayard, 2006.

THE EIGHTH COMMANDMENT AND CIVIL LAW

BIBLICAL FAITH AND ENGAGEMENT IN THE SHAPING OF PUBLIC POLICY

BRET SCHUNDLER

BRET SCHUNDLER

Bret Schundler most recently served as the Commissioner of Education in New Jersey, where he marshaled broad stakeholder support for a comprehensive package of systemic education reforms. Prior to that stint, Schundler was the Chief Operating Officer of The King's College in Manhattan, where he oversaw that entrepreneurial college's accreditation by the Middle States Commission on Higher Education and implemented student recruitment and business plans that accelerated student enrollment growth and improved the college's finances.

In his younger years, Schundler built a successful career on Wall Street at Salomon Brothers and C. J. Lawrence. He then became the first Republican since World War One to be elected the Mayor of Jersey City – a community of 250,000 that is 65% minority and only 6% Republican. In 1993, he was re-elected with 69% of the vote, the largest margin of victory for a Mayor in that city's history. In 1997, he was re-elected in another landslide to become Jersey City's longest serving Mayor in 50 years. Choosing not to run for Mayor a fourth time, he won the Republican nomination for Governor of New Jersey in 2001, but he did not succeed in the general election, nor in 2005 when he ran for Governor a second time.

Bret Schundler's innovative policies in Jersey City were called a "national model for urban reform" by Time magazine. His policing policies reduced crime by over 40%. His tax cuts saved residents their homes. And a Harvard University study said that during Schundler's tenure, Jersey City led the 100 largest cities in America in job growth and poverty reduction.

This conference session is unique. The rest of this conference is about the implications of the Eighth Commandment, "Thou Shall Not Steal," for the business ethics of Christians. It is about what the Eighth Commandment suggests you should do or not do in regard to your business practices.

But this session is about the implications of the Eighth Commandment for civil law and public policy. It is about what the Commandment suggests Christians should seek to have *government* do, require, or encourage, and what Christians should seek to have *government* not do, prohibit, or discourage in regard to business practice or economic policy.

There is a huge difference between what is morally wrong and what government should make illegal, and between what you should do out of love for your neighbor and what government should do or make you do.

We'll talk about where to draw these lines momentarily. It first warrants mentioning that when exercising their rights as citizens to influence public policy, it is fully appropriate for Christians to bring their biblical values with them into the public square.

The Framers of our American Constitution, who were mostly Christians of the Reformed tradition, believed as a function of their faith in the separation of church and state. They believed that government should be controlled not by church bodies, but by the people acting through their democratically elected representatives, and that church bodies should be controlled not by politicians, but by believers.

That said, the Framers understood that when people enter into political discourse, they necessarily argue from a foundation of axiomatic values which are essentially religious in character. The American people have made murder illegal because they believe that life has value and that ending an innocent life should therefore be prohibited. Their belief that life has value is not a scientific conclusion; it is an axiomatic statement of faith. When secular Democratic Socialists argue for the redistribution of wealth, it is because they believe, as an article of faith, that income equality is good. Their belief in this regard is essentially a religious conviction. All people have an equal right to support the implementation of public policies that will advance their concept of the just society, even though such conceptions are the product of axiomatic values that are, whether their holders acknowledge it or not, essentially religious in character.

Now let's try to work through what the Eighth Commandment suggests about the laws and economic policies of the just society. To start, let's consider what the Eighth Commandment commands.

What the Eighth Commandment Commands

The Westminster Larger Catechism goes through an extensive cataloging of sins forbidden by the Eighth Commandment. The list includes "theft," "robbery," "receiving anything that is stolen," "fraudulent dealing," and "all other unjust...ways of taking or withholding from our neighbor what belongs to him." The linkage of these prohibitions with the Eighth Commandment is consistent with our contemporary definition of stealing as "taking the property of another without right or permission."

But the Larger Westminster Catechism goes on. It also lists among the sins condemned by the Eighth Commandment, "covetousness," "inordinate prizing...of worldly goods," "distracting...studies in getting [and] keeping" (watch out, business school students), and "envying the prosperity of others." The catechists see these sins as stealing from God the focus and abiding gratefulness He is due.

Then the catechists continue even further, listing the sins of "idleness," "prodigality," "wasteful gaming," and "all other ways whereby we do unduly prejudice our own outward estate"—in other words, by which we waste our abundance, lives, and potential and, in effect, steal from ourselves.

To understand the Eighth Commandment as the catechists understand it, in the context of the entire Bible and all of its teachings, is to realize that God desires not just that we abstain from robbing or otherwise hurting each other, but that we rejoice in Him and, energized by such joy, live responsibly in a way that promotes not just our spiritual well-being, but also our material well-being. To lack gratitude, to weigh down our spirits with envy, to impoverish ourselves through irresponsible, prodigal-living, is to steal from God and to steal from ourselves, and is as sinful as stealing from others.

Given this deeper understanding of the Eighth Commandment's prohibition on stealing, should Christians endeavor to make envy and idleness illegal? The Bible does not directly address the question, but prudence suggests that the answer is "No;" the spiritual and material suffering that result are mostly the sinner's and justice does not require restitution or further punishment. But stealing from others mostly causes harm to others, so here prudence and justice argue for making such stealing illegal.

We will look at instances where prudence does argue for making some forms of stealing from God or stealing from oneself illegal. But first let's look more closely at stealing from others, appreciating the fact that all unjust ways of taking or withholding from our neighbor what belongs to him or her are wrong, and typically should be illegal.

On Stealing From Others

Inherent in the biblical idea that a thing can justly belong to a person is the concept of property. Some conception of property rights exists in all societies, but such conceptions are not always the same. There is general agreement that government should not permit individuals to take away others' property on their own authority. This kind of stealing is condemned by nearly everyone, since permitting it would lead to a state of never-ending warfare between people. But there is a difference in opinion relating to the essential nature of property rights, and whether government itself is bound to respect them.

Jean Jacques Rousseau, in *The Social Contract*, argues that people have a collective right to establish the laws under which they will live, and that the laws they establish are by definition just. If a democratic society chooses to define civil property rights narrowly and to have government socialize control of certain natural resources or industries, or to have it place confiscatory taxes upon the wealth of the rich, it can justly do so, Rousseau would argue.

Bible-believing Christians, affirming the sovereignty of God in all things, do not cede to popular majorities the authority to determine what is right or wrong, just or unjust. They hold that God is the ultimate authority in such matters. Thus to Christians, the fact that slavery might have been supported by a majority of Alabamans before the Civil War, does not mean it was a just institution. Moreover, they hold that Christians who found the institution a gross injustice – a stealing of the most basic property of all, the property a person has in him or herself – had a moral obligation to seek the institution's abolition.

The biblical ideas 1) that every individual has certain fundamental rights that are ordained, as Thomas Jefferson put it, by "Nature and Nature's God," 2) that these rights include not just a right to life and liberty, but also rights in regard to property, and 3) that justice demands that government secure these fundamental rights, have historically led most Bible-believing Christians to support the enshrinement of a rather broad conception of property rights in civil law.

The Social Contract and the Bible, and the two very different conceptions of property rights they uphold, have largely established the parameters of American political debate In regard to what constitutes economic justice. The Democratic Socialist Left, believing Society itself is the highest authority, rejects the very concept of inalienable rights that come from Nature and Nature's God. It believes a society's people, exercising their collective will through the state, can justly define civil property rights however they choose, and acting through government can justly confiscate and redistribute material wealth however they choose. The Christian Right, believing that God is the highest authority, affirms the existence of inalienable human rights, and believes that for a society to be civilly just, its government must secure these inalienable human rights – rights that belong to each of us simply because we are human, whether or not our society or government chooses to affirm these rights.

Christians have *not* held that the natural, human right to property is limitless. The Larger Westminster Catechism condemns as stealing only "*unjust*...ways of taking or withholding from our neighbor what belongs to him." There can be times, Christians have believed, when a taking can be just, as has been reflected, historically, in our laws relative to eminent domain. But even under eminent domain, our courts, under the influence of our Christian heritage, have historically held that government can seize private property only for public uses, and when seizing such property, must fully compensate the property owner. The intensity of the eminent domain debate today reflects the great distance between the views of those who hold that government can justly seize private property for whatever purposes it chooses – including the purpose of giving such property to another private owner – and those who hold that government can justly seize private property only for public uses, and even then must respect the private owner's rights to due process and full compensation.

The clash between Democratic Socialist and Christian ways of thinking also plays itself out in political fights over welfare. The Westminster Larger Catechism's condemnation of "ways whereby we do unduly prejudice our own outward estate" – in other words, by which we waste or destroy our own material well-being – highlights the Christian belief that our material well-being matters to God, a belief supported by innumerable Bible verses. But nowhere does the Bible endorse welfare as a way to remedy poverty. The Bible says that with man's banishment from the Garden, God declared man would have to toil for material wealth. Meanwhile, 2 Thessalonians 3:10 says explicitly, "If a man will not work, he shall not eat." From these and other scriptures, Bible-believing Christians have historically concluded that while a man has a need and a right to labor for sustenance, he has no right to welfare – not if he is *able* to work, at least. Government should secure people's right to work, Christians have argued, and some say that when times necessitate, it should provide people with jobs whereby they can earn their daily bread. But able-bodied people have no right to welfare benefits for which they do not work, funded by the labor of others – not even when those who would be taxed have achieved considerable wealth and can arguably afford it.

This tees-up the question of redistributionist taxation – taxation which explicitly endeavors to equalize wealth through reducing the wealth of some people (e.g., the rich) to increase the wealth of others (e.g., the poor). For the Democratic Socialist Left, income equality is a fundamental value, and income equalization is a primary public policy goal. But throughout most of American history, most Christians have believed that a tax policy aimed at nothing more than equalizing incomes unjustly tramples upon the property rights of those from whom it expropriates wealth. They have pointed out that wealth is *not* decried as evil by the Bible; material abundance is good. It is *coveting* money, or *envying* the wealth of others, that is repeatedly condemned. They point to verse after verse indicating that the Bible's conception of justice is one which focuses not on income equality, but on fair treatment – e.g., that an employer not withhold from a laborer the payment it was agreed the laborer would receive for work the laborer has provided.

In response, Christians who support income redistribution highlight the biblical prophets' frequent condemnation of social conditions where while the rich gorge themselves, the poor starve, and they point to the institution of the Jubilee Year in ancient Israel (when, every fifty years, land was redistributed) as biblical evidence that justice demands income redistribution.

Looking at all of the scriptures typically cited by the different sides, and listening to all of the different arguments advanced, many Christians have come to believe that the Bible supports what might be described as a middle-ground position. The Jubilee Year did not produce equality of income; it just ensured that people would have an opportunity to work the land and grow the food they need. In today's economy, ensuring that everyone can obtain a high quality education and get a job where they will be able to earn life's necessities provides that kind of guarantee.

Some Christian Libertarians reject this middle ground position. The Bible teaches that government has a just purpose, they say, but that just purpose is limited to the securing of people's lives, liberty and property. They say that any expansion of government's dominion ultimately represents a diminution of the people's God-given liberties and equates to government working against its own just purposes. These Christians argue against things like government funding for education, highlighting that education is not a natural right, it is not a gift from God that you are born possessing and will continue to naturally possess unless it is unjustly taken away from you; it is a human-provided good. Government cannot, they argue, justly coerce people to provide or pay for others' goods. You have a right to life, liberty and property, they say, you don't have a right to force others to serve you involuntarily or to give you stuff. When government begins forcing people into involuntary servitude or unjustly taking their property, it becomes not a securer of justice for all, but a weapon of the majority, or the politically powerful, against the minority or those less powerful.

This last argument may be correct in many elements, but may still be wrong in its conclusion. The Bible does suggest that securing people's God-given rights is the fundamental purpose of government, and reason does suggest that to keep government from trampling on people's natural liberties, or from laying waste to their wealth through overly expansive government and economically destructive tax burdens, the dominion and powers of government must be limited. Yet prudence arguably finds that public policies which cost-effectively expand opportunity or provide a social safety net serve to increase domestic tranquility and social stability, and are thus every bit as critical to the securing of people's lives, liberties, and property as are a police force, court system, and national defense capability (all government operations which Christian Libertarians typically acknowledge as just). Thus, a social program which does work to expand opportunity and increase prosperity may be as justly funded by coercive taxation as a nation's defense forces.

My personal conclusions relative to these economic policy questions are likely obvious from the preceding paragraphs. I believe that in regard to the Eighth Commandment's prohibition upon stealing from others, our traditional American regard for property rights, our traditional support for people enjoying a fair opportunity to work and earn (but not for welfare or income equalization policies), and our traditional support for social programs that expand opportunity (but not for social programs that necessitate such high tax rates that they actually work to reduce economic prosperity and opportunity), are all reflective of biblical values.

Given the American people's religious heritage, and their historic regard for the authority of the Bible, it should not be surprising that this nation's traditional economic values appear well-aligned with biblical principles. I and other contemporary Christians who are led by our study of Scripture to endorse these traditional economic principles as biblical may be wrong in our interpretation of the Bible's teachings, but given that so many Christians throughout history have come to the same conclusions, it is also possible that we are right.

Christians were on both sides of the slavery issue, but most Christian thinkers throughout the millennia have seen the Bible proclaiming universal human dignity. Christians are on both sides of the abortion issue, but most Christian thinkers throughout the millennia have seen the Bible proclaiming a universal right to life. The existence of differences of opinion on the proper interpretation of Scripture does not preclude the prospect that one side is right, nor does it necessarily mean that Scripture is unclear on a question: it may just mean that one side doesn't want to acknowledge what Scripture has to say.

Some people, of course, don't care what the Bible has to say. Some people assail it as a reactionary document. But it seems to me that regard for the biblical values of life, liberty, and property has been the greatest driver of social progress – of human freedom and dignity – in history.

On Stealing From God

Turning to the Eighth Commandment's prohibition on stealing from God, I have already stated that while covetousness and envy might be sinful, justice argues against Christians trying to make them illegal. God naturally punishes such stealing from Him – these sins make the sinner miserable – and the biblical principal of proportionality (an eye for an eye, not two eyes for an eye) argues against the adding of civil punishment.

But there are civil laws called for by the Eighth Commandment's prohibition on stealing from God. The First Amendment of the United States Constitution is one example. It separates church and state to prevent politicians from endeavoring to steal from God the worship He is due. Allow me to provide a bit of history on this point.

Most pre-historic religions were nature cults. People in awe of the power of the sun, of the sea, and of other natural objects, worshipped these objects. With the development of powerful civilizations, emperors became the incarnation of a civilization's power and often demanded that their subjects worship them.

Jews and Christians refused, believing that emperors were but fellow human beings and that to give emperors worship was to steal from that which belongs to God. They went even further, rejecting the religious authority of the emperor's priests and recognizing their own ecclesiastical authorities. European monarchs might establish a Christian sect as the state religion, and some monarchs succeeded in making themselves the head of their state church, but in most instances, Christian monarchs were simply accorded respect as protectors of the Church. The spiritual head, according to believers, was Christ; the head of the earthly Church in most of Christendom was an ecclesiastical authority independent of the local king: for instance, the Pope for Catholics, or a body of elected Elders for Christian congregations of the Reformed tradition.

The separation of secular and religious authority in Europe did not guarantee religious freedom – but it did in post-Revolution America. The Framers of our Constitution did not want to replicate the political and re-ligious architecture of Europe, so greatly influenced by the continent's pre-Christian heritage. They wanted to create a new society upholding biblical principles of justice. Accordingly, they wanted to deny political leaders the power to be able to steal from God the worship He is due. In addition, they believed people were naturally born with freedom of conscience and that God intended for them to have it. They turned the Eighth Com-mandment's prohibition on stealing the rightful property of God (the free-willed worship He is due), or the rightful property of one's neighbor (his liberty) into the First Amendment of the United States Constitution.

Through this limit on the powers of government, reflecting their belief that God is sovereign, not the state, the Framers gave us the free-dom of conscience that under lays all political freedom. Christians should engage politically to preserve this freedom. It is foundational to the just society and it is under attack.

Efforts to take "In God We Trust" off of our money and the phrase "one nation under God" out of the Pledge of Allegiance may seem consis-tent with the separation of church and state, but in fact they are an attack upon that biblical principle. They seek to eliminate not just words, but our government's upholding of the idea that there is a moral authority greater than human will. If they succeed, if our legal system becomes dedicated to the idea that government can justly do whatever the majority dictates, instead of the idea that justice requires government limit itself out of respect for the people's inalienable rights, then all of our liberties will rapidly erode.

Thomas Jefferson, who authored the language "separation between church and state," and who together with his peers believed there should be such separation, believed that to preserve it, our government must remain dedicated to the idea that there is a higher moral authority than human will. "Can the liberties of a nation be thought secure," he asked, "when we have removed their only firm basis, a conviction in the minds of the people that these liberties are the gift of God?" He didn't want any church in control of our government and he believed people had a right to reject belief in God altogether. But he wanted our government, at least, dedicated to the idea that people have rights which come from "Nature and Nature's God," and which it cannot justly take from us.

Attacks upon our freedom of conscience come in many forms. In 1819, Chief Justice of the Supreme Court John Marshall wrote that "the power to tax is the power to destroy." But in a scholarship tax credit case decided just this spring, the plaintiffs sought to turn that ruling on its head. They argued that exemption from taxation equals government support. More specifically, the plaintiffs argued that when people get a tax credit for contributing to a scholarship foundation, and then children use some of the scholarships to attend church-affiliated schools, the government is subsidizing churches. It is a radical argument.

The United States Supreme Court has long held that while the government cannot directly give money to church-affiliated schools or colleges, it can make tuition assistance available to students, and any students receiving such assistance have a First Amendment right to use it at church-affiliated institutions if they choose. This does not equate to government support for churches, the Court has repeatedly held, it equates to respect for the people's religious liberty. Frighteningly, four Supreme Court justices sided with the plaintiffs' radical attack on this long-cherished principle of freedom. By only the barest court majority, does this bedrock principle still survive – and the chipping at it will continue.

In Democratic Socialist states, such as China, there is no religious freedom. Unsurprisingly, there is no political freedom either. If we don't want a similar situation here, Christians should engage politically to keep America dedicated to its historic understanding of what the First Amendment means and keep politicians from endeavoring to steal what belongs to God.

On Stealing From Ourselves

Libertarians believe that the government has no right to prevent people from doing harm to themselves. Christians, while believing in liberty and limited government, have not typically taken this absolutist position. Some have supported a substantial degree of governmental "nannyism." Others have only supported what I call "cliff railings" – laws that allow people to make decisions for themselves, good or ill, up to a boundary beyond which they might easily kill themselves or lose control of their ability to make rational decisions.

The Bible, while stating that the road of righteousness is straight and narrow, does not suggest government should bar and punish all wayward wandering. I have mentioned the idea that when people do harm to themselves, justice does not call for them to be further harmed by the state. Prudence too argues against excessive nannyism. On what biblical basis, then, do Christians justify even cliff railings?

The answer is that in the Bible, God gives us not just a right to life and liberty, but life and liberty themselves, and God wants us to possess them. Since in the Bible, God's will (not our own) determines what is just, life and liberty, unlike property, cannot justly be given away. (Property can be given away because by definition it is not what God gives us, but what we fashion out of God's creation or gain a right to through the application of our labor.)

The Christian who views things from this perspective argues that the law ought to permit people to contract for the sale of their labor, but not in such a way that they enslave themselves and lose the ability to make any further decisions relating to their lives. A society ought to permit people to do dangerous things, but not permit them to commit suicide. A society ought to permit people to use certain drugs for certain purposes, but not, for recreational purposes, to use drugs which are so controlling and addictive that users will lose the ability to make rational decisions for themselves.

The Law of Love

Libertarians are apt to argue that the middle-ground positions I have favored in this essay amount to mush. They will say you either have the right to make decisions about your life, or you don't; government either has an unlimited right to tax, or its right to tax is strictly limited to a few, just purposes, such as paying for a police force and national defense system in order to secure people's inalienable rights to life, liberty, and property.

Coercively taxing people for other purposes, some Libertarians say, is using government to effectuate theft.

Christians often see this Libertarian position as being ideological – as putting an idea above the more balanced public policies for which experience and prudence might argue. In his book, *Intellectuals*, Paul Johnson writes: "Above all, we must at all times remember what intellectuals habitually forget: that people matter more than concepts and must come first. The worst of all despotisms is the heartless tyranny of ideas."

This notion, that what truly matters is the actual well-being of people, is also how Christians respond to the Redistributionists' critique of income inequality. The latter argue that if extremely high tax rates, implemented for the purpose of income redistribution, ultimately reduce productive investment and labor, if they ultimately make a society poorer, if they ultimately reduce the living standards even of the poor, so be it, because a greater good, the narrowing of material inequality, will have been achieved. Christians argue that a concept such as income inequality should not be more important than the well-being of flesh and blood people.

In the end, no amount of economic research will be able to end this dispute because the argument is fundamentally a religious one. By faith, these camps have committed themselves to different first values. This causes them to answer the question, "What is the cornerstone of justice?" differently.

The Libertarian answers "individual liberty." The Democratic Socialist says "popular sovereignty" (though, one notes, he often seems committed to income equality regardless of what people want). The Bible-believing Christian says "love."

Loving one's neighbor, caring about others as completely as one cares about oneself, appreciating that each individual's well-being has infinite value, is what the Bible's law of love commands. Justice, the Bible suggests, requires the social application of this moral law.

If the just government must treat a minority even as the majority wants to be treated, if it cannot be in the business of harming innocent people (no matter what the utilitarian justification), if its policies must benefit everyone, then one is led to a vision of the just society in which:

- Government secures each person's life, liberty, and property (even as we want it to secure our own);

o It does this by preventing people from taking others'
lives, liberty, and property;

o And by preventing people from killing or enslaving
themselves;

- Government may exercise eminent domain against a person's property for the public's benefit, but it does not favor one private individual at the expense of another, and whenever it takes anyone's
property, it provides that person full compensation and accords
him or her due process rights, so the person is not harmed by the
action;

- Government may institute taxes to provide goods and services that
benefit all people, but it does not take the fruit of one person's labor
to give it to another who has not labored, nor set itself to benefit-
ting some people at the expense of others, nor institute policies
that, in practice, serve to harm everyone.

Christians, Engage!

The Bible is not a political treatise, but it does speak of what characterizes
the just society, not just what is morally right and wrong for individuals.
Since reasonable people interpret the teachings of the Bible relative to the
mandates of social justice in different ways, we should each be humble in
our personal conclusions in this regard and be open to others' arguments.
But that doesn't mean Christians should be politically disengaged. At stake
here are not merely academic questions. At stake is whether our society
will be just.

I believe we can look to Martin Luther King, Jr., as a role model
for Christian engagement in the sphere of public policy. In his *Letter
From a Birmingham Jail*, King responded to Christians who thought he
was pushing things too fast. He didn't disregard their arguments that his
actions were stirring up reaction that would just make things worse for
African-Americans. He considered their arguments fully; he wrestled with
them. But in the end, he came to the conclusion that he should continue
pushing for the full civil enfranchisement of all Americans.

In King's last sermon, he spoke about his eventual death, not
knowing how close it was. He said that he didn't want it mentioned at his
funeral that he had won the Nobel Prize; he just wanted it mentioned that
he had *tried*, in his life, to help his neighbor. I suspect he chose his words

carefully and did not say that he *had* helped his neighbor because he believed only God knows if our ideas of how to advance justice are correct. I suspect that he did not say he just wanted to help his neighbor because he believed merely wanting to advance justice is not enough. God calls us as Christians to love our neighbor. Being faithful to that command requires that we actually try to build the just society.

We should think about the Eighth Commandment and its implications not just for our personal business ethics, therefore, but also for the kinds of public policies that we, as Christians, should work to shape.

I see the Commandment as upholding a conception of justice that is founded on the cornerstone of love and that demands we endeavor via our civil institutions to secure each person's life, liberty, and property.

Mine is a fairly traditional interpretation, I admit. But in my opinion, it is this age-old, biblical conception of justice which still drives social and economic progress in the world.

ARE PROFITS MORAL?

Answers from a Comparison of Adam Smith, Max Weber, Karl Marx, and the Westminster Larger Catechism

This text was taken from Business Ethics Today: Foundations, *a text published in 2010 as the culmination of white papers and presentations produced for the 2010 conference entitled: "Business Ethics Today: Adding a Christian Worldview as Found in the Westminster Confession of Faith."*

PHILIP CLEMENTS, PETER LILLBACK, WAYNE GRUDEM & JOHN WEISER

PHILIP CLEMENTS

Philip J. Clements is the managing director of the Center for Christian Business Ethics Today, LLC. Clements has been a leader in the business community for over thirty years. He has held the position of Executive Vice President of Standard & Poor's Corporate Value Consulting ("CVC") division. He led the transition of CVC to S&P, after S&P acquired CVC from PricewaterhouseCoopers LLP (PwC). Prior to joining Standard & Poor's, Clements was the Global Leader of the CVC practice of PwC. He also served on the U.S. boards of Coopers & Lybrand and Pricewaterhouse Coopers and the global board of PwC. He was a member of the Finance Committees of both firms. Clements was Chairman of the Board of Trustees of the National Bible Association. Seattle University School of Law Board of Visitors, International Leadership Board of Advisors, and HOPE Bible Mission board are others boards that Clements has served or is serving on. In addition to founder and CEO of the Center, Philip J. Clements is also Managing Direcotor at Cathedral Consulting Firm.

PETER LILLBACK

Doctor Peter A. Lillback is President and Professor of Historical Theology at Westminster Theological Seminary. Lillback also serves as the President of The Providence Forum, the nonprofit organization that is committed to preserving and promoting America's spiritual roots of religious and civil liberties.

Living between Philadelphia and Valley Forge for many years, Dr. Lillback has pursued an avid interest in the history of the Judeo-Christian heritage of the United States. He has done much research and study on the founding and Founders of our nation through examination of original source documents in numerous libraries and archives. His books Freedom's Holy Light *and* Proclaim Liberty *are outgrowths of his research. In 2006, Dr. Lillback's bestseller on the Christian faith of George Washington was released.* George Washington's Sacred Fire *represents the culmination of over twenty years of original research and scholarship. In May 2010, the paperback reached #1 on Amazon.com.*

WAYNE GRUDEM

Wayne Grudem is Research Professor of Theology and Biblical Studies at Phoenix Seminary in Phoenix, Arizona. Prior to Phoenix Seminary he taught for twenty years at Trinity Evangelical Divinity School, Deerfield, Illinois, where he was chairman of the department of Biblical and Systematic Theology. He received a BA from Harvard University, an MDiv from Westminster Seminary, Philadelphia, and a PhD (in New Testament) from the University of Cambridge, England. He has published sixteen books, including Systematic Theology, Recovering Biblical Manhood and Womanhood (co-edited with John Piper), The TNIV and the Gender-Neutral Bible Controversy (co-authored with Vern Poythress), The First Epistle of Peter (Tyndale NT commentary), *and* Business for the Glory of God. *He was also the General Editor for the* ESV Study Bible (published October 2008).

He is a past president of the Evangelical Theological Society, a co-founder and past president of the Council on Biblical Manhood and Womanhood, and a member of the Translation Oversight Committee for the English Standard Version *of the Bible.*

JOHN WEISER

John Weiser spent his first twenty-one years in Bloomington, Indiana, as the son of a professor of music at Indiana University. There he graduated from IU in business administration and began his business career with National City Bank in Cleveland, Ohio, where he was first exposed to the realm of institutional investments and has never left that path. With several intermediate stops, he has spent the last twenty-three of thirty-five years in this field and continues to work in his specialty of global fixed income investments with a private "hedge fund" in Texas.

John was a founder and Elder at Fort Worth Presbyterian Church, PCA, until his recent move to Charlottesville, Virginia. He has served on the Board of Trustees at Westminster Theological Seminary for fourteen years and currently serves on the board of In Medias Res, a support foundation for the Institute for Advanced Studies in Culture at the University of Virginia.

INTRODUCTION

W
e live in a time when business and business profits are routinely challenged as to morality. The Middle Ages had similar perspectives. Part of the outcome of the Reformation was a new respect for business and its appropriateness for all members of a community.

Why does society struggle with the question, "Are profits moral?" As with so many things, a review of the past sheds real light on both the reasons and implications. This paper presents a collection of material from the past to show the perspectives that lead up to the current views. Please read on; the message will shock you.

The paper starts with a brief look at the *Westminster Larger Catechism* (hereinafter called *Catechism*)[1] questions and answers surrounding the Ten Commandments. We start with the *Catechism* because it articulates well the Reformed Christian perspectives on business and profits. This perspective lays the foundation for the following authors' material, which supports and contrasts the Christian worldview. There is much more richness in the *Catechism* than papers such as this one, can fully explore; so, we encourage the reader to study the *Catechism* for the wisdom it contains.

The first author is Adam Smith and *The Wealth of Nations*.[2] Smith framed the essence of business and how business contributes to the progress in a society. Smith, a professor of moral philosophy at Glasgow, studied the business activities of his day, which were done in a culture that was essentially Christian. Space does not allow an exploration of the distinctives of the Christianity of his time. However, we will touch on the connection to the *Catechism*. Next up is Max Weber and *The Protestant Ethic and the Spirit of Capitalism*.[3] Weber was a social scientist and not a Christian. However, Weber's thesis was that Reformed Christianity did indeed change the way in which business was engaged and how it was viewed in the period following the Reformation. Weber cited the *Westminster Confession of Faith* as the theology of Reformed Christianity, but he decidedly rejected its application later. Many protest Weber's findings, but they are most useful in comparing them to the next author, Karl Marx and *Communist Manifesto*.[4] Marx can be said to have turned the world upside down in his writings. Marx rejected religion, particularly Christianity, and the capitalism that underlies the Reformed orientation to commerce. This paper quotes extensively Marx's writings because they speak quite clearly and are decidedly reflected in the rhetoric we see today about business and profits.

Before jumping into the topic, we would call to remembrance that the Bible is God's revealed Word. It is God's provision of redemption for mankind and the history of that provision. The Bible is not a book on economics. Yet, even in its role, the Bible provides insights into the realities of human existence. Part of man's existence is commercial activity; therefore it is reasonable to anticipate that the Bible contains principles and illustrations of man's commercial activities, pursuit of wealth, and the rights of individual private property.[5]

WESTMINSTER LARGER CATECHISM

The *Catechism* contains 196 questions and answers designed to lead the believer into a deeper and fuller understanding of Christian faith and its blessings, duties, and practices. Each question and answer contains Bible verses that tie the principles to Scripture so that the studious Christian can know for himself the Word of God on the matter. It is in this spirit that we pride here a selection of the *Catechism* questions and answers that related to the first, fifth, eighth, and tenth commandments. These commandments and questions have been selected because these most crisply highlight the Bible's view on private property, business, and profits. Of particular significance is Question 141. Especially note the italicized text at the end of the answer where it is declared to be a moral duty before God to "further the wealth and outward estate of others, as well as our own." We have highlighted works and phrases to draw your attention to the portions most applicable to this topic.[6]

> **Question 99:** What rules are to be observed for the right understanding of the ten commandments?
> **Answer:** For the right understanding of the ten commandments, these rules are to be observed: That *the law is perfect*, and binds everyone to full conformity in the whole man unto the righteousness thereof, and unto entire obedience forever; so as to require the utmost perfection of every duty, and to forbid the least degree of every sin. That *it is spiritual*, and so reaches

the understanding, will, affections, and all other powers of the soul; as well as words, works, and gestures. That one and the same thing, in divers respects, is required or forbidden in several commandments. That as, where a duty is commanded, the contrary sin is forbidden; and, *where a sin is forbidden, the contrary duty is commanded*: so, where a promise is annexed, the contrary threatening is included; and, where a threatening is annexed, the contrary promise is included. That: What God forbids, is at no time to be done; What he commands, is always our duty; and yet every particular duty is not to be done at all times. *That under one sin or duty, all of the same kind are forbidden or commanded; together with all the causes, means, occasions, and appearances thereof, and provocations thereunto.* That: What is forbidden or commanded to ourselves, we are bound, according to our places, to endeavor that it may be avoided or performed by others, according to the duty of their places. That in: What is commanded to others, we are bound, according to our places and callings, to be helpful to them; and to take heed of partaking with others in: What is forbidden them.

Question 99 has been included to set the stage for the specifics of those commandments, questions, and answers that most bear upon the question of profits and business.

> *Question 103:* Which is the first commandment?
> *Answer:* The first commandment is, Thou shall have no other gods before me.

> *Question 104:* What are the duties required in the first commandment?
> *Answer:* The duties required in the first commandment are, the knowing and acknowledging of God to be the only true God, and our God; and to worship and glorify him accordingly, by thinking, meditating, remembering, highly esteeming, honoring, adoring, choosing, loving, desiring, fearing of him; believing him; trusting, hoping, delighting, rejoicing in him; being zealous for him; calling upon him, giving all praise and thanks, and yielding all obedience and submission to him

with the whole man; *being careful in all things to please him, and sorrowful when in anything he is offended;* and walking humbly with him.

Question 105: What are the sins forbidden in the first commandment?

Answer: The sins forbidden in the first commandment are, atheism, in denying or not having a God; idolatry, in having or worshiping more gods than one, or any with or instead of the true God; the not having and avouching him for God, and our God; the omission or neglect of anything due to him, required in this commandment; ignorance, forgetfulness, misapprehensions, false opinions, unworthy and wicked thoughts of him; bold and curious searching into his secrets; all profaneness, hatred of God; *self-love, self-seeking, and all other inordinate and immoderate setting of our mind, will, or affections upon other things, and taking them off from him in whole or in part;* vain credulity, unbelief, heresy, misbelief, distrust, despair, incorrigibleness, and insensibleness under judgments, hardness of heart, pride, presumption, *carnal security,* tempting of God; using unlawful means, and *trusting in lawful means; carnal delights and joys;* corrupt, blind, and indiscreet zeal; lukewarmness, and deadness in the things of God; estranging ourselves, and apostatizing from God; praying, or giving any religious worship, to saints, angels, or any other creatures; all compacts and consulting with the devil, and hearkening to his suggestions; making men the lords of our faith and conscience; *slighting and despising God and his commands;* resisting and grieving of his Spirit, *discontent and impatience at his dispensations,* charging him foolishly for the evils he inflicts on us; and *ascribing the praise of any good we either are, have, or can do, to fortune, idols, ourselves, or any other creature.*

Question 106: What are we specially taught by these words before me in the first commandment?

Answer: These words before me, or before my face, in the first commandment, teach us, that God, *who sees all things,* takes special notice of, and is much displeased with, the sin of having any other God: that so it may be an argument to dissuade from it, and to aggravate it as a most impudent provocation: *as also to persuade us to do as in his sight, Whatever we do in his service.*

The first commandment lays a foundation for man's relationship to his God. Question 106 captures the implications of this first commandment for those engaged in business: God *"sees all things"* and *"persuade[s] us to do as in his sight, whatever we do in his service."* All bosses know that being present changes behavior. Christian behavior should be grounded in the knowledge of the ever presence of our Creator God. This directly affects the importance of understanding His charge and expectation of engaging in business and making a profit. The fifth, eighth, and tenth commandments bear directly on the commercial activity.

> **Question 122:** What is the sum of the six commandments which contain our duty to man?
> **Answer:** The sum of the six commandments which contain our duty to man is, *to love our neighbor as ourselves, and to do to others: What we would have them to do to us.*

Here we find stated the "golden rule." John Maxwell's book *There's No Such Thing as "Business" Ethics: There's Only One Rule for Decision Making*[7] adopts this golden rule as the rule for business.[8] But as will be seen below, the commandments have a richness in application that needs the separate analysis and consideration given by those who assembled the *Catechism.*

> **Question 126:** What is the general scope of the fifth commandment?
> **Answer:** The general scope of the fifth commandment is, the performance of those duties which we mutually owe in our several relations, as inferiors, superiors, or equals.

> **Question 127:** What is the honor that inferiors owe to their superiors?
> **Answer:** The honor which inferiors owe to their superiors is, all due reverence in heart, word, and behavior; prayer and thanksgiving for them; imitation of their virtues and graces; willing obedience to their lawful commands and counsels; due submis-

sion to their corrections; fidelity to, *defense and maintenance of their persons and authority*, according to their several ranks, and the nature of their places; bearing with their infirmities, and covering them in love, that so they may be an honor to them and to their government.

Question 128: What are the sins of inferiors against their superiors?

Answer: The sins of inferiors against their superiors are, all neglect of the duties required toward them; *envying* at, contempt of, and rebellion against, their persons and places, in their lawful counsels, commands, and corrections; cursing, mocking, and all such refractory and scandalous carriage, as proves a shame and dishonor to them and their government.

Question 129: What is required of superiors towards their inferiors?

Answer: It is required of superiors, according to that power they receive from God, and that relation wherein they stand, to love, pray for, and bless their inferiors; to instruct, counsel, and admonish them; countenancing, commending, and *rewarding such as do well*; and discountenancing, reproving, and chastising such as do ill; *protecting, and providing for them all things necessary for soul and body*: and by grave, wise, holy, and exemplary carriage, to procure glory to God, honor to themselves, and so to preserve that authority which God has put upon them.

Question 130: What are the sins of superiors?

Answer: The sins of superiors are, besides the neglect of the duties required of them, an *inordinate seeking of themselves, their own glory, ease, profit, or pleasure; commanding things unlawful, or not in the power of inferiors to perform; counseling, encouraging, or favoring them in that which is evil; dissuading, discouraging, or discountenancing them in that which is good*; correcting them unduly; careless exposing, or leaving them to wrong, temptation, and danger; provoking them to wrath; or any way dishonoring themselves, or lessening their authority, by an unjust, indiscreet, rigorous, or remiss behavior.

Question 131: What are the duties of equals?
Answer: The duties of equals are, to regard the dignity and worth of each other, in *giving honor to go one before another; and to rejoice in each other's gifts and advancement, as their own.*

Question 132: What are the sins of equals?
Answer: The sins of equals are, besides the neglect of the duties required, *the undervaluing of the worth, envying the gifts, grieving at the advancement of prosperity one of another; and usurping preeminence one over another.*

Not all of the questions related to the fifth commandment have been included, but we see here great guidance and affirmation of the roles of superiors and their reports in a business context.

Questions 131 and 132 are very telling in today's world, that we should celebrate success, not envy or usurp preeminence one over another. Such a contrast to what we will see below.

Question 140: Which is the eighth commandment?
Answer: The eighth commandment is, Thou shalt not steal.

Question 141: What are the duties required in the eighth commandment?
Answer: The duties required in the eighth commandment are, *truth, faithfulness, and justice in contracts and commerce between man and man; rendering to everyone his due; restitution of goods unlawfully detained from the right owners thereof; giving and lending freely, according to our abilities, and the necessities of others; moderation of our judgments, wills, and affections concerning worldly goods; a provident care and study to get, keep, use, and dispose these things which are necessary and convenient for the sustentation of our nature, and suitable to our condition; a lawful calling, and diligence in it; frugality; avoiding unnecessary lawsuits and suretyship, or other like engagements; and an endeavor, by all just and lawful means, to procure, preserve, and further the wealth and outward estate of others, as well as our own.*

Question 142: What are the sins forbidden in the eighth commandment?

Answer: The sins forbidden in the eighth commandment, besides the neglect of the duties required, are, *theft, robbery, man stealing, and receiving anything that is stolen; fraudulent dealing, false weights and measures, removing land marks, injustice and unfaithfulness in contracts between man and man, or in matters of trust; oppression, extortion, usury, bribery, vexatious lawsuits, unjust enclosures and depopulations; engrossing commodities to enhance the price; unlawful callings, and all other unjust or sinful ways of taking or withholding from our neighbor: What belongs to him, or of enriching ourselves; covetousness; inordinate prizing and affecting worldly goods; distrustful and distracting cares and studies in getting, keeping, and using them; envying at the prosperity of others; as likewise idleness, prodigality, wasteful gaming; and all other ways whereby we do unduly prejudice our own outward estate, and defrauding ourselves of the due use and comfort of that estate which God has given us.*

Clearly the eighth commandment is a centerpiece for understanding God's perspective on commercial relations. Throughout modern history and across the globe, the role of private property in commercial development of a society or country affirms that the principles in the eighth commandment on the respect for private property are universal and essential. In the discussions on alienation of poverty through economic activity, Hernando De Soto noted that there is plenty of capital in the developing world; it is just trapped in poor ownership/legal structures.[9] De Soto's point is that where private property is respected and ownership is clear, the values created in building businesses or enhancing property become transferable or form collateral for loans to increase economic activity. In short, private property creates the framework for profits that create the economic activity that create blessed communities. But where private property is not respected or ownership is not clear, the enhancements or businesses have no value, because they cannot be transferred or become collateral for financing. While this seems a simple set of statements, De Soto properly highlights what the Bible had addressed thousands of years before. It is essential to economic development and the profitability of a community, that property rights be clear and respected. The eight commandment questions of the *Catechism* capture the richness of this respect and the comfort that following this commandment brings to individuals and communities.

The contrasts of the obligations set forth in these questions and answers with the views of Marx could not be more graphic. Clearly there are simply different and irreconcilable worldviews between the *Catechism* and the *Communist Manifesto*.[10]

> **Question 146:** Which is the tenth commandment?
> **Answer:** The tenth commandment is, Thou shalt not covet thy neighbor's house, thou shalt not covet thy neighbor's wife, nor his manservant, nor his maidservant, nor his ox, nor his ass, nor any thing that is thy neighbor's.

> **Question 147:** What are the duties required in the tenth commandment?
> **Answer:** The duties required in the tenth commandment are, *such a full contentment with our own condition, and such a charitable frame of the whole soul toward our neighbor, as that all our inward motions and affections touching him, tend unto, and further all that good which is his.*

> **Question 148:** What are the sins forbidden in the tenth commandment?
> **Answer:** The sins forbidden in the tenth commandment are, *discontentment with our own estate; envying and grieving at the good of our neighbor, together with all inordinate motions and affections to anything that is his.*

> **Question 149:** Is any man able perfectly to keep the commandments of God?
> **Answer:** *No man is able, either of himself, or by any grace received in this life, perfectly to keep the commandments of God;* but does daily break them in thought, word, and deed.

The tenth commandment gets somewhat short attention in the *Catechism*. In part, much of its charge seems to be covered elsewhere. But in today's business world the specifics of this commandment should challenge us to the same depth of thinking on behavior and duties as those of the other commandments. Space in this paper limits our ability to cover the application of contentment in our business as we operate in the competitive marketplace, but the reader is encouraged to meditation on this commandment with the spirit of the *Catechism*.

We would summarize these passages as to the question of the morality of profits by noting that profits and wealth creation cannot become an idol, to displace God. Nowhere in these questions and answers are profits treated as an error or immoral. Rather, instruction and caution are given as to both the pursuit and the treatment of our and others' assets and wealth accumulations. We should be content with what we have been given by God. But we have a responsibility to make it productive, which generally means creating increase, or more profits.

ADAM SMITH, THE WEALTH OF NATIONS, AND THE BASIS OF PROFITS

We leave the *Catechism* and look to the work of Adam Smith. The classic capitalistic insights of labor, profits, and supply and demand were stated by Adam Smith in his seminal work, *The Wealth of Nations*. Smith's work shows that man is by nature of necessity, a businessman. The following excerpts are provided from book 1, chapter 2, and chapter 3. These show the basics of the need for barter and the benefits, he found, from division of labor or making labor more productive.[11] An added concept embedded in Smith's findings are the effects of the economic law of supply and demand. Highlights have been provided to draw the reader's attention to portions that provide contrasts with other material in this paper:

> [Chapter 2] In civilized society he stands at all times in need of the cooperation and assistance of great multitudes, while his whole life is scarce sufficient to gain the friendship of a few persons. In almost every other race of animals each individual, when it is grown up to maturity, is entirely independent, and in its natural state has occasion for the assistance of no other living creature. *But man has almost constant occasion for the help of his brethren, and it is in vain for him to expect it from their benevolence only. He will be more likely to prevail if he can interest their self-love in his favour, and show them that it is for their own advantage to do for him what he requires of them.* Whoever offers

to another a bargain of any kind, proposes to do this. *Give me that which I want, and you shall have this which you want, is the meaning of every such offer; and it is in this manner that we obtain from one another the far greater part of those good offices which we stand in need of.* It is not from the benevolence of the butcher, the brewer, or the baker, that we expect our dinner, but from their regard to their own interest. We address ourselves, not to their humanity but to their self-love, and never talk to them of our own necessities but of their advantages. Nobody but a beggar chuses to depend chiefly upon the benevolence of his fellow-citizens. Even a beggar does not depend upon it entirely. The charity of well-disposed people, indeed, supplies him with the whole fund of his subsistence. But though this principle ultimately provides him with all the necessaries of life which he has occasion for, it neither does nor can provide him with them as he has occasion for them. The greater part of his occasional wants are supplied in the same manner as those of other people, by treaty, by barter, and by purchase. With the money which one man gives him he purchases food. The old cloaths which another bestows upon him he exchanges for other old cloaths which suit him better, or for lodging, or for food, or for money, with which he can buy either food, cloaths, or lodging, as he has occasion.

As it is by treaty, by barter, and by purchase, that we obtain from one another the greater part of those mutual good offices which we stand in need of, so it is this same trucking disposition which originally gives occasion to the division of labour. In a tribe of hunters or shepherds a particular person makes bows and arrows, for example, with more readiness and dexterity than any other. He frequently exchanges them for cattle or for venison with his companions; and he finds at last that he can in this manner get more cattle and venison, than if he himself went to the field to catch them. From a regard to his own interest, therefore, the making of bows and arrows grows to be his chief business, and he becomes a sort of armourer. Another excels in making the frames and covers of their little huts or moveable houses. He is accustomed to be of use in this way to his neighbours, who reward him in the same manner with cattle and with venison, till at last he finds it his interest to dedicate himself entirely to this employment, and to become a sort of house-carpenter. In the same manner a third becomes a smith or a brazier; a fourth a tanner or dresser of hides or skins, the principal part of the clothing of savages. And thus the certainty of being able to exchange all that surplus part of the produce of his own labour, which is over and above his own consumption, for such parts of the produce of other men's labour as he may have occasion for, encourages every man to apply himself to a particular occupation, and to cultivate and bring to perfection whatever talent or genius he may possess for that particular species of business.

The difference of natural talents in different men is, in reality, much less than we are aware of; and the very different genius which appears to distinguish men of different professions, when grown up to maturity, is not upon many occasions so much the cause, as the effect of the division of labour. *The difference between the most dissimilar characters, between a philosopher and a common street porter, for example, seems to arise not so much from nature, as from habit, custom, and education.* When they came into the world, and for the first six or eight years of their existence, they were perhaps, very much alike, and neither their parents nor playfellows could perceive any remarkable difference. About that age, or soon after, they come to be employed in very different occupations. The difference of talents comes then to be taken notice of, and widens by degrees, till at last the vanity of the philosopher is willing to acknowledge scarce any resemblance. But without the disposition to truck, barter, and exchange, every man must have procured to himself every necessary and conveniency of life which he wanted. All must have had the same duties to perform, and the same work to do, and there could have been no such difference of employment as could alone give occasion to any great difference of talents.

[Chapter 3] As it is the power of exchanging that gives occasion to the division of labour, *so the extent of this division must always be limited by the extent of that power, or, in other words, by the extent of the market.* When the market is very small, no person can have any encouragement to dedicate himself entirely to one employment, for want of the power to exchange all that surplus part of the produce of his own labour, which is over and above his own consumption, for such parts of the produce of other men's labour as he has occasion for.

There are some sorts of industry, even of the lowest kind, which can be carried on no where but in a great town. A porter, for example, can find employment and subsistence in no other place. A village is by much too narrow a sphere for him; even an ordinary market town is scarce large enough to afford him constant occupation. In the lone houses and very small villages which are scattered about in so desert a country as the Highlands of Scotland, every farmer must be butcher, baker and brewer for his own family. In such situations we can scarce expect to find even a smith, a carpenter, or a mason, within less than twenty miles of another of the same trade. The scattered families that live at eight or ten miles distance from the nearest of them, must learn to perform themselves a great number of little pieces of work, for which, in more populous countries, they would call in the assistance of those workmen. Country workmen are almost every where obliged to apply themselves to all the different branches of industry that have so much affinity to one another as to be employed about the same sort of materials. A country carpenter deals in every sort of work that is made of wood: a country smith in every sort of work that is made of iron. The former is not only a carpenter, but a joiner, a cabinet maker, and even a carver in wood, as well as a wheelwright, a ploughwright, a cart and waggon maker. The employments of the latter are still more various. It is impossible there should be such a trade as even that of a nailer in the remote and inland parts of the Highlands of Scotland. Such a workman at the rate of a thousand nails a day, and three hundred working days in the year, will make three hundred thousand nails in the year. But in such a situation it would be impossible to dispose of one thousand, that is, of one day's work in the year.

This division of labor that is inherent in human commerce which is coupled with the law of supply and demand, also ultimately creates human profits. For example, in book 1, chapter 9, he declares:

> It is not easy, it has already been observed, to ascertain what are the average wages of labour even in a particular place, and at a particular time. We can, even in this case, seldom determine more than what are the most usual wages. But even this can seldom be done with regard to the profits of stock. *Profit is so very fluctuating, that the person who carries on a particular trade cannot always tell you himself what is the average of his annual profit.* It is affected, not only by every variation of price in the commodities which he deals in, but by the good or bad fortune both of his rivals and of his customers, and by a thousand other accidents to which goods when carried either by sea or by land, or even when stored in a warehouse, are liable. It varies, therefore, not only from year to year, but from day to day, and almost from hour to hour. To ascertain what is the average profit of all the different trades carried on in a great kingdom, must be much more difficult; and to judge of what it may have been formerly, or in remote periods of time, with any degree of precision, must be altogether impossible.
>
> But though it may be impossible to determine with any degree of precision, what are or were the average profits of stock, either in the present, or in ancient times, some notion may be formed of them from the interest of money. It may be laid down as a maxim, that wherever a great deal can be made by the use of money, a great deal will commonly be given for the use of it; and that wherever little can be made by it, less will commonly be given for it. *According, therefore, as the usual market rate of interest varies in any country, we may be assured that the ordinary profits of stock must vary with it, must sink as it sinks, and rise as it rises. The progress of interest, therefore, may lead us to form some notion of the progress of profit.*

Thus profits and labor go hand in hand, when the actual forces of the market itself determine their activities. Competition, supply and demand, and the inherent instinct of the human soul to engage in commerce are bread-and-butter concepts for Western modern and postmodern civilization. But are such profits in themselves moral? Are profits a good thing, or just a necessary evil that must be controlled by competition, government intervention, or even revolution? Note that Smith did not answer these questions. Rather he recorded his observations as a scientist of the functioning of the world around him.

MAX WEBER AND THE DEVELOPMENT OF THE ETHICS OF CAPITALISM

The American principle of the propriety of the economic pursuit of profits is well captured by Max Weber's *The Protestant Ethic and the Spirit of Capitalism*. Interestingly, his assessment focuses on the great American Founding Father, Ben Franklin, and argues that there is a direct connection between Franklin's capitalism that sees profits as a moral pursuit, and the Puritan tradition as represented by Richard Baxter. Weber wrote:

> [Chapter 2] In the title of this study is used the somewhat pretentious phrase, the spirit of capitalism. What is to be understood by it? The attempt to give anything like a definition of it brings out certain difficulties which are in the very nature of this type of investigation. . . .
>
> We turn to a document of that spirit which contains what we are looking for in almost classical purity, and at the same time has the advantage of being free from all direct relationship to religion, being thus for our purposes, free of preconceptions.
>
> "*Remember, that time is money. He that can earn ten shillings a day by his labor, and goes abroad, or sits idle, one half of that day, though he spends but sixpence during his diversion or idleness, ought not to reckon that the only expense; he has really spent, rather thrown away, five shillings,* besides.
>
> "Remember, that credit is money. If a man lets his money lie in my hands after it is due, he gives me interest, or so much as I can make of it during that time. This amounts to a considerable sum where a man has good and large credit, and makes good use of it.
>
> "Remember, that money is of the prolific, generating nature. *Money can beget money, and its offspring can beget more, and so*

on. Five shillings turned is six, turned again it is seven and three pence, and so on, till it becomes a hundred pounds. The more there is of it, the more it produces every turning, so that the profits rise quicker and quicker. He that kills a breeding sow, destroys all her offspring to the thousandth generation. He that murders a crown, destroys all that it might have produced, even scores of pounds."

"Remember this saying, *The good paymaster is lord of another man's purse. He that is known to pay punctually and exactly to the time he, promises, may at any time, and on any occasion, raise all the money his friends can spare.* This is sometimes of great use. After industry and frugality, nothing contributes more to the raising of a young man in the world than punctuality and justice in all his dealings; therefore never keep borrowed money an hour beyond the time you promised, lest a disappointment shut up your friend's purse for ever.

"The most trifling actions that affect a man's credit are to be regarded. The sound of your hammer at five in the morning, or eight at night, heard by a creditor, makes him easy six months longer; but if he sees you at a billiard table, or hears your voice at a tavern, when you should be at work, he sends for his money the next day; demands it, before he can receive it, in a lump. *'It shows, besides, that you are mindful of what you owe; it makes you appear a careful as well as an honest man, and that still increases your credit.'*

"Beware of thinking all your own that you possess, and of living accordingly. It is a mistake that many people who have credit fall into. *To prevent this, keep an exact account for some time both of your expenses and your income.* If you take the pains at first to mention particulars, it will have this good effect: you will discover how wonderfully small, trifling expenses mount up to large sums, and will discern what might have been, and may for the future be saved, without occasioning any great inconvenience.

"For six pounds a year you may have the use of one hundred pounds, provided you are a man of known prudence and honesty.

"He that spends a groat a day idly, spends idly above six

pounds a year, which is the price for the use of one hundred pounds.

"He that wastes idly a groat's worth of his time per day, one day with another, wastes the privilege of using one hundred pounds each day.

"He that idly loses five shillings' worth of time, loses five shillings, and might as prudently throw five shillings into the sea.

"He that loses five shillings, not only loses that sum, but all the advantage that might be made by turning it in dealing, which by the time that a young man becomes old, will amount to a considerable sum of money."

It is Benjamin Franklin who preaches to us in these sentences. . . . Let us pause a moment to consider this passage, the philosophy of which Kurnberger sums up in the words, "They make tallow out of cattle and money out of men." The peculiarity of this philosophy of avarice appears to be the ideal of the honest man of recognized credit, and above all the idea of a duty of the individual toward the increase of his capital, which is assumed as an end in itself. *Truly what is here preached is not simply a means of making one's way in the world, but a peculiar ethic.* The infraction of its rules is treated not as foolishness but as *forgetfulness of duty.* That is the essence of the matter. It is not mere business astuteness, that sort of thing is common enough, it is an ethos. This is the quality which interests us. . . .

The concept spirit of capitalism is here used in this specific sense, it is the spirit of modern capitalism. For that we are here dealing only with Western European and American capitalism is obvious from the way in which the problem was stated. Capitalism existed in China, India, Babylon, in the classic world, and in the Middle Ages. But in all these cases, as we shall see, this particular ethos was lacking . . .

In fact, the *summum bonum* of his ethic, the earning of more and more money, combined with the strict avoidance of all spontaneous enjoyment of life, is above all completely devoid of any eudaemonistic, not to say hedonistic, admixture. It is thought of so purely as an end in itself, that from the point of view of the happiness of, or utility to, the single individual, it appears entirely transcendental and absolutely irrational. Man is dominated by the making of money, by acquisition as the ultimate purpose of his life. Economic acquisition is no longer subordinated to man as the means for the satisfaction of his material needs. This reversal of what we should call the natural relationship, so irrational from a naive point of view, is evidently as definitely a leading principle of capitalism as it is foreign to all peoples not under capitalistic influence. At the same time it expresses a type of feeling which is closely connected with certain religious ideas. If we thus ask, *why* should "money be made out of men," Benjamin Franklin himself, although he was a colorless deist, answers in his autobiography with a quotation from the Bible, which his strict Calvinistic father drummed into him again and again in his youth: "Seest thou a man diligent in his business? He shall stand before kings" (Prov. xxii. 29). The earning of money within the modern economic order is, so long as it is done legally, the result and the expression of virtue and proficiency in a calling; and this virtue and proficiency are, as it is now not difficult to see, the real Alpha and Omega of Franklin's ethic . . .

For the purposes of this chapter, though by no means for all purposes, we can treat ascetic Protestantism as a single whole. *But since that side of English Puritanism which was derived from Calvinism gives the most consistent religious basis for the idea of the calling, we shall, following our previous method, place one of its representatives at the centre of the discussion.* Richard Baxter stands out above many other writers on Puritan ethics, both because of his eminently practical and realistic attitude, and, at the same time, because of the universal recognition accorded to his works, which have gone through many new editions and translations. . . . His Christian Directory is the most compendium of Puritan ethics, and is adjusted to the practical experiences of his own ministerial activity . . .

Now, in glancing at Baxter's Saints' Everlasting Rest, or his Christian Directory, or similar works of others,' *one is struck at first glance by the emphasis placed, in the discussion of wealth and its acquisition,* on the ebionitic elements of the New [T]estament. Wealth as such is a great danger; its temptations never end and its pursuit is not only senseless as compared with the dominating importance of the Kingdom of God, but it-is morally suspect. Here asceticism seems to have turned much more sharply against the acquisition of earthly goods than it did in Calvin, who saw no hindrance to the effectiveness of the clergy in their wealth, but rather a thoroughly desirable enhancement of their prestige. Hence he permitted them to employ their means profitably. Examples of the condemnation of the pursuit of money and goods may be gathered without end from Puritan writings, and may be contrasted with the late mediaeval ethical literature, which was much more open-minded on this point. Moreover, these doubts were meant with perfect seriousness; only it is necessary to examine them somewhat more closely in order to understand their true ethical significance and implications. *The real moral objection is to relaxation in the security of possession, the enjoyment of wealth with the consequence of idleness and the temptations of the flesh, above all of distraction from the pursuit of a righteous life. In fact, it is only because possession involves this danger of relaxation that it is objectionable at all.* For the saints' everlasting rest is in the next world; on earth man must, to be certain of his state of grace, "do the works of him who sent him, as long as it is yet day." Not leisure and enjoyment, but only activity serves to increase the glory of God, according to the definite manifestations of His will.

Waste of time is thus the first and in principle the deadliest of sins. The span of human life is infinitely short and precious to make sure of one's own election. Loss of time through sociability, idle talk, luxury, even more sleep than is necessary for health, six to at most eight hours, is worthy of absolute moral condemnation. It does not yet hold, with Franklin, that time is money, but the proposition is true in a certain spiritual sense. It is infinitely valuable because every hour lost is lost to labour for the glory of God. Thus inactive contemplation is also valueless, or even directly reprehensible if it is at the expense of one's daily work. For it is less pleasing to God than the active performance of His will in a calling. Besides, Sunday is provided for that, and, according to Baxter, it is always those who are not diligent in their callings who have no time for God when the occasion demands it.

Accordingly, Baxter's principal work is dominated by the continually repeated, often almost passionate preaching of hard, continuous bodily or mental labour. . . . "Work hard in your calling." *But the most important thing was that even beyond that labour came to be considered in itself the end of life, ordained as such by God. St. Paul's "He who will not work shall not eat" holds unconditionally for every-one. Unwillingness to work is symptomatic of the lack of grace.*

Here the difference from the *medieval view-point* becomes quite evident. Thomas Aquinas also gave an interpretation of that statement of St. Paul. But for him labour is only necessary naturali ratione for *the maintenance of individual and community. Where this end is achieved, the precept ceases to have any meaning.* Moreover, it holds only for the race, not for every individual. It does not apply to anyone who can live without labour on his possessions, and of course contemplation, as a spiritual form of action in the Kingdom of God, takes precedence over the commandment in its literal sense. *Moreover, for the popular theology of the time, the highest form of monastic productivity lay in the increase of the Thesaurus ecclesie through prayer and chant.*

Now only do these exceptions to the duty to labour naturally no longer hold for Baxter, but he holds most emphatically that wealth does not exempt anyone from the unconditional command. Even the wealthy shall not eat without working, for even though they do not need to labour to support their own needs, there is God's commandment which they, like the poor, must obey. *For everyone without exception God's Providence has prepared a calling, which he should profess and in which he should labour.* And this calling is not, as it was for the Lutheran, a fate to which he must submit and which he must make the best of, but God's commandment to the individual to work for the divine glory. This seemingly subtle difference had far-reaching psychological consequences, and became connected with a further development of the providential interpretation of the economic order which had begun in scholasticism.

The phenomenon of the division of labour and occupations

in society had, among others, been interpreted by Thomas Aquinas, to whom we may most conveniently refer, as a direct consequence of the divine scheme of things. But the places assigned to each man in this cosmos follow ex causis naturalibus and are fortuitous (contingent in the Scholastic terminology). The differentiation of men into the classes and occupations established through historical development became for Luther, as we have seen, a direct result of the divine will. The perseverance of the individual in the place and within the limits which God had assigned to him was a religious duty. This was the more certainly the consequence since the relations of Lutheranism to the world were in general uncertain from the beginning and remained so. Ethical principles for the reform of the world could not be found in Luther's realm of ideas; in fact it never quite freed itself from Pauline indifference. Hence the world had to be accepted as it was, and this alone could be made a religious duty—But in the Puritan view, the providential character of the play of private economic interests takes on a somewhat different emphasis. True to the Puritan tendency to pragmatic interpretations, the *providential purpose of the division of labour is to be known by its fruits. On this point Baxter expresses himself in terms which more than once directly recall Adam Smith's well-known apotheosis of the division of labour. The specialization of occupations leads, since it makes the development of skill possible, to a quantitative and qualitative improvement in production, and thus serves the common good, which is identical with the good of the greatest possible number.* So far, the motivation is purely utilitarian, and is closely related to the customary view-point of much of the secular literature of the time.

But the characteristic Puritan element appears when Baxter sets at the head of his discussion the statement that "*outside of a well-marked calling the accomplishments of a man are only casual and irregular, and he spends more time in idleness than at work,*" and when he concludes it as follows: "*and he [the specialized worker) will carry out his work in order while another remains in constant confusion, and his business knows neither time nor place . . . therefore is a certain calling the best for everyone.*"

Irregular work, which the ordinary labourer is often forced to accept, is often unavoidable, but always an unwelcome state of transition. A man without a calling thus lacks the systematic, methodical character which is, as we have seen, demanded by worldly asceticism.

The Quaker ethic also holds that a man's life in his calling is an exercise in ascetic virtue, a proof of his state of grace through his conscientiousness, which is expressed in the care and method with which he pursues his calling. What God demands is not labour in itself, but rational labour in a calling. In the *Puritan concept of the calling the emphasis is always placed on this methodical character of worldly asceticism, not, as with Luther, on the acceptance of the lot which God has irretrievably assigned to man.*

Hence the question whether anyone may combine several callings is answered in the affirmative, if it is useful for the common good or one's own, and not injurious to anyone, and if it does not lead to unfaithfulness in one of the callings. Even a change of calling is by no means regarded as objectionable, if it is not thoughtless and is made for the purpose of pursuing a calling more pleasing to God, which means, on general principles, one more useful.

It is true that the usefulness of a calling, and thus its favour in the sight of God, is measured primarily in moral terms, and thus in terms of the importance of the goods produced in it for the community. But a further, and, above all, in practice the most important, criterion is found in private profitableness. For if that God, whose hand the Puritan sees in all the occurrences of life, shows one of His elect a chance of profit, he must do it with a purpose. Hence the faithful Christian must follow the call by taking advantage of the opportunity. "*If God show you a way in which you may lawfully get more than in another way (without wrong to your soul or to any other), if you refuse this, and choose the less gainful way, you cross one of the ends of your calling, and you refuse to be God's steward, and to accept His gifts and use them for Him, when He requireth it: you may labour to be rich for God, though not for the flesh and sin.*"

Wealth is thus bad ethically only in so far as it is a temptation to idleness and sinful enjoyment of life, and its acquisition is bad only when it is with the purpose of later living merrily and without care. But as a performance of duty in a calling it is not only morally permissible, but actually enjoined. The parable of the servant who was rejected because he did not increase the talent which was entrusted to him seemed to say so directly. To wish to be poor was, it was often argued, the same as wishing to be unhealthy; it is objectionable as a glorification of works and derogatory to the glory of God. Especially begging, on the part of one able to work, is not only the sin of slothfulness, but a violation of the duty of brotherly love according to the Apostle's own word. The emphasis on the ascetic importance of a fixed calling provided an ethical justification of the modern specialized division of labour. In a similar way the providential interpretation of profitmaking justified the activities of the business man. The superior indulgence of the seigneur and the parvenu ostentation of the nouveau riche are equally detestable to asceticism.

But, on the other hand, it has the highest ethical appreciation of the sober, middle-class, self-made Man. "God blesseth His trade" is a stock remark about those good men who had successfully followed the divine hints. The whole power of the God of the Old Testament, who rewards His people for their obedience in this life, necessarily exercised a similar influence on the Puritan who, following Baxter's advice, compared his own state of grace with that of the heroes of the Bible, and in the process interpreted the statements of the Scriptures as the articles of a book of statutes. . . .

The idea of a man's duty to his possessions, to which he subordinates himself as an obedient steward, or even as an acquisitive machine, bears with chilling weight on his life. The greater the possessions the heavier, if the ascetic attitude toward life stands the test, the feeling of responsibility for them, for holding them undiminished for the glory of God and increasing them by restless effort. The origin of this type of life also extends in certain roots, like so many aspects of the spirit of capitalism, back into the Middle Ages. *But it was in the ethic of ascetic Protestantism that it first found a consistent ethical founda-*

tion. Its significance for the development of capitalism is obvious. This worldly Protestant asceticism, as we may recapitulate up to this point, acted powerfully against the spontaneous enjoyment of possessions; it restricted consumption, especially of luxuries. On the other hand, it had the psychological effect of freeing the acquisition of goods from the inhibitions of traditionalistic ethics. It broke the bonds of the impulse of acquisition in that it not only legalized it, but (in the sense discussed) looked upon it as directly willed by God. The campaign against the temptations of the flesh, and the dependence on external things, was, as besides the Puritans the great Quaker apologist Barclay expressly says, not a struggle against the rational acquisition, but against the irrational use of wealth.

But this irrational use was exemplified in the outward forms of luxury which their code condemned as idolatry of the flesh, however natural they had appeared to the feudal mind. On the other hand, they approved the rational and utilitarian uses of wealth which were willed by God for the needs of the individual and the community. They did not wish to impose mortification on the man of wealth, but the use of his means for necessary and practical things. The idea of comfort characteristically limits the extent of ethically permissible expenditures. It is naturally no accident that the development of a manner of living consistent with that idea may be observed earliest and most clearly among the most consistent representatives of this whole attitude toward life. Over against the glitter and ostentation of feudal magnificence which, resting on an unsound economic basis, prefers a sordid elegance to a sober simplicity, they set the clean and solid comfort of the middle-class home as an ideal. . . .

When the limitation of consumption is combined with this release of acquisitive activity, the inevitable practical result is obvious: accumulation of capital through ascetic compulsion to save. The restraints which were imposed upon the consumption of wealth naturally served to increase it by making possible the productive investment of capital. How strong this influence was is not, unfortunately, susceptible to exact statistical demonstration. In New England the connection is so evident that it did not escape the eye of so discerning a historian as Doyle. But also in Holland, which was really only dominated by strict Calvinism for seven years, the greater simplicity of life in the more seriously religious circles, in combination with great wealth, led to an excessive propensity to accumulation...

We may hence quote here a passage from John Wesley himself which might well serve as a motto for everything which has been said above. For it shows that the leaders of these ascetic movements understood the seemingly paradoxical relationships which we have here analysed perfectly well, and in the same sense that we have given them. He wrote:

> *I fear, wherever riches have increased, the essence of religion has decreased in the same proportion.* Therefore I do not see how it is possible, in the nature of things, for any revival of true religion to continue long. For religion must necessarily produce both industry and frugality, and these cannot but produce riches. But as riches increase, so will pride, anger, and love of the world in all its branches. How then is it possible that Methodism, that is, a religion of the heart, though it flourishes now as a green bay tree, should continue in this state? For the Methodists in every place grow diligent and frugal; consequently they increase in goods. Hence they proportionately increase in pride, in anger, in the desire of the flesh, the desire of the eyes, and the pride of life. So, although the form of religion remains, the spirit is swiftly vanishing away. Is there no way to prevent this— this continual decay of pure religion? We ought not to prevent people from being diligent and frugal; we must exhort all Christians to gain all they can, and to save all they can; that is, in effect, to grow rich.

There follows the advice that those who gain all they can and save all they can should also give all they can, so that they will grow in grace and lay up a treasure in heaven. It is clear that Wesley here expresses, even in detail, just what we have been trying to point out. As Wesley here says, the full economic effect of those great religious movements, whose significance for economic development lay above all in their ascetic educative influence, generally came only after the peak of the purely religious enthusiasm was past. Then the intensity of the search for the Kingdom of God commenced gradually to pass over into sober economic virtue; the religious roots died out slowly, giving way to utilitarian worldliness. . . .

One of the fundamental elements of the spirit of modern capitalism, and not only of that but of all modern culture: rational conduct on the basis of the idea of the calling, was born—that is what this discussion has sought to demonstrate-from the *spirit of Christian asceticism.* One has only to reread the passage from Franklin, quoted at the beginning of this essay, in order to see that *the essential elements of the attitude which was there called the spirit of capitalism are the same as what we have just shown to be the content of the Puritan worldly asceticism, only without the religious basis, which by Franklin's time had died away.* . . .

The Puritan wanted to work in a calling; we are forced to do so. For when asceticism was carried out of monastic cells into everyday life, and began to dominate worldly morality, it did its part in building the tremendous cosmos of the modern economic order. This order is now bound to the technical and economic conditions of machine production which today determine the lives of all the individuals who are born into this mechanism, not only those directly concerned with economic acquisition, with irresistible force. Perhaps it will so determine them until the last ton of fossilized coal is burnt. In Baxter's view the care for external goods should only lie on the shoulders of the "saint like a light cloak, which can be thrown aside at any moment." But fate decreed that the cloak should become an iron cage.

While the above is a long and full citation of Weber's thinking, it omits the citation of the other chapter in his work of the *Westminster Confession of Faith.* Some observations are useful here. First, the action and attitude findings of asceticism and stewardship of time, talent, and goods is consistent with the questions and answers in the Ten Commandments cited above. Weber finds these as the grounding for modern capitalism and modern business. Second, Weber finds that profits form a fundamental moral dimension to the Protestant belief. He does not find it immoral, but does note that before the Reformation, profits were consumed, not reinvested, which then creates more profits. Third, we should see that Weber misses the essential reason for why the Protestant is hardworking and a bit ascetic—he serves his Creator God, question 106. It is the love of God, found in the magnificence of our salvation and the assurance that we will spend eternity with our Savior that compels the Protestant. Unfortunately, Weber did not see this; rather, he applied humanistic interpretations to actions in order to explain the Protestant's motive as a self-interest action as found in the Smith quotation.

So Weber affirms profits are moral and fundamental and derived from an ethic that is grounded in hard work and thriftiness. It is useful to note that these principles remain valid today. So we turn to the last author to get a complete contrast.

KARL MARX'S REPUDIATION OF CAPITALISM AND PROFITS

The Communist agenda is clearly defined in Marx's *Communist Manifesto*.[12] To gain a sense of Communism's hostility to private property and therefore to the whole notion of capitalism and private property, consider this selection from *The Communist Manifesto*. The italicized portions are added to aid the reader in the points being made:

> In this sense, the theory of the Communists may be summed up in the single sentence: *Abolition of private property.*
>
> We Communists have been reproached with the desire of abolishing the right of personally acquiring property as the fruit of a man's own labor, which property is alleged to be the groundwork of all personal freedom, activity and independence.
>
> Hard-won, self-acquired, self-earned property! Do you mean the property of petty artisan and of the small peasant, a form of property that preceded the bourgeois form? There is no need to abolish that; the development of industry has to a great extent already destroyed it, and is still destroying it daily.

Or do you mean the modern bourgeois private property?

But does wage labor create any property for the laborer? Not a bit. It creates capital, i.e., that kind of property which exploits wage labor, and which cannot increase except upon conditions of begetting a new supply of wage labor for fresh exploitation. Property, in its present form, is based on the antagonism of capital and wage labor. Let us examine both sides of this antagonism.

To be a capitalist, is to have not only a purely personal, but a social STATUS in production. Capital is a collective product, and only by the united action of many members, nay, in the last resort, only by the united action of all members of society, can it be set in motion.

Capital is therefore not only personal; it is a social power.

When, therefore, capital is converted into common property, into the property of all members of society, personal property is not thereby transformed into social property. It is only the social character of the property that is changed. It loses its class character.

Let us now take wage labor.

The average price of wage labor is the minimum wage, i.e., that quantum of the means of subsistence which is absolutely requisite to keep the laborer in bare existence as a laborer. What, therefore, the wage laborer appropriates by means of his labor merely suffices to prolong and reproduce a bare existence. We by no means intend to abolish this personal appropriation of the products of labor, an appropriation that is made for the maintenance and reproduction of human life, and that leaves no surplus wherewith to command the labor of others. *All that we want to do away with is the miserable character of this appropriation, under which the laborer lives merely to increase capital, and is allowed to live only in so far as the interest of the ruling class requires it.*

In bourgeois society, living labor is but a means to increase accumulated labor. In communist society, accumulated labor is but a means to widen, to enrich, to promote the existence of the laborer.

In bourgeois society, therefore, the past dominates the present; in communist society, the present dominates the past. In bourgeois society, capital is independent and has individuality, while the living person is dependent and has no individuality.

And the abolition of this state of things is called by the bourgeois, abolition of individuality and freedom! And rightly so. The abolition of bourgeois individuality, bourgeois independence, and bourgeois freedom is undoubtedly aimed at.

By freedom is meant, under the present bourgeois conditions of production, free trade, free selling and buying.

But if selling and buying disappears, free selling and buying disappears also. This talk about free selling and buying, and all the other "brave words" of our bourgeois about freedom in general, have a meaning, if any, only in contrast with restricted selling and buying, with the fettered traders of the Middle Ages, but have no meaning when opposed to the communist abolition of buying and selling, or the bourgeois conditions of production, and of the bourgeoisie itself.

You are horrified at our intending to do away with private property. But in your existing society, private property is already done away with for nine-tenths of the population; *its existence for the few is solely due to its non-existence in the hands of those nine-tenths.* You reproach us, therefore, with intending to do away with a form of property, the necessary condition for whose existence is the non-existence of any property for the immense majority of society.

In one word, you reproach us with intending to do away with your property. Precisely so; that is just what we intend.

From the moment when labor can no longer be converted into capital, money, or rent, into a social power capable of being monopolized, i.e., from the moment when individual property can no longer be transformed into bourgeois property, into capital, from that moment, you say, *individuality vanishes.*

You must, therefore, confess that by "individual" you mean no other person than the bourgeois, than the middle-class owner of property. This person must, indeed, be swept out of the way, and made impossible.

Communism deprives no man of the power to appropriate the products of society; all that it does is to deprive him of the power to subjugate the labor of others by means of such appropriations.

It has been objected that upon the abolition of private property, all work will cease, and universal laziness will overtake us.

According to this, bourgeois society ought long ago to have gone to the dogs through sheer idleness; *for those who acquire anything, do not work.* The whole of this objection is but another expression of the tautology: There can no longer be any wage labor when there is no longer any capital.

All objections urged against the communistic mode of producing and appropriating material products, have, in the same way, been urged against the communistic mode of producing and appropriating intellectual products. Just as to the bourgeois, the disappearance of class property is the disappearance of production itself, so the disappearance of class culture is to him identical with the disappearance of all culture.

That culture, the loss of which he laments, is, for the enormous majority, a mere training to act as a machine.

But don't wrangle with us so long as you apply, to our intended abolition of bourgeois property, the standard of your bourgeois notions of freedom, culture, law, etc. Your very ideas are but the outgrowth of the conditions of your bourgeois production and bourgeois property, just as your jurisprudence is but the will of your class made into a law for all, a will whose essential character and direction are determined by the economical conditions of existence of your class.

The selfish misconception that induces you to transform into eternal laws of nature and of reason the social forms stringing from your present mode of production and form of property—historical relations that rise and disappear in the progress of production—this misconception you share with every ruling class that has preceded you. What you see clearly in the case of ancient property, what you admit in the case of feudal property, you are of course forbidden to admit in the case of your own bourgeois form of property. . . .

[Omitted are precepts on family, marriage, and nations.]

"Undoubtedly," it will be said, "religious, moral, philosophical, and juridical ideas have been modified in the course of historical development. But religion, morality, philosophy, political science, and law, constantly survived this change.

"*There are, besides, eternal truths, such as Freedom, Justice, etc.*, that are common to all states of society. But communism abolishes eternal truths, it abolishes all religion, and all morality, instead of constituting them on a new basis; it therefore acts in contradiction to all past historical experience."

What does this accusation reduce itself to? The history of *all past society has consisted in the development of class antagonisms,* antagonisms that assumed different forms at different epochs.

But whatever form they may have taken, one fact is common to all past ages, viz., *the exploitation of one part of society by the other.* No wonder, then, that the social consciousness of past ages, despite all the multiplicity and variety it displays, moves within certain common forms, or general ideas, which cannot completely vanish except with the total disappearance of class antagonisms.

The communist revolution is the most radical rupture with traditional relations; no wonder that its development involved the most radical rupture with traditional ideas.

But let us have done with the bourgeois objections to communism.

We have seen above that the first step in the revolution by the working class is to raise the proletariat to the position of ruling class to win the battle of democracy.

The proletariat will use its political supremacy to wrest, by degree, all capital from the bourgeoisie, to centralize all instruments of production in the hands of the state, i.e., of the proletariat organized as the ruling class; and to increase the total productive forces as rapidly as possible.

Of course, in the beginning, this cannot be effected except by means of despotic inroads on the rights of property, and on the conditions of bourgeois production; by means of measures, therefore, which appear economically insufficient and untenable, but which, in the course of the movement, outstrip themselves, necessitate further inroads upon the old social order, and are unavoidable as a means of entirely revolutionizing the mode of production.

These measures will, of course, be different in different

countries.

Nevertheless, in most advanced countries, the following will be pretty generally applicable:

- *Abolition of property in land and application of all rents of land to public purposes.*
- *A heavy progressive or graduated income tax.*
- *Abolition of all rights of inheritance.*
- *Confiscation of the property of all emigrants and rebels.*
- *Centralization of credit in the banks of the state, by means of a national bank with state capital and an exclusive monopoly.*
- *Centralization of the means of communication and transport in the hands of the state.*
- *Extension of factories and instruments of production owned by the state; the bringing into cultivation of waste lands, and the improvement of the soil generally in accordance with a common plan.*
- *Equal obligation of all to work. Establishment of industrial armies, especially for agriculture.*
- *Combination of agriculture with manufacturing industries; gradual abolition of all the distinction between town and country by a more equable distribution of the populace over the country.*
- *Free education for all children in public schools. Abolition of children's factory labor in its present form. Combination of education with industrial production, etc.*

When, in the course of development, class distinctions have disappeared, and all production has been concentrated in the hands of a vast association of the whole nation, the public power will lose its political character. Political power, properly so called, is merely the organized power of one class for oppressing another. If the proletariat during its contest with the bourgeoisie is compelled, by the force of circumstances, to organize itself as a class; if, by means of a revolution, it makes itself the ruling class, and, as such, sweeps away by force the old conditions of production, then it will, along with these conditions, have swept away the conditions for the existence of class antagonisms and of classes generally, and will thereby have abolished its own supremacy as a class.

In place of the old bourgeois society, with its classes and class antagonisms, we shall have an association in which the free development of each is the condition for the free development of all.

CONCLUSION

Clearly, in the biblical system of ethics, profit is godly if it is gained in God's way. And surprisingly, this means that *not* making a profit may also be a sin against God, one's neighbor and oneself!

Adam Smith established by rational evaluation that profit making was an inherent part of human conduct as it worked itself out in the social environment of human culture. What Adam Smith described was actually a traditional perspective of the Reformed tradition as evidenced by Max Weber. This is not only evident in Weber's analysis, however. It is in fact established by a careful reading of the Reformed tradition's classic ethical treatise, the *Westminster Larger Catechism.* And this serves to underscore how an inherent hostility to profits gained in a just manner is actually an expression of the socialistic spirit that emanates from Marx's *Communist Manifesto.*

While there clearly can be "obscene profits" under the Calvinistic system, that is, a violation of one's duty to God and man in acquiring profits, it must also be maintained that profit making itself is not inherently obscene. If such were not the case, the parable of the talents given by our Lord could not righteously include the words to the unfaithful steward in Matthew 25:26–27, "His master replied, 'You wicked, lazy servant! So you knew that I harvest where I have not sown and gather where I have not scattered seed? Well then, you should have put my money on deposit with the bankers, so that when I returned I would have received it back with interest'" (NIV).

We trust that this study has been a *profitable* undertaking for all who have engaged the business themes of this article!

Notes

1. *Westminster Confession* (Glasgow: Bell and Bain first published 1646, repr. 2001 containing the *Westminster Larger Catechism* approved 1648).
2. Adam Smith, *The Wealth of Nations,* (New York: Bantam Classic, first published 1776, repr. 2003).
3. Max Weber, *The Protestant Ethic and the Spirit of Capitalism* (NewYork: Scribner, 1958). *The Protestant Ethic and the Spirit of Capitalism* was first published in German in 1904.
4. Karl Marx and Friedrich Engels, *Communist Manifesto,* public domain, first published in German in1848.

5. The following Bible passages illustrate such principles:
   - Second Kings 6:24–7:20 manifests the laws of supply and demand, profits, and just war.
   - Acts 5:1–11 emphasizes the rights of private property and stands as an apostolic indictment against Christian communitarian or communistic economic ethics.
   - Exodus 20:15 commands man not to steal from his neighbor, thus emphasizing, when expressed positively, the right to private property. The story of Naboth's vineyard in 1 Kings 21 stands as a condemnation of the greed of the state over against the property rights of the individual.
   - Paul's teaching in 1 Timothy 6:3–19 shows that wealth is a gift of God and that compassion is a choice of the believer, not a mandate of the church or the state.
6. Because of the use of the Internet to find material such as the *Catechism* and the number format of the questions, no page references to the published book are given in footnote 1.
7. John C. Maxwell, *There's No Such Thing as "Business" Ethics: There's Only One Rule for Making Decisions* (New York: Warner Books, 2003).
8. A number of other books endeavor to take similar use of the Ten Commandments as a model for business ethics, such as Wes Cantrell and James R. Lucas, *High-Performance Ethics: 10 Timeless Principles for Next-Generation Leadership* (Carol Stream: Tyndale, 2007).
9. Hernando De Soto, *The Mystery of Capital: Why Capitalism Triumphs in the West and Fails Everywhere Else* (New York: Basic, 2003).
10. The ninth commandment questions and answers are included here due to space limitations. But the reader is encouraged to see the depth of care we are to take in our dealings with our business colleagues.

Question 143: Which is the ninth commandment?

Answer: The ninth commandment is, Thou shalt not bear false witness against thy neighbor.

Question 144: What are the duties required in the ninth commandment?

Answer: The duties required in the ninth commandment are, the preserving and promoting of truth between man and man, and the good name of our neighbor, as well as our own; appearing and standing for the truth; and from the heart, sincerely, freely, clearly, and fully, *speaking the truth, and only the truth, in matters of judgment and justice, and in all other things: Whatsoever; a charitable esteem of our neighbors; loving, desiring, and rejoicing in their good name; sorrowing for, and covering of their infirmities; freely acknowledging of their gifts and graces, defending their innocency; a ready receiving of a good report, and unwillingness to admit of an evil report, concerning them; discouraging talebearers, flatterers, and slanderers; love and care of our own good name, and defending it when need requires; keeping of lawful promises; studying and practicing of: Whatsoever things are true, honest, lovely, and of good report.*

Question 145: What are the sins forbidden in the ninth commandment?

Answer: The sins forbidden in the ninth commandment are, *all prejudicing the truth, and the good name of our neighbors, as well as our own, especially in public judicature; giving false evidence, suborning false witnesses, wittingly appearing and pleading for an evil cause, outfacing and overbearing the truth; passing unjust sentence, calling evil good, and good evil; rewarding the wicked according to the work of the righteous, and the righteous according to the work of the wicked; forgery, concealing the truth, undue silence in a just cause, and holding our peace when iniquity calls for either a reproof from ourselves, or complaint to others; speaking the truth unseasonably, or maliciously to a wrong end, or perverting it to a wrong meaning, or in doubtful and equivocal expressions, to the prejudice of truth or justice; speaking untruth, lying, slandering, backbiting, detracting, tale bearing, whispering, scoffing, reviling, rash, harsh, and partial censuring; misconstructing intentions, words, and actions;*

flattering, vainglorious boasting, thinking or speaking too highly or too meanly of ourselves or others; denying the gifts and graces of God; aggravating smaller faults; hiding, excusing, or extenuating of sins, when called to a free confession; unnecessary discovering of infirmities; raising false rumors, receiving and countenancing evil reports, and stopping our ears against just defense; evil suspicion; envying or grieving at the deserved credit of any, endeavoring or desiring to impair it, rejoicing in their disgrace and infamy; scornful contempt, fond admiration; breach of lawful promises; neglecting such things as are of good report, and practicing, or not avoiding ourselves, or not hindering: What we can in others, such things as procure an ill name.

11. A Christian worldview discussion of the implications of the concepts underlying division of labor are beyond the scope of this paper. However, the concept of increasing the productivity of labor is indeed consistent with the *Catechism* and is noted in Weber's material.

12. Although lesser-known communist movements have existed, the type we know of today is best explained by Karl Marx in his treatise *The Communist Manifesto* (in Karl Marx, *Selected Writings*, ed. David McLellan [Oxford, UK: Oxford University Press, 1977], 221–47) The Communist league was started largely under the leadership of Marx and Engels in June 1847. It linked the main centers of Communist activities in Paris, London, Brussels, and Cologne. At the request of this League, Marx wrote the Manifesto, which was first published in Brussels in February 1848. Marx wrote: "I. Communism is already acknowledged by all European Powers to be itself a Power. II. It is high time that Communists should openly, in the efface of the whole world, publish their views, their aims, their tendencies, and meet this nursery tale of the Spectre of Communism with a Manifesto of the party itself" (222). With the Bolshevik Revolution in 1917, seventy years after the Communist League was formed, the czar of Russia was toppled and the world experienced the first Communist nation in history.

The fact that Christianity has been open to the allure of Communism under the cloaks of "Christian Communism" or "Liberation Theology" or "Christian Socialism" is anticipated by Marx's remarks in the *Manifesto*: "Nothing is easier than to give Christian asceticism a socialist tinge. Has not Christianity declaimed against private property, against marriage, against the state? Has it not preached in the place of these, charity and poverty, celibacy and mortification of the flesh, monastic life and Mother Church? Christian socialism is but the holy water with which the priest consecrates the heart-burnings of the aristocrat."

FOR LOVE OR MONEY?
THE ETHICS OF PROFITS
IN GOD'S WORLD

DR. PETER A. LILLBACK
EDITED BY PHILIP CLEMENTS

PETER LILLBACK

Doctor Peter A. Lillback is President and Professor of Historical Theology at Westminster Theological Seminary located in Philadelphia and the senior pastor of Proclamation Presbyterian Church in Bryn Mawr, Pennsylvania. Lillback also serves as the President of The Providence Forum, the nonprofit organization that is committed to preserving and promoting America's spiritual roots of religious and civil liberties.

Living between Philadelphia and Valley Forge for many years, Dr. Lillback has pursued an avid interest in the history of the Judeo-Christian heritage of the United States. He has done much research and study on the founding and Founders of our nation through examination of original source documents in numerous libraries and archives. His books Freedom's Holy Light *and* Proclaim Liberty *are outgrowths of his research. In 2006, Dr. Lillback's bestseller on the Christian faith of George Washington was released.* George Washington's Sacred Fire *represents the culmination of over twenty years of original research and scholarship. In May 2010, the paperback reached #1 on Amazon.com.*

Lillback is a frequent lecturer on many worldview issues and has debated Barry Lynn, president of Americans United for the Separation of Church and State and appeared on panels broadcast by C-Span. He is the voice of Proclaiming the Word, *a fifteen-minute Bible teaching radio and television program, which airs weekdays across the country.*

His primary passion in life is serving the Lord wherever he is called. As a result of being in ministry, he has enjoyed the privilege to teach and preach in numerous missions, popular and scholarly contexts. These experiences have only increased his love for travel.

He has an avid interest in all things historical—especially theology and American history—and enjoys researching original sources. For fun, he plays a Liberty Tree Guitar. He loves to hike when possible, both locally and on vacations, and has hiked up mountainsides around the globe.

In addition to Greek and Hebrew, he reads French for fun and continues to improve his speaking ability, aiding in his role with the Huguenot Fellowship.

Dr. Lillback considers himself a "generalist." Those who work with him see him as a "servant leader" who seeks to do any job that is required, including taking out the trash, moving boxes, cleaning floors, etc. He is known for his gifts as a teacher, preacher, and mediator. He is a visionary who can see potentials and connections which are not always obvious to others and, thus, has been successful at starting many new ministries and initiatives.

Doctor Lillback grew up in Painesville, Ohio, the middle of three boys. He lives in Wayne, Pennsylvania, with his wife, Debbie. They have two grown daughters.

The story is told of a youthful capitalist university student who attended a convention of socialist economists. The Master of Ceremonies of the convention called on the throng to raise their hands if they were committed to the tenets of socialism. A sea of hands was thrust into the air. Then the MC asked if there were any capitalists in the crowd, and if so that they too should raise their hands. Sheepishly, the student raised his hand—the only one visible in the entire hall. At this the MC laughingly asked, "Why in the world are you a capitalist?" The student hesitatingly, but clearly replied, "My great grandfather was a capitalist. My grandfather was a capitalist. My father was a capitalist. So that's why I'm a capitalist." Without missing a beat, the MC thundered, "If your great grandfather was a fool, and your grandfather was a fool and your father was fool, what would that make you?" To which the student answered, "A socialist, I guess."

I am not sure how many here today are capitalists or socialists, but we do know that a great deal of economic folly from capitalists and socialists alike parades before us wearing the masks of wisdom.

I. Can Capitalism Be Done to the Glory of God?

The question before us is "Do we do business for love or for money?" Is the profit motive the reason for business, or, is love the motive for profits? Is our entrepreneurial activity the pursuit of gold or the pursuit of God? Scripture's warning and commands concerning what we are to love are clear:

The love of money is the root of all kinds of evil.

Love your neighbor as you love yourself.

Love the Lord your God with all your heart, with all your soul and with all your mind and with all your strength.

Such love glorifies God. There are other ways to state our concern here: "Can one glorify God in God's world through business success and profitability?" Can this be done if our enterprises are motivated by the golden rule instead of the rule of gold? The golden rule, after all, is not, the man with the gold makes the rules, rather it is, "Do unto others as you would have them do unto you." In this context, the motive for profit is not greed or the love of money. Instead the motive for profits is love for God and love for one's neighbor.

The historic Judeo-Christian perspective holds that the Ten Commandments should be the paradigm of business ethics. With that commitment in mind, this study seeks to remove the ignorance regarding the legitimate creation of wealth and profit which is sounder assault today. Here we seek to arm business and theological leaders with the basic insights they need to justify and defend the free enterprise system. Specifically, we look at the shifting social foundations in which business operates today, including continued adoption of communistic ideals and post modern selfishness. Then we review the reasons that schools cannot teach ethics. Finally, we see the importance of understanding the balance between self-interest and selfishness in God's world.

II. The Ethical Crisis at the Heart of the Business Crisis of 2008

Everyone knows that business is about making money. But the business crisis emanating from the real estate market that has swept the global economy has highlighted other economic concerns as well, such as bail-outs, constructive destruction of competitors; survival of the fittest; anti-trust laws, the governmental control of private enterprises. The profit motive has fallen under severe scrutiny with demands for more government controls for a more equitable distribution of wealth.

But do all profits require the adjectives dirty or obscene? What are the ethics of profits in God's world? Is the love of money, which according to Scripture is the root of all kinds of evil, indistinguishable from making money by loving God and one's neighbor?

As socialist economics continues to see personal profit as wrong and social or community enrichment as the only grounds for business, the need has arisen for a renewed analysis of the ethics of profits so that one can clearly distinguish moral business from immoral business. It has been argued that when businesses make profits in an immoral way, they will eventually fail. As Sir John Templeton noted, "if a business is not ethical, it will fail, perhaps not right away, but eventually." [1] Simply put, for capitalism to succeed there must be a virtuous circle of everyday trust between the people who conduct business.

Consider the contrast between the following:

> The evolution of capitalism has been in the direction of more trust and transparency and less [purely]self-serving behavior; not coincidentally, this evolution has brought with it greater productivity and economic growth…Not because capitalists are naturally good people, [but] because the benefits of trust – of being trusting and of being trustworthy are potentially immense, and because a successful market system teaches people to recognize those benefits…a virtuous circle in which an everyday level of trustworthiness breeds an everyday level of trust. [2]

> The public lost trust in business and some of our graduates seem to be responsible for that." [3]

The wealth and greatness of America can be traced, in part, to the economic fundamentals of the free market system which were embraced from the earliest days of the founding of this nation. And while the free enterprise economic system has always had detractors, the financial meltdown of 2009 has even ardent free enterprise advocates questioning the ethics and societal benefits of this system. However, to argue that the free enterprise system is morally bankrupt, one has already assumed that the system has moral and ethical principles and brings value to society.

For example, the Templeton Prize for Ethics and Values states,

> Ethical behavior tends to be rewarded in a free market, since business success requires establishing trust, finding profitable

opportunities to provide value to others, and delaying gratification in order to save and invest. At the same time, institutions of free enterprise themselves depend upon ethical practices, and can be seriously undermined by unethical practices.

It is clear that the debate on the merits of an economic system that many consider soulless is going to continue, particularly as the competing economic system of socialism continues to gain adherents in American government and society. It is critical thus not only to understand the history and basis of the American free enterprise system, but more importantly to see if the nature of this economic system can indeed provide instruction in the very ethics that are required to sustain itself.

Congressman Ron Paul said in 2002:

> Ignorance, as well as disapproval for the natural restraints placed on market excesses that capitalism and sound markets impose, cause our present leaders to reject capitalism and blame it for all the problems we face. If this fallacy is not corrected and capitalism is even further undermined, the prosperity that the free market generates will be destroyed.

III. The Socialist Challenge to the Capitalistic View of Profits: Marx, Alinsky and Tucson's Ethnic Studies Program

But it's not just the destruction of the prosperity of the free market that is at stake, but the destruction of the free market itself. This, of course, was the revolutionary vision of Karl Marx, the father of dialectical materialism or Communism as it is more popularly called. [4]

The Communist league was started largely under the leadership of Marx and Engles in June 1847. It linked the main centers of Communist activities in Paris, London, Brussels, and Cologne. At the request of this League, Marx wrote the *Manifesto* which was first published in Brussels in February 1848.

Marx wrote: "I. Communism is already acknowledged by all European Powers to be itself a Power. II. It is high time that Communists should openly, in the face of the whole world, publish their views, their aims, and their tendencies, and meet this nursery tale of the Spectre of Communism with a Manifesto of the party itself." (P. 222.)

With the Bolshevik Revolution in 1917, 70 years after the Communist League was formed, the Czar of Russia was toppled and the world experienced the first Communist nation in history.

Marx explained the basic conception of Communism in terms of class struggle: the class struggle between the Bourgeois (Industrialists/Capitalists) and Proletarians (modern working class or laborers). He declares, "The history of all hitherto existing society is the history of class struggles." (p. 222)

The Aims of Communism according to Marx can be summarized by the following points:
1. "The immediate aim of the Communists is...overthrow of the bourgeois supremacy, conquest of political power by the proletariat."
2. "In this sense, the theory of the Communists may be summed up on the single sentence: Abolition of private property."
3. "Abolition of the Family! Even the most radical flare up at this infamous proposal of the Communists.
4. "On what foundation is the present family, the bourgeois family, based? On capital.
5. "But, you will say, we destroy the most hallowed of relations, when we replace home education by social....
6. "But you communists would introduce community of women.
7. The Communists are further reproached with desiring to abolish countries and nationality.
8. The charges against Communism made from a religious, a philosophical, and generally, from an ideological standpoint, are not deserving of serious examination. (Pp. 222ff.)

And Marxist ideology has had its impact in America in various forms as well. Consider, for example, Saul Alinsky's *Rules for Radicals*. [5] Alinsky's socialistic thought has been seen by many as an American application of Marx's call for revolution to create economic change. Alinsky explains the purpose of his book when he writes,

> What follows is for those who want to change the world from what it is to what they believe it should be. *The Prince* was

written by Machiavelli for the Haves on how to hold power. *Rules for Radicals* is written for the Have-Nots on how to take it away....We are talking about a mass power organization which will change the world into a place where all men and women walk erect, in the spirit of that credo of the Spanish Civil War, "Better to die on your feet than to live on your knees." This means revolution. (p.3.)

The back cover of a recent printing of Alinsky's *Rules* quotes the *Chicago Sun-Times* that notes his significant influence on leading American political leaders:

> Alinsky's techniques and teaching influenced generations of community and labor organizers, including the church-based group hiring a young [Barack] Obama to work on Chicago's South Side in the 1980's....Alinsky impressed a young [Hillary] Clinton, who was growing up in Park Ridge at the time Alinsky was the director of the Industrial Areas Foundation in Chicago."

A foundational aspect of Alinsky's *Rules* is an emphatic call for a reappraisal of the ethics of the means and the ends of political or social action.

> That perennial question, "Does the end justify the means?" is meaningless as it stands; the real and only question regarding the ethics of means and ends is, and always has been, "Does this *particular* end justify this *particular* means?" (p. 23.)

> I present here a series of rules pertaining to the ethics of means and ends: first, that *one's concern with the ethics of means and ends varies inversely with one's personal interest in the issue.* When we are not directly concerned our morality overflows; as La Rochefoucauld put it, "We all have strength enough to endure the misfortunes of others." Accompanying this rule is the parallel one that *one's concern with the ethics of means and ends varies inversely with one's distance from the scene of conflict.* (p. 26.)

Life and how you live it is the story of means and ends. The end is what you want, and the means is how you get it. Whenever we think about social change, the question of means and ends arises. The man of action views the issue of means and ends in pragmatic and strategic terms. He has no other problem; he thinks only of his actual resources and the possibilities of various choices of action. He asks of ends only whether they are achievable and worth the cost; of means, only whether they will work. To say that corrupt means corrupt the ends is to believe in the immaculate conception of ends and principles. The real arena is corrupt and bloody. Life is a corrupting process from the time a child learns to play his mother off against his father in the politics of when to go to bed; he who fears corruption fears life. The practical revolutionary will understand Goethe's "conscience is the virtue of observers and not of agents of action"; in action, one does not always enjoy the luxury of a decision that is consistent both with one's individual conscience and the good of mankind. The choice must always be for the latter. Action is for mass salvation and not for the individual's personal salvation. (pp. 24-25).

But even if means and ends are entirely relative in his rules for radicals, the appearance of morality is still "indispensable at all times".

Moral rationalization is indispensable at all times of action whether to justify the selection or the use of ends or means. Machiavelli's blindness to the necessity for moral clothing to all acts and motives—he said "politics has no relation to morals"—was his major weakness. (p. 43.)

If this appears rather diabolical in character, Alinsky would likely count that epithet as something of a compliment given that his dedication in *Rules for Radicals* asserts:

Lest we forget at least an over-the-shoulder acknowledgment to the very first radical: from all our legends, mythology, and history (and who is to know where mythology leaves off and history begins—or which is which), the first radical known to man who rebelled against the establishment and did it so effectively that he at least won his own kingdom—Lucifer. (opening quotes.)

A direct result of the Marx-Alinsky assault on American capitalism and the celebration of the socialist perspective has been the development of educational materials that take this perspective. A recent example of Alinskyesque socialist thought in the American context can be found in "An Epic Poem" that is included in a Tucson, Arizona ethnic studies program designed for third to twelfth grades that attacks capitalism claiming that it is an assault on chicanos and is based on greed. This poem says in part:

> We have to destroy capitalism…The Declaration of Independence states that we the people have the right to revolution, the right to overthrow a government that has committed abuses and seeks complete control over the people. This is in order to clean out the corrupted, rotten officials that developed out of any type of capitalistic systems. [6]

IV. "Greed Is Good": The Impact of Post-Modernity on Popular Culture and Business Ethics

But simultaneously with the emergence of socialistic and Marxist economics, we are also living in the aftermath of a great sea change that occurred in the sixties as the cultural expression of Christianity began to evaporate from our popular culture. I grew up in the 60's when our present culture was then known as the "counter-culture." Jim Morrison from the Doors sang songs like, "Hello, I love you won't you tell me your name?" Love had become erotic in meaning. More recently we've seen a move in our culture beyond erotic love to include narcissistic love. Witness here Whitney Houston's song, "I've found the greatest love of all, it's happening to me. . . it's deep inside of me."

And we must not think that this influence is not impacting the Church in our day. J.I. Packer writes, "Modern Christians tend to make satisfaction their religion. We show much more concern for self-fulfillment than for pleasing God." (*Keep in Step with the Spirit.*) David Wells states the following significant observations:

> In 1983, 87.8% of titles published by the eight largest religious publishers in America "dealt with subjects related to the self, its discovery and nature and the resolution of its problems and tensions." (p. 175.)

> In 1987 a study revealed "an accentuation of subjectivity and the virtual veneration of the self, exhibited in deliberate efforts to achieve self-understanding, self-improvement, and self-ful-fillment" (*No Place for Truth* (Eerdmans, 1992), Chapter IV entitled "Self-piety", p. 176, quoting James Hunter's *Evangeli-calism: The Coming Generation*, p. 65.)

Our modern world's hostility to the Judeo-Christian ethic grounded upon God's moral law found in the Ten Commandments became public and powerful in the revolutionary Sixties. The Courts and both our univer-sity and media intellectuals began to sing the Humanist chorus of human autonomy, values clarification, and a non-absolute or relativistic ethic. All references to God, the Bible, prayer, and the Ten Commandments had to go. As one of the founders of the sexual education program in America said, "The 'Thou shalt nots don't apply anymore."

But we've moved beyond the modern world into the post-modern era. What marks post-modernity? While this is a question that will be given various answers by scholars, appropriately so according to the spirit of post-modernity, it is both a rejection of the optimism of the scientific enterprise that was so much a part of modernity, and it is also a profound affirmation of expressive individualism and the inherent relativism that accompanies the claim that the self is the only truth in a world where there can be no truth except that which one makes for oneself. As Allan bloom wrote in *The Closing of the American Mind,*

> . . . today's university student believes one thing deeply. It has reached the status of an axiom. He is absolutely convinced that truth is relative, and he is astonished if anyone is fool-ish enough to challenge the point. This relativism is not the product of theoretical reasoning. It is, so the student believes, a moral postulate of a free society. He has been taught from childhood that the danger of absolutism is not error but intol-erance. Thus in our democratic society, openness is the highest virtue . . . the supreme insight is not to think you are right at

all.

In the postmodern view of tolerance, contemporary expressive individualism and relativism consider all truth claims as mere preferences and thus allow there to be many truths even though there is no truth.

But if the "Thou shalt nots" don't apply anymore, then why are we surprised that the first American generation to be raised without a moral compass finds it entirely within their prerogatives to pursue business goals simply for greed and self-enrichment?

And while our post-modern world has rejected truth claims it is simultaneously deeply influenced by philosophical materialism or atheism as well. Thus the rejection of God is either explicit as can be seen in the new atheism, or more subtle as in the overt secular commitment to a determinate materialism that only allows for time, change, matter and energy to interpret reality. Nevertheless, with C. S. Lewis, theists assert, "A creature revolting against a creator is revolting against the source of his own powers—including even his power to revolt...It is like the scent of a flower trying to destroy the flower." (*Preface to Paradise Lost*).

Chuck Colson in his classic article, "The Problem of Ethics: Why Good People Do Bad Things" writes,

> *Time* magazine, in its cover story on ethics, said what's wrong: "Hypocrisy, betrayal and greed unsettle a nation's soul." The *Washington Post* said that the problem has reached the point where "common decency can no longer be described as common." The *New Republic* magazine said, "There is a destructive sense that nothing is true and everything is permitted." I submit to you that when the *Washington Post*, the *New Republic* magazine, and Time magazine—which have never been known as bastions of conservative, biblical morality—begin to talk about some sort of ethical malaise, a line has been crossed. These aren't simply isolated instances, but rather a pattern emerging in American life. No institution has been more sensitive to this than Harvard. Former President Bok has given some extraordinary speeches decrying the loss of ethics in the American business community. I think some of you have seen the recent polls finding that business school students across America, by a two-to-one margin, believe that businesses

are generally unethical. It's a very fragile consensus that holds together trust in our institutions. When most business school students believe there aren't any ethical operations, you begin to wonder if something isn't affecting us a lot more broadly than isolated instances of misbehavior that have been exposed.... How can you have ethical behavior? The crisis of character is totally understandable when there are no absolute values. [7]

Greed and lust seem to be the engines for many as they redefine the American dream as a way to get everything one can to make them happy in the belief that the one who dies with the most toys wins.

Is there any surprise then that an increasing number of our leaders in Church, State and Business are often implicated in some type of ethical failure? We can sense this in accounts from the evening news frequently emanating from the business sphere: Enron, Tyco, Ponzi schemes, subprime mortgages, corporate bail-outs and trillions of dollars of federal international debt. Perhaps we are beginning to understand just how wrong the noted business leader Ivan Boesky was. Speaking at a UCLA Business School some years ago, he declared, "Greed is a good thing." Even Boesky has had substantial time to reconsider his business philosophy since he eventually spent three years in a federal prison.

V. "Intelligent Selfishness"? Why Harvard Business School Hasn't Taught Ethics

The development of the business school is an important and fascinating story. [8] The oldest top five business schools in America are The Wharton School of the University of Pennsylvania (1881), The University of Chicago Booth School (1898), The Hass School, Berkley (1898), The Tuck School at Dartmouth (1900), and Harvard Business School (1906). But our focus here, however, will be the history of teaching ethics at Harvard. [9]

In his "The Problem of Ethics: Why Good People Do Bad things", Charles Colson speaks of a "crisis in character" that is facing our country and America's business schools such as Harvard.

I believe we are experiencing today in our country what I choose to call a crisis of character: a loss of those inner restraints and virtues that prevent Western civilization from pandering to its own darker instincts.

If you look back through the history of Harvard, you'll see that President Elliott was as concerned about the development of character as he was about education. Plato once said, if you asked why we should educate someone "We educate them so that they become a good person, because good persons behave nobly." I believe we should be deeply concerned about the loss of what Edmund Burke called the traditional values of republican citizenship—words like value, honor, duty, responsibility, compassion, civility....

Why has this happened? I'm sure many of you studied philosophy in your undergraduate courses, and, if so, you are well aware that, through twenty-three centuries of Western civilization, we were guided by a shared set of assumptions that there was a transcendent value system. This was not always the Judeo-Christian value system, though I think the Judeo-Christian values were, as the eminent historian Christopher Dawson wrote, "the heart and soul of Western civilization." [10]

Colson notes that this has been a recent concern of Harvard's leadership: "No institution has been more sensitive to this than Harvard. Former President Bok has given some extraordinary speeches decrying the loss of ethics in the American business community." [11] As Nitin Nohria, the current President of Harvard Business School, recently said, "The public lost trust in business and some of our graduates seem to be responsible for that." [12] The ethical crisis facing business and the problems surrounding the teaching of business ethics have been broadly recognized by American Business Schools. [13]

In fact, Harvard's concern for ethics is not new and reflects the early Puritan tradition of Boston.

An 1846 pamphlet—entitled "Our First Men, A Calendar of Wealth, Fashion and Gentility"...reflected Boston's Puritan tradition: "It is no derogation, then, to the Boston aristocracy that it rests upon money. Money is something substantial. Every body knows that and feels it. Birth is a mere idea which grows every day more and more intangible." With wealth, however, came responsibilities. One such obligation was ethical conduct in business: for example, most business transactions in Boston were concluded with a handshake. One merchant of the period suggested that mercantile honor could only be compared with a woman's: "delicate and fragile," as he put it, the merchant's honor could not "bear the slightest stain." [14]

The ethical underpinnings of American business were boldly confirmed when George Baker, a prominent Boston banker and supporter of the Harvard business school spoke in Congressional hearings in December, 1912 in Congress' investigation of the famous "Money Trust". In his testimony, George Baker said, "There would not be much business done if it was not done on confidence." Baker's answer followed financier J. P. Morgan, who when asked to confirm that commercial credit was based on money or property, replied, "No, sir, the first thing is character." [15]

Throughout the history of the Harvard Business School, a concern for teaching ethics has been expressed. For example, F. W. Bird an early donor to the business school wrote, "Something should be done to teach a higher code of business morals." [16] But little headway was made on the project:

> When paper manufacturer F. W. Bird contributed $500 to the original subscription for the Business School, he took the opportunity to lobby for instruction in a "higher code of business morals." President A. Lawrence Lowell agreed—but suggested that such training should appear "an integral part of the principles that are explained or demonstrated."

> Thus began a debate that continues to this day. What is the appropriate place in a business school curriculum for "business morals"—which in today's terminology might include both ethics and certain aspects of human resource management?

> Dean Gay faced the question in the summer of 1908, as he drew up the School's initial curriculum. His decision to omit a course specifically devoted to ethical conduct caused some

consternation among the School's supporters. Boston lawyer Frederick P. Fish, for one, argued strongly in favor of ethical instruction, and particularly in the field of corporate finance. But Gay held firm.

"I decided not to have any courses on Business Ethics in the Business School," he explained, "but I have tried to choose our lecturers with reference to their standards in conduct of business. I believe with you that we should give some occasional lectures which seek to give our students some light on what is at present a very perplexing and not wholly solved problem. The difficulty is to find lecturers who can handle this theme in the proper spirit, at once practical and elevating, without being 'preachy.'" [17]

But the ethical crisis became even more intense as the developments of modern science began to impact the ethical arena. This reality prompted Harvard's President Abbott Lawrence Lowell and Business School Dean Wallace Donham to invite retiring British philosopher, Alfred North Whitehead to join the Harvard faculty.

First, and most important, was [Donham's] conviction that the industrialized nations of the West were facing a crisis—social, economic and spiritual—of unprecedented dimensions. This apocalyptic perception was shared by many intellectuals in the decades between the two world wars: that something at the core of Western society was unraveling. Many observers, including Wallace Donham, attributed that unraveling to the ascent of science and industry, and the concomitant decline of religion.

Donham had been impressed by his reading of British philosopher Alfred North Whitehead, who joined the Harvard University faculty in the fall of 1924…In the interests of both science and religion, Whitehead had argued, society needed to recognize the dangers inherent in scientific materialism, and guard against the misapplication of technologies. "It may be," wrote Whitehead, "that civilization will never recover from the bad climate which enveloped the introduction of machinery."...

The problems created by scientific materialism were human problems. Society had once turned to the legal profession for its "wise counselors" in these matters; but the law had lost its independent professional status, to a very large extent, by allowing itself to be transformed in the late 19th century into a servant of industry. Because religion was not likely to be reinstated to its position of moral authority, and because science and law could not lay claim to such authority, it fell to the business community to face what Donham saw as the critical social problem: the "control of the consequences of scientific development."...

...a student asked Donham how he reconciled this "social point of view" with the profit motive. It was, the dean admitted, a difficult question: "intelligent selfishness"—the stance of the enlightened capitalist of the early 20th century—was of only limited usefulness. "Getting control of all these forces is not a simple problem," he concluded. "It took two centuries for the English-speaking part of the race to get control of credits, of bills, mortgages, notes and so forth, to the point that they ceased to be weapons of oppression of the most serious sort, and the results of the industrial revolution are far more complicated. We face the necessity of socializing the results of science." [18]

Ultimately, Harvard's experiments at teaching business ethics have failed.

Instruction in business ethics had been an issue since the School's founding. Harvard President A. Lawrence Lowell had argued against a separate course on the subject, suggesting that students should instead encounter ethical questions in all their courses. Edwin Gay contemplated such a course in his original curriculum for the School, but concluded that it would be very difficult to teach.

Early in his tenure as Dean Wallace Donham decided that such a course could and should be taught. In his 1922 report to Lowell, he noted that instruction in business ethics was "much on the minds" of his faculty, and that the case method seemed to be the only sure means to the end. The professionalization of business demanded "a collection of cases on this subject and adequate class-room instruction to give it proper emphasis."

By 1924, however, Donham was not so confident in a March interview with the Boston *Globe*, he suggested that business as a profession was barely out of the "frontier stage," and that while some aspects of business, such as banking, had developed clear codes of conduct, the wide variety of business activities hindered the formulation of an effective, all-encompassing ethical code.

As was true of other subjects investigated by the School's field agents, business ethics had proved immensely complicated. "Imagine you are employed by an automobile plant which is experimenting with four-wheel brakes," Donham suggested to the Globe reporter. "Suppose a friend in a rival establishment catches you unprepared and suddenly inquires point-blank: 'Is your concern experimenting with four-wheel brakes?'

"Now, I'm not suggesting what your answer should be, but I do suggest that you have many conflicting obligations to consider when you reply…. Obviously, even so simple a problem requires some thought."…

"The history of every profession contains plenty of evidence," Donham suggested…."that it will be practically impossible to get great groups of men acting from pure altruism. The hope for ethical progress lies, as I see it, in tying the institutional point of view into current business policies, and it is for this reason that the big, stable companies in this country have been most influential in building up ethical standards."

But the School, nevertheless, had a role to play; and in recognition of this fact, the faculty had in 1928 authorized a second-year elective in Business Ethics. Carl F. Taeusch, who held a doctorate in philosophy from Harvard, was hired from the State University of Iowa to conduct this first formal experiment in the teaching of business ethics. "Although moral fiber can scarcely be created in the student," Donham wrote of the course in his 1929 report to Lowell, "the more common ethical dilemmas of business can be presented to him while he has time for deliberate consideration free from the pressure of circumstance." Taeusch's course, however, remained more theoretical than practical , and never won sufficient student support. Even Donham's strong advocacy for the experiment could not save the course, which was discontinued in 1935.

"It is the opinion of those who remember Dr. Taeusch's course on ethics," wrote one observer many years later, "that it was unsuccessful because it was perceived as 'Sunday School talk.' Indeed that effort and another in the middle Thirties appear to have set back the desire to tackle the subject at all."

Events in the world of affairs had, in fact, bypassed Taeusch's modest efforts. "There was a steady improvement in ethical standards [in business] up to something like the year 1926," Donham wrote in a 1934 letter to a critic of the School, reflecting on the lessons of a decade. The effects of the Depression, and federal responses to the economic crisis, were by then lending a new urgency to the quest for ethical standards. "I think from 1926 to 1929 a good many business men, like an even larger percentage of the rest of the community, were swept off their feet by a sudden apparent expansion in the wealth of the nation, and [contributed to] a temporary reduction in ethical standards.

"Since the crash in the fall of 1929 I think there has been an even more rapid improvement in ethical standards in business than in the period preceding 1926. Adversity has at least this advantage." ...

Derek Bok...president of Harvard...also raised the issue of ethics and their proper place in the Business School curriculum. "While Cummins Engine Company has actually hired a moral philosopher to participate in many aspects of corporate planning," wrote Bok in his 1977-78 report to Harvard's Board of Overseers, "few business schools, if any, have yet seen fit to appoint a professor of comparable background to serve on their faculties." Bok was evidently unaware of Carl Taeusch's unhappy experience in precisely that role; he nevertheless correctly identified a longstanding inability on the part of Harvard's business school—and other schools in the field—to teach ethics effectively.

"Desire outruns performance," Wallace Donham conduced in 1933, "all along the line." [19]

In the context of this long and unsuccessful attempt to teach ethics in the Business School at Harvard, we as theists declare that this is God's world whether men admit it or not. And since business operates in God's world, no one can escape the need for ethics. Calvin declares as he begins his *Institutes of the Christian Religion*: "Nearly all the wisdom we possess, that is to say, true and sound wisdom, consists of two parts: the knowledge of God and of ourselves." As C.S. Lewis wrote, "We may ignore, but we can nowhere evade, the presence of God." (*Letters to Malcolm*). This is true not just in the broader sphere of life and culture, but also in the narrower context of our economic and business pursuits. Lewis said it well when he observed, "Atheism turns out to be too simple. If the whole universe has no meaning, we should never have found out that it has no meaning...." "When you are arguing against Him [God] you are arguing against the very power that makes you able to argue at all." What is needed to have a sound theory of business ethics is a clear understanding of God's moral order revealed in the Ten Commandments.

There are, nevertheless, many ethical theories that develop from the philosophical arena that make no recognition of God's moral law. [20] The plethora of ethical alternatives is part of the crisis. Which of these multiple possibilities is the ethical system that one should follow? It is important to recognize, however, that each of these theories have to wrestle with the ideas of goal, motive and standard.

VI. The Profit Motive Requires Self-Interest. Can There Be Godly Self-Interest?

In Matthew 22:39 Jesus teaches the standard for our love for our neighbor is to love them "as we love ourselves." This, however, may be a *confusing* standard in our self-oriented age. Self-love has the sense of selfishness or a radical commitment to self-fulfillment. Sociologist Daniel Yankelovich has observed that self-fulfillment has become the new religion of our culture, i.e., there is no higher cause than your own personal self-actualization, peace, comfort and fulfillment. He writes on p. 242 of *New Rules: Searching for Self-Fulfillment in a World Turned Upside Down,*

> By concentrating day and night on your feelings, potentials, needs, wants, and desires, and by learning to assert them more freely, you do not become a freer, more spontaneous, more creative self; you become a narrower, more self-centered, more isolated one. You do not grow, you shrink.

C. S. Lewis wrote, "The natural life in each of us is something self-centred, something that wants to be petted and admired, to take advantage of other lives, to exploit the whole universe."

But having said that, we must recognize that there is a godly and an ungodly self-love. [21]
Augustine writes in *The Morals of the Catholic Church,*

> Now you love yourself suitably when you love God better than yourself. What, then, you aim at in yourself you must aim at in your neighbor, namely, that he may love God with a perfect affection. For you do not love him as yourself, unless you try to draw him to that good which you are yourself pursuing. (chap.26).

Again, Augustine explains,

> After all, why are you afraid to give yourself, as though you may waste yourself? .... Charity herself speaks through wis-

dom, and tells you something to save you from panicking at being told, "Give yourself.",…"Give me your heart," she says; "let it be mine and it won't be lost to you." ...

But you will answer, 'When did I not love myself?' You may be quite sure you weren't loving yourself when you weren't loving the God who made you. When in fact you were hating yourself, you imagined you were loving yourself. Whoever loves iniquity, you see, hates his own soul (Ps 11:5). Augustine, "Sermon 34: Sermon Preached in Carthage at the Ancestors," in *Sermons*, vol. 2, translated by Edmund Hill, edited by John E. Rotelle (Brooklyn, NY: New City Press, 1990), pp. 169-70.

Augustine argues that humans go to great lengths to get what we love, whether for good or for evil, which creates two types of love for oneself:

Reflect on this, then (and see the differences). Think of all the evils that greedy men are prepared to face. Think how they will put up with hardship, in order to win the things they are greedy for—things that seem unbearable to people who don't share their greed. But love makes them brave. Love of evil, though, is called "greed," love of good is called "charity." (Sermon 335C, p. 53.)

The love of evil is greed and the love of good is charity for Augustine. Anders Nygren in his *Eros and Agape* points out that on the one hand the love of oneself "is the real sin and root of all evil; on the other, self-love is the presupposition and criterion of our love for our neighbor." [22]

The point here is simply this: all of us as humans—including business people—are willing to suffer for whatever we love. Augustine argues that we must carefully choose the right cause for which to suffer.

Augustine sees a proper balance of man's obedience to Christ's command to the triple love of God, himself and neighbor resulting in true peace, especially in one's home.

But as this divine Master inculcates two precepts,—the love of God and the love of our neighbor,—and as in these precepts a man finds three things he has to love,—God, himself, and his neighbor,—and that he who loves God loves himself thereby, it follows that he must endeavor to get his neighbor to love God, since he is ordered to love his neighbor as himself. He ought to make this endeavor in behalf of his wife, his children, his household, all within his reach, even as he would wish his neighbor to do the same for him if he needed it; and consequently he will be at peace, or in well-ordered concord, with all men, as far as in him lies. And this is the order of this concord, that a man, in the first place, injure no one, and, in the second, do good to every one he can reach. Primarily, therefore, his own household are his care, for the law of nature and of society gives him readier access to them and greater opportunity of serving them. And hence the apostle says, "Now, if any provide not for his own, and specially for those of his own house, he hath denied the faith, and is worse than an infidel." [1] This is the origin of domestic peace, or the well-ordered concord of those in the family who rule and those who obey. For they who care for the rest rule,—the husband the wife, the parents the children, the masters the servants; and they who are cared for obey,—the women their husbands, the children their parents, the servants their masters. But in the family of the just man who lives by faith and is as yet a pilgrim journeying on to the celestial city, even those who rule serve those whom they seem to command; for they rule not from a love of power, but from a sense of the duty they owe to others—not because they are proud of authority, but because they love mercy. (*City of God*, Book XIX, Chapter xiv.)

Similarly, William Ames, the great Puritan divine, wrote:

This is the order of love: God is first and chiefly to be loved and is, as it were, the formal reason of love towards our neighbor. After God, we are bound to love ourselves with the love of true blessedness, for loving God with love of union, we love ourselves directly with that greatest love which looks toward our spiritual blessedness. Secondarily, as it were, we ought to love others whom we would have to be partakers of the same good with us. For others may be deprived of blessedness without our fault, but we cannot be. Thus we are more bound to desire and seek it for ourselves than for others. Hence it is that love of ourselves has the force of a rule or measure for the love of others, "You shall love your neighbor as yourself." (*Marrow of Theology*, II. xvi. 13-14.)

Matthew Henry comments on Matt. 22:39:

> It is implied, that we do, and should love ourselves. There is a self-love which is corrupt, and the root of the greatest sins, and it must be put off and mortified: but there is a self-love which is natural, and the rule of the greatest duty, and it must be preserved and sanctified. We must love ourselves, that is, we must have a due regard to the dignity of our own natures, and a due concern for the welfare of our own souls and bodies.

John Calvin was most careful to point out the sinful dangers of self-love, yet he understands that we must raise our neighbor to "equal rank with us":

> But as we are too much devoted to ourselves, Moses, in correcting this fault, places our neighbours in an equal rank with us; thus forbidding every man to pay so much attention to himself as to disregard others, because kindness unites all in one body. (Commentary on Matt. 22:39.)

The Westminster Larger Catechism says it well when it answers Question #131,

> What are the duties of equals? The duties of equals are, to regard the dignity and worth of each other, in giving honour to go one before another; and to rejoice in each others' gifts and advancement, **as their own**. (Emphasis added.)

An instructive parallel may be helpful here. The love for God, for others and for one self are inseparable like the heat, light and energy of the sun. But, they must be in proper order.

First: The sun's invisible energy = the love for God.
Second: The sun's light = the love for neighbor.
Third: The sun's warmth = the godly love for oneself.

The Scriptures teach that there is an inseparable connection of our love for God and love for neighbor (1 John 4:10-12; 20-21; 5:2-3). Contrary to Whitney Houston's hit song, the greatest love of all is found first in God's love for us. John 3:16 says, "For God so loved the world, He gave His only begotten Son;" and 1 John 4:19 declares, "We love Him because He first loved us. " And while the Bible recognizes that there is a godly love of self, this is by no means the greatest love of all. Jesus tells us, "Greater love has no one than this, that he lay down his life for his friends." (John 15:13.) Our neighbors are those who have need that we love. They are spiritually speaking our friends. And as we see them in their need, we are to meet those needs if we can. That is how we love them as ourselves. This is the only way we will truly love God first, others next and ourselves last.

Greatness in the kingdom is not found in the greatness of the gifts we possess, but in the loving use of those gifts, whatever size and quality they may be. Robert Murray M'Cheyne wrote, "It is not great talent God blesses so much as great likeness to Jesus. A holy minister is an awful weapon in the hand of God." Could we also say a holy businessman is an awful weapon in the hand of God? As theoretical as this may sound, there is good evidence that "religion can have very positive impacts on corporate life." [23]

VII. The Eighth Commandment: Why The Ten Commandments Are Relevant for Business

For people in business to be endued with the holiness of God's love, they must integrate the wisdom of God's law into their lives and business practices. For starters, they must recognize that the pursuit of riches requires a realistic and godly attitude. As Proverbs 23:4-5 teaches, "Do not wear yourself out to get rich; have the wisdom to show restraint. Cast but a glance at riches, and they are gone, for they will surely sprout wings and fly off to the sky like an eagle."

C. S. Lewis put it this way, "All that we call human history—money, poverty, ambition, war, prostitution, classes, empires, slavery—[is] the long terrible story of man trying to find something other than God which will make him happy."

Specifically, business persons need to master the teachings of the Eighth Commandment that declares "Thou shalt not steal." When this Commandment is stated in a positive way it means that we are to preserve personal property. This fact undercuts any effort to establish a Biblical legitimacy to a thoroughgoing socialistic economic policy. The story of Ananias and Sapphira in Acts 5 supports this understanding. Acts 5:1-4 (KJV) says,

> But a certain man named Ananias, with Sapphira his wife, sold a possession, and kept back part of the price, his wife also being privy to it, and brought a certain part, and laid it at the apostles' feet. But Peter said, Ananias, why hath Satan filled thine heart to lie to the Holy Ghost, and to keep back part of the price of the land? While it remained, was it not thine own? And after it was sold, was it not in thine own power? Why hast thou conceived this thing in thine heart? Thou hast not lied unto men, but unto God. And Ananias hearing these words fell down, and gave up the ghost; and great fear came on all them that heard these things.

Ananias and Sapphira were under no obligation to sell their land or to give the proceeds of the sale to the church. Before the sale, "it remained [his] own" and "after it was sold, [it was] ... in [his] own power." The right to private property here is underscored. There is no socialism here.

Socialism denies the right to private property, which is protected by the Eighth Commandment. As such socialism undermines an aspect of how God has created the world. The denial of private property tends to destroy people's personal productivity by removing the motivation for success. In fact, one of the curses of Scripture is that the fruits of one's labors are enjoyed by another rather than the one who labored for them. Eccl. 6:1-2 (ESV) declares, "There is an evil that I have seen under the sun, and it lies heavy on mankind: a man to whom God gives wealth, possessions, and honor, so that he lacks nothing of all that he desires, yet God does not give him power to enjoy them, but a stranger enjoys them. This is vanity; it is a grievous evil." (See also Deuteronomy 28:30-34; Psalm 69:25; 109:8; Isaiah 65:21-22; Amos 5:11; Matthew 8:10-12; 25:28-30; Acts 1:20.)

The Eighth Commandment teaches that profits can be moral when there are godly standards for the practice of capitalism. This Commandment does not support the claim that there are sufficient self-correcting moral limits that operate inherently and independently in the market itself. Rather, the necessary godly standards for just capitalism and ethical profits are discovered in the Law of God that teaches us to love our neighbor as we love ourselves.

There is a biblical legitimacy for profits in a capitalistic sense in the perspective of historic Christianity as represented by the *Westminster Larger Catechism*. However, there are also necessary moral principles that must govern this business activity. In the teaching of the *Larger Catechism*, for there to be a just capitalism, there must be more than Adam Smith's invisible hand of the market[24] to govern the ethics of a just capitalistic system. And hence, for there to be ethical profits there must also be the ethical teachings of the Ten Commandments as applied to business.

These ethical teachings call for more than what Timothy Fort calls a bare "hard trust" in regard to corporate legal compliance. The commitment to ethical principles must become "good trust" or a matter of the employees' and the company's heartfelt internal commitment to be good. Fort explains,

> At the risk of undermining my credibility completely, let me give an example that, in teaching at least, seems to have significantly helped explain the differences between Hard, Real, and Good Trust as well as how these forms of trust can build on each other. It's a cheesy example
>
> For eleven years, I was a professor at the University of Michigan, where I got into a lot of trouble for never wavering from my football loyalties to my alma mater, Notre Dame. When the Enron scandals hit, it suddenly dawned on me that the arguments I had been making about ethics, and analyzing Enron in particular, were nicely summarized by a play on the Notre Dame-Michigan rivalry. I began to tell audiences that the key to ethics was understanding a hidden truth in the game. I would explain why I thought it was a great game, which is pretty easy to do, but then I got to the heart of the issue, which was that even if the two schools didn't have such magnificent football traditions, it was worth going to the game every year

simply to hear the bands play the two school songs. Some have argued that Michigan's "The Victors" and the "Notre Dame Victory March" are the two greatest school songs ever.

The two bands have a nice tradition in which each plays the other school's song before playing its own. When a band plays the other school's song, you hear Hard Trust and Real Trust. That is the band follows all the rules of music, and rules are what Hard Trust is about. The band plays the right notes, the right rhythm, the right key signature, the right time signature; it does everything "right" and will be rewarded for doing so The fans whose band just played aren't going to boo their own band, and the fans whose songs was just played aren't going to boo their own song. So there will be an alignment of values and actions, which is what Real Trust is about. The band will have done something "nice" and "polite."

But then listen to the band play its own song. It is a totally different rendition because then it is played with heart, with pride, with passion, and with identity. That is when chills go up and down one's spine. Passions are engaged. That is Good Trust. Good Trust is when people and companies are ethical not just because it is the a law or because it pays but because people are sincerely passionate about being ethical and good as part of their very identity.

There is something to be said for a company that follows the law. There is something more to be said about a company that integrates its strategies and operations to make ethics good business. But the motivation for getting people to care about ethics in the first place and for getting them to embrace trustworthy behavior as part of their very identity is much more aesthetic and spiritual. My claim is that companies have a reason to listen to spiritual ideas because such ideas unleash the passions that create trustworthiness, which has direct economic and social (legal) value.

Companies are aware of the importance of trust. It has become an important emphasis following the scandals at the start of the twenty-first century. Look at just about any company's Web site, and you will see some mention of "trust" or "integrity" or "ethics." A 2006 U.S. chamber of Commerce conference was dedicated to the question of how to foster trust in business. Executives regularly say that ensuring customer's trust—and society's trust more generally—is vital. Yet what business executives mean by trust tends to be a bit narrow. They typically recognize the legal (Hard Trust) and economic (Real Trust) dimensions, but they miss the underlying aesthetic and spiritual motivations that effectuate compliance and strategy and shortchange the possibilities for moral excellence that create even stronger forms of trustworthiness. Understanding and integrating all three aspects of trust makes companies stronger and more trustworthy. [25]

In biblical terms, this is the result when the law is written upon the heart rather than on legal tablets of stone.

VIII. Conclusion

Our culture and our courts have required us to take down the law of God from our public lives. But let us not take down the law from our homes (Deuteronomy 6:4-9) or from our businesses. Let us not erase the law written upon our hearts by the Holy Spirit through the New Covenant and the Gospel (Jeremiah 31:31-34; 2 Corinthians 3:3-6.) Let us understand the trends in society, but let us be faithful in our hearts to the commandments God would have us show in His world as we do our business.

Our first President warned our nation of the danger of seeking to conduct our lives without the wisdom of God. In his Farewell Address published on September 17, 1796, Washington declared:

Of all the dispositions and habits which lead to political prosperity, Religion and Morality are indispensable supports. In vain would that man claim the tribute of Patriotism, who should labor to subvert these great pillars of human happiness, these firmest props of the duties of Men and Citizens. The mere Politician, equally with the pious man, ought to respect and to cherish them. A volume could not trace all their connections with private and public felicity. . . . And let us with caution indulge the supposition that morality can be maintained without religion. Whatever may be conceded to the influence of refined education on minds of peculiar structure, reason and experience both forbid us to expect that national morality can prevail in exclusion of religious principle.

When retiring from his command of the Revolutionary Army, General Washington wrote to the Governors of all thirteen states the following Christ-honoring prayer calling for charity (love), humility and peace which is based on Micah 6:8 [26] :

I now make it my earnest prayer, that God would have you, and the State over which you preside, in his holy protection, that he would incline the hearts of the Citizens to cultivate a spirit of subordination and obedience to Government, to entertain a brotherly affection and love for one another, for their fellow Citizens of the United States at large, and particularly for their brethren who have served in the Field, and finally, that he would most graciously be pleased to dispose us all, to do Justice, to love mercy, and to demean ourselves with that Charity, humility and pacific temper of mind, which were the Characteristics of the Divine Author of our blessed Religion, and without an humble imitation of whose example in these things, we can never hope to be a happy Nation.

Every American business person should still be able to say "Amen" to that. When we do, we no longer are business people who are mere lovers of money. Instead we can truly answer the question with which we began this study. Do we do business for love or for money? The answer is both, but our business activities must be conducted in that order. We are to do business for Love first and then Money second. This, then, is how we do business to the glory of God.

Notes

1. *Banner*, March 11, 2011, a publication of the Union League of Philadelphia.
2. James Surowiecki, *Forbes*, "A Virtuous Circle" Dec. 23, 2002, p. 248
3. Nitin Nohria, President, Harvard Business School as quoted in the *Wall Street Journal*, "Harvard Changes Course", Feb. 3, 2011.
4. See Karl Marx, *The Communist Manifesto* in Karl Marx, *Selected Writings*, ed. David McLellan, Oxford University Press, 1977, pp. 221-47.
5. Saul D. Alinsky, *Rules For Radicals: A Pragmatic Primer for Realistic Radicals* (New York: Vintage Books, 1989).
6. Raven Clabough wrote in "Tucson Parents Challenge Ethnic Studies Curriculum":

    Parents in Tucson, Arizona, are beyond disgruntled over the content of an anti-capitalist, anti-American textbook used in an ethnic studies curriculum for grades 3–12. At a Tucson board meeting on May 10 parents articulated their anger over the curriculum's content, and read aloud excerpts from the controversial book

    One mother began the tirade against the curriculum by asking, "I want to know why books like this one are being taught to our kids." She explained that she confronted the issue with administrators at the school, and was told that the book was used in at least five classes, including third graders.

    She then proceeded to read jaw-dropping excerpts from the textbook, including "An Epic Poem," which states:

    > I shed tears of sorrow, I sow seeds of hate
    > The force of tyranny of men who rule by farce and hypocrisy,
    > In a country that has wiped out all my history, stifled all my pride....
    > My land is lost and stolen, My culture has been raped
    > Poverty and city-living under the colonial system of the Anglo has frustrated our people's culture

    One note, especially to those young chicanos, hard drugs and the drug culture is the invention of the gringo because he has no culture.

    We have to destroy capitalism...The Declaration of Independence states that we the people have the right to revolution, the right to overthrow a government that has committed abuses and seeks complete control over the people. This is in order to clean out the corrupted, rotten officials that developed out of any type of capitalistic systems.

    Another section of the textbook indicates, "Today I have a message....to the children, the students, the workers, the masses, and to the bloodsuckers, the parasites, the vampires who are the capitalists of the world: The schools are tools of the power structure that blind and sentence our youth to a life of confusion, and hypocrisy, one that preaches assimilation and practices institutional racism. http://thenewamerican.com/culture/education/7452-tucson-parents-challenge-ethnic-studies-curriculum

7. Charles Colson, "The Problem of Ethics: Why Good People Do Bad Things" in *Business Ethics*

Today:Foundations, (Westminster Seminary Press, 2011), pp. 39-42

8. See, for example, Paul A. Moreland, *A History of Business Education* (Toronto: Pitman Publishing, 1977) and Wayne G. Broehl, Jr., *Tuck & Tucker: The Origin of the Graduate Business School* (Hanover and London: University Press of New England, 1999).

9. This discussion relies upon Jeffrey L. Cruikshank, *A Delicate Experiment: The Harvard Business School, 1908-1945*, (Boston: Harvard Business School Press, 1987).

10. Colson, "The Problem of Ethics", p. 40.

11. See note 4 above.

12. Nitin Nohria, President, Harvard Business School as quoted in the *Wall Street Journal*, "Harvard Changes Course", Feb. 3, 2011.

13. See, for example, Rakesh Khurana, *From Higher Aims to Hired Hands: The Social Transformation of American Business Schools and the Unfulfilled Promise of Management as a Profession* (Princeton and Oxford: Princeton University Press, 2007), pp. 364-366.

14. Cruikshank, *A Delicate Experiment*, p. 13.

15. Ibid., p. 100. When the request for support of the business school was made to Baker, Bishop William Lawrence made the ask. Lawrence explains, "The point that I tried to make was that with the enormous development of business, and the hundreds of thousands of business men, small and great, a definite forward step had got to be made in sustaining the ethical standards of himself, and those of other days; and that the one spot from which that influence was to come, at all events at first, was the Graduate Business School of Harvard University." Ibid., p. 106.

16. Ibid., p. 37.

17. Ibid, p. 84.

18. Ibid, pp. 154-155.

19. Ibid, pp.168-69. Other professors have sought to bring ethical studies to aspects of the Harvard Business School programs. Sumner H. Slichter, head of the Trade Union Fellowship Program at Haravard said, "The School should also aim much more than in the past, to be a center of research and ideas—the sponsor and the supporter of the most significant research in the world on the subject of administration and on the problems of business and the originator of the most significant appraisals of the new responsibilities of business and of the kind of job that business is doing. This last means that the School should be a leader both in scientific investigations and in ethical thinking about business." Ibid, p. 265. Similarly, Harvard Professor Louis E. Kirstein "believed that business had a special responsibility to shape both social and economic progress ,and that the school should offer its students training in ethical business conduct." Ibid, p. 276.

20. Ethics is one of the great philosophical questions: metaphysics, ontology, epistemology, the mind/body problem, ethics and aesthetics. While we cannot present a study of ethics here, an overview of some of the basic concerns of ethics is presented below.

Main Schools of Ethical Theory

A. Power – Dynamism – might makes right
B. Happiness – Eudaemonism – happiness is the test of what is good
C. Pleasure – Hedonism – if it feels good, it's ok
D. Practical – Pragmatism – if it works, it is good
E. Be a part of the Culture – Conventionalism – the majority view is right
F. No Absolutes – Relativism – no right or wrong, just preferences
G. What ever you can get away with – Anarchism – wrong only if caught
H. Economic necessity – Dialectical Materialism – private property is evil and the source of all evils

I.   Materialism of Nietzsche—will to power.

J.   Logically necessary moral absolutes – Idealism – logic alone is needed to dis cover absolutes

K.   Evolutionary or Dialectical Ethics – ethics change from generation to generation

L.   Personal Decision – Existentialism – one's definitive personal choice establishes personal ethics

M.   Christian Theistic Ethics. The Revealed Will of God in Christian Theism holds that the Bible gives standards of morality. Moreover, woven into very fabric of reality are "creation ordinances".

21. For a helpful consideration of the history of the idea of self-love in Christian thought as it develops from Jesus' teaching that we are to love our neighbors as we love ourselves, see, G. C. Berkouwer, *Studies in Dogmatics: Sin* (Grand Rapids: Eerdmans, 1971), pp. 249-253.

22. Berkouwer, *Sin*, p. 251, n. 48.

23. See Timothy L. Fort, *Prophets, Profits, and Peace: The Positive Role of Business in Promoting Religious Tolerance* (New Have and London: Yale University press, 2009), pp. 33-35.

24. Adam Smith writes in *An Inquiry Into the Nature and Causes of the Wealth of Nations*,

Secondly, every individual who employs his capital in the support of domestic industry, necessarily endeavours so to direct that industry, that its produce may be of the greatest possible value.... As every individual, therefore, endeavours as much as he can, both to employ his capital in the support of domestic industry, and so to direct that industry that its produce maybe of the greatest value; every individual necessarily labours to render the annual revenue of the society as great as he can. He... neither intends to promote the public interest, nor knows how much he is promoting it. By preferring the support of domestic to that of foreign industry, he intends only his own security; and by directing that industry in such a manner as its produce may be of the greatest value, he intends only his own gain; and **he is in this, as in many other cases, led by an invisible hand to promote an end which was no part of his intention**. Nor is it always the worse for the society that it was no part of it. By pursuing his own interest, he frequently promotes that of the society more effectually than when he really intends to promote it.... (Emphasis added.)

25. Timothy Fort, *Prophets, Profits and Peace*, pp. 58-59.

26. Micah 6:1-8 presents the Law's holistic provision for His people and its exacting requirements upon mankind:

A. The Lord calls Israel to account for their behavior with respect to His Covenant. Vv. 1-2.

B. The Lord asks if they can show any failure on His part toward Israel in light of all His grace. Vv. 3-5.

C. The Prophet's message of repentance with respect to the Law of God. Vv. 6-8.

1. Human works of merit are not the answer. Vv. 6-7. Our works do not save our souls.

2. He has showed you, O man, what is good. V. 8a. God has provided our salvation.

A. Consider God's works of redemption cited in verses 4-5.

B. Jesus' work on the cross shows God's justice in salvation by redemption from sin. (Romans 3:22-26.)

3. *And what does the Lord require of you?*

A. To act justly--the Second Table of the law defines "justice." Commandments 6-10.

B. To love mercy--The Golden rule or love of neighbor summarizes these commandments. Compare Matthew 7:12; Matthew 22:34-40; Romans 13:8-10. The law as standard is inseparable from the motive of love. To "love mercy" is to "love love!"

C. <u>To walk humbly with your God</u>--The First table of the law (Commandments 1-4) defines how we worship, how we walk in love with our God. "Walking with" is the life that is in covenant with God (Gen. 2:8; 6:21-24; 17:1.) Note that he is "*your*" God that you are to love according to the first great commandment (Matthew 22:24-40; Deuteronomy 6:4-5).

MORALITY OF PROFITS

DR. JOHN TEMPLETON

JOHN TEMPLETON

John M. Templeton, Jr. has been actively involved in the Foundation since its inception in 1987. He retired from his medical practice in 1995. He directs all of the Foundation's activities and works closely with the Foundation's staff, Trustees, and Board of Advisors.

A graduate of Yale University, he earned his medical degree from Harvard Medical School. He completed his internship and residency in surgery at the Medical College of Virginia in Richmond and subsequently trained in pediatric surgery under Dr. C. Everett Koop at The Children's Hospital of Philadelphia. After serving two years in the U.S. Navy, he returned to The Children's Hospital of Philadelphia in 1977, where he served on the staff as pediatric surgeon and trauma program director. He also served as professor of pediatric surgery at the University of Pennsylvania.

Dr. Templeton was board certified in pediatric surgery and surgical critical care and is a fellow of the American College of Surgeons. He serves as Vice Chairman of the American Trauma Society and as a president of its Pennsylvania division. He has published numerous papers in medical and professional journals, in addition to two books, Thrift and Generosity: The Joy of Giving *(2004) and* A Searcher's Life *(2008).*

> *The following speech was given by Dr. Jack Templeton, Keynote Speaker for the 2011 Business Ethics Conference. The Conference took place at the Union League in Philadelphia, PA on June 10-11, 2011, and was entitled "Business Ethics Today Conference: Business and the Eighth Commandment." Any Conference materials referenced in this paper can be made available on request. Email: info@cfcbe.com*

Good morning, everyone. It is a real honor to have an opportunity to share with you some perspectives on an immensely neglected, feared and therefore almost completely ignored topic – namely, the "morality of profits". While I personally have had only limited experience in any sort of business – except for a small start up business – I think that it is still helpful to ask among ourselves: Why does anyone chose to "do business"? Actually, there is most assuredly a complex of factors from the often quite strong psychological factors of what it can mean to be a part of seeing ideas – perhaps from meeting an unfulfilled need – as real-life opportunities to both sense and feel that one can really make a difference. Added to this is that innate, human quality of the spirit of competition.

At this point, however, I would like to shift the emphasis for a moment to accentuate the critical role that free enterprise business – whether small or large – can provide and has historically played in America as the single most reliable and the most sustainable vehicle for the well being of millions and millions of Americans. Many of these millions of Americans, of course, have been multiple beneficiaries of for-profit businesses in the context of providing for the basic well being of individuals and families. For many such persons there has also been the phenomenon of how a variety of jobs in the for-profit world earlier in many peoples' lives provide frameworks for subsequent stepping-stones for later education and the development of added skills and thus a much wider range of even hundreds of thousands of opportunities.

But, however, it is very critical for all of us not to become a willing, or even unconscious, ally of legions of social planners who have for several decades been trying to wear down the for-profit world and tens of millions of citizens as a whole that businesses or corporations have only one valid justification for existence. That justification is couched in terms of "social responsibility". The advocates for this relatively new phenomenon in America in history derive from a whole range of self-elevated "experts" who want, in effect, to produce an encompassing system of top down control and engineering of the lives of people at all levels – not the least those who are the genesis and the engine of creativity and productivity.

Instead, I would like to set forth a quite different world view regarding the morality of for-profit business. In that regard, first and foremost, the true calling, or the true role, of business is not to provide jobs or to become activist agents of government which makes proliferating "green" policies, or for business to become agents of many other forms of government political agendas.

Thus, I would like to propose a worldview in regard, first of all, to for-profit businesses, in general, but more particularly for business entrepreneurs from every area. That specific worldview is that each business person or corporation is not some isolated entity in a sea of relativism. This is critical because the overwhelming majority of self-proclaimed opinion leaders widely propagate concepts that all of us as individuals have little significance in the face of mass movements or external events which are presented as proliferating completely beyond our control. Thus, in this pervasive campaign of "learned or taught helplessness" - individuals with distinctive values are irrelevant.

Instead, even though it does admittedly represent an unfathomable miracle – each and every one of us is not solely "dust to dust" as the materialists strongly advance, but instead, each and every one of us are unequivocally a unique creation in the image of a loving God. Thus, we each have that distinctiveness called "Imageo Deo" – or, in the "image of God". When the emphasis is properly placed on each person as a unique loving intentionality of God – then the logic is clear. The Lord God does not love amorphous concepts of people as mass collections of beings or even pulsating herds. In contrast, God has created every single person from the entire past history of humanity, in our present time and for all of future history – that every person is individually a unique child of God. For each of his Children, he has blessed each one with remarkable, different, truly unique gifts of mind and spirit. He loves each one of us here today, and every other person, unreservedly. Thus, it is not for nothing that He also gives each one of us special personal gifts.

The extraordinary range of gifts the Lord has bestowed on each of us has never been, nor ever will be, a matter of a one way street of God's love and even blessings radiating out to us. In other words, it is clear from God's Word that He never intended the flow of love to be uni- directional. In fact, He created each one of us with a unique purpose and meaning which we have to seek and acknowledge and to do so – from a baseline of concentrated love. When each child or adult accepts with profound gratitude the free, unreserved totality of God's love – thus, it is just not logical that any one of us could be passive in return, nor especially, that we could ever imagine being fatalistic.

He created us, instead, to respond, to be proactive in many ways and thus to love the Lord and to never fail in serving Him. Thus, again, it is not for nothing that the Lord called Moses as one of His earliest servants on earth and gave to Moses the eternal gift of what we call the Ten

Commandments. Just so – we ourselves have the added gift of what Jesus reminded us – as the two most cardinal and central commandments - commandments which are both of obligation and duty, but also as a springboard for joy. That first commandment, as was stated by Jesus is, and will always be: "Love the Lord your God with all your heart and with all your soul and with all your mind."

We might pause at this moment and hopefully agree that this very short commandment of only 19 words is not some waffling, relativistic "suggestion". There is simply no wiggle room in this commandment. This commandment is both an expectation and a duty of a profoundly moral nature – namely, that however undeservedly, if we are indeed individually so overwhelmingly loved – that simple "gratitude" impels us to love in return. (Thus, the second commandment so strongly stressed by Jesus).

In contrast, our culture shouts out in varying degrees that are reflective of the complex and often contrary components of human nature – a human nature that keeps asserting from dozens and dozens of vantage points, that human beings can never be, nor become, anything more than millions and millions of declarations of "Me, Me, Me" – a perfect squawking voice of narcissistic relativism.

Christ knew very well the unrelenting nature of this narcissistic relativistic impulse. And yet by His Father's hand, He descended to a suffering and lost world to call forth an awakening of His Lordship. He came to a culture that – like our own – was recognized by many ancient Jewish prophets as other self-important people who are "stiff – necked" – that is, too narcissistic to ever think of bowing ones head. But more largely, God, through His Word, also called us as individuals not to be self-focused – especially when even in trying to honor the first commandment – only then to convey an ungenerous self-righteousness. Instead, God calls us to that second accountability which is why Jesus told the Pharisees that the second commandment is like the first: "Love your neighbor as yourself, (and that) all the Law and the Prophets hang on these two commandments." Thus both the first and second commandments are an unequivocal call to love – a calling that Christ reinforced to an infinite degree through His model of total, self-denying Eternal Love.

With this as a common frame of reference for all of us – I want to come back, therefore, to several key premises already suggested, and to add to these several other premises:

- First – each person is indeed a unique creation as Imageo Deo.

- Second – God's love for each one of us is personal and direct.

- Third - He calls each one of us to complete service in honor of Him and that what we do - will always be in His Name.

- Fourth – that biologically and morally each person – even in the case of identical twins – is, in fact, blessed as a unique combination of mental and other skills.

- Fifth – that the prospering of these gifts is a genuine "charge to us" as to what God expects of each one of us.

Therefore, God calls each one of us, and indeed all of those who "do business" to first and foremost, give thanks to our Lord God for every breath of life; to give thanks for our mind – especially that we intentionally conform ourselves as loving gardeners of our mind and to prosper our minds by repetitive faithful cultivation. This process engulfs the intentionality of creating within ourselves a far ranging intellectual, moral and spiritual curiosity through the asking of questions. It also involves a willingness to challenge assumptions. Furthermore, it involves an embracing and even joyful giving of thanks for adversity; and finally, it involves a determination never to bury any of our talents in the ground as one man did in the Parable of the Talents, but instead to prosper opportunity for ourselves and for others.

Just as it is true for all of you – namely, that in addition to our heavenly Father, we have, or share, or hopefully gain from different attributes from our "earthly fathers", I also cannot help appreciating the fact that my father, Sir John Templeton, as a teenager took on the responsibility of being superintendent of his church's Sunday School as a service to his neighbors. Later in life my father began to accumulate a growing number of lessons that he often said he wished he had fully understood and appreciated when he was 20 years of age. I have, therefore, provided in a handout, a number of these accumulated insights on a variety of themes including competition, creativity, freedom, gratitude, reliability, thrift and wisdom.

But, perhaps as significant as all of these is the fact that my father felt that next to God's unreserved love for each one of us, God's second most enormously dimensional love-gift is that of our Minds. I have included in your handouts as a small reflection of Dad's viewpoint on this theme in the form of a Christmas message that my father sent to friends and family in 1962. As you can see, what this Christmas message accentuates is the concept of not only the preciousness of each of our Minds, but also the concept of being a loving proactive gardener of our Minds. Among several of the quotations from my father's writings about the Mind include:

- "The more knowledge we gain, the more we can see the extent of the unknown. As we grow in knowledge (therefore) we grow in humility."

- Also that: "Our minds are filled with ideas and thoughts that show us how to build or create the things our imaginations can conceive. If our attitude is open for new understanding, fresh stimulation, and acceleration of discovery, we currently have no idea of what (extraordinary) discoveries can be accomplished."

- One other example among many others states: "The more we know, the more we do not know. This is what gives life spice. In fact, in order to grow, we must daily become more humble and honest in admitting the paucity of our knowledge. This humble admission of ignorance is what increases progress, what keeps man searching, what makes life as we know it exciting and challenging."

And so, is it not logical that God, in giving each of us different instinctive abilities and skills has also provided one of the most profound forms of creativity – namely how to take an initial, not fully formed idea, such as in business, coupled with imagination, initiative, hard work, discipline and drive and to convert that idea into one of the most remarkable forms of creativity there is – namely, the ministry of a successful, for-profit business? Might we then give due respect and thus learn and honor the word "profit" when we explore its origins from Latin, which accentuates the concept of "gain". Stated more broadly, profit is "an advantageous gain or return".

When we recast the word "profit" into the word "gain" we find, in fact, that the Bible has a great deal to say about "gain". Most of these statements are admonitions in regard to distinctions between honesty and dishonesty. For example, in Titus (1:7) it says: "Since an overseer (or what we might call a steward) is entrusted with God's work, he must be blameless…not pursuing dishonest **gain**."

- Isaiah (33:15) asserts: "He who walks righteously and speaks what is right, who rejects gain from extortion and keeps his hand from accepting bribes… is the man who will dwell on the heights; his refuge will be the mountain fortress."

- In the famous love passages of 1 Corinthians, chapter 13, we have, in contrast, a powerful, centralizing message that what must prevail in all things is LOVE. Verse three says: "If I give all I possess to the poor and surrender my body to the flames, but I have not love, I gain nothing." It is this critical matter of the centralizing aspect of love for God and for others that we will come to in a moment in regard to the honorable role of "profit" in business and society.

- Thus, we might look at just two other passages that accentuate the word "gain" to understand much of the essence of what we have already suggested as a cardinal principle of the morality of profits – namely, do your "profits" capture you and burden you, your mind and your soul, or in contrast - do your "profits" liberate you and empower others? In the first matter in Mark (8:36) it says: "What good is it for a man to **gain** the whole world, yet forfeit his soul?"

- Instead, when we move from Mark to the final gospel of Luke, we hear instead: "By standing firm, we will **gain** life."

Now that we have more confidently opened the door to the matter of the "morality of profits", we need to consider and answer several questions (some of which I have at least partially already put forward):

- First, is it God Himself who created freedom and liberty and does He intend for each one of us to live in liberty"?

- Second, does God intend for you and me and everyone to be passive and fatalistic, or instead, to be proactive in all that we do – a proactivity that is tempered by prudence - which we shall touch on a bit later?

- Third, does God not only call us to dedicate ourselves to sincere commitment to prosper everything that we do including everyone we "touch – in word and deed"?

Therefore, there is a corollary in God's eyes – does He call us to see all honest work as honorable? And, moreover, does he call us to honor all others who bless our lives and the lives of countless others including those such as cleaners of offices, cleaners of streets, deliverers of the mail and also the hard but very honorable work of trash removal?

- Lastly, does God just call we, ourselves, to do work, to create, to invent, to see and pursue opportunities where others only see defeat, and overall, to create and do things that have such merit that they can be either virtually or in reality the two most pivotal, unifying aspects of "beneficial profit". The first criteria of "beneficial profit" is "sustainability" and the second, which as an outgrowth of sustainability, is "generativity".

I have provided as a part of the handouts for today, a sequence of thoughts which first began to dwell in my mind just over a year ago in regard to "morality of profits". I would like to share with you not only a sequence of thoughts that are contained in this handout, but also to suggest that just as we explored the powerful Biblical insights regarding the "gain", likewise, there are a significant range of multi-dimensional, but beneficial, relevant factors in regard to a fuller understanding of "profits":

- First, without thrift itself – a powerful part of stewardship, we need to open our minds to the much neglected but very compelling Biblical concept of "skeptical stewardship". Thus, while pondering these two words of "Skeptical Stewardship" – might we all agree that there can be little or no generosity, especially in the form of sustainable voluntary generosity – if thrift does not prevail over all?

Time does not permit me to explore more than very briefly how important the Biblical concept of "skeptical stewardship" is in regard to "profits". To help I have provided a paper that Peter Lillback provided approximately a year and a half ago that puts forth a remarkable continuity between the

Old Testament and the New Testament regarding "skeptical stewardship". The depth of wisdom that Peter Lillback brings forth in this handout starts not surprisingly, first, from Proverbs including (14:15) "A simple man believes anything, but a prudent man gives thoughts to his steps." From this ancient wisdom of Solomon we move through the Gospels to Acts in chapter 20 where it asserts that "our own fallen nature requires that we are all accountable – that we are to watch over ourselves and others".

With this hopefully strongly embedded concept of accountability, we move to the next logical sequence of: - next – "with no profits, there can be no free enterprise".

- Likewise – with no free enterprise – or with no core virtues like honesty, diligence, thrift and accountability – then poverty, sustenance living, selfishness and vulnerability are assured.

- Thus, among many overall timeless virtues like love, honesty, generosity, diligence, beneficial purpose and humility, we arrive at those much deeper and powerful underlying pillars for morality which asks, for example: Is morality in finance and business almost meaningless – if, as suggested, it is not deeply rooted in thrift and future mindedness?

- Thus, is there a profound, vastly significant "morality of profits", and if so, what would encapsulate the essential, moral dimensions of "profits". The first answer I have already suggested is genuine "sustainability" – an essential element which includes the critical concept of receiving nothing artificial, including no favoritism of any form from others including the government; no subsidies; and overall, no form of support that is not also available to others.

- The other critically related component of morality of profits is best expressed by the word "generativity". This latter concept, which envisions something, that is living and is growing, involves not only being "self-sustaining", but more importantly, providing a proliferation of dynamic, expanding approaches to meeting larger and even bigger real needs and wants.

Therefore, if we give due respect to our minds as already suggested, and the often untapped, latent potentialities of our minds – no matter how high or lofty or visionary our goals may be, it is God Himself who expects everyone involved to uphold the true spiritual sense of a "calling" in the for-profit world to be an exemplar of accountability.

On a certain basic level, of course, the very concepts of "profit" and "profit-making" involve a quantifiable and often objective measure of results to assess success. In fact, if you do not pursue in multiple ways, an accountability in regard to results, one may not be acting as fully morally as one might.

Thus, in the one domain in which "profit" may be accountable in dollars and cents, there are still other forms of beneficial quantifiable accountability. If, for example, you are a teacher of inner city, underprivileged kids – would you not set for both yourself and for the kids you teach the highest possible, quantitative standards for beneficial results of your teaching?

Lastly, in regard to those critical, dual criteria for "morality of profits" – namely, "sustainability" and generativity" – profits with such a strong dual framework are, in fact, likely to contribute to a liberation from self-dependency, hopelessness and especially soul destroying ENVY – and its self-defeating perpetual assertions of "Them Versus Me!"

At this point, I would like to ask you to walk with me in the manner of a "thought experiment" involving a real world, true "case study" of success in the world of profit. As you will quickly recognize when I cover these steps from this now immensely successful global company – as is true for many thousands of other for profit successful endeavors, the key components for the "morality of profits" keep bringing us back to the concepts of "sustainability" and "generativity".

I would like to ask you then to take this brief excursion with me by thinking of yourself as a 25-year old who had an excellent high school education and a perfect 4.0 school grade average, but because of a variety of economic limitations, neither further education nor a so-called "good job" is available. Therefore, lacking any other choices, you decide to take a job as a food service person, taking orders behind the counter of your local McDonald's store. From the very first day, there is an internal attitude of strong character and a passion for excellence and care for others that impels you to provide outstanding service, in a warm, friendly and welcoming manner. As a result, your manager soon notices that if one of your fellow workers has a problem, or is impeded in some way, that you readily pitch in to help your fellow worker. In fact, with that same drive and your own internal standards, you continue to impress your manager, such that, a month later, when he wishes to take a 4 day weekend – and having no one else to turn to – he asks if you would consider being acting manager of the store for 4 days.

When he returns, he is quite struck to find that not only is the store cleaner and brighter but that there is a more palpable sense of "How can I help you?" service at the store, which causes him to watch you even more closely. This pattern of exemplary service including your routinely coming to work 20 or more minutes before each work day, comes quickly to your manager's mind, when after 2 more months you come to him and say that you have learned about McDonald's University and would the manager help you in some way to attend the 2 month course at McDonald's University. Actually, the manager indicates that he would not like to lose such a valuable employee; but in fact, he goes out of his way to get you a place to stay and to work out with the McDonald's organization to help with funding for their very intense 2 month training period.

At the end of this 2 month program, you have, in fact achieved extraordinarily high standards for mastery of new skills and even have suggested one or two possible areas for improvement. Thus, when you ask the McDonald's organization if you might then be allowed to be a manager of one of your own company stores, they quite readily agree.
It turns out that the store you have been given has been a fairly lack luster store, but within two months, the profits each month from this store have now increased consistently at about 30% more per month. Moreover, on regular, unscheduled inspection visits, the McDonald's inspector notes in his report: "an exceptionally cheery, clean, efficient and quite pleasant atmosphere in addition to McDonald's always consistent highest quality standards for food preparation and delivery".

After two years of continued increased levels of profitability at the store you manage, you then decide to go back to the McDonald's organization and ask them if they might, in some way, assist you with some appropriate financing whereby you might acquire your own franchise store. Indeed, they are quite happy to support you in this regard, and because of their high confidence in you, they actually provide one of their more promising outlets in an area with no other nearby McDonald's. The company management is not disappointed. The same high quality standards, and cheerful attitude of "How can I help you?", plus the ever present McDonald's standards of excellence, allows you within 2 years to pay off your entire loan from the McDonald's organization at which point you are a franchise owner free and clear. It is then only a year later in which in this same continued trajectory of personal care, concern for not only your store and also the customer but your workers as well – that it becomes possible for you to become the owner of a second and eventually a third and fourth McDonald's franchise.

This phenomenon was first appreciated by me when I attended several meetings a number of years ago made up of very successful entrepreneurial business persons – almost all of whom started with next to nothing and over time became extraordinarily successful across a range of perhaps 100 or 200 different types of businesses. I was especially impressed, when during a few of these meetings I met four different individuals who I gathered were clearly quite substantial multi-millionaires. When I asked them what their business was, they said: "Why, I own 40 McDonald's franchises."

As I suggested earlier, everything in life, but especially with regard to the topic of morality in business, "perspective" is a very important thing to bring to bear. First, the man who produced the extraordinary world-wide success of McDonald's was Ray Kroc who opened an initial franchise McDonald's restaurant in Illinois in 1955. This success in his adding more and more franchise outlets led eventually to his ability to buy out the original McDonald's Brothers. From that point, up to the present, McDonald's has become the leading global food service retailer with more than 82,000 local restaurants serving more than 64 million people in 117 countries each day. More to the point, is that 80% of McDonald's restaurants worldwide are owned and operated by independent local men and women.

This is of particular note when one considers that even countries like America have certain population groups that have historically had trouble in breaking out of patterns of economic, and other forms of being under resourced and under privileged. It is quite notable, therefore, that USA Today reported that McDonald's had been selected by the National Minority Franchise Initiative as one of the top 50 Franchises for Minorities. More specifically, Black Enterprise Magazine – listed McDonald's as one of the 40 best franchises for African-Americans.

To have such a track record of success is quite notable, but perhaps the most significant factor in a corporate culture which did not exist even some 60 years ago, is its impact on other even non-Western cultures and countries. Specifically – a group of anthropologists in a study entitled "Golden Arches East" looked at the impact McDonald's had on East Asia and Hong Kong in particular. When McDonald's opened several initial stores in Hong Kong in 1975, McDonald's was quickly recognized as the first restaurant in Hong Kong to consistently offer clean restrooms, as well as, exemplary service – thus, driving customers to demand the same bright, clean bathrooms from other restaurants and institutions in Hong Kong.

In summary, while there are ever present a number of vociferous and even harsh critics of McDonald's – which has over the years not only changed its packaging of the food but also diversified its food menu – it is quite impressive that over the first 40 years of McDonald's history, some 20 million Americans have worked at McDonald's. Over the entire 56 years since Ray Kroc opened his first store – a conservative estimate is that McDonald's has given employment lasting from months to many, many years to some perhaps 30 million people worldwide. Not only were many of these job holders youngsters who were first getting their foot in the door for "work ethic" and for understanding what high standards of account-ability and responsibility look like when one is part of an organization that expects nothing less than excellence – but that indeed, as reflected in the story I shared with you, there may very well be today some 30,000 persons who are multi-millionaires from having their own franchises. Moreover, might many of these other now successful entrepreneurs have also started out taking orders behind the counter of one of McDonald's outlets. If you had perhaps listened carefully at certain points, many of these individual steps for both individuals and as well for the corporation, epitomize both "sustainability" and "generativity".

Besides the points that we have already tried to bring forth in re-gard to the remarkable story of McDonalds, we might now be able to pull together the various threads we have been discussing to assert that perhaps the most significant basis of the "morality of profits" for McDonalds and for millions of other successful, self-sustaining for-profit businesses is when optimized "empowerment", even in creating, or running a business – that every business leader and every member of the business team are parts of a greater "empowerment of opportunity"; specifically, that what you are doing may indeed prosper because it passes that first critical hurdle of sustainability.

There is also the aspect that the business person hopefully will al-ways bear in mind that even the jobs that he or she provides should at least be thought of in the context of "empowering others" such as a supervisor or a worker – that in addition to creating quality products that bless and improve the lives of others – we also empower both workers and customers through quality products or even critical services, whereby each "contribution" truly creates a framework for expanded opportunities for others.

In short, in the entirety of the ethics and morality of for-profit business – it is indeed this matter of the empowerment of others – including the empowerment that may, in some circumstances, be as basic as food and shelter, or an empowerment for a wider and longer range goals and vision for education – including for workers or managers who have goals for "callings" to be pastors; or to become expert, and often highly profitable, business persons; or for a drive for future contributions to science; or for creating beauty as a designer, etc. – all of which, in real ways, also enrich the lives of others.

To conclude, through the practical and very understandable concreteness of profits – there is a love-gift that offers the prospects of the sort of "empowerment" that the highest and best prospects for sustainability – are genuine, realistic prospects for endurance, self-respect and resiliency. From that critical platform, doors may open widely to "generativity" in that what began today or is done today, may prosper in multiple, growing and unforeseen ways – ways that may, in fact, bless and empower perhaps millions of others, whom no one could have imagined at any given moment in time.

Thus, we have gone from God as a loving creator of the uniqueness of each individual person; to freedom as a fully intended gift of God; to a range of how vast our sense of gratitude should be in all things; to being proactive and not passive; to the non-waffling importance of accountability of every person and every endeavor (especially when there arises that special quantification of accountability that one finds in measurable profits; and lastly, not just the vast potentialities for empowerment itself – but most especially when the empowerment that is evoked is driven by Christian love.

It might be best, therefore, to both look for and to accentuate a LOVE that does not overlook a multiplicity of beneficial impacts but that also respects others by continuing to ask himself: Does Christian love ask of each one of us to always strive to be optimizers of opportunity – while never forgetting the specific wisdom of Proverbs to be realistic, and prudent Skeptical Stewards?

Thus, with any one of thousands of different for-profit endeavors, all of which typically contribute to a growing spectrum of empowerment of others – and, in fact, even whether or not, any sense of love of God or love of others was intended – **nevertheless,** might the **love of God** and a

love of others be an even more powerful springboard for a truly intended "love-witness" of Christian love in all that we say or do.

Thus, in the entirety of this worldview of morality – with God at the helm – we have Christ's own calling to us: (KJV) Matthew 6:19-21:

> (19) Lay not up for yourselves treasures on earth, where moth and rust doth corrupt, and where thieves break through and steal: (20) But lay up for yourselves treasures in heaven, where neither moth nor rust doth corrupt, and where thieves do not break through nor steal: (21) For where your treasure is, there will your heart be also.

And so, thank you, first, for the life-changing sense of "high calling" that each of you – yourselves – bring to bear as honest, accountable business persons, and, second, thank you for the compelling role model you convey when every aspect of your business is a tangible witness to your faith.

SECTION 4

SPECIFIC EXAMPLES FOR THE APPLICATION OF THE EIGHTH COMMANDMENT TO BUSINESS

SECTION 4: SPECIFIC EXAMPLES FOR APPLICATION OF THE EIGHTH COMMANDMENT TO BUSINESS

PHILIP J. CLEMENTS

The Introduction frames that the Christian worldview holds that God, as Creator, owns everything and gives it to whom He pleases. The individual recipient has responsibility to God for the stewardship, employment and enjoyment of what God has given him. Section 1 covers the theology underlying the commandment not to steal, including that what can be stolen is more than property; stealing includes time, and talent and opportunity. These framing thoughts are not repeated here. Rather the principles here go to the effect on an individual and the individual's community when these basic principles are respected. Section 2 presents the role of property rights as an essential element of human flourishing. Section 3 considers the challenges of social structures and the Eighth Commandment. Social structures necessarily lead to contemplations on the role of government and its actions. Underlying governments are the community itself and the differing views on how a community should be structured. All of these principles relate to our conduct of business today.

The six papers in Section 4 explore a series of business situations where stealing occurs that go beyond the normal parameters for the Eighth Commandment. A detailed listing of the topic the Reformers believed to be included in the Eighth Commandment can be found in the Appendix: Chart on the Eighth Commandment and Business Practices. To help the reader utilize the cases of conscience, as the Reformers would call the specific situations, a listing of the business situations addressed in this text are also included in the Appendix: List of Business Cases and Examples.

The first paper, "Contracts and the Destructive Effects of Unfaithfulness," by Vern S. Poythress and John Coors, uses three cases to consider the implications of violating the Eighth Commandment. Before delving into the cases, the paper presents an excellent overview of God's world and how the CoorsTek company values stack up. For those in business, this is an excellent analysis of comparing our value statements to biblical principles. Then the fallen nature of man is compared to the Eighth Commandment's requirements for respecting property ownership, with biblical references underlying each principle. The overview closes with an important look at the fact that "evil has consequences."

By way of principle application, each of the three cases is analyzed with these principles. But Poythress and Coors do not stop there, but inquire as to what our response should be. After considering the usual human responses to evil, the authors help us to understand what does work.

> "Biblically based ethics requires a response that is robust enough to interact with the full dimensions of moral challenge. Moral challenge confronts us in three interlocking dimensions: in our attitudes and motives; in the standards that we follow; and in our reckoning with the situations."

The paper closes with "We must pray. We must ask God to bring justice, not only in governments and in nations, but in companies and individuals."

The second[1] and third[2] papers show how businesses should evaluate compliance with government regulations while holding to a biblical worldview. When analyzing a business problem against God's principles, these papers highlight the need to first understand the facts, then to understand the law currently applicable. From there research is done into God's Word to see what principles God would have us apply. In these papers, the law is compared to the Eighth Commandment and God's framework for proper behavior. The papers present a conclusion of God's standards for the business situation.

In business today, business behavior is increasingly legislated or regulated. Neither paper fully addresses the interplay of government and business from an ethical perspective, i.e., when a business must comply with the laws as written, because the papers assume the need to follow the law. Bret Schundler's paper, "The Eighth Commandment and Civil Law: Biblical Faith and Engagement in the Shaping of Public Policy," in Section 3 does explore this important topic a bit further. In many cases the law will be a minimum standard for behavior with the biblical worldview raising the bar. In rare cases, not illustrated here, there may be a conflict between the law and God's requirements.[3]

Also in the public company space, Steve Austin, Keith Krzewski, and Andrew Peterson join to consider the problem of fraud in financial reporting in their paper, "Fraud And Resolution In The Public Company: Keeping The Eighth Commandment With Heart And Hand." This team opens with an important discussion of the relevance of public companies for God's world. Using an appendix, the authors provide useful insights on "principles, operating, and practices to be applied by the Christian to a business ethic for the public company." Three cases are used to illustrate both situations and analyses. The paper closes with a discussion of tools available for the prevention of fraud and the resolution of situations. Calvin Chin and William Goligher explore the Eighth Commandment's implications for the entrepreneur in the Eighth Commandment and Respect for Capital. Capital and stewardship merge in unique ways as we start companies. At the same time, operating a company in a startup environment poses real challenges for applying biblical principles such as the Eighth Commandment. This paper is particularly good for highlighting some of the due diligence required when investing, even with family members. The Reformers held that the Eighth Commandment requires us to procure, preserve and further our estate, but failure to do due diligence can lead to unwise investments and losses.

Capital requires a return. Modern social discourse and Liberation Theology has held this not to be the case. Yet, Jesus in His parables makes the required return on capital so important that He uses it to illustrate the Kingdom of God. In Matthew 21:33-46 the parable of the landowner indicates that the landowner deserved the rents on the vineyard he had leased out. In Matthew 25:14-30, Jesus uses the illustration of a master-servant relationship to show that capital given to servants requires a return. Too often entrepreneurs view startup capital, particularly friends and family capital, as high risk, therefore subject to loss and are not focused on both getting the capital back plus giving it a return. The result is that little caution is used in their investment and no passion is shown for earning the funds back, let alone a profit on them. What Christian entrepreneurs need to see in these parables is that the principles are at the very highest standards of behavior. Therefore, when friends and family funds are used to start a business, the responsibility to use them wisely and to create a return of and on is just as high as other principles about the kingdom of heaven. The sixth paper, "Effects of Ignoring God's Counsel: An Analysis of 2007-2008 Financial Crisis" by Philip J. Clements, further shows that God's Word holds much wisdom for business activities. This paper was prepared for general distribution and was posted on *CFO Magazine* website, being the most downloaded paper through the end of 2008. The paper explores the business activities leading up to the 2007-2008 financial crisis and how these activities violated clear counsel of God. The counsel was given some 3,000 years ago, yet remains fully applicable to the modern finance practices and modern finance theory.

This "Effects" ends with a look to the future. It is easy to take a negative perspective on the ethics of business and culture. Instead, Clements affirms that God is in control and His providence remains in the world He created. Therefore, Christians should have a positive outlook on the future. Like other papers in this section, the message for the business person is that God's Word does hold timeless counsel on how business should be conducted in God's world.

Notes

1. Julius J. Kim and John R. Mesher, "Thou Shall Not Steal – From Your Customers and Competitors: The Eighth Commandment and Antitrust Legislation."

2. Mark Futato and Philip J. Clements, "Material Nonpublic Information, Insider Trading, and the Eighth Commandment."

3. An example of this conflict is the legal requirement that all licensed physicians perform abortions, when requested by a patient. Most Christian doctors would view that the Sixth Commandment, Thou shall not kill, contravenes this law. In refusing to do an abortion, the doctor would accept the risk of losing his license to practice medicine.

Contracts and the Destructive Effects of Unfaithfulness

VERN S POYTHRESS AND JOHN COORS[1]

VERN POYTHRESS

Vern S. Poythress was born in 1946 in Madera, California, where he lived with his parents, Ransom H. Poythress and Carola N. Poythress, and his older brother, Kenneth R. Poythress. The family lived on a farm until he was five years old. When he was nine years old he made a public commitment to Christ and was baptized in Chowchilla First Baptist Church, Chowchilla, California. The family later moved to Fresno, California, and he graduated from Bullard High School in Fresno.

He earned a BS in mathematics from California Institute of Technology (1966) and a PhD in mathematics from Harvard University (1970). After teaching mathematics for a year at Fresno State College (now California State University at Fresno), he became a student at Westminster Theological Seminary, where he earned an MDiv (1974) and a ThM in apologetics (1974). He received an MLitt in New Testament from University of Cambridge (1977) and a ThD in New Testament from the University of Stellenbosch, Stellenbosch, South Africa (1981).

He has been teaching in New Testament at Westminster Theological Seminary in Philadelphia since 1976. In 1981 he was ordained as a teaching elder in the Reformed Presbyterian Church Evangelical Synod, which has now merged with the Presbyterian Church in America. More information about his teaching at Westminster can be found at the Westminster Seminary website.

Doctor Poythress studied linguistics and Bible translation at the Summer Institute of Linguistics in Norman Oklahoma in 1971 and 1972, and taught linguistics at the Summer Institute of Linguistics in the summers of 1974, 1975, and 1977. He has published books on Christian philosophy of science, theological method, dispensationalism, biblical law, hermeneutics, Bible translation, and Revelation.

Doctor Poythress married his wife, Diane, in 1983, and they have two children, Ransom and Justin. He has side interests in science fiction, string figures, volleyball, and computers.Doctor Lillback grew up in Painesville, Ohio, the middle of three boys. He lives in Wayne, Pennsylvania, with his wife, Debbie. They have two grown daughters.

JOHN COORS

John Coors is the Chairman of the Board, President and Chief Executive Officer of CoorsTek, Inc. Dr. Coors assumed the role of Chief Executive Officer and Chairman of the Board in October of 2000, after serving as President of the company since October of 1998 and as a Director since January of 2000.

Prior to assuming these positions, from January 1997 to October 1998, Dr. Coors served as the Chief Executive Officer of Golden Genesis Company, a former publicly traded subsidiary of Graphic Packaging, and a distributor and integrator of remote solar power applications. Dr. Coors grew the company from a small start-up to the largest public solar electric integrator in the country, with sales of $32.8 million in 1997. From July 1992 to January 1997, Dr. Coors served as President of Golden Photon, Inc., a manufacturer and developer of photovoltaic solar modules.

Dr. Coors began his career with Coors Brewing Company in 1979, and held various positions of increasing responsibility within the company in areas ranging from R&D and Engineering to Project Management and Human Resources. He left Coors Brewing Company in 1992, after having served as Vice President of Global Brewing Operations and Vice President and Plant Manager of the Memphis, Tennessee Brewery.

Dr. Coors holds a Bachelor's degree in Chemical Engineering from the Colorado School of Mines, a Master's degree in Biochemistry from the University of Texas and a Doctorate in Engineering from the Technical University of Munich. He currently serves on the Colorado School of Mines Board of Governors. Recently he has established the Advantage Energy Fund LLLP for investing in businesses providing modern energy services in Kenya.

W hat goes wrong when God's ways are ignored or violated? In particular, what goes wrong in business practice when people do not follow the eighth commandment, "You shall not steal" (Ex.20:15)?

From his experience at CoorsTek, Inc., and Community Uplift Ministries, a public charity, John Coors has provided three cases that illustrate the vital role of the eighth commandment.

BACKGROUND

CoorsTek is a privately owned custom manufacturer of ceramics and other high-tech products (http://www.coorstek.com/about.asp). It has a statement of core values that reflects concern for faithfulness:

In everything, we do to others what we would have them do to us
We do what we say, and say what we mean
We create outstanding value for our customers
We work together to make our company the best [2]

A second company, Community Uplift Ministries, founded by John Coors, was started to implement the Circle of Light program to provide a sustainable supply of modern energy to rural Africans.

What happens when people try to follow values like these and engage in a world whose values may violate God's standards?

PART 1: THREE CASES

Here are three cases from actual business practice.

Case 1. Foreign agents and governments not dealing squarely

Community Uplift Ministries partnered with a Kenyan Christian organization for a nonprofit program in Kenya. Following five years of collaborative work, the Kenyan "partner" decided to take over the program and all its assets, with the attitude "It is a good thing to steal from the West. They owe us." Once program support was cut off, the program quickly collapsed. The result was the failure of seven years development work, millions of dollars lost and 100,000 people defrauded and discouraged. The Kenyan government was asked to intervene on behalf of the donors. The response from the Kenyan government to this was "tough luck." Because John participated with a venture that claimed to be a Christian ministry, the name of Jesus was sullied. It was said, "If this is what Christians are like, we want no part."

Case 2. Contracts

CoorsTek had as their largest customer a company that wanted them to sign a global supply agreement. CoorsTek would not sign because they could see there were provisions in the contract that they would not be able to fulfill. The customer maintained, "Well, just sign it, because no one cares what it says, and we won't enforce the contract anyway." The customer threatened to replace CoorsTek as a supplier if they would not sign the agreement. (And the customer had backing in his experience dealing with other companies. All the competitors of CoorsTek were willing to sign.) Five to six years time and considerable back-and-forth negotiation was necessary before a contract was produced that CoorsTek could enter into, fully prepared to live by its terms.

John Coors reflects more broadly:

> We often compete with companies that promise customers what cannot be delivered, either by selling what they cannot make, or pricing in such a way as knowingly to lose money to get the business and eliminate the competition. After eliminating the competition they plan on raising prices and more than recouping their loss. This is a very typical business practice out of Asia (Japan and China), although the Japanese seem to be improving in this area. CoorsTek will normally lose this business rather than chase it, but at a significant loss. More often than not, our customers will return, because they know (or learn) they can trust us, but there is significant damage done to both parties. The "professional buyers" at large companies encourage these kind of tactics from suppliers because they are rewarded based on the price they pay for a part, not on the value a part provides. That is one of the reasons a one-dollar part can be responsible for the failure of a multimillion-dollar piece of equipment.

Case 3. Purchase agreements and paying suppliers

Standard agreements specify that the customer receiving goods must pay his supplier within a certain period, typically 30 days. Customers unilaterally extend the length of the period and delay payment, or sometimes do not pay at all or only after lengthy negotiations. Oftentimes they withhold payment until after the quarter or the year ends, allowing them to show to public markets artificially inflated cash balances. These practices get especially tested when times get harder. In short, actual practice of customers renders the contractual terms (30 days) meaningless.

Meanwhile the supplier suffers. The supplier has spent money for materials, labor, plant maintenance, and so on. He is being charged for the capital invested during the whole time while his customers are delaying payment. The charge comes either in the form of interest on a loan, or the unavailability of the expected money to use for further investment. If the delay is severe, and money does not come in return for what he has supplied, he can even be forced into bankruptcy.

PART II: THEOLOGICAL AND ETHICAL ANALYSIS

Ever since the fall of man into sin and rebellion (Genesis 3), we have been in flight from God and have been practicing ways of excusing ourselves. The Bible is a realistic book in depicting the record of sin through the centuries, even sin in the midst of God's own people, in the Old Testament and in the New. Over 2000 years ago, Amos and Proverbs indicted those who use two sets of weights, one in buying and the other in selling, so that they surreptitiously gain extra profit (Amos 7:5-6; Prov. 11:1; 20:10). [3] James indicts exploitative business practice (James 5:4). Sin penetrates and corrupts every area of life, including our dealing with money, profit, success, and business. God sees injustice in business and pronounces it "an abomination" (Prov. 20:10).

Background of God, man, and the world God has made

Modern "shady" and unscrupulous business practices typically assume that God is irrelevant, absent, or nonexistent. Even people who consider themselves "religious" may in practice confine their religion to Sunday or to some narrow sphere of life. They tell themselves that "Business is business." They mean that they adopt a different set of rules in the business world than what their conscience would dictate in another context. Or they say, "Everyone is doing it," more or less the way the customer in Case 2 excused an unreasonable contract. It is "typical business practice," the Asian businessman may tell himself in Case 2.

God is not mocked (Gal. 6:7). Even within this life, God frequently brings consequences for secret sins. "Whoever walks in integrity walks securely, but he who makes his ways crooked will be found out" (Prov. 10:9 ESV). "The righteous is delivered from trouble, and the wicked walks into it instead" (Prov. 11:8). We can see a degree of operation of such consequences in the second case study. Customers end up coming back to a company that deals honestly, because they gradually learn from experience that they are better off. But justice within this life is very uneven. Sometimes customers learn. But even these instances take time. Moreover, the Kenyan government did not bring justice in Case 1. The Kenyan partner "got away with one."

The Bible proclaims the reality of final judgment, when *every* sin and *every* injustice will receive due judgment at the hand of God: "he will judge the world with righteousness, and the peoples with equity" (Ps. 98:9; see Rev. 20:11-15). "... he [God] has fixed a day on which he will judge the world in righteousness by a man whom he has appointed; and of this he has given assurance to all by raising him from the dead" (Acts 17:31). The "man" of whom this passage speaks is Jesus Christ, who is not only the final judge but also the unique savior. We need to be saved not only from consequences of our sins within this world, but from the impending wrath of God. God himself has provided the one remedy through Christ.

Those who come to Christ in faith come to him as Lord as well as Savior (Rom. 10:9). He is Lord, meaning that we must obey him. So a follower of Christ needs to turn away from his sins, in the realm of business as well as every other realm. This deliverance is actually the one stable rock on which to build sound business practices (Matt. 7:24-27). Yet even people outside Christ can have a sense of their moral obligations and do external good. We can be thankful for all those whose business practices conform to God's standards, even if it is only because they are guided by a broad cultural atmosphere that has been touched by the influence of Christian faith or by common grace that God gives to people who are still in rebellion against him.

Business practices involving contracts take place in God's world, and so they are answerable to God. In particular, they are responsible to the eighth commandment, which says, "You shall not steal." The Kenyan example (Case 1) is a particularly egregious case of just running off with the money--it is stealing. But contracts also come under the scope of the eighth commandment, because contracts spell out legal obligations in matters of property. Contractual unfaithfulness is a form of stealing. The

Westminster Larger Catechism rightly includes among the violations of the eighth commandment "injustice and unfaithfulness in contracts between man and man."[4] Contracts also involve a verbal dimension, and so they bring us into interaction with the ninth commandment, "You shall not bear false witness against your neighbor" (Ex. 20:16). The immediate focus of the ninth commandment is on bearing witness in a court case. But contracts are made partly in case they come to court. They are serious. And the implications of the ninth commandment extend out quite broadly. God is a God of truth, and so he wants us to honor him and reflect his character by practicing truth in our lives. This principle is pertinent to Case 2. We cannot promise what we cannot give, even if we are assured that our promise will not be "enforced."

Analysis of business values

Now let us begin to analyze the challenges that arise in business practice. First, let us look at the "values" that CoorsTek has set forth. Those values resonate with biblical principles in a number of ways. The first principle is "... we do to others what we would have them do to us ." It is a reiteration of the Golden Rule, which comes from Jesus (Matt. 7:12; Luke 6:31).

The second principle is "We do what we say, and say what we mean ." The principle of telling the truth is deeply embedded in the Bible (Ex. 20:16; Prov. 12:17-20; Matt. 5:33-37; Eph. 4:25).

The third principle is "We create outstanding value for our customers." This principle is really a positive rewording of the principle, "You shall not steal." Positively, you look out for the good of your neighbor, who in this case is your customer. You provide "outstanding value," so that both seller and customer should be satisfied that the product is worth what is paid for it.

The fourth principle is "We work together to make our company the best." We strive for excellence, in order that God may be glorified, and our Master may say, "Well done, good and faithful servant. You have been faithful over a little; I will set you over much. Enter into the joy of your master" (Matt. 25:21).

The the core values of CoorsTek express biblical principles. We should be glad when we see such principles expressed, whether the principles are written by people who get their instruction directly from the Bible, or whether they come from a broader atmosphere, the influence of what we have called "common grace." People in their conscience know about the standards of God, even though their conscience is not infallible and can be distorted by sin. This inner knowledge from conscience can become embodied in the policies of companies and their customers. It is a benefit from God.

Broader implications of the eighth commandment

Other sessions for our conference on business ethics will delve more into the rich implications of the eighth commandment for business practices. But it is worth underlining some of this richness when we analyze the three cases we have set out above. The eighth commandment originated when God spoke to the people of Israel at Mount Sinai (Ex. 19-20). It was not just an impersonal moral rule or an arbitrary invention or a cultural convention. Rather, God spoke. And when he spoke, what he said expressed his character. God is a God of truth, and so he commands us to be truthful in the ninth commandment. God is the owner of the whole world, and he gives as gifts whatever we have. So God calls on us to respect human ownership, which is derivative from and reflective of God's original divine ownership. God's ownership is thus the foundation for the eighth commandment.

People may for awhile respect human ownership after they have managed to suppress and "forget" God's original ownership. But human ownership then no longer has a solid foundation. Why should I respect what someone claims to be his own, if the claim is merely his personal opinion or a social convention? And why may I not go along with the crowd if a general disrespect for ownership of property creeps in? We will consider later on the importance of a larger cultural atmosphere.

So the eighth commandment comes in a context where God's will defines its scope and purpose. We do not have the right to re-interpret and re-define it according to our own selfish desires. This principle is relevant for business, where each party is tempted to define moral standards in his own favor.

Moreover, the eighth commandment has positive implications for looking out for what is due to others. [5] For example, the Mosaic law has a specific provision telling people to pay what they owe:

> The wages of a hired servant shall not remain with you all night until morning (Lev. 19:13).

> You shall not oppress a hired servant who is poor and needy, whether he is one of your brothers or one of the sojourners

who are in your land within your towns. You shall give him his wages on the same day, before the sun sets (for he is poor and counts on it), lest he cry against you to the LORD, and you be guilty of sin (Deut. 24:14-15). [6]

The provision in Deuteronomy 24 speaks specifically of a laborer who "is poor." This statute might not seem to apply to the case of modern companies and corporations. But it is quite relevant to Case 3. In Case 3, the supplier depends on the customer for payment--he needs the payment. The broader principle, behind the specific provision in Deuteronomy 24, still requires that the customer be timely in his payment. Otherwise, the word "oppress" is appropriate.

Leviticus in the context of chapter 19 specifically sets the principle of payment in the context of larger principles of justice. Look at the whole passage:

> 11 "You shall not steal; you shall not deal falsely; you shall not lie to one another.
> 12 You shall not swear by my name falsely, and so profane the name of your God: I am the LORD.
> 13 "You shall not oppress your neighbor or rob him. The wages of a hired servant shall not remain with you all night until the morning.
> 14 You shall not curse the deaf or put a stumbling block before the blind, but you shall fear your God: I am the LORD.
> 15 "You shall do no injustice in court. You shall not be partial to the poor or defer to the great, but in righteousness shall you judge your neighbor (Lev. 19:11-15).

Verse 11 begins with a repetition of the eighth commandment: "You shall not steal." It thus indicates that Verse 13 concerning withholding wages is intended to be seen as an implication of the eighth commandment. It also puts the eighth commandment together with the ninth ("you shall not lie to one another") and the temptation to deceit ("you shall not deal falsely"), both of which address business practices. [7]

Verse 14 talks about sins that are not likely to be caught. The deaf person cannot hear your curse; the blind cannot see the stumbling block or who put it there. In these case it superficially looks as though you can "get away with one." Likewise the Kenyan "partner" must have felt that he could "get away with one." But God's response is, "You shall fear your God: I am the LORD." The obligations for contracts are ultimately set in the context of God himself. God sees and hears, though the blind and deaf do not. He is to be feared because he is a righteous judge. He will judge the world in righteousness (Ps 96:13). He is the LORD. We are meant to relate to him in his whole character.[8] And the way for such relationship has been opened to us through Christ the Savior.

In the USA and other well-developed market economies, we deal with corporations. It is easy for people to want to rip off a corporation, because, they tell themselves, it is rich and does not need what it has. They tell themselves that corporations are unscrupulous and so they deserve it. In addition, a corporation is impersonal and it will not matter. But it does matter to God. And as we shall see in our further reflections, a wide-spread breakdown to moral conviction destroys business. Vern Poythress has seen retail chain stores go out of business in circumstances in which he suspected they were being ripped off by their own employees carting away goods or stealing time, and by shoplifters who were "sticking it to the man." The businesses did not survive, and the neighborhood then suffered from being deprived both of their services and the opportunities for employment.

The failure to carry through principles

Even if we have before us admirable values like those that CoorsTek has put in place, challenges remain. It is one thing to express values in conformity with God's standards. It is another actually to practice them. Not all companies that have "values" are trustworthy companies. The Bible complains repeatedly that the Jews honored the law with their words but failed in their deeds: "You who boast in the law dishonor God by breaking the law" (Rom. 2:23; see Matt. 15:8). An individual or a company can pretend to be upright in business practices, and loudly proclaim its honesty, only in order to deceive more effectively those whom it will exploit. John's "partner" Kenya (Case 1) claimed to be Christian in spirit. This claim was only part of the game of exploitation.

We also must deal with circumstances where there may be no pretense of uprightness. People may admit, either to themselves or to others, that they are entering a relationship only for their own benefit. Some of the Kenyans doubtless admitted later on that they were ripping off the West.

Consequences of evil

Evil has consequences. We have mentioned the final judgment of God. But consequences work themselves out even within this world. People who plan evil can fall into their own pit: "He makes a pit, digging it out, and falls into the hole that he has made" (Ps. 7:15; see Prov. 26:27; 28:10; Eccles. 10:8). "Such are the ways of everyone who is greedy for unjust gain; it takes away the life of its possessors" (Prov. 1:19). We can see the operation of this principle in Case 2. The businesses who promise what they cannot deliver eventually get a reputation for not delivering. Their customers may wake up and search for someone they can trust. The greedy business may go out of business. But what if no honest business is available, because a whole culture has gone corrupt? Then the culture as a whole may spiral downward.

The principle of consequences is also operative with the making of unreasonable contracts, mentioned in Case 1. Time and money and opportunity were wasted through the customer who proposed the unreasonable contract. Unfortunately, the waste also effected CoorsTek, because they had to spend more time and money and lose opportunity through the back-and-forth negotiations that eventually led to something reasonable.

The principle is a general one. The person who wants to behave with integrity in business is still hurt by people who are operating with less worthy principles. Such people waste time and money and energy and opportunity. But the atmospheric effects are even worse, because the multiplication in numbers of unscrupulous people poisons the whole atmosphere for business. Why start a business as an entrepreneur if you must repeatedly confront the prospect of being ripped off? And if you are ripped off too many times, the company cannot be a financial success, and it has to close. All prospective customers then lose the opportunity to receive the company's services and products.

We can see large-scale effects in a situation like Case 1 in Kenya. A cultural atmosphere encourages people to excuse false dealing with Western companies. It goes through people's minds, "Everyone is doing it." People may think, "This is our country, and we have a distinctive allegiance. We are justified in not extending loyalty to Western companies, because Western colonialism has exploited us and impoverished us." Whatever may be the details of excuse-making, such an atmosphere bars the door to business. It takes away the incentive for any Western country to try to help in Kenya. Everyone in the country, good or bad, suffers effects corporately and nationally from this kind of atmosphere. There may indeed have been colonial exploitation in the past, but the desire to strike back at the West is also a desire for injustice to pay back previous injustice, and its reaps consequences in the form of prolongation of misery.

The Kenyan government did not enforce a contract with a Western company. The loss in Case 1 was catastrophic: millions of dollars and 100,000 people defrauded and discouraged. But this is only one case. More ominous still is the perpetuation of a pattern. Western companies soon learn that they cannot do business in Kenya. Neither can Kenyans benefit from any of the positive business developments that might follow. How many more millions of dollars have been lost, and how many more hundreds of thousands of people discouraged, because of projects that never got started? They never got started because the Kenyan government and the atmosphere of ripping off the West have closed the door.

Atmospheric effects extend even more broadly. A wide-spread attitude of ignoring or violating the eighth and ninth commandments encourages everyone in the culture to fall in with the attitude. There is pressure from peers: "My son, if sinners entice you, do not consent" (Prov. 1:10). Even citizens of Kenya who might want to start new businesses cannot trust an atmosphere that excuses injustice, favoritism, and deceit. What if they become the next object of the same exploitation?

Business cannot function and flourish without the practice of justice and a cultural atmosphere that affirms justice. A business cannot make money when its customers do not pay (Case 3). People find it difficult to take initiative and improve their property if the government makes it too difficult for them to obtain property to which they have a clear title, property for which the government will defend the rights. The consequence is that business in a whole country may become problematic. As a result, there are few businesses within the country, and these struggle if they are trying to be honest. Other businesses may thrive because they receive government favoritism. But the thriving is then a thriving for the benefit of a few rather than serving every customer. The nation reaps cultural disaster.

USA and Western world

We might be tempted to think complacently, "At least the problem is in other countries." The most severe problems are typically found in countries like Kenya whose industrial and business development is not robust. But what about Japan and China? Japanese practices have somewhat improved, according to Case 2. But Japan and China show us that unethical practices can crop up even where business development is already in motion. And what about the USA? Case 2 and Case 3 belong to the USA. Here as well as overseas businessmen can experience the temptation to do whatever they can "get away with."

In our cultural atmosphere as a whole, confidence about the presence of God, the coming judgment of God, and the validity of the Ten Commandments is gradually evaporating. But the problem is even deeper and broader than general cultural conviction. Within business there is pressure for performance, particularly financial performance, and that pressure frequently takes the form of demanding performance *regardless of moral principle.*[9] Pure pragmatism comes in: whatever works is OK. This pure pragmatism can then be excused by the motto, "Business is business." Pressure to perform and the temptation to bend to the pressure is always there. God have mercy on us; Jesus, revive our hearts and the hearts of many in our culture.

Conclusion

Evil produces damage, and the damage spreads. "Like a roaring lion or a charging bear is a wicked ruler over a poor people" (Prov. 28:15). "A ruler who lacks understanding is a cruel oppressor, but he who hates unjust gain will prolong his days" (Prov. 28:16). "When the righteous triumph, there is great glory, but when the wicked rise, people hide themselves" (Prov. 28:12).

Sin has corporate consequences on a neighbor, a city, a nation. Business does not work without the foundation of God himself. And the real God of the universe is the God who reveals himself in the Bible, not a god as we might imagine him to be, a god who overlooks sin and winks at unscrupulous business. God who is righteous is our foundation; but business in practice will not flourish unless God is known among people. Business does not flourish without respect for the eighth commandment in the consciences of the multitude, both inside and outside business.

Response

How do we respond? Should we just get more and more depressed by the prospect of cultural disintegration? We should be depressed if we expect merely human technique and human problem-solving and three-step remedies to pull us out of the mire. The mire at the bottom of our difficulty is the mire of human sin--people in flight from God. But that bottom-layer corruption does not get acknowledged very often. One part of our cultural atmosphere is is an attitude of self-help and technical "fixes." We will have a better set of company values. We will train our sales negotiators more effectively and make them more winsome. We will train our executives on how to recognize bad deals. We will get better laws from the government.

Yes and no. Technical improvements do have value. But we must face the fact that the deepest remedy is spiritual, and that such a message does not find ready acceptance with the glitzy side of modern culture. We must come to Christ to be reconciled to God. And the name of Christ does not find ready acceptance in our postmodern pluralism, which would prefer a bland talk about spirituality.

Biblically based ethics requires a response that is robust enough to interact with the full dimensions of moral challenge. Moral challenge confronts us in three interlocking dimensions: in our attitudes and motives; in the standards that we follow; and in our reckoning with the situation.[10]

First, moral action includes attitudes. It is not enough to "go through the motions" of adhering to God's law in outward forms. If you do not literally steal, but try to trap people into business deals that work in ways that undermine their well-being, your attitudes show deviation from God's ways. Moral action must be serving God, not merely conforming to God's commandments as if they were rules detached from the God who speaks them and whose character they reflect. We must seek God ourselves, and we must encourage others to seek him personally, not merely to "behave morally." We must encourage others to do the same.

Second, moral action includes adherence to God's standards, not merely standards that we make up or that society makes up or that we change when convenient. Even if a whole society endorses violations of the eighth commandment, the commandment remains as a standard. We must articulate a stance differing radically from the moral relativism and pragmatism that crops up today.

Third, moral action thinks wisely about the situation. The atmosphere of moral decay or of pragmatism or of lack of integrity in customers and businesses matters because it is part of the situation to which we must respond. We must try to find wise ways to act that encourage societies and cultures as a whole to turn in godly and pure directions. At the same time, we must be realistic about cultural influence, and not think of ourselves more highly than we ought (Rom. 12:3). God may or may not put us in a position where we can have serious cultural influence.

We must be aware of the ways in which sin infiltrates even Christian people and the church. We can make excuses for sleazy behavior (we at most call it "sleazy," not sinful). We can be oblivious to the pressure for "performance" that confronts businessmen.

We must be "wise as serpents and innocent as doves" (Matt. 10:16). One side of this principle is that we must be wise as serpents. With the Bible to equip us with a knowledge of sin, we must steel ourselves to detect and resist unscrupulous practices from suppliers, customers, and employees. We must not be naive. On the other hand, we must be innocent as doves. We must speak truth and respect others' property. We must not use the jungle-like character of some of modern business as an excuse to adopt the ethics of the jungle ourselves. May Christ through his resurrection power empower us to new living.

We must pray. We must ask God to bring justice, not only in governments and in nations, but in companies and in individuals. We must work for justice through being just in our dealings. "May the God of peace who brought again from the dead our Lord Jesus, the great shepherd of the sheep, by the blood of the eternal covenant, equip you with everything good that you may do his will, working in us that which is pleasing in his sight, through Jesus Christ, to whom be glory forever and ever. Amen" (Heb. 13:20-21).

Notes

1. Both authors have been over this whole paper. But John Coors has primary responsibility for the case studies (Part I), and Vern Poythress for the theological and ethical analysis (Part II). Bible passages are quoted from the English Standard Version (ESV).

2. <http://www.coorstek.com/about/vmv.asp>, accessed 2011 Jan. 25. The webpage includes along with a statement of values the company "Vision" and "Mission."

3. The *Westminster Larger Catechism*, Answer #142, includes "false weights and measures" among the sins forbidden by the eighth commandment.

4. The *Westminster Larger Catechism*, Answer #142.

5. See the *Westminster Larger Catechism*, Answer 99, #4: "[in interpreting the Ten Commandments] That as, where a duty is commanded, the contrary sin is forbidden; and, where a sin is forbidden, the contrary duty is commanded. Also, Answer #142, "The sins forbidden in the eighth commandment, besides *the neglect of the duties required, are* ...."

6. See also James 5:4.

7. See *Westminster Larger Catechism*, Answer #142, "fraudulent dealing," "all other unjust or sinful

ways of taking or withholding from our neighbour what belongs to him."

8. See *Westminster Larger Catechism*, Answer 99, #2: "That it [the law] is spiritual, and so reacheth the understanding, will, affections, and all other powers of the soul; as well as words, works, and gestures."

9. See *Westminster Larger Catechism*, Answer #142: among the sins are "covetousness; inordinate prizing and affecting worldly goods; distrustful and distracting cares and studies in getting, keeping, and using them."

10. These three elements correspond to the three perspectives on ethics worked out by John Frame in *The Doctrine of the Christian Life* (Phillipsburg, NJ: Presbyterian and Reformed, 2008). The perspectives in question are called the personal perspective (focusing on attitudes), the normative perspective (focusing on God's standards), and the situational perspective (focusing on the situation in which action is about to take place).

  3. *And what does the Lord require of you?*

  A. To act justly--the Second Table of the law defines "justice." Commandments 6-10.

  B. To love mercy--The Golden rule or love of neighbor summarizes these commandments. Compare Matthew 7:12; Matthew 22:34-40; Romans 13:8-10. The law as standard is inseparable from the motive of love. To "love mercy" is to "love love!"

  C. To walk humbly with your God--The First table of the law (Commandments 1-4) defines how we worship, how we walk in love with our God. "Walking with" is the life that is in covenant with God (Gen. 2:8; 6:21-24; 17:1.) Note that he is *"your"* God that you are to love according to the first great commandment (Matthew 22:24-40; Deuteronomy 6:4-5).

Thou Shall Not Steal–From your Customers and Competitors

The Eighth Commandment and Antitrust Legislation

JULIUS KIM & JOHN MESHER

JULIUS KIM

Prior to taking his current position at Westminster Seminary California (WSC), Dr. Kim ministered in a variety of ecclesiastical and academic settings. He has served in Presbyterian Church in America churches in California and Illinois. His current church calling is as Associate Pastor of New Life Presbyterian Church in Escondido, CA. While in Illinois, he taught undergraduate communications at Trinity International University and church history at Trinity Evangelical Divinity School. Following a brief tenure as Visiting Scholar with the Faculty of Divinity at Cambridge University, Dr. Kim returned to Southern California to serve as Dean of Students and to teach Practical Theology at WSC.

Dr. Kim also directs the Center for Pastoral Refreshment at WSC, a unique institute funded by the Lilly Endowment, Inc., dedicated to helping sustain pastoral excellence among Korean-American pastors. As a result of this work, he was able to pursue further research as a Visiting Professor at the Torch Trinity Graduate School of Theology, located in Seoul, South Korea, where he also lectured on history, preaching, and missions. He is a founding board member of a new resource center called the Council on Asian-American Reformed Leadership, a ministry dedicated to foster the biblical call, character, and competency of Reformed Asian-American pastoral leaders. He has served on several boards, including Peacemaker Ministries, Covenant College, Edmund P. Clowney Legacy Foundation, and the Cambridge Classical School.

Dr. Kim also continues to serve the broader Christian community as a preacher, speaker, and ministry consultant—recently participating in the Desiring God 2009 National Conference and the Together for the Gospel 2010 Conference. In addition to his doctoral concentration on English church history during the Restoration, his research interests include the history of preaching, homiletics, and Asian-American Christianity. His goals are to contribute both to the church and the academy through his teaching, preaching, and writing. He is the author of The Religion of Reason and the Reason for Religion: John Tillotson and the Latitudinarian Defense of Christianity, 1630–1694 and a contributor to Covenant, Justification, and Pastoral Ministry: Essays by the Faculty of Westminster Seminary California and Heralds of the King: Christ-centered Sermons in the Tradition of Edmund P. Clowney.

JOHN MESHER

Mr. Mesher is currently an Adjunct Professor at Philadelphia Biblical University in Langhorne, Pennsylvania. He teaches business law and corporate transactions in the undergraduate and graduate programs of the University's School of Business and Leadership.

Mr. Mesher retired in 2009 as the Senior Vice President, General Counsel and Corporate Secretary of Saint-Gobain Corporation, a $7 billion company with 19,000 employees at over 350 locations in the U.S. and Canada. Headquartered in Valley Forge, Pennsylvania, Saint-Gobain Corporation is the holding company for the North American activities of Compagnie de Saint-Gobain, the world leader in the habitat and construction markets, with annual sales of $40 billion and 190,000 employees in 65 countries. At Saint-Gobain, Mr. Mesher was responsible for the legal affairs, government relations, business ethics and corporate governance of Saint-Gobain Corporation, heading a staff of 23 in-house lawyers and four paralegals in four locations. He was also the Corporate Secretary for a multi-national Board of Directors, and was the company's chief compliance officer.

Mr. Mesher serves on the Board of Directors of Good Works, Inc., a nonprofit home repair agency for low income residents in Chester County, Pennsylvania. He is also a Quality Control Examiner for the IRS's Volunteer Income Tax Assistance Program. Mr. Mesher has been a panel member for various Philadelphia Bar Association programs, as well as the Argyle Executive Forum in New York City. He was the featured in-house counsel in the May 2006 edition of the National Law Journal.

INTRODUCTION

D o companies really steal from their customers? Why? How? Do they get caught? What are the consequences? These and other questions will be addressed in detail in this paper. At the outset, however, the answer to the initial question is unfortunately a resounding "YES."

This became quite evident in a fairly recent FBI sting operation in which members of an international cartel were caught red-handed on video and audio tapes in the act of fixing prices and carving up the worldwide market for lysine, a feed additive used by farmers around the world. The tapes demonstrated that employees of these companies, like other criminals, were brazen in their conduct, contemptuous of others, heartless about their impact, and fearless of detection. The executives and companies captured on these tapes stole money from farmers around the world just as if they had taken cash out of the farmers' worn blue jeans.

Not only did they violate man-made law, but they also completely ignored the Eighth Commandment's simple, but powerful, admonition – "Thou shall not steal." Public companies operating both in the United States and around the world engage in a number of unique practices that challenge business principles found in the Bible. One of those practices is compliance with antitrust legislation and one of the principles is found in the Eighth Commandment.

In the Old Testament, the Ten Commandments have traditionally been divided into two categories, or "Tables" (Exodus 20:2-17; Deuteronomy 6:5-21). The First Table spells out the duties we are to render God himself in the first four commandments: honor God only, worship God only, revere His name, and keep the Sabbath. The Second Table outlines the remaining duties we have toward our neighbors: do not murder, commit adultery, steal, lie, and covet. What Jesus does in the New Testament, however, is reveal that these duties to God and neighbor are essentially two sides of the same coin. In summarizing the Decalogue, Jesus states,

> "You shall love the Lord your God with all your heart and with all your soul and with all your mind. This is the great and first commandment. And a second is like it: You shall love your neighbor as yourself. On these two commandments depend all the Law and the Prophets" (Matthew 22:37-40). [1]

Thus, when we do not honor, worship and revere God only, we, for example, essentially break the Eighth Commandment. We steal from God what is rightly due to him alone. After all, the Westminster Shorter Catechism Question and Answer 1 succinctly teaches us that we were created "to glorify God and enjoy him forever." Furthermore, the Bible teaches us that because we were created in the image of God, in knowledge, righteousness, and holiness, we are called to honor, value and respect our neighbors since they are also God's image-bearers. John Calvin argued that we must treat even our enemies with righteousness and justice because of the divine image every person bears. [2] Thus, whether our "neighbor" is a customer or a competitor, the public company has a duty to not steal by honoring who they are and what they possess.

As this paper will argue, since we are created in the image of God and are given an inheritance as the children of God, we must not steal from our customers and our competitors in the context of antitrust legislation and practices. The remainder of the paper will answer two main questions: (1) What are the biblical **principles** involved in the Eighth commandment in the context of antitrust legislation? (2) What are the best **practices** involved with antitrust legislation for Christians seeking to honor God and neighbor, customers and competitors?

BIBLICAL PRINCIPLES

Two primary biblical principles serve as the foundation for understanding the Eighth commandment and its implications to antitrust legislation and practices that honor both God and neighbor, whether the neighbors are customers or competitors: (1) honoring the person as created in the image of God and (2) honoring their property as an inheritance from God.

Honor the Person (Who They Are): Created in the Image of God
One of the central truths of the Bible is that as humans we were created in distinction from the rest of creation, for we were created *imago Dei*, in the image of God. Genesis 1:26-27 states:

> Then God said, "Let us make man in our image, after our likeness. And let them have dominion over the fish of the sea and over the birds of the heavens and over the livestock and over

all the earth and over every creeping thing that creeps on the
earth." So God created man in his own image, in the image of
God he created him; male and female he created them.

Humans possess something that animals do not: a covenantal relationship
with God. Being created in the image of God means that humans are
intrinsically related to God. Patterned after Ancient Near Eastern trea-
ties between the conquering King and the vanquished King, the covenant
between God and man included the promises of blessing if the stipula-
tions of the arrangement were kept and the warnings of curses if they were
violated.[3] So serious was God in this covenantal arrangement, that he was
willing to suffer the consequences of the violations, that is death itself, if
man were to break the covenant in any way. This is graphically portrayed
in Genesis 15 where God reveals to Abram both the blessings and curses
involved in this unique covenantal relationship. This, of course, anticipates
the sacrificial death of Christ as a substitution for our covenant breaking.

Being in covenant characterizes human relationships created in the
image of God, first towards God and then to one another. We are not created as autonomous individuals who may or may not enter into a relationship with God. One scholar writes, "From the moment of conception,
each of us is already a participant in the web of human histories, relationships, genetics, and nurture that condition our personal identity." [4]

It must be remembered that the creation account of origins found
in the opening chapters of Genesis is primarily written with a theological
purpose, not a scientific one. God wants to reveal his eschatological purposes of creation, that is, that he has both a beginning and an end to what
he is creating. In Acts 17:26-27, the Apostle Paul argues that humans were
created for the purpose of having fellowship with God: "And he made from
one man every nation of mankind to live on all the face of the earth, having determined allotted periods and the boundaries of their dwelling place,
that they should seek God, in the hope that they might feel their way
toward him and find him."

Theologian Michael Horton summarizes the implications of this covenantal relationship in loving God and also neighbor:

> As a legal command to love God and neighbor and to subdue
> any ethical threat to this reign of God, this original covenant is
> indelibly written on the human conscience. All people retain

some sense of God as their lawgiver and judge and of the obligation to love. It is not that this religious and moral sense is
lost in the fall, but it has been gravely distorted and depraved.
Although we invest tremendous industry, creativity, and inge-
nuity in suppressing our identity as God's image-bearers, the
covenantal relationship between God and human beings is
ineradicable. [5]

This is why being created in the image of God not only includes the idea
of relationship, but also relationship that leads to ethics. When we were
created *imago Dei*, we were called into communion with God. At creation,
God speaks us into existence; it is his covenantal speech that is the source
of our personhood. [6] Without imparting divine faculties in our body and
soul, God reveals truth to us, primarily in the law written on our hearts.
This truth thus has an ethical component. God reveals, we must respond;
covenantal relationship implies ethics. Horton again is helpful here: "Human beings are those who reflect God's image not chiefly in *what they are
essentially but in how they reply ethically.*" [7]

John Calvin reiterates these same points in his *Institutes*. He
argued that the covenantal relationship, and not the imparting of some
divine essence or faculty into man, is the primary meaning of being created in the image or likeness of God.[8] This is why Calvin would speak of
the necessity of Christ's work on the cross to repair and restore the image
of God that was marred by sin. He writes, "Now we see how Christ is the
most perfect image of God; if we are conformed to it, we are so restored
that with true piety, righteousness, purity, and intelligence we bear God's
image." [9] This is not to say that God did not impart any traits into man.
Calvin rightly describes the communicable attributes that are given to man
at creation. Nevertheless, he argued that what separated man from the rest
of creation was the covenantal and ethical relationship as a result of being
created in the image of God.

In conclusion, every person has the rights and privileges of being
an image-bearer of God. Our responsibilities and duties to our neighbors,
however, flow out of this truth. Though my abilities to follow the law are
marred by sin and the fall, I still possess in my personhood this relational
essence and ethic. I honor my covenantal relationship with God by honoring my fellow image-bearing man. Since other humans also possess God's
image in relationship, I have a responsibility to do everything in my power
to love and honor them. This duty to love God and neighbor is established at creation and is thus binding to all humans, not just to Christians

who have put their faith in Christ and his work on the cross.

Honor their Property (What They Have): Receivers of an Inheritance from God

The first principle that serves as a foundation for understanding the implications of the Eighth Commandment is honoring the **person** as an image-bearer of God. The second biblical principle is honoring **property** as an inheritance from God.

The Bible has much to say regarding the nature and role of inheritance and the resulting stewardship of those gifts. First, the Bible teaches that God has the ultimate **ownership** of all that exists. Psalm 89:11 says, "The heavens are yours; the earth also is yours; the world and all that is in it, you have founded them." As sovereign creator and Lord, God rules and reigns over all of creation. This includes the pinnacle of his creation, mankind. Created in the image of God for relationship, mankind can rightly be called a possession of the Lord, for he is the potter and we are the clay (Isaiah 64:8). The Apostle Paul picks up this idea of inheritance and stewardship in his letter to the Ephesians when he writes, "For we are his workmanship, created in Christ Jesus for good works, which God prepared beforehand, that we should walk in them" (Ephesians 2:10).

Part of what God possesses is both corporate Israel and individual Christians. In the Old Testament, Israel was chosen out of all other nations to be his possession and inheritance solely out of his gracious love for them:

> For you are a people holy to the Lord your God. The Lord your God has chosen you to be a people for his treasured possession, out of all the peoples who are on the face of the earth. It was not because you were more in number than any other people that the Lord set his love on you and chose you, for you were the fewest of all peoples, but it is because the Lord loves you and is keeping the oath that he swore to your fathers (Deuteronomy 7:6-8).

In the New Testament, we read that his people were chosen in Christ (John 17:6; John 10:27-30) and that because of Christ's work, they become God's treasure, the pearl beyond price (Matthew 13:45-46; see also Psalm 28:9). Thus, God is the ultimate ruler and possessor of all things, including us.

Secondly, the Bible teaches that God gives to us everything that we possess as an **inheritance**. In the Old Testament, for example, we read that the Israelites were given the land that was already cultivated (flowing with milk and honey) as an inheritance (see Numbers 36; cf. Psalm 78:55; Psalm 16:5-6). The land was a "gift" given to them by their Father God, something they did not earn. The land was also proportioned equally among the tribes and was to be utilized for their benefit. The Year of Jubilee in Israel's history was another example of land inheritance as property was redistributed (Leviticus 25).

Third, in the same pattern seen at creation when Adam and Eve were called to have dominion over all that God gave them, the Israelites were expected to be **stewards** of the land that they were given as a gift from God. In Genesis 2:15 we read, "The Lord God took the man and put him in the Garden of Eden to work it and keep it." The language here of "work" and "keep" is the same language used for the priests and their work in the temple. Thus, just as the priests were to labor in extending God's kingdom of righteousness, justice and peace, man was called to steward the gift of the land as part of his covenantal relationship and responsibility. [10]

John Calvin writes of this dominion and stewardship given to man:

> The custody of the garden was given in charge to Adam, to show that we possess the things which God has committed to our hands, on the condition, that being content with a frugal and moderate use of them, we should take care of what shall remain. Let him who possesses a field, so partake of its yearly fruits that he may not suffer the grounds to be injured by negligence; but let him endeavour to hand it down to posterity as he received it, or even better cultivated. [11]

One scholar states it this way: "To fail in our stewardship, either in our duty to our neighbor or in our duty to God on behalf of our environment, is to steal from God, from ourselves, and from future generations."[12] So in sum, the right to private property as an gift of God and the responsibility for careful stewardship of our inheritance are key principles that flow out of the Eighth Commandment.

The Israelites knew, however, that the land of Canaan was not the final gift of inheritance. When the land was distributed among the tribes, one tribe did not receive any property—the Levites—for they were promised God himself as their inheritance. Furthermore, the civil and ceremonial laws found in the Old Testament (including the case-law applications of the Ten Commandments to political and judicial affairs) were part of the unique theocratic relationship that God had with Israel. All of this would anticipate the fulfillment of these land promises and laws in the promise of God himself as our inheritance through the work of Christ.

In the New Testament, the land symbolically and typologically pointed forward to the eternal Promised Land—heaven itself—as an inheritance, a gift we did not earn. The Scriptures teach that the entrance into the heavenly land is a gift of grace purchased for us through the sinless life, sacrificial death and inheritance-earning resurrection of Christ. The promise given to the Levites is ultimately fulfilled through Christ, who earns our inheritance for us—eternal communion with God himself.

We also read in the New Testament that the Holy Spirit is our "cash" down payment of this full inheritance (Ephesians 1:13-14). As Christians, though we "already" have this promise of the gift of God himself through Christ's finished work, this inheritance is "not yet" fully experienced in this life. But as we await the full consummation of this gift, God the Father and God the Son send us the Holy Spirit as a guarantee that this reality will come to full fruition.

Thus, we are God's own treasured property, the inheritance of the land, earned through the sacrifice of Christ himself. What is amazing about this transaction is that Christ then becomes our property, our inheritance. Edmund Clowney wrote succinctly yet profoundly, "As we are the inheritance, the property of the Lord, so too, we possess our inheritance in Christ. We belong to Jesus; he belongs to us."[13] This is inheritance and extravagance.

The Apostle Paul continues the idea of working faithfully and giving extravagantly because what we have is ultimately God's gift of inheritance. Negatively, in Ephesians 4:28, he states it this way, "Do not steal." Positively, however, he states, "Work; do something useful, and share with those in need." Which brings us to another principle: gift receivers are gift givers.

The Apostle Paul makes clear that the opposite of stealing is giving (Ephesians 4:28). We can, therefore, deduce that one of the principle applications of the Eighth Commandment is to be generous with our time, talent and treasure. In his advice to thieves, Paul calls them to stop stealing and work hard so they can earn money to give away! Clearly, Paul was following the teachings of Jesus himself who gave an illustration of extravagant giving in the story of the Good Samaritan (Luke 10:25-37).

Jesus tells a remarkable tale highlighting the unexpected generosity found in the Samaritan. After the expert in the law correctly responded that loving God and loving neighbor was the expectation of God, Jesus expands the boundaries of extravagance by redefining "neighbor." In this familiar story, a traveler on a dangerous road from Jerusalem to Jericho was ambushed, beaten and robbed, left by the side of the road to die. Two people consecutively encountered the assaulted man in their travels, a priest and a Levite. Though both knew their duty to care for those in need, they quickly passed by on the other side of the road. The one who did stop, however, was a Samaritan, someone who would never be considered a "neighbor" by Jews—such was the animosity and contempt that the Jews had for Samaritans.

The Samaritan stopped, tended to the wounds, took him on his own donkey to Jericho, and left him only after he had nursed him back to health. Such was his extravagance that he paid for the entire stay in the motel and promised to pay more if it was needed. Clowney summarizes this point well when he states:

> Jesus showed how he transformed the law [loving neighbor] by this story and by the question he asked. Jesus said, "Which of these three do you think was a neighbor to the man who fell into the hands of the robbers" (Luke 10:36)? Jesus does not suggest that we ask, "Who is my neighbor? How many must I love?" He wants us to ask, "To whom am I a neighbor? To how many can I show unmeasured love?" [14]

While this a wonderful story highlighting the extravagant model of love, we as Christians need to remember that Jesus is not just promoting love here, he is foreshadowing the extravagant love that will cost him his own perfect life as a substitutionary sacrifice for sinners. It is Jesus Christ's life, death and resurrection that transforms the Eighth Commandment. When we begin to see how it was his own love for us that took him to the cross, we begin to see not only the message of the Eighth Commandment but also the motivation. Because of the reality of the inheritance of Christ himself for us, we can give of ourselves with extravagance to those around us—especially to our customers and our competitors in the context of antitrust legislation.

BEST PRACTICES

The Eighth Commandment's principles of respect and value for others and their property have been embodied in the U.S. antitrust laws for over a century. The fundamental thrust of the antitrust laws is that the free enterprise system depends upon a marketplace that is devoid of collusion, market dominance, price discrimination and exclusionary business practices. Through this "_free_ enterprise" system, companies are able to enter and thrive (and, sometimes, fail) in the marketplace, competitors are able to compete vigorously, but fairly, for customers, and customers pay market-driven prices for the products they purchase. All of this is intended to result in economic efficiency (_i.e._, getting the most output from the least input). Just like the Eight Commandment's admonition of "Thou shall not steal," the antitrust laws prohibit theft from, and demand respect and value for, customers and competitors, as well as their property.

Major U.S. Antitrust Laws

The U.S. antitrust laws cover a myriad of prohibited business practices. Either directly or indirectly, this prohibited activity includes the "theft" of someone else's property through monopolization, barriers to entry, and artificially high prices for customers and consumers.

The **Sherman Act**, which is a criminal statute enacted in 1890, prohibits agreements or understandings (whether written or oral, expressed or implied) between two or more persons to restrain trade or competition in any product or service. An _agreement_ is any understanding between two or more parties. It may be wholly or partly written or oral, tacit, or implied by parallel behavior. No formal agreement is necessary to prove a conspiracy in restraint of trade. Rather, the existence of a conspiracy is often proven from the surrounding circumstances and subsequent events. A general discussion between competitors, followed by common action, is frequently enough to establish the basis of an unlawful agreement. Accordingly, every communication between a firm's representatives and those of its competitors, whether oral or written, is subject to close scrutiny in an antitrust investigation.

The Sherman Act also makes it illegal for any person, acting alone or with another, to monopolize or attempt to gain a monopoly over a particular product or service.

The **Clayton Act** was enacted in 1914 and prohibits (i) exclusive dealing arrangements where the supplier conditions the sale of products or services upon the buyer's refusal to purchase such products or services from a competing supplier, and (ii) tying arrangements in which the supplier conditions the sale of a desired product or service on the purchase of a separate (and often less desirable) product or service, where such arrangements may substantially lessen competition. The Clayton Act also prohibits acquisitions or mergers that may substantially lessen competition in the relevant market.

The **Robinson-Patman Act** was enacted in 1936 to prohibit a supplier from discriminating in the price charged for the same product sold to two or more customers where the effect of such discrimination may be to injure competition, or favoring one customer over another in the granting of promotional services or allowances, unless certain statutory exceptions or defenses apply. This Act also prohibits a supplier from selling products at unreasonably low prices for the purpose of destroying competition or eliminating a competitor.

The **Federal Trade Commission Act** was enacted in 1914 and prohibits unfair methods of competition and unfair or deceptive acts or practices.

While each of these statutes applies to domestic interstate commerce, they also apply in many cases to any international business transaction that involves imports into or exports from the U.S. For instance, competing companies may not divide world business in such a way as to affect substantially the foreign trade of the U.S.

In addition, most states have adopted their own antitrust laws that are very similar to the federal statutes.

Is the Fear of Punishment the Beginning of Wisdom?

It has often been said that, "The fear of punishment is the beginning of wisdom." [15] Whether this is true or not, the antitrust laws certainly use this "stick" to force firms and their employees to comply with the law. The consequences of a violation of the U.S. antitrust laws can be severe, both for the firm and the employees involved.

Prison Sentences: Violations of the Sherman Act are serious crimes. Prison sentences of up to ten years per offense may be imposed on any individual found guilty of violating the Sherman Act.

Fines: Fines of up to $100 million for each criminal offense or twice the violator's gross gain or the victim's gross loss may be imposed on a firm, and fines of up to $1 million for each criminal offense may be imposed on an individual participating in a violation.

Injunctions and Decrees: The government may obtain an injunction that may be broader in its prohibition of certain activities than would seem to be warranted by the illegal conduct itself. In addition, the government may enter a decree against the firm that enjoins specific future activities. These injunctions and decrees can restrain severely the legitimate business activities of a firm and place the firm at a substantial competitive disadvantage.

Treble Damages: Any person or class of persons who are financially injured by an antitrust violation may recover in a civil suit **three times** the amount of damages actually suffered (also known as "treble damages").

Legal Fees: In addition to paying its own legal expenses, which can be very substantial, a losing party in an antitrust action also will have to reimburse all of the legal fees of the successful claimant or claimants. These are in addition to the payment of any final award of treble damages granted to a successful claimant.

Government Contractor Debarment: A firm may be prohibited from contracting with the U.S. government following any criminal or civil violation of the antitrust laws where the violation involved the submission of bids to the government.

Personal Costs: When an employee is a party in a criminal or civil antitrust case, the employee's legal expenses, as well as any fine that is imposed, may not be reimbursed by the firm. And, it almost goes without saying that involvement in a violation may also lead to the termination of the employee's employment.

The U.S. and foreign antitrust regulators have been rigorous in their enforcement of the antitrust laws in recent years, imposing significant fines for violators. In fiscal year 2009,[16] the Antitrust Division of the U.S. Department of Justice obtained criminal fines of over $1 billion. Although criminal fines dropped to $555 million in 2010, jail time for individual criminal antitrust defendants increased over the prior two years, reaching an average jail term of 30 months – the second highest ever. Public antitrust enforcement by jurisdictions outside of the United States (particularly in Europe) has also been significant, with the European Union imposing fines of €3 billion (about $4 billion) in 2010. In Brazil, the antitrust regulators levied the highest fine of any competition authority in 2010 in their investigation of an alleged industrial gas cartel. Five companies and seven executives were fined 2.9 billion Brazilian reais (about $1.7 billion).

Public Companies

In the antitrust arena, public companies are particularly vulnerable to wayward employees (especially, salespeople and management). Employee bonuses are frequently determined quarterly or monthly on the basis of sales and/or profit for the period - - a compensation system that can sometimes reward short-term (and illegal) manipulation of the market. When coupled with frequent opportunities for inappropriate contacts and discussions with employees of competitors (such as at otherwise legitimate trade shows or industry association meetings), this profit-at-all-cost motive meets opportunity, creating a recipe for disaster. Not only are employees themselves rewarded too readily for short-term results, but the public companies for which they work are judged by financial analysts on the basis of brutal quarter-by-quarter performance indicators. All of this can foster short-term decisions without regard to the long-term negative impact that an antitrust violation will have on a public company's stock price, reputation, corporate image and customer relations. Despite a public company's best efforts to educate its employees about the antitrust laws and to maintain a rigorous compliance program, this explosive mix of greed and willing participants from other companies has unfortunately ensnared even the most reputable companies.

Disdain for Customers and Love of Competitors

In the 2009 movie, *The Informant*, Matt Damon plays the character of an executive (Mark Whitacre) with a large company in which he participates in a conspiracy to illegally fix the prices of an animal food additive (lysine) with other business rivals around the world. Matt Damon ultimately assists the FBI in a sting operation and surreptitiously attends, and lets the FBI listen in on, the cartel's meetings in cities such as Tokyo, Paris, Mexico City and Hong Kong. During the undercover operation, the FBI collects hundreds of hours of video and audiotapes that document price-fixing crimes committed by executives from around the world. These tapes show the distain the price-fixers had not only for the law, but also their own customers. While waiting for other price-fixers to arrive at one of the cartel's meetings, these executives are shown saying, "We have a couple other people joining [our meeting]," and then they are heard joking that "one will be from the FBI and seven more from the FTC!" At another meeting, one executive is caught on tape saying, "[Our customers] are not our friends. Thank God we gotta have 'em, but they are not . . . our friend. I want to be closer to you [the competitors] than I am to any customer."

This is hardly the respect and value for the law and customers demanded by the Eighth Commandment.

Unfortunately, Matt Damon's role was not based on fiction - - it was based on true events. The lysine price-fixing conspiracy was an organized effort during the mid-1990s to raise the price of lysine. The cartel was very successful, having been able to raise lysine prices 70% within their first nine months of cooperation. The criminal investigation ultimately yielded $105 million in criminal fines and significant prison sentences for three executives of one of the firms involved in the price-fixing conspiracy. Buyers of lysine in the United States and Canada also sued and recovered hundreds of millions of dollars in civil damages.

Ten Commandments of Antitrust Compliance
Although the antitrust laws can be complex in their application to specific facts, compliance with the antitrust laws can be generally assured by adhering to the following Ten Commandments of Antitrust Compliance, each of which has its origins in one or more of the Federal antitrust laws.[17]

"Thou Shall Not" . . . .

I. **Discuss prices, terms of sale or other competitively sensitive information with competitors.**

II. **Obtain market information (e.g., price lists) directly from competitors, or use an external consultant or other agent to obtain it for you.**

III. **Divide customers, markets or territories with competitors.**

IV. **Agree upon, or attempt to control, a customer's resale price without first consulting a lawyer with antitrust expertise (in some cases, this activity may be illegal).**

V. **Attempt to restrict a customer's resale activities without first consulting a lawyer with antitrust expertise (in some cases, this activity may be illegal).**

VI. **Talk to customers about the resale practices (e.g., pricing) or other activities of other customers.**

VII. Offer a customer prices or terms more favorable than those offered to competing customers, unless a legitimate meeting competition exception applies and proper paperwork is completed.

VIII. Require a customer to buy one product in order to purchase another without first consulting a lawyer with antitrust expertise (in some cases, this activity may be illegal).

IX. Agree with a customer on another customer's pricing or agree that its margin in the resale of your products will always be a certain amount or percentage higher than the margins of other customers buying your products.

X. "Bad mouth" a competitor's product unless you have documented test results or other objective proof that the statements are true.

CONCLUSION

The Bible's Ten Commandments must not be read as a list of things we are owed by others; rather, they stress what we owe our neighbor. In the Eighth Commandment, God teaches us both the requirements involved in the simple yet poignant statement "thou shall not steal" as well as the prohibitions. Several answers from the Westminster Larger Catechism are helpful in its summary of both the duties and sins involved with the Eighth Commandment:

Question 141: What are the duties required in the eighth commandment?

Answer: The duties required in the eighth commandment are, truth, faithfulness, and justice in contracts and commerce between man and man; rendering to everyone his due; restitution of goods unlawfully detained from the right owners thereof; giving and lending freely, according to our abilities, and the necessities of others; moderation of our judgments, wills, and affections concerning worldly goods; a provident care and study to get, keep, use, and dispose these things which are necessary and convenient for the sustentation of our nature, and suitable to our condition; a lawful calling, and diligence in it; frugality; avoiding unnecessary lawsuits and suretyship, or other like engagements; and an endeavor, by all just and lawful means, to procure, preserve, and further the wealth and outward estate of others, as well as our own.

Question 142: What are the sins forbidden in the eighth commandment?

Answer: The sins forbidden in the eighth commandment, besides the neglect of the duties required, are, theft, robbery, man-stealing, and receiving anything that is stolen; fraudulent dealing, false weights and measures, removing land marks, injustice and unfaithfulness in contracts between man and man, or in matters of trust; oppression, extortion, usury, bribery, vexatious lawsuits, unjust enclosures and depopulations; engrossing commodities to enhance the price; unlawful callings, and all other unjust or sinful ways of taking or withholding from our neighbor: What belongs to him, or of enriching ourselves; covetousness; inordinate prizing and affecting worldly goods; distrustful and distracting cares and studies in getting, keeping, and using them; envying at the prosperity of others; as likewise idleness, prodigality, wasteful gaming; and all other ways whereby we do unduly prejudice our own outward estate, and defrauding ourselves of the due use and comfort of that estate which God has given us

Public companies have much to gain by incorporating into their mission and practice the truths involved in the Eighth Commandment. By increasing their knowledge of biblical principles and antitrust practices found in the Eighth Commandment, they will experience an increase in reputation, clients, and quite reasonably, revenue. Conversely, without this knowledge and know-how, companies, and by extension, our society, have much to lose.

Notes

1. All Scripture quotations are from the *English Standard Version*.
2. John Calvin, *Institutes of the Christian Religion*, 3.7.6.
3. See Meredith Kline, *Kingdom Prologue*, for more on this covenantal framework of creation.
4. Michael Horton, *The Christian Faith*, 380.
5. Horton, 384.
6. Ibid., 388.
7. Ibid., 389; emphasis his.
8. See Calvin, *Institutes of the Christian Religion*, 1.15.
9. Ibid., 1.15.4.
10. Horton, 398-9.
11. Calvin, *Commentaries on the Book of Genesis*, vol. 1, 125.
12. Michael Horton, *The Law of Perfect Freedom*, 204-5.
13. Clowney, 115.
14. Clowney, 120.
15. This notion may have its origins (although somewhat misguided) in the Bible where it is said that, "The fear of the Lord is the beginning of wisdom; all who follow his precepts have good understanding" (Psalm 111:10).
16. The fiscal year for the U.S. Department of Justice runs from October 1 through September 30.
17. These Ten Commandments, as well as the summary of the U.S. antitrust laws, are taken from Saint-Gobain Corporation's Antitrust Compliance Policy and Guidelines (used with permission). Mr. Mesher was Senior Vice President and General Counsel of Saint-Gobain Corporation before he retired in 2009. He used these "Ten Commandments" frequently as part of the company's antitrust compliance educational programs.

FRAUD AND RESOLUTION IN THE PUBLIC COMPANY

KEEPING THE EIGHTH COMMANDMENT WITH HEART AND HAND, "THOU SHALT NOT STEAL"

KEITH KRZEWSKI, ANDREW J. PETERSON & STEVE AUSTIN

KEITH KRZEWSKI

Keith Krzewski is a Partner and Chief Operating Officer with Swenson Advisors, LLP. In his capacity as Partner and COO, Keith manages all financial and administrative operations for the firm.

Prior to joining Swenson, Keith was Chief Operating Officer for the San Diego office of Baker & McKenzie LLP, one of the world's largest law firms. Prior to Baker & McKenzie LLP he was the Chief Operating Officer for Directed Electronics Inc., where he was responsible for assisting in the management of a multi-million dollar electronics manufacturing company with 175 employees. Prior to Directed Electronics, he worked a total of 8 years as an Audit Manager in the public accounting sector both in the U.S. and Australia, for Coopers & Lybrand and Nelson Parkhill BDO.

Keith graduated from Walsh College of Accountancy and Business Administration and attained his Certified Public Accountant status in Michigan.

Keith serves as Treasurer for Community Christian Church and is a Board Member for Community Christian School and the Downtown YMCA. He also serves as Treasurer for San Diego County Citizens Against Lawsuit Abuse (CALA) and is President for Women's Resource Committee.

ANDREW PETERSON

Since 1997, Dr. Peterson has directed distance education for graduate theological education from Charlotte, North Carolina, for Reformed Theological Seminary, Virtual Campus. Additional professional work includes business consulting with Cathedral Consulting Group, LLC, and educational technology with Digital Vistas Carolina, LLC.

Over the past dozen years, Andy has developed a "virtual campus" for the education of hundreds of graduate students at a school in the Southeast USA, Reformed Theological Seminary. With headquarters in Charlotte, the student body is worldwide. This formal degree program makes the most use of distance education of any accredited seminary in the world. Using online promotion, sales, and delivery, positive net revenue has been gained year to year. To date, RTS/Virtual has over thirty courses, including church history, systematic theology, biblical studies, pastoral counseling, Christian education, and online Greek and Hebrew language instruction.

Andy's professional road map has been from licensed psychologist in Pennsylvania at a community mental health center, to a professor of psychology for business psychology and teacher training courses for Grove City College, a four-year liberal arts college north of Pittsburgh, to a professor of practical theology at Westminster Seminary in California and educational technologist at Santa Fe Foundation in Solana Beach, and then to University of California, San Diego, in 1995 to establish the first Multimedia Development Center for faculty development of digital presentations (just as the Internet hit!). While in southern California, he consulted with businesses and schools on the use of educational technology. He continues to do that with the "virtual campus" concept now as well as doing business reviews and board services. Long-term professional themes are education, counseling, and business with help from theology as well as technology. Tours in higher education have been at Western Washington University (BA, Psychology), University of California, Berkeley (MA, Educational Psychology), and University of Pittsburgh (PhD, Educational Communications and Technology).

STEVE AUSTIN

Steve Austin services audit and business consulting engagements with a focus on technology, manufacturing, telecom, software, drug discovery, and medical device companies. He is the author of the book, "Rise of the New Ethics Class," with a focus on Sarbanes-Oxley regulations.

Prior to joining Swenson Advisors, LLP Steve had over 22 years of experience as an Audit Partner with Price Waterhouse LLP, and with McGladrey & Pullen, LLP serving both public and private companies. While at Price Waterhouse, Steve also worked in the New York National Office, where he addressed complex accounting and reporting issues for companies, including ESOPs, software cost capitalization, business combinations, income taxes and leading edge business transactions. Steve worked with various members of the FASB and EITF staffs. At McGladrey & Pullen, LLP he focused on high tech, manufacturing, and real estate companies as well as managed the audit department in San Diego.

Steve has experience with emerging, middle market, and large private and public companies. He has significant IPO and secondary offering experience with high technology, biomedical, software and real estate companies.

Steve is a Certified Public Accountant in California and Georgia and is a member of the California Society of CPAs and the American Institute of Certified Public Accountants. He is the past Global Chairman of Integra International and a member of their Global Executive Committee (in charge of Asia). He is a member and supporter of the Corporate Directors Forum, Global CONNECT, CONNECT, San Diego Venture Group, San Diego Software Industry Council, and past committee member of The San Diego Mayor's Pension Reform Committee. He serves on the Board of Directors of Family Heritage Foundation, Pinnacle Networking Group, Sharp Healthcare Foundation, American Heart Association in San Diego (past Chairman), Santa Fe Christian Schools Endowment Fund and serves as an Elder at Faith Community Church. He is Audit Committee Chairman of World Trade Center San Diego and Avanir Pharmaceuticals (a NASDAQ Company).

> *4 Rejoice in the Lord always; again I will say, Rejoice. 5 Let your reasonableness be known to everyone. The Lord is at hand; 6 do not be anxious about anything, but in everything by prayer and supplication with thanksgiving let your requests be made known to God. 7 And the peace of God, which surpasses all understanding, will guard your hearts and your minds in Christ Jesus. 8 Finally, brothers, whatever is true, whatever is honorable, whatever is just, whatever is pure, whatever is lovely, whatever is commendable, if there is any excellence, if there is anything worthy of praise, think about these things. 9 What you have learned and received and heard and seen in me—practice these things, and the God of peace will be with you. (Philippians 4:4-9)*

PURPOSE

The aim of this paper is to present apt Christian principles, some biblical practices, and the peace that can help avoid fraud and promote resolution in the public company. By seeing the world with biblical assumptions, one sees the violation of Christian ethics in a wide range of corporate deceptions and the point-by-point remedies for effective response and future prevention. It is in God's law, properly understood as a grace and in step with God's love, that we see simple standards versus fraud, especially in the eighth commandment and its related case laws. Training of behavior is necessary, but not sufficient – business ethics is a matter of the heart, too (Edgar, 2006). The need is for a culture of people who resist theft and resolve fraud. We ought to trust and obey God's Word rather than worry and scheme.

The *Westminster Larger Catechism* unpacks many of the implications of this eighth commandment in life, including the marketplace. There is a set of wrong attitudes as well as definitions of the sins that are variations on the theme of stealing. That culture has been called the *Protestant Ethic and the Spirit of Capitalism* (Weber, 1914, Landes, 2002, Huntington, 2004). Cases from the extant literature and the actual practice of public accounting illustrate the use of Christian principles in action. Hope and help are given for "overcoming evil with good" in business situations with God's norms and a heart that is holy and happy and at peace in a stressful world. Theologically and professionally, we see that theft is a "get rich quick scheme" that defies God and leads to disaster. There is a slide from the sin of worry to the sin of stealing. We begin by thinking about business in God's world from a robust perspective based on God's Word.

BIBLICAL PRESUPPOSITIONS FOR PUBLIC COMPANIES

Relevance of God's Word in the Business Ethics of the Public Company
The apostle Paul reminds Christians to rejoice in all situations because the Lord is near and the effect will be a good witness of a positive lifestyle for all to see. Note the transparency in the biblical way of life. No secret formulas for success. No shadowy conspiracies for power. Just upright living in the confidence that the Judge is near who sees all and looks right into the heart of every human actor. He is not the "watchmaker God" who has created the world and now walks away from his production. He sustains all things, including large public companies. These ancient truths are brought into the pressure of the modern world of big business. And they are perspicuous, i.e. clear and understandable. The truth is near ... "it is in your mouth" (Deuteronomy 30:14).

Given that the Christian worldview is the valid way to see God's world in general and in detail, we ought not to steal because of this commandment, at least. Even a non-believer has to admit to the wisdom of the prohibition on theft. As the apostle Paul reminds us in Colossians 1, all things are understood in Christ. Do you see the Lord in the business world? What is His character and scope? What is your response? Is it to rejoice? If not, … let's try again. Or do you insist to take things into your hands … even when others own them!

Categories for thinking about commerce are found in the Bible as an important human activity with personal, church, family and state dimensions. The ways to think about the players and the processes are presented in the Bible. Plus, the right ethics for response to our world are given, too. Adam's task was to care for a growing Garden of Eden. That dominion mandate remains in effect for us. In II Timothy 3:16, 17, there is a four-stage analysis for implementing business ethics from Scripture:

1. Teaching
2. Conviction
3. Correction
4. Training

The teaching is based in God-breathed Scripture shows how to think about a problem. The conviction is the personal impact of the truth as revealed by the Spirit. The correction is taking out the error and replacing with a righteous response. And training is to establish godly routines that prevent a repetition of the sinful response. This paper applies this biblical sequence to the problem of fraud in a public company as "cases of conscience", cf. the Puritan father Richard Baxter.

The abundance of Eden (Hall and Burton, 2008, p. 15) is the beginning of understanding our environment for business in any location or culture. Subsequently, the Fall resulted in the depravity of the owner, an effect on the environment, the nature of man and the new nature of nature. It was bad for business. The Fall was a fraudulent arrangement with Satan, Adam and Eve. They chose to steal the one thing that was prohibited in order to steal all of God's glory. Yet, still, God's people have an ongoing mandate to make things better as part of the victory of Christ over sin.

This mandate, along with the Great Commission, is the necessary godly motivation for business: The pressure of challenges and threats are met with trust in God to be able to complete the stewardship of life in all of its rich dimensions. The motivation of knowing his presence even in the midst of business pressure sends the Christian on a new trajectory in stewardship. The peace of knowing God's presence gives stability for composure in the business setting, regardless of size or complexity. There is a big picture that puts the "ups and downs" of business into perspective.

Biblical principles and practices can be found in God's Word for all of life, including business operations. Both general principles with manifold application and illustrative examples are available in Scripture. His Word is sufficient as well as necessary. Other non-Christian approaches may have "glimmers of truth" from common grace, but still require discernment with biblical standards. The Eighth Commandment is clear: private property is a fact and must be respected.

As a currently popular movie, *Inception* (2010) with Leonardo DiCaprio is an example of the tricky combination of a contrived "objective" reality, corporate fraud, and stealing a birthright. Entering into fraud is like going into an alternate universe, a house of mirrors. The storyline for the film was for a consultant to cause an heir to reject "willingly" the ownership in a mega-corporation. The competitors, from another country, gain advantage with this discontinuity. The consultant's method is to affect dream life as a process of planting suggestions. In the end, the effect is actually the same result as more ordinary methods of fraud. To be grounded in God's Word is to be protected from the ordinary temptation to deceive as well as a so-called, "Inception."

Relevance of the Public Company in God's World

Publically traded companies are usually large organizations, involve many stakeholders, and based on complicated financial arrangements. Even in such complexity, Christian theology notices the attention to detail ... "everything by prayer" and "your requests" are noted as specific details in God's world. Notice the blessing of "guard your hearts and your minds" for focus and its effect on motivation in any workplace. The Christian can analyze in peace and fearlessly look at the consequences with denial (Collins, p. 19). There is no valid reason to steal anything, large or small. It is sinful, lazy, and stupid.

Theologically, the key institution in God's world today and in eternity is the church. Regarding prayer, the church is the locale of corporate worship, which has corporate and individual prayer as a central feature. Prayer involves resisting anxiety, supplication, thanksgiving, and sense of peace and safety beyond expectation. Business is often where the needs and answers of prayer are seen. Business done to God's glory is a blessing in personal achievement, family prosperity, church life and community progress and the public company.

For example, reflecting on the family business at Clearfield Wholesale Paper Company in central Pennsylvania, one remembers grandparents giving glory to God for the provision of daily bread from " the store." Many hours were spent in the business in doing ordering, selling, fulfilling, delivering and supporting necessary products for day-to-day life. At the large-sized corporate level, we see Wal-Mart worldwide as the number one retailer today. It is a true blessing to millions of people when through organization and work, products are sold for affordable prices by a public company with such scale in a free market. In fact, the occasional threatening of anti-trust prosecution is another example of violation of the eighth commandment by the State.

Biblical institutions for the government of business in God's World are personal, family, church, and civic patterns. Self-government is the beginning of ethics as motivated by the fear of the Lord (Proverbs 1:7) and matured via apt biblical education and training. We spend more time on our vocational work than any other activity, so, time-wise, it is the most common venue for obedience to the Lord. The cultural mandate of dominion is most focused through the family with business as central to stewardship and increasing control over the earth under God. As any nation has less theft throughout society, the work and effort in business are rewarded with compensation that can be maintained and enjoyed. This is necessary to start and maintain public companies.

As the church baptizes and disciples people worldwide, business is a key social area for loving God and neighbor as well as a source of material support through the tithe. Business is a cultural activity where godly living takes place. For the church, among other things, it is a major source of the tithe through the members that is the financial model for funding its operations. The connections from church to business life are manifold. Many congregants work at successful public companies in their daily vocation.

We pray for our government leaders that there might be justice for persons and families as well as an environment for the growth of the church and her evangelism (I Timothy 2:1-2). The statist has a biblical version of the Marxist counterfeit motto in God's Free World, "according to our abilities, and the necessities of others; WLC, Q141." In context, the phrase is introduced in this confession with the idea of "giving and lending freely," which is hindered greatly by a collectivist government. The government "bears the sword" to punish "evildoers," including thieves and frauds. Thus, it ought to protect citizens from real theft rather than directing culture and the economy.

Westminster Larger Catechism, Q140 – 142

See Appendix A for tables of principles, operations, and practices to be applied by the Christian to a business ethic for the public company. The WLC contains the biblical elements for a rich training program in the workplace. Consider these principles and practices in the confrontation with a possible culture of theft in a society or a public company.

Cases Of Conscience With Fraud And Resolution

In his 17th century classic, Richard Baxter addressed the "cases of conscience" from everyday life and particularly in the marketplace. With a biblical worldview, this Puritan father applied Scripture-based thinking to the whole range of social interaction in family, church and community, including business. By practicing this biblical worldview, the element of trust for Puritans was steadily built up in their economy. As this culture comes over to the New World, there will be opportunity where the customs and creeds build both social trust and personal responsibility. Each participant in the market is accountable before the Lord to obey the commandments, including "Thou shalt not steal."

Again, especially for business ethics, the Bible is eminently practical. To quote Professor John Frame, "all good theology is applied theology." The following sections are three contemporary "cases of conscience" with the public company and a pattern of intentional stealing. They will illustrate diagnosis and treatment for fraud and theft in public companies. Note that each of the three cases reveals stealing that is directed from senior management. Indeed, "tone at the top" as emphasized in COSO will be important for resolution in the public company every time. Comprehensive recommendations from the biblical approach will focus on leadership and training in ethics and discipleship.

Case One: Financial Statement Manipulation at WorldCom

For our main illustrations, the first case of conscience with a modern public company will be WorldCom. This darling of Wall Street in the mid-90s was a real cowboy in the technology space. From trading with a chain of motels in Mississippi to the purchase of UUNET, it was the amazing and unlikely story of Bernie Ebbers, an unorthodox entrepreneur. In the late 1990's one of the exciting new players in the high-powered technology sector of the American economy was WorldCom of Jackson, Mississippi. This company was led by the iconic Bernie Ebbers, a basketball coach turned entrepreneur and eventual telecom titan of the early days of the carriers for the Internet. MFS services which had just complete the purchase of UUNET was purchased. With UUNET's CEO, John Sidgemore, WorldCom vaulted to the lead of the infrastructure for the explosion of the World Wide Web. Acquisition of UUNET was genius as it did bring the advantage of tremendous growth in the connectivity for the Internet.

Before there was a WorldCom, Mr. Charles Cannada was originally the CFO of LDDS Communications, the predecessor of WorldCom but no other relationship with Bernie Ebbers. Scott Sullivan took over the CFO job from Cannada in January 1995. As the long-distance business changed and expanded, he helped to build a company that grew quite large. One of his employees in finance was Cynthia Cooper. He mentored her through the build up in WorldCom. But as the business grew larger and ran into difficulty making the change from landlines to the cell phone era, Cannada left for other opportunities. In 2008, Cynthia Cooper published her *Extraordinary Circumstances: The Journey of a Corporate Whistleblower*. Cannada reviewed the manuscript several times and is satisfied with this account (Personal communication, 2011).

Cooper had good training from Price Waterhouse before joining Bernie Ebbers. But as business results turned downward, then pressure was applied to record numbers with a biased slant. An important note is that WorldCom had a season of very bad business results as well as the fraudulent reporting under Ebbers and Scott Sullivan. The long distance industry changed rapidly from landlines to cell phones in the mid- to late-90s. Also, the Telecom Act (1996) was a game changer for the industry and the leading players. The fraud covered up poor results. Some investors lost money because of the stock going down later than would have occurred while others actually profited. Theoretically, those long-term investors would have lost their money anyway, just a little sooner, because the company's financial condition had gone to pieces primarily due to Tech bubble of 2000 but also the migration to cheaper long-distance rates and cell phones. The fraud began in late 2000.

According to Charles Cannada, upon reflection about the World-Com matter, the engagement and expertise of the CEO is the most important factor. Sarbanes-Oxley applies pressure on the signature of the CEO for the financial statements. His observation was that Bernie Ebbers may or may not have understood the financial reports. He is reported to be good with numbers, but perhaps did not have the background or interest for understanding the trends in the overall financial picture of a company. Bernie's college training was in Physical Education and he was a sports coach before moving into business. He is reported to tend to micro-manage on a multitude of small items at times. An innovative businessman, however, he was not engaged beyond a 40-hour week. Today, Cannada continues to work with public companies on their boards and on audit committees.

In addition to the CEO, the board and audit committee must be engaged, informed, and open to data and concerns from anyone. This would include a "hotline" for anonymous tips. Cannada has that in place today in a couple of his current corporate efforts. Anxiety about the Street's reaction, satisfying managers or covering up falsehoods must be resisted and replaced with trust in the Lord and doing the right thing. In fact, a positive aspect of Sarbanes-Oxley and the Dodd-Frank Act is that it is much easier for whistleblowers to come forward and have a level of protection against retaliation from the company they are pointing a spotlight on.

At World Com we see the sins of making top-line journal entries to adjust the published financials by the capitalization of what should have been items that are normally expensed. The role of the two WorldCom bookkeepers who finally talk about the burden of their guilt was dramatic (Austin, 2004, p. 38). Bernie Ebbers and Scott Sullivan, the CEO and CFO of WorldCom, had created an organizational ideology, or culture, in which leaders and managers were not to be doubted or questioned. A great deal of focus was put on "team work" and being a strong "team player". In one instance, following attempts of certain employees to establish a corporate Code of Conduct, Bernie Ebbers reportedly described this effort as a "colossal waste of time"!

This negative "Tone at the Top" attitude weighed heavily on the WorldCom accounting team who knew what they were doing was wrong, but yet still decided to go along with management's wishes and make the fraudulent accounting entries. This collusion was primarily accomplished through under reporting line costs, by capitalizing them on the balance sheet rather than properly expensing, with $9 billion being adjusted from 1999 through the first quarter of 2002.

When first asked to make the necessary accounting entries to meet market expectations the accounting team rationalized this would be a one-time event and that results would turn around the next quarter. Yet their consciences at that time told them what they were doing was wrong. In fact, two of the accounting managers drafted letters of resignation that they never turned in. Both were breadwinners in the home and knew it would be very difficult to find another position in Jackson, Mississippi that paid anywhere near their income at WorldCom. Eventually, as this "cooking of the books" continued over numerous quarters, the emotional toll on the controller caused him to become seriously depressed, to the point of contemplating taking his own life. The decision by WorldCom's management to generate misleading financial statements ultimately resulted in the stealing of millions of dollars from investors (in many instances the bulk of their retirement funds), the layoff of thousands of employees, and the imprisonment of senior management and the accounting team.

Case Two: Asset Misappropriation at Tyco

Looking to cultural patterns and religious effects in society is not to miss individual greed and failure of trust. Tyco was a vast company of five large divisions, 260,000 employees with 25 languages in 100 countries. While he continues to protest his innocence, the public accounts of Dennis Kozlowski show an abuse of corporate assets. There were a reported 600 million dollars of fraud of stock transactions and wire transfers to personal accounts. Loans received in the corporation were written off without board approval. Sadly, there never was a whistleblower who stepped forward as did Cynthia Cooper at WorldCom. Later analysis would show weakness of controls. In due course, both CEO and CFO were charged with crimes.

The resolution program began in August 2002. Ed Breen was selected to be the new chairman. He hired Eric Pillmore and others to address the crisis. In an excellent article in *Harvard Business Review* December 2003, Pillmore describes, "How we're fixing up Tyco." In November 2002, he was Senior Vice President for corporate governance and a leader on the "turnaround team." Structural changes had to be made at the top, certainly, but a culture of business ethics was required at all levels of the corporation as well. Needed was a strategy to "strengthen business practices across all fronts." Implementing this new culture was important beyond Sarbanes Oxley requirements and even board reconstitution. Every senior manager at Tyco was replaced by Breen. Yet the changes had to go even deeper to be effective. Governance changes would address leadership, policy, and communications. Management improvements had to encompass values and life, worldwide response to more breaches, implementing the Code, and practical metrics. Ethics training was mandated as part of the program.

The strength in the turnaround was that unlike WorldCom, Tyco was a solid, profitable business with its range of products such as building materials, consumer necessities and security systems. Tyco did not need to file bankruptcy so there was no financial reorganization. The company had to make changes right now in real-time in the business processes. In broad strokes, the approach was to determine the wrong done, make a break from the past, and prepare for a new start with a new ethical culture. In a sense, this was a positive challenge to turnaround with something akin to a 35 billion start-up. The idea was to making Tyco more operations-driven and less of a Merger & Acquisition business.

First of all, values driving the whole resolution process were intentional integrity, excellence, teamwork, and accountability. The actual work of resolution was with a Phase 1 that was an investigation of former senior executives. The clear challenges were to order a plan of action, review the board and operations, carry out a thorough investigation, develop some new policies, and communication and training processes. That due diligence of Phase 1 was followed by Phase 2 with its review of the 15 largest acquisitions on their controls and reporting. Not a "white-wash," the investigation included very explicit questions.

A major theme for the implementation of the resolution was a clear separation of finance and operations. This distinction resulted in a brand new organization chart with CFOs reporting to one main CFO vs. to the presidents of business units. Throughout Tyco there was a greater controllership with this new corporate structure. Rather than getting deals done, the focus was on controlling assets. Now the emphasis would be on reconciling bank accounts and doing physical inventory. We know that people do whatever is emphasized, measured and rewarded. Thus, the program could be effective.

By looking at the basic "blocking and tackling" of business, ethics in operations can really be improved. Board membership moved from financial deal making experience to operational history. There was a greater operations background on the board, cf. Frame's situational perspective on biblical business ethics. The resolution program included important details such as authorization of transactions and a new policy manual. Checks and balances and written regulations are needed for an impact on day-to-day business.

While the key to change was to include the operational processes, structural leadership was not avoided. For example, in a dramatic and major change, audit functions were reported directly to the board audit committee, not the company's CFO. Three senior positions reported directly to the board: SVP of Governance, Ombudsman, and Corporate Audit. As recommended by Charles Cannada as a best practice, a toll-free number for reporting abuses was instituted. And there was a careful use of expert consultants and other industry benchmarks, for example, General Electric, Johnson & Johnson, and Coca-Cola. Finally, succession planning and leadership mentoring began to be taken seriously in top and middle management, including an emphasis on ethical standards and practice.

Training was more challenging with the need to bring the policy manual to life: enter dramatic vignettes, case scenarios. It is important to note that it was observed that the more interactive the training, the more effective ... even with online technologies. And in a big corporation with 260,000 employees, there is the imperative to be scalable. Supervision and instruction were a more difficult approach to managing with the new reporting paths and the committees. Leaders did meet with the managers, hear objections and defend policies and adapt them to the best criticisms. The results of training must be "embedded in our operations." That is high and valid standard for any good instructional program.

Leadership confirmation was required at all levels. As in most ethical systems, there had to be a code. As the Bible would term it, this is a vow. The statement was involved daily application, consistent routines, all channels of the business, and an affirmation of no violations by self or others. It was named *the Tyco Guide to Ethical Conduct.*

I confirm that I have read and understand the Tyco Guide To Ethical Conduct (Guide) and I commit to embrace and utilize the Guide principles in my daily work activities. I understand that consistent with applicable local law every Tyco employee is required to comply with the policies in the Guide. I am not aware of any unreported violations of these principles. Should I have a concern about a possible violation of Tyco policy, I will raise the concern through the appropriate channels as outlined in the Guide. I acknowledge my leadership responsibility in the annual Commitment Statement process.

Within my organization there is an established process to ensure that employees:
　•Have read and understood the Guide; and
　•Confirmed their commitment to the Guide through a signed Commitment Statement

Based on this process, and my review of the information gathered from this process, I am not aware of any violations of the Guide, other than those that have been raised through those avenues that Tyco has made available.

Results for Tyco were very good and actually quite prompt from 2002 to 2007. Based on industry surveys, the company went from worst in terms of business ethics to most improved to best. This was a remarkable record. Even so, Pillmore does note a tendency to underestimate time required for culture change. Sending out the instructions and making sure that they are realistic and helpful takes a lot of time. Much downline help was needed. That all did require significant resources for the distributed locations and the overall persuasion.

　　Training was a crucial aspect of the resolution program. It worked best when interactive and social. Online interactive video social simulation is a preferred use of media for training with dynamic case studies (Peterson, DeHart and Rees, 2009). Alongside mentoring, there is the increasing the role of training and a more dynamic instructional design for increased effectiveness and speed. Rather than just new behavior, the element of personal character should not be overlooked.

Case Three: Corruption at Parmalat, "Europe's Enron"
When the Parmalat scandal broke it was quickly dubbed "Europe's Enron", suggesting that multi-billion dollars frauds are not, after all, a predomi-

nately American phenomenon. Parmalat, Enron, and other American companies such as WorldCom and Tyco all have number-fudging at their core – efforts to make the companies look healthier than they really were. They all raise questions about the behavior of accountants, auditors, management, and underwriters who might have, should have, or did know that something was wrong.

Parmalat was an Italian food giant employing 36,000 employees in 29 countries until it unraveled in December 2003 with the revelation of a $19 billion dollar hole in its financing. The company's financial woes had been covered up by major falsifications of balance sheets and sophisticated financial fiddling coupled with a simple "cut and paste" forgery of a bank letter.

In any large business under global capitalism there is enormous pressure to "perform" in the global market, to bring favorable returns that meet investors' expectations. Not surprisingly, the details that surfaced indicated that Parmalat's fraudulent activities really "took off" when its stock went public in 1990. In the early 1990's the company launched a massive acquisition drive to spread its business through Europe, Latin America, and Africa. This rapid expansion was facilitated by huge borrowings from banks and financial institutions, complex international organizational structure and financial wizardry to minimize tax liability and cover losses over the years.

The company was running a strong business in manufacturing and trading of food and dairy products and had a large market share in many countries. The collapse was indirectly caused by recent underperforming Latin American acquisitions but more directly by the deliberate misappropriation of funds by management through complex financial instruments (particularly derivatives) and siphoning funds through its subsidiaries located in the Cayman Islands.

Most intriguing with this case was the common forgery of a bank document that was deemed acceptable by the auditors. Parmalat's finance director participated in a "cut and paste" forgery, in which a document with Bank of America letterhead was scanned and then added to a document verifying a deposit account with that bank holding over $4.98 billion. The document was then passed through a fax machine several times in order to appear authentic. Yet the basic issue on Parmalatt is one of poor auditing and deception. The auditors, Grant Thornton in Italy, failed to adequately confirm substantial Bank of America cash assets (a basic audit step) in the Bahamas. The auditors were not doing their jobs and an apparent laziness contributed to the massive fraud.

There were two items that caused Parmalat's schemes to be exposed. First, the firm changed its outside auditors. According to Italian law, this must be done every nine years, and in 1999 Parmalat changed from the up-and-coming firm Grant Thorton to Deloitte, on of the "big four" auditing companies. Although the law is clear on the nine-year rule, it has no provision against a parent company using the same auditor for concerns it spins off. Grant Thorton, which had been struggling for years to compete against giant multinational firms, was desperate to keep one of its most valuable and high profile clients. Rather than lose Parmalat, the accounting firm suggested that Parmalat spin off its travel business and a few other businesses, and allow these to remain under its watch.

In this way, Parmalat could maintain a fair degree of propriety in its main division, which was now monitored by Deloitte, and use the spun-off concerns to generate illicit payments to the parent firm. The executives would create debts owed to Parmalat by the subsidiaries, and the latter would create false accounts from which to pay debts. Grant Thorton accountants presented records of these transactions to Deloitte accountants, who rubber-stamped most of them. Grant Thorton's accountants were intimately aware of the shell games being played by Parmalat's executives. No doubt, the pressures to compete exerted on both companies by global markets drove the two into each other's arms.

The second item occurred when the head of Parmalat, Calisto Tanzi, met with the private equity firm Blackstone Group in New York to discuss selling all 51 percent of the family's stake in the food empire. During their conversation, in preparation for the opening of their books to a transition team from Blackstone, Tanzi let slip that cash on hand was somewhat less than the 3 billion euros listed in the company's annual report. He also admitted that, in fact, there were hardly any liquid assets, and the company was 10 billion euros in debt. The SEC was alerted to these discrepancies, and within two weeks Parmalat was under bankruptcy protection, with Tanzi in custody, and the company's stock worth pennies a share. As one of the lead investigators, Lucia Russo, would say during the trial, "Parmalat was the symbol of a sick system and the biggest debt factory of European capitalism."

Techniques And Tools For Resolution And Prevention Of Fraud

Fraud is any intentional act or omission designed to deceive others, resulting in the victim suffering a loss and/or the perpetrator achieving a gain. All organizations are subject to fraud risks. Large frauds have led to the downfall of entire organizations, massive investment losses, significant legal costs, incarceration of key individuals, and erosion of confidence in capital markets. Publicized fraudulent behavior by key executives has negatively impacted the reputations, brands, and images of many organizations around the globe. Regulations such as the U.S. Foreign Corrupt Practices Act of 1977 (FCPA), the 1997 Organization for Economic Co-operation and Development Anti-Bribery Convention, the U.S. Sarbanes-Oxley Act of 2002, the U.S. Federal Sentencing Guidelines of 2005, and similar legislation throughout the world have increased management's responsibility for fraud risk management.

Reactions to recent corporate scandals have led the public and stakeholders to expect organizations to take a "no fraud tolerance" attitude. Good governance principles demand that an organization's board of directors, or equivalent oversight body, ensure overall high ethical behavior in the organization, regardless of its status as public, private, government, or not-for-profit; its relative size; or its industry. The board's role is critically important because historically most major frauds are perpetrated by senior management in collusion with other employees. Vigilant handling of fraud cases within an organization sends clear signals to the public, stakeholders, and regulators about the board and management's attitude toward fraud risks and about the organization's fraud risk tolerance.

In addition to the board, personnel at all levels of the organization – including every level of management, staff, and internal auditors, as well as the organization's external auditors – have responsibility for dealing with fraud risk. Particularly, they are expected to explain how the organization is responding to heightened regulations, as well as public and stakeholder scrutiny; what form of fraud risk management program the organization has put in place; how it identifies fraud risks; what it is doing to better prevent fraud, or at least detect it sooner; and what process is in place to investigate fraud and take corrective action. Only through diligent and ongoing effort can an organization protect itself against significant acts of fraud. The most effective fraud prevention tool is education. The more businesses, employees, and auditors know about fraud, the less likely they will become victims.

There are three general categories of fraud; financial statement manipulation, asset misappropriation, and corruption. Financial statement manipulation represents only 4% of overall fraud cases, but generally results in the largest amount of losses. As publically traded companies try to meet market expectations the resulting adjustment of "rainy day" accounts begins small but generally become quite large over time. Asset misappropriations represent 74% of all fraud cases and normally occur in private industry where the business owner has implicit trust in the financial staff. Unfortunately this trust is often misplaced and cash and/or assets of the company are stolen. The final category is corruption which generally occurs outside of the U.S. where paying bribes and receiving kickbacks is considered a normal part of doing business.

The perception by average citizens is that the external auditor's main job is to detect fraud. Yet external audits account for less than 5% of the overall frauds that are detected. Most frauds (40%) are detected through tips that are received by management. The ranking of other forms of fraud detection are as follows: management review (15%), internal audits (14%), by accident (8%), account reconciliation (6%), and document examination (5%). Although external audit fraud detection ranks seventh on this list, frauds at audited companies were caught more quickly and resulted in smaller losses than in non-audited companies. Therefore an audit is an excellent fraud prevention tool. "In God we trust, audit everyone else!"

When detected it is important that the following steps are taken in response to the fraudulent activity: investigation of the fraud with corrective action; perform a thorough review of existing internal controls; assist management with fraud risk. The investigation should quickly put a "fence" around the type and extent of damages experienced by the company, identifying all individuals involved in the activity. Remove those responsible for the fraud from their positions and find replacements to mitigate the impact on day-to-day operations. A thorough review of internal controls should include: the identification of key business processes; performance of walk throughs of key controls; preparation of narratives identifying key controls; performing testing of key controls; recommending ways to strengthen internal controls; utilizing Swentrack™ to electronically document the above steps regarding internal controls.

For example, Swentrack™ is a proprietary comprehensive web-based tool designed to assist management oversee the internal control compliance process. This web-based tool streamlines the whole process of defining, evaluating, documenting, testing and reporting internal controls. Swentrack™ guides management through a proven SOX methodology developed by Swenson Advisors LLP, all the while monitoring progress and simultaneously organizing documents in a secure, convenient location that is accessible through any web browser. Access to particular components can be assigned to process owners, external auditors, audit committee members, or any others that may require it.

The final step in the investigation of fraud and corrective action is to assist management with developing a fraud risk program. Key principles for proactively establishing an environment to effectively manage an organization's fraud risk include:

- Suitable fraud risk management oversight and expectations exist (governance)
- Fraud exposures are identified and evaluated (risk assessment)
- Appropriate processes and procedures are in place to manage these exposures (prevention and detection)
- Fraud allegations are addressed, and appropriate corrective action is taken in a timely manner (investigation and corrective action)

Fraud Risk Governance

As part of an organization's governance structure, a fraud risk management program should be in place, including a written policy (or policies) to convey the expectations of the board of directors and senior management regarding managing fraud risk. Corporate governance is the manner in which management and those charged with oversight accountability meet their obligations and fiduciary responsibilities to business stakeholders (e.g. church members, employees, vendors, governmental entities, and media). Effective boards and organizations will address the issue of ethics and the impact of ethical behavior on business strategy, operations, and long-term objectives. Effective business ethics programs can serve as the foundation for preventing, detecting, and deterring fraudulent and criminal acts. An organization's ethical treatment of employees, church members, vendors, and other partners will influence those receiving such treatment. These ethics programs create an environment where making the right decision is implicit.

To help ensure an organization's fraud risk management program is effective, it is important to understand the roles and responsibilities that personnel at all levels of the organization have with respect to fraud risk management. Policies, job descriptions, and/or delegations of authority should define roles and responsibilities related to fraud risk management. In particular, the documentation should articulate who is responsible for the governance oversight of fraud controls (i.e. the role and responsibility of the board of directors and/or designated committee of the board). Documentation should reflect management's responsibility for the design and implementation of the fraud risk strategy, and how different segments of the organization support fraud risk management. The board of directors, audit committee, management, staff, and internal auditing, all have key roles in an organization's fraud risk management program.

Most organizations have written policies and procedures to manage fraud risks, such as codes of conduct, expense account procedures, and incident investigation standards. They usually have some activities that management has implemented to assess risks, ensure compliance, identify and investigate violations, measure and report the organization's performance, and communicate expectations. However, few have developed a concise summary of these documents and activities to help them communicate and evaluate their processes. Generally this is referred to as a fraud risk management program. The following elements should be found within a fraud risk management program: commitment from the top, fraud awareness, affirmation process, conflict/independence disclosure, fraud risk assessment, whistleblower procedures, investigation process, corrective action, and process evaluation and improvement (quality assurance) with continuous monitoring.

Fraud Risk Assessment

Fraud risk exposure should be assessed periodically by the organization to identify specific potential schemes and events that the organization needs to mitigate. The foundation of an effective fraud risk management program should be seen as a larger enterprise risk management (ERM) effort and is rooted in a risk assessment that identifies where fraud may occur and who the perpetrators might be. To this end, control activities should always consider both the fraud scheme and the individuals within and outside the organization who could be the perpetrators of each scheme. If the scheme is collusive, preventive controls should be augmented by detective controls, as collusion negates the control effectiveness of segregation of duties.

A fraud risk assessment generally includes three key elements:

1. Identify inherent fraud risk – Gather information to obtain the population of fraud risks that could apply to the organization. Included in this process is the explicit consideration of all types of fraud schemes and scenarios; incentives, pressures, and opportunities to commit fraud; and IT fraud risks specific to the organization.

2. Assess likelihood and significance of inherent fraud risk – Assess the relative likelihood and potential significance of identified fraud risks base on historical information, known fraud schemes, and interviews with staff.

3. Respond to reasonably likely and significant inherent and residual fraud risks – Decide what the response should be to address the identified risks and perform a cost-benefit analysis of fraud risks over which the organization wants to implement controls or specific fraud detection procedures.

While ongoing worry and insecurity is a general problem, motives for committing fraud are numerous and diverse. The fraud risk identification process should include an assessment of the incentives, pressures, and opportunities to commit fraud. These factors can impact an employees' behavior when conducting business or applying professional judgment. Opportunities to commit fraud are greatest in areas with weak internal controls and a lack of segregation of duties. It is also important to consider the potential for management override of controls established to prevent or detect fraud. It is reasonable to assume that individuals who are intent on committing fraud will use their knowledge of the organization's controls to do it in a manner that will conceal their actions. An anti-fraud control is not effective if it can be overridden easily.

Fraud Prevention
Prevention techniques to avoid potential key fraud risk events should be

established, where feasible, to mitigate possible impacts on the organization. Although preventive measures cannot ensure that fraud will not be committed, they are the first line of defense in minimizing fraud risk. One key to prevention is making personnel throughout the organization aware of the fraud risk management program, including the types of fraud and misconduct that may occur. This awareness should enforce the notion that all of the techniques established in the program are real and will be enforced. The ongoing communication efforts could provide information on the potential disciplinary, criminal, and civil actions that the organization could take against the individual. If effective preventive controls are in place, working, and well-known to potential fraud perpetrators, they serve as strong deterrents to those who might otherwise be tempted to commit fraud.

Fraud risks, although a form of business risk, necessitate specific controls to mitigate them, which makes an organization's fraud risk assessment process essential to fraud prevention. In addition to implementing fraud preventive controls, it is important that the organization assess and continuously monitor their operational effectiveness to help prevent fraud occurring. Prevention is the most proactive fraud-fighting measure. An organization should address all identified risks, design and implement the control activities, and ensure that the techniques used are adequate to prevent fraud from occurring in accordance to the organization's risk tolerance.

The ongoing success of any fraud prevention program depends on continuous communication and reinforcement. Stressing the existence of a fraud prevention program through a wide variety of media – posters on bulletin boards, flyers included with vendor payments, and articles in internal and external communications – gets the message out to both internal and external communities that the organization is committed to preventing and deterring fraud.

Fraud Detection
Detection techniques should be established to uncover fraud events when preventive measures fail or unmitigated risks are real. Having effective detective controls in place and visible is one of the strongest deterrents to fraudulent behavior. Used in tandem with preventive controls, detective controls enhance a fraud risk management program's effectiveness by providing evidence that preventive controls are working as intended and identifying fraud that occurs. Although detective controls may provide

evidence that fraud is occurring or has occurred, they are not intended to prevent fraud. As with fraud prevention, it is important that the organization assess and continuously monitor its fraud detection techniques to help detect fraud.

Organizations can never eliminate the risk of fraud entirely. There are always people who are motivated to commit fraud, and an opportunity can arise for someone in any organization to override a control or collude with others to do so. Therefore, detection techniques should be flexible, adaptable, and continuously changing to meet the various changes in risk. While preventive measures are apparent and readily identifiable by employees, third parties, and others, detective controls are clandestine in nature. This means they operate in the background and are not evident in the everyday business environment. Important detection methods include anonymous reporting mechanism (whistleblower hotline), process controls, and proactive fraud detection procedures specifically designed to identify fraudulent activity.

Fraud Investigation and Corrective Action

A reporting process should be in place to solicit input on potential fraud, and a coordinated approach to investigation and corrective action should be used to help ensure potential fraud is addressed appropriately and timely. It is essential that any violations, deviations, or other breaches of the code of conduct or controls, regardless of where in the organization, or by whom, they are committed, be reported and dealt with in a timely manner. Appropriate punishment must be imposed, and suitable remediation completed. The board should ensure that the same rules are applied at all levels of the organization, including senior management.

The investigation and response system should include a process for the following:
- Categorizing issues
- Confirming the validity of the allegation
- Defining the severity of the allegation
- Escalating the issue or investigation when appropriate
- Referring issues outside the scope of the program
- Conducting the investigation and fact-finding
- Resolving or closing the investigation
- Listing types of information that should be kept confidential
- Defining how the investigation will be documented

- Managing and retaining documents and information
- Consult with legal counsel before taking disciplinary action

A proactive approach to managing fraud risk is one of the best steps organizations can take to mitigate exposure to fraudulent activities. Although complete elimination of all fraud risk is most likely unachievable or uneconomical, organizations can take positive and constructive steps to reduce their exposure. The combination of effective fraud risk governance, a thorough fraud risk assessment, strong fraud prevention and detection (including specific anti-fraud control processes), as well as coordinated and timely investigations and corrective actions, can significantly mitigate fraud risks.

Although fraud is not a subject that any organization wants to deal with, the reality is most organizations experience fraud to some degree. The important thing to note is that dealing with fraud can be constructive, and forward-thinking, and can position an organization in a leadership role within its industry or non-profit business segment. Strong, effective, and well-run organizations exist because management takes proactive steps to anticipate issues before they occur and to take action to prevent undesired results. Implementation of a fraud risk program should help establish a climate where positive and constructive steps are taken to protect employees and ensure a positive culture. It should be recognized that the dynamics of any organization require ongoing reassessment of fraud exposures and responses in light of the changing environment the organization encounters.

Biblical Perspectives for Hope and Help in Public Companies in the "New Normal"

As in a previous study (Conway and Peterson, 2010) we take a biblical, tri-perspectival approach to business ethics that is compatible with the Westminster Larger Catechism (WLC). God's Word is clear and objective to all, but there are at least three vantage points from which to appreciate and understand His instruction to us: Normative, Situational and Heart (Frame, 2008). For example, in business ethics we read the propositional commandments in the Bible, we evaluate the goals in a business situation, and we assess the intentions of our hearts.

Interestingly, this biblical approach is parallel to the three dimensions of Michael Sandel's recent study, *Justice: What's the Right Thing to Do?* In a secular context, Sandel presents the three perspectives of freedom, welfare, and virtue. In philosophy these emphases follow the schools of the ontological, utilitarian, and existential frameworks for ethics. It seems that there are three similar facets in secular ethics with respective emphases on obeying cultural norms, maximizing happiness in a situation, and being a good person. Sandel, the Anne T. and Robert M. Bass Professor of Government at Harvard University, explores the meaning of these three directions and their inter-relation. In his teaching and writing, attention is paid to the principles of justice, the benefit to society, and the cultivation of moral dispositions and attitudes. This whole bundle is reminiscent of the age-old Stoic version of natural law from the Greeks going forward.

Normative Standards for Practice and Training

No doubt, the Bible gives us clarity in a complex world. It is sufficient for life albeit not exhaustive for every possible question, situation and strategy. The Christian can have a coherence in a chaotic world. The biblical "ought" trumps "is" as ethics actually determines epistemology. To know a fact is to believe in a way to know reality … which is an ethical commitment. From this vantage, the issue is about obeying God's Law.

On all three biblical perspectives, Richard Baxter does the work of applying Scripture to the marketplace. With the normative approach he writes in *The Practical Works of Richard Baxter: A Christian Directory, Volume 1* as follows: "Direct. VI. Therefore have a special regard to the laws of the country where you live; both as to your trade itself, and as to the price of what you sell or buy" P. 827. The normative biblical perspective for business ethics looks directly to God's commands and a biblical understanding of the meaning of those directives. The theological study of Scripture yields a hermeneutical guide for interpreting the precepts relevant to any ethical decision. As we gain experience in reading and applying biblical texts to everyday life, then our facility for business ethics matures along with our personal sanctification as a whole. With this understanding comes an appreciation for writing and defending just laws.

Laws against theft are simply to be obeyed, regardless of the circumstances in the public company. Rationalization of theft must be resisted strongly! Corporate resources must not be stolen for personal enjoyment or even fulfilling of great need for a person, but ownership must be respected. And even if others are working hard, or offering brilliant ideas or rainmaking with abandon, in principle, the passive shareholder's property should be valued and cared for, nonetheless.

Situational Goals for Practice and Training

A second perspective involves the respect for experience in similar situations and expertise brought to a situation. When CEO Ed Breen hired Eric Pillmore to help at Tyco in the recovery, he was accessing years of professional skill and trust. The issue is that we can know much about God's world, which is a place of cause and effect. Knowledge of the common situations in a public company is vital to making good ethical decisions.

Once again we hear from Baxter with a relevant directive: In Chapter XIX we read of general directions and particular cases of conscience, about contracts in general, and about buying and selling, borrowing and lending, usury, in particular, are given. He gives general directions against injurious bargaining and contracts in business situations.

- "Direct. IV. Understand your neighbor's case aright, and meditate on his wants and interest."
- "Direct. V. Regard the public good above your own commodity."

Business ethics is more than just applying explicit rules to commercial behavior. While computer information processing remains a popular paradigm for the study of some human cognition, it is insufficient to expect an algorithm for right behavior to suit every moral dilemma. One of the reasons that artificial intelligence cannot sufficiently cover business ethics is the variety of unique circumstances in any case study. "Thou shalt not steal" is a clear imperative.

But how does this apply to common property, projects in collaboration, and unneeded waste of materials. Actually, the gleaning process in Old Testament scripture had an ambiguous element to it for the owner, workers, harvesters, et al. What about efforts in the heat of high stakes negotiation? Is it wrong to play hard-ball dealmaking? What about if due to your knowledge or persistence the acquisition is a "steal!" Is that cause for repentance and rescinding your signature on the papers in the name of "full disclosure?" In regard to these Godly goals and questions in each situation were there any "sins of omission? The Christian is careful to take positive loving steps as well as avoid overt transgressions in a business question.

Heart Motives for Practice and Training

The third nuance that is critical when teaching on business ethics for the public company is the intentional dimension. The Bible is not merely an instruction book for experts in their field. It is more than the ancient or modern Stoic version of natural law where cognition, best practices and power determine doing the right thing. One's heart must also be right in the situation and with the norms. There must be a God-given integrity of faith and love for neighbor. A prayerful will is necessary when coping with stress and turning threats into challenges. A regenerate heart makes this love possible, although the question of motives must be asked of any actor in an ethical dilemma. Baxter, p. 823, discusses the heart of the matter as follows in Chapter XVIII. Directions against all theft and fraud, or injurious getting and keeping that which is another's, or desiring it."

Furthermore, can one know the right scripture passages, and be an industry expert in a well-worn situation, and still fall short of ethical thinking and action? Yes, if the heart is not right before God and neighbor, the apparently right actions and right immediate effects can be part of a larger fraud in a relationship and in one's stewardship for the business. Do you have the email track that evidences your honesty in a transaction, despite a series of motives that wish ill for the other party? But are there other actions and communication that did commit fraud against a business partner or employee, in fact. Human beings can be quite insightful and deceitful in pursuit of a long-term outcome through a series of moves over several months that end a successful collaboration or withdraw an opportunity long-promised? "The heart is deceitfully wicked, who can know it?" The perpetrator may even be self-deceived to not see what he has done in willful ignorance. In pastoral counseling, it can become clear that there is need for teaching, confession and repentance. Then, maturity of character advances to God's glory. Great blessings in history and eternity result from such ... teaching, conviction, correction and training in righteousness.

In terms of prevention of fraud and engineering resolution in the public company, the long-term firewall is a new heart obedient to God's law by His grace. As Baxter recorded, p. 823. "Direct. I. Cure covetousness, and you will kill the root of fraud and theft." The link from Commandment 8 to Commandment 10 is quite clear and compelling. With this teaching of biblical norms and we pray that the Holy Spirit will convict the heart of each employee. Then they will practice correction of wrong actions with an ongoing training process of replacing the sins with righteous action to the benefit of neighbor and the glory of God. For business ethics in the public company that is truly "the right thing to do."

REFERENCES

Austin, Stephen. (2004). *Rise of the New Ethics Class: Life after Enron, not Business as Usual.* Lake Mary, Florida: Charisma House.

Baxter, Richard. (1673). *The Practical Works of Richard Baxter: A Christian Directory, Volume 1.* Morgan Run, PA: Soli Deo Gloria.

Cannada, Charles. (2011). Personal communication. April 11, 2011.

Collins, Jim. (2009). *How the Mighty Fall and Why Some Companies Never Give In.* NY: HarperCollins.

Cooper, Cynthia. (2008). *Extraordinary Circumstances: The Journey of a Corporate Whistleblower.* Hoboken, New Jersey:; John Wiley.

Edgar, William. (2006). *Reasons of the Heart: Recovering Christian persuasion.* Phillipsburg, NJ: P & R.

Forbes, Steve and Prevas, John. (2009). *Power Ambition Glory: The Stunning Parallels between Great Leaders of the Ancient World and Today . . . and the Lessons You Can Learn.* NY: Crown.

Frame, John (1987). *The Doctrine of the Knowledge of God.* Phillipsburg, NJ: P & R.

Frame, John. (2008). *The Doctrine of the Christian life.* Phillipsburg, NJ: P & R.

Hall, David and Burton, Matthew. (2009). *Calvin and Commerce: The Transforming Power of Calvinism in Market Economies.* Phillipsburg, NJ: P & R.

Huntington, Samuel. (2004). *Who are We?: The Challenges to America's National Identity.* NY: Simon and Schuster.

Landes, David. (2002). *The Wealth and Poverty of Nations.* NY: Norton.

Morecraft, Joseph C. III. (2009). *Authentic Christianity: An Exposition of the Theology and Ethics of the Westminster Larger Catechism.* Powder Springs, GA: American Vision Press.

Peterson, Andrew, DeHart, Donn and Rees, Dennis. (2009). Online interactive video social simulations for theological training. *Bank of America Day of Training.* Charlotte, North Carolina, March 15.

Pillmore, Eric M. (2003). How we're fixing up Tyco. *Harvard Business Review*, December.

Sandel, Michael J. (2010). *Justice: What's the right thing to do?* NY: Farrar, Straus and Giroux.

Weber, Max. (1904, 1920). *The Protestant Ethic and the Spirit of Capitalism.* NY: Routledge Classics.

Westminster Larger Catechism.

APPENDIX A

WESTMINSTER LARGER CATECHISM (Q140 – 142)
Q. 140. Which is the eighth commandment?
A. The eighth commandment is, Thou shalt not steal.

Q. 141. What are the duties required in the eighth commandment?
A. The duties required in the eighth commandment are, truth, faithfulness, and justice in contracts and commerce between man and man; rendering to every one his due; restitution of goods unlawfully detained from the right owners thereof; giving and lending freely, according to our abilities, and the necessities of others; moderation of our judgments, wills, and affections concerning worldly goods; a provident care and study to get, keep, use, and dispose these things which are necessary and convenient for the sustentation of our nature, and suitable to our condition; a lawful calling,

and diligence in it; frugality; avoiding unnecessary lawsuits, and suretiship, or other like engagements; and an endeavor, by all just and lawful means, to procure, preserve, and further the wealth and outward estate of others, as well as our own.

Q. 142. What are the sins forbidden in the eighth commandment?
A. The sins forbidden in the eighth commandment, besides the neglect of the duties required, are, theft, robbery, man-stealing, and receiving anything that is stolen; fraudulent dealing, false weights and measures, removing landmarks, injustice and unfaithfulness in contracts between man and man, or in matters of trust; oppression, extortion, usury, bribery, vexatious lawsuits, unjust enclosures and depredation; engrossing commodities to enhance the price; unlawful callings, and all other unjust or sinful ways of taking or withholding from our neighbor what belongs to him, or of enriching ourselves; covetousness; inordinate prizing and affecting worldly goods; distrustful and distracting cares and studies in getting, keeping, and using them; envying at the prosperity of others; as likewise idleness, prodigality, wasteful gaming; and all other ways whereby we do unduly prejudice our own outward estate, and defrauding ourselves of the due use and comfort of that estate which God hath given us.

MATERIAL NONPUBLIC INFORMATION, INSIDER TRADING AND THE 8TH COMMANDMENT

MARK FUTATO & PHILIP CLEMENTS

MARK FUTATO

Dr. Mark D. Futato is Robert L. Maclellan Professor of Old Testament and Academic Dean at Reformed Theological Seminary in Orlando, Florida. He received his Ph.D. from The Catholic University of America, in Washington, DC, his M.Div. from Westminster Theological Seminary in Philadelphia, PA, and his B.A. from Geneva College in Beaver Falls, PA.

Dr. Futato has published: Psalms: Cornerstone Biblical Commentary (Tyndale House), Interpreting the Psalms: An Exegetical Handbook (Kregel), Joy Comes in the Morning: Psalms for All Seasons (P&R), Transformed By Praise: The Purpose and Message of the Psalms (P&R), Beginning Biblical Hebrew (Eisenbrauns), and Creation: A Witness to the Wonder of God (P&R). Mark has also served on the translation team for the Book of Psalms in the New Living Translation (Tyndale House), wrote the study notes to the Books of Ezra and Nehemiah in Spirit of the Reformation Study Bible (Zondervan) and to the Book of Jonah in the ESV Study Bible, and contributed to The New International Dictionary of Old Testament Theology and Exegesis (Zondervan). He has written numerous other articles and is currently writing a book on the theology of the Book of Jonah.

Dr. Futato is a Minister in the Presbyterian Church in America. He was ordained in 1983 as a Minister in the Orthodox Presbyterian Church, and was pastor of Covenant OPC in Burtonsville, MD, from 1983-88. He taught at Westminster Theological Seminary in CA from 1988-99.

PHIL CLEMENTS

Phil Clements is the managing director of the Center for Christian Business Ethics Today, LLC. Phil has been a leader in the business community for over thirty years. In 2003, Jack Templeton, a fellow board member of the National Bible Association, challenged Phil with a question of the role of faith in commerce. Phil's research affirmed the foundational importance of the principles of our Christian faith and the quality of business commerce. That research confirmed the changes he has experienced during his business career as the world moves away from these Christian principles.

Phil founded the Center to meet this concern that is articulated in Judges 2:10–11.

From September 2001 to October 2004 Phil held the position of Executive Vice President of Standard & Poor's Corporate Value Consulting ("CVC") division. He led the transition of CVC to S&P, after S&P acquired CVC from PricewaterhouseCoopers LLP (PwC). Prior to joining Standard & Poor's, Phil was the Global Leader of the CVC practice of PwC. During FY'99 and FY'00, Global CVC grew to a fully integrated global service unit. Prior to becoming Global Leader for CVC at the formation of PwC, Phil ran the Coopers & Lybrand's Corporate Finance Practice for the U.S. This practice included CVC, investment banking, transaction structuring, due diligence and bankruptcy turnaround services.

From 1989 to 2000, Phil served on the U.S. boards of Coopers & Lybrand and Pricewaterhouse Coopers and the global board of PwC. Phil was a member of the Finance Committees of both firms. The board experience included the board approvals of the merger of C&L and PW to form PwC and the oversight of the transition to PwC operations globally. Finance committee work included the capital structure of the firms and financial reporting. Although both firms were private, they had substantial numbers of partners for whom financial results were very relevant. Community service plays an important role in Phil's life. At Grace Bible Chapel, a non-denominational evangelical church, Phil has been the High School Sunday School teacher for the past thirteen years, an Elder, and part of the touring praise and worship team, PowerSurge. Phil was Chairman of the Board of Trustees of the National Bible Association. Seattle University School of Law Board of Visitors, International Leadership Board of Advisors, and HOPE Bible Mission board are others boards that Phil has served or is serving on.

Phil has three daughters and lives with his wife in Chester, New Jersey. He has a passion for the water, which drives his two favorite pastimes—sailing and sea-plane piloting.

Introduction

The CEO of Company A knows that Company A will soon be taken over by Company B and believes that as a result the share price of Company A will go up, so the CEO buys additional shares of stock in Company A. A retired financial journalist who is now an at-home day trader is researching Company C, observes various interactions between Company C and Company D, and comes to the conclusion that the share price of Company C will soon go up, so the at-home day trader buys shares of stock in Company C. Are either of these individuals guilty of breaking God's law as found in the 8th Commandment?

God himself said it first, "You shall not steal" (Exodus 20:15; ESV). Moses repeated God's commandment in Deuteronomy 5:19 and Leviticus 19:11. The prophet Ezekiel included keeping the 8th commandment as one characteristic of the person who "is righteous and does what is lawful and right" (NRSV). Jesus reminded the rich young man that "you shall not steal" was a commandment still in need of keeping in his day (Matthew 19:18). And Paul listed the 8th Commandment among the commandments "summed up in this one word: 'You shall love your neighbor as yourself'" (Romans 13:9; ESV). But the ancient world knew nothing of material nonpublic information (MNPI hereafter) or insider trading, so how does the 8th Commandment apply to these issues?

We will begin by defining key terms and concepts. This will be followed by a discussion of the application of the 8th Commandment to MNPI and insider trading. We will conclude with a brief consideration of the two greatest commandments.

Key Terms and Concepts

Material Nonpublic Information

By the word "material" we are referring to information that would be deemed important to the investment decision of a reasonable investor. Some examples of "material" information would be financial results, mergers, acquisitions or divestitures, a new line of business or new products, projections and earnings forecasts, corporate events, changes in financial condition, dividends or changes in dividend policy, major inventions, significant contracts, unusual gains or losses, negotiations of agreements regarding significant projects, financings, major management changes, gaining or loosing a significant customer, impending bankruptcy or liquidity issues, and major litigation or related exposure. The "material" nature of information is, of course, subject to reassessment on a regular basis, as information may become stale or subsequent situations may supersede prior ones, and subject to the facts of the situation related to the information.

By the word "nonpublic" we are referring to information that is not generally available to the investing public or known to the marketplace. Information would no longer be "nonpublic" if, for example, that information were published in a newspaper or filed with Securities and Exchange Commission (SEC hereafter) and sent to security holders. Moreover, a period of time must elapse after the public release of material information to allow for the adequate dissemination of the information and adequate evaluation by the investor community.

Insider Trading

The law defines insider trading as the trading of a security "on the basis of material nonpublic information about that security or issuer, in breach of a duty of trust or confidence that is owed directly, indirectly, or derivatively, to the issuer of that security or the shareholders of that issuer, or to any other person who is the source of the material nonpublic information" [Paragraph (a) of 17 C.F.R. 240.10(b)5-1, generally referred to as Rule 10(b)5-1]. This language incorporates all theories of insider trading liability under the case law: classical insider trading, temporary insider theory, tippee liability, and trading by someone who misappropriated the inside information. A trade is "on the basis of" MNPI, if the trader "was aware of" the information when he or she made the purchase or sale [Paragraph (b) of Rule 10b5-1], and the SEC asserts that "awareness" of MNPI inevitably leads to use of MNPI, and provides a sufficient basis for liability. Mark J. Astarita lists the following as general examples of insider trading:

- Corporate officers, directors, and employees who traded the corporation's securities after learning of significant, confidential corporate developments;
- Friends, business associates, family members, and other "tippees" of such officers, directors, and employees, who traded the securities after receiving such information;
- Employees of law, banking, brokerage and printing firms who

were given such information to provide services to the corporation whose securities they traded;

• Government employees who learned of such information because of their employment by the government;

• Employees of financial printers who learned of the information during the course of their employment; and

• Other persons who misappropriated, and took advantage of, confidential information from their employers. [1]

Importance of Information in Transactions

A basic theory of valuation is that the buyer and seller have relevant information upon which to make their valuation or pricing decision. For example, according to the U.S. Internal Revenue Service the definition of fair market value is "the price at which the property would change hands between a willing buyer and a willing seller, neither being under any compulsion to buy or to sell and both having reasonable knowledge of relevant facts."[2] For our discussion the key phrase is "knowledge of the relevant facts."

For those with insider knowledge the ability to trade in advance of the publication of information that will likely cause a price movement, whether the trade is one of buying in or selling out, allows the insider to gain at the expense of the public shareholder. In this situation to buy in is to take from the seller and to sell out is to take from the buyer. In either case the insider is taking advantage of information over the general public investor. In promulgating Rule 10(b)5 the SEC adopted the concept that buyers and sellers of securities should have equal access to information. Therefore, a person with material information must either disclose it or forgo trading in the security until the information becomes public.

APPLICATION OF THE 8TH COMMANDMENT

One of the challenges of securities laws is their relationship to morality as compared to orderly operations of the market. Underlying the market activity is a desire to create fairness in the market, where the buyer and seller are on more equal terms. Given the complexity of the various financial instruments, the impersonal nature of modern trading, and the speed of trading activity, the SEC is enacting increasingly detailed laws to address what are deemed inappropriate activities, both from the perspective of fairness and from the perspective of efficiency or orderliness. In this paper, the focus is on overarching principles, such as those contained in the 8th Commandment. This paper recognizes that the starting point for this analysis must be that the trader be in compliance with the law or SEC rules [3]. This paper now explores whether the 8th Commandment includes or even expands the duties imposed by the insider trading rules. Please note that this paper necessarily limits this consideration to insider trading and does not address any of the many other SEC rules. All of these rules warrant a similar look by the studious Christian. It is hoped that this paper will lay a measure of foundation for such a review. The authors would welcome comments in this regard.

Before looking into the 8th Commandment, the reader is challenged to note that we conduct our commercial activities in God's world. The *Westminster Confession of Faith* is a wonderful articulation of this important principle (see, for example, chapter 5), which is clearly revealed in the Bible (see, for example, Psalm 104). God further declares that He is present in this world, is watching our every action and every thought, and will hold each of us accountable for our thoughts and actions (see, for example, Ecclesiastes 12:14 and 2 Corinthians 5:10).[4] The relevance of God's presence to proper behavior is fundamental to understanding why a Christian community should exhibit a different ethic. Those in the community should be aware of and practice the presence of God, which in turn should lead to the respecting of positions of trust such as those involving MNPI. A modern example is traffic slowing when a police car is parked along the side of the road. The SEC is effectively trying to create the same ethics by enacting laws.

The *Westminster Larger Catechism* asks two questions with regard to the application of the 8th Commandment:

Question 141: What are the duties required in the eighth commandment?
Question 142: What are the sins forbidden in the eighth commandment?

Although the catechism gives detailed answers to these questions, for historical reasons no mention is made of the wrongful use of MNPI or insider trading. At least one preacher, however, has suggested that to "bring the catechism up to date, we should also include insider trading...."[5] Like all of the Ten Commandments, the 8th Commandment has many applications,[6] and it certainly applies to the wrongful use of MNPI and insider trading. Even though the catechism does not explicitly mention insider trading, some of what it does mention has a direct bearing on the subject.

In commenting on the 8th Commandment, J. G. Vos asks, "What is the general scope of the eighth commandment?" His answer:

> The general scope of the eighth commandment is respect for the sanctity of property....Property or wealth is created by God and entrusted to man for his use in glorifying and serving God. It is therefore a stewardship committed to man, and for this reason must be respected. Thus the eighth commandment requires not only that we refrain from stealing our neighbor's property, but that we acquire and take care of our own.[7]

On a most fundamental level, then, the wrongful use of MNPI fails to respect the wealth of others, in particular the wealth of other investors.

More particularly, the answer to Question 141 says that we are duty bound to endeavor by "...all just and lawful means, to procure, preserve, and further the wealth and outward estate of others, as well as our own." Procuring, preserving, and furthering our own wealth is a good thing, but not when carried out with disregard for the wealth of others. Insider trading takes no thought for furthering the wealth of other public shareholders, but thinks only of the self. As with Question 141 and the duties required by the 8th Commandment, so Question 142 pertaining to sins to avoid lists "all other unjust or sinful ways...of enriching ourselves...."

Again, the answer to Question 142 says that we are duty bound to avoid "unfaithfulness...in matters of trust." This strikes at the heart of insider trading, since insider trading is:

> ...the buying or selling of a security, in breach of a fiduciary duty or other relationship of trust and confidence, while in possession of material, nonpublic information about the security.[8]

And as we have seen, the SEC itself defines insider trading in part as "breach of a duty of trust" [Paragraph (a) of Rule 10b5-1].

This breach of trust in human relationships is rooted in a breakdown of trust in the human/divine relationship. In his exposition of the Ten Commandments, Thomas Watson asks, "Whence does theft arise?" His first answer is:

> Unbelief...A man has a high distrust of God's providence... Can God spread a table for me, says the unbeliever? No, he cannot. Therefore he is resolved he will spread a table for himself, but it shall be at other men's cost...."[9]

Breaking faith with God leads to breaking faith with shareholders.

Watson's second reason is equally illuminating:

> Covetousness...an immoderate desire of getting...is the root of theft. A man covets more than his own, and this itch of covetousness makes him scratch what he can from another. [10]

In this same vein, the answer to Heidelberg Catechism Question 110, "What does God forbid in the eighth commandment?" mentions "all covetousness." Unbelief and covetousness are a powerful one-two that has led to the knock-out of more than one or two traders along the way.

SCENARIOS

The scenarios presented here are designed to show two poles associated with MNPI and insider trading. These scenarios are fictional and intended to set the parameters for discussing the application of the 8th Commandment to MNPI and insider trading. These scenarios are not intended to correspond to true events in any way. Papers such as this necessarily must simplify the details, but with these scenarios the authors endeavor to set forth events that could transpire in the real world of trading securities, not only as examples to be analyzed in their own right but also as examples that provide grist for further reflection on other scenarios, be they real or imagined.

Scenario #1: The CEO

The CEO of Company A, a publically traded company that trained real estate agents in how to do business by referral, was accused of violating insider trading rules based on her purchase of additional shares of Company A stock. In her role as CEO she was in possession of confidential information regarding the acquisition of Company A by Company B, a large real estate company that was looking to bring the training of its agents in house and was looking to diversify into the real estate training market. The CEO had every reason to believe that this acquisition was going to result in a substantial rise in the value of Company A stock.

Because the CEO held this information with regard to the acquisition in trust, she had a fiduciary responsibility not to use this information for her own personal gain. The use of this information in the purchase of additional stock was a violation of the 8th Commandment in at least three ways. One, the CEO failed to "avoid unfaithfulness…in matters of trust (Westminster Larger Catechism, Q/A 142). Two, the CEO stole the increase in stock value from others who did not hold the same information and could not, therefore, benefit from it. She failed to avoid "all other unjust and sinful ways…of enriching [herself]" (Westminster Larger Catechism, Q/A 142). Three, the CEO failed to fulfill the positive aspect of the 8th Commandment in that she did not employ "all just and lawful means, to procure, preserve, and further the wealth and outward estate of others [i.e., the public shareholders]" (Westminster Larger Catechism, Q/A 141).

Scenario #2: The At-home Trader

A retired journalist had spent his career investigating and writing on a variety of financial issues, including the trading of securities. Now retired, he sought to earn some additional income as an at-home day trader. He had recently become interested in Company C, a software development company that focused on, among other things, audio/video software for use over the internet. While sitting outside the offices of Company C, as he used to do at times as a journalist, he recognized business executives from Company D, a large social networking company, entering the offices of Company C. Intrigued by this he began to research the audio/video software of Company C and the audio/video capabilities of Company D. He surmised that Company D was in the process of acquiring Company C, so that it could own the proprietary software developed by Company C. Based on this hunch, he not only bought substantial stock in Company C just days before it was announced publically that Company D was in the process of acquiring Company C, but he also recommended the purchase of this stock to several of his friends and family members, who likewise purchased stock.

Because the at-home day trader had no fiduciary responsibility to either company and had no access to MNPI but made his decision to purchase stock based on information that could have been ascertained by any diligent and inquisitive investor, the at-home day trader was not guilty of insider trading and did not violate the 8th Commandment by stealing from anyone. In fact, the at-home day trader fulfilled the positive aspect of the 8th Commandment in that he employed "all just and lawful means, to procure, preserve, and further the wealth and outward estate of others [i.e., his friends and family], as well as [his] own" (Westminster Larger Catechism, Q/A 141).

Conclusion: The Two Greatest Commandments

In the introduction, we mentioned that the Apostle Paul listed "you shall not steal" among the commandments "summed up in this word: 'You shall love your neighbor as yourself'" (Romans 13:9). The wrongful use of MNPI is in short a failure to love neighbor as self. The failure to love neighbor as self, moreover, is a failure to love God, for love of God and love of neighbor cannot be separated. As 1 John 2:20 reminds us,

> Whoever claims to love God yet hates a brother or sister is a liar. For whoever does not love their brother and sister, whom they have seen, cannot love God, whom they have not seen. (NIV)

Likewise, James 2:10-11 says,

> For whoever keeps the whole law and yet stumbles at just one point is guilty of breaking all of it. For he who said, "You shall not commit adultery," also said, "You shall not murder." If you do not commit adultery but do commit murder, you have become a lawbreaker. (NIV)

In other words,

> ...the law is a unity... and in one sense each commandment

requires of us the same thing. What each commandment requires is a loyalty toward God (i.e., a love for God) that issues in godly behavior…each commandment mandates the law of love (i.e., covenant loyalty) from a different perspective.[11]

Thus the best antidote for resisting the temptation to misuse MNPI is "this command: Anyone who loves God must also love their brother and sister" (1 John 2:21; NIV). To love God and neighbor is to keep the 8th Commandment.[12] To love God and neighbor is keep trust with God and with neighbor and thus to rightly use material nonpublic information.

WORKS CITED

- Astarita, Mark J. "Insider Trading - The Legal and Illegal", n.d. http://www.seclaw.com/docs/insidertrading033104.htm.
- Frame, John M. *The Doctrine of the Christian Life*. Phillipsburg, N.J: P & R Publishing, 2008.
- Garrison, Jeff. "The Pulpit: The Eighth Commandment", August 19,2007.http://hastingspresbyterian.blogspot.com/2007/08/eighth-commandment.html.
- Vos, Johannes Geerhardus. *The Westminster Larger Catechism: A Commentary*. Edited by G. I. Williamson. Phillipsburg, N.J: P & R Publishing, 2002.
- Watson, Thomas. *The Ten Commandments*. Revised. Carlisle, PA: The Banner of Truth Trust, 1965.

Notes

1. Mark J. Astarita, "Insider Trading - The Legal and Illegal", n.d., http://www.seclaw.com/docs/insidertrading033104.htm.
2. Revenue Procedure 59-60.
3. The concepts found in Acts 4 about public disobedience do not seem to apply to securities trading.
4. While this paper addresses a commercial issue, the reader is encouraged to understand that the Bible makes it clear that every person needs to place his faith in the finished work of Jesus Christ in payment for his sins. This fundamental truth transcends the matters at hand.
5. Jeff Garrison, "The Pulpit: The Eighth Commandment", August 19, 2007, http://hastingspresbyterian.blogspot.com/2007/08/eighth-commandment.html.
6. John M. Frame, *The Doctrine of the Christian Life* (Phillipsburg, N.J: P & R Publishing, 2008), 796.
7. Johannes Geerhardus Vos, *The Westminster Larger Catechism: A Commentary* (ed. G. I. Williamson;

Phillipsburg, N.J: P & R Publishing, 2002), 377.

8. Astarita, "Insider Trading - The Legal and Illegal."

9. Thomas Watson, *The Ten Commandments* (Revised; Carlise, PA: The Banner of Truth Trust, 1965), 121.

10. Watson, *The Ten Commandments,* 121.

11. Frame, *Christian Life,* 396.

12. See Frame, *Christian Life,* 395-396, for more on the relation of love for God and neighbor to the keeping of the Ten Commandments.

The Eighth Commandment and Respect for Capital

CALVIN CHIN & WILLIAM GOLIGHER

CALVIN CHIN

Calvin is the Entrepreneurship Initiative Director at the Center for Faith and Work. Before joining the Center for Faith and Work, Calvin worked in the finance industry for seventeen years. Most recently, he spent seven years with Burnham Securities, Inc. as a director with its investment banking group where he focused on a range of activities for clients in multiple industries. His experience at the boutique enabled him to work with start ups as well as small cap public entities. Calvin also has investment advisory experience at Chase Manhattan and Sanford C. Bernstein & Co., Inc. where he managed relationships with high net worth individuals. Calvin received a B.A. from the University of Buffalo and an MBA from The NYU Stern School of Business. He also serves on the board of Hope for New York as well on the University of Buffalo's Dean of the College of Arts and Sciences' Advisory Council.

WILLIAM "LIAM" GOLIGHER

Dr. Liam Goligher was born and raised in Glasgow, Scotland in a Christian family. At the age of 11 he attended an event where a film of the Reverend Billy Graham had a profound impact on his life. He had never before heard a person preach with such passion and conviction, and from that point forward, he knew that God had called him to preach too. On his own initiative he began to study theology from whatever books he could get his hands on. Before long, he realized that he was a Calvinist, though he didn't know another living person with similar beliefs, and he was unsure of exactly what to call his beliefs. After College in Glasgow he graduated in Theology from the Irish Baptist Theological College in 1973, and in 2004, he earned his Doctor of Ministry degree from the Reformed Theological Seminary in Jackson, Mississippi.

Since April 2000, Dr. Goligher has served as Senior Minister at Duke Street Church, an independent Reformed evangelical church in West London. During his ministry Duke Street has seen significant growth among young professionals, young families, and in cultural diversity. The number of church employees has also grown from 3 to 15. Through Liam's leadership, Duke Street Church began a trainee system and instituted an eldership within the church. He also led the church to adopt the Westminster Confession of Faith and recently directed it through a capital campaign, where the equivalent of $6 million dollars was raised to restore and upgrade the church. Liam preaches both morning services and the evening service.

Duke Street is a metropolitan church that draws its people from a wide area of West London. The church has sought to build a community of believers who are devoted to the making and maturing of fully committed followers of Jesus Christ. The church has a long history with a gospel witness since the middle of the 19th century and began when C.H. Spurgeon sent one of his students to found a new church in the borough of Richmond, London. The website writes of the church's legacy: Since its earliest days, Duke Street has faithfully maintained its witness to the message of Jesus Christ — in days of spiritual decline and of revival.

Duke Street has had a history of innovation when it comes to getting the Christian message out to the community and the world. This outreach to and engagement with the city of London targets several key areas, including the business community, families, and the homeless. The church has a growing number of young families living near the church, so they have various programs for mothers, children, and youth throughout the week as well as on Sundays.

Liam Goligher has been closely involved in Bible teaching and evangelistic ministry among college students. He has spoken at conventions throughout the world, and he has preached regularly at conferences and churches in the United States. Liam has contributed to more than ten books and authored four, including The Fellowship of the King, (Carlisle, 2003), The Jesus Gospel (Milton Keynes, 2006), and Joseph — The Hidden Hand of God (Fearn, 2008). He has spoken at pastor training conferences in Ireland and Scotland, and his Sunday morning sermon is heard on radio throughout the United Kingdom and through satellite and cable channels.

H ow did it come to pass that 'a minority of people stuck out on the extreme western end of the Eurasian landmass came to dominate the world in cultural, political and economic terms for more than half a millennium?' In his book, *Civilization: the West and the Rest*, [1] Niall Ferguson offers an explanation. The west's ascendancy, he argues, is based on six attributes that he labels its "killer apps": competition, science, property, medicine, consumption and the work ethic. Ferguson who is the Laurence A. Tisch Professor of History at Harvard University and William Ziegler Professor at Harvard Business School, argues that above all the other factors it has been the respect for private property and the Protestant work ethic that made economic growth in the West far more robust than anywhere else. He writes: 'Why did the empire established by the English in North America in the 17th century ultimately prove so much more successful than that established by the Spanish in South America a century earlier? It was, Ferguson contends, because the English settlers brought with them a particular conception of widely distributed property rights and democracy, inherited from John Locke. And he quotes Max Weber's thesis that Protestantism was a form of Christianity that encouraged hard work (and just as importantly, Ferguson adds, reading and saving). It isn't a coincidence, he says, that the decline of religion in Europe has led to Europeans becoming the "idlers of the world" (while the more religious US has remained hardworking). We have a similar crisis brewing in America , the likes of which I have not seen in my lifetime. The structures of freedom and democracy have been severely weakened over the last fifty years, and in the last couple of years at an increasingly rapid rate. Yet, there is a tsunami building five hundred miles away at sea, and when it arrives, it will demolish our health care and our pensions, and freedom and democracy will go by the boards. We saw what happened in Haiti when the structures of the buildings were weak. The buildings collapsed. We have a number of weak structures holding up democracy, and they will surely collapse unless all of us suit up and take appropriate coordinated actions.

In discussing the growing success of China, Ferguson points to the growth of Protestant Christianity in that country and cites Wenzhou, China's most entrepreneurial city, which has 1400 churches. North America still retains the advantage of having all these 'killer apps' which the rest of the world wants to imitate. If we are not to lose our competitive advantage, we need to recover the heartbeat of the Reformation and the dynamic of the gospel that drove the growth of the Western world. We need to believe that 'the gospel that changes your heart can change your world.' The gospel gives us freedom in Christ and sends us back to the law to learn what loving God and our neighbor looks like in our business as well as our personal lives.

The eighth commandment says, 'you shall not steal,' but behind the simplicity of the command lies a wealth of practical inferences. What these are is clarified in the exposition of this commandment found in the Westminster Larger Catechism:

Question 141: What are the duties required in the eighth commandment?

Answer: The duties required in the eighth commandment are, truth, faithfulness, and justice in contracts and commerce between man and man; rendering to everyone his due; restitution of goods unlawfully detained from the right owners thereof; giving and lending freely, according to our abilities, and the necessities of others; moderation of our judgments, wills, and affections concerning worldly goods; a provident care and study to get, keep, use, and dispose these things which are necessary and convenient for the sustentation of our nature, and suitable to our condition; a lawful calling, and diligence in it; frugality; avoiding unnecessary lawsuits and suretyship, or other like engagements; and an endeavor, by all just and lawful means, to procure, preserve, and further the wealth and outward estate of others, as well as our own.

Question 142: What are the sins forbidden in the eighth commandment?

Answer: The sins forbidden in the eighth commandment, besides the neglect of the duties required, are, theft, robbery, man stealing, and receiving anything that is stolen; fraudulent dealing, false weights and measures, removing land marks, injustice and unfaithfulness in contracts between man and man, or in matters of trust; oppression, extortion, usury, bribery, vexatious lawsuits, unjust enclosures and depopulations; engrossing commodities to enhance the price; unlawful callings, and all other unjust or sinful ways of taking or withholding from our neighbor: What belongs to him, or of enriching ourselves; covetousness; inordinate prizing and affecting worldly goods; distrustful and distracting cares and studies in getting, keeping, and using them; envying at the prosperity of others; as likewise idleness, prodigality, wasteful gaming; and all other ways whereby we do unduly prejudice our own outward estate, and defrauding ourselves of the due use and comfort of that estate which God has given us.

High on the agenda of the eighth commandment is the issue of respecting others' person and property and a responsible use of the resources of time, property, money and opportunity. It addresses such areas as working and earning, saving and spending, giving and lending, borrowing and repaying, speculating and investing. It presupposes that God is the owner of all things and that we are stewards of his good gifts.

DIVINE PROVIDENCE

An ethical society does not have any disagreement with the principles of the second table of the law. In fact, it affirms them. What it objects to is the religious context in which they are presented. Yet the Ten Commandments include integrally the preface or prologue, "I am the Lord your God who brought you out of the land of Egypt, out of the house of bondage. You shall have no other gods before me." Who is the author of The Ten Commandments? It is the God of Abraham, Isaac, and Jacob; the God and Father of our Lord Jesus Christ. These are the ten words that out of the whole Bible were spoken and then inscribed by God Himself. The Bible presumes that ultimately everything and everyone belongs to God, for 'the earth is the Lord's and everything in it' (Ex.19:5; Psa.24:1; 50:10). He calls human beings to take dominion over the earth, to care for it in his name, and makes them trustees of whatever he lends them, whether time, money, goods, legal rights and titles. In the language of Jesus' parable, these are talents, lent by the Lord on a temporary basis for us to use for him, for ourselves and for others.

In His Providence God gives people property so in the Old Testament we find each family in Israel given a portion of land in Canaan (Exod. 33:1-3; Lev.25:10-55) while, in the New Testament, believers own houses and lands (Acts 12:12; 16:14; 21:8). Abraham makes a business deal with the Hittites to buy a burial plot for his wife Sarah, while Paul ply's his trade as a tentmaker to support his gospel work. And His generosity is not confined only to his own people but, He shows common grace to the family of unbelieving Cain so that they become innovators in the areas of agriculture and metallurgy for Jabal 'was the father of all those who dwell in tents and have livestock,' while Tubal-Cain 'was the forger of all instruments of bronze and iron' (Gen. 4:20-22). Common grace would bring forth the argument that there is no sacred and secular divide. We are to be God's instruments and work with all people, in our communities, to bring glory to the King.

It is possible to steal from God, ourselves and others.

How do we steal from *God*? We steal the worship due his name by bowing down to idols. We defraud God of His rights when we deny Him the day he has set aside for public worship or by withholding from him the tithe, time and talents on which he has a rightful claim. And we take from God the glory we owe to his name when we accept for ourselves the praise and admiration which is rightly due to him. False prophets and faithless teachers steal God's word from people when they distort His word or withhold it from the people or proclaim their own words as God's (Jer.23:30). Jesus called false religious leaders 'thieves and robbers' (John 10:1).

In Malachi's time people were offended at the thought that they would rob God. But the Lord answered their complaint: 'Will man rob God? Yet you are robbing me. But you say, 'How have we robbed you?' In your tithes and contributions. You are cursed with a curse, for you are robbing me, the whole nation of you. Bring the full tithe into the storehouse, that there may be food in my house. And thereby put me to the test, says the LORD of hosts, if I will not open the windows of heaven for you and pour down for you a blessing until there is no more need' (Mal.3:8-10). This is one subject that is often avoided in churches because it seems to be in bad taste – 'how much should I give to God through his church?' In the New Testament Jesus assumes that his people will tithe. While he criticizes the Pharisees for neglecting 'the weightier matters of the law: justice, mercy and faithfulness,' he nonetheless commends their tithing and adds, 'These you ought to have done, without neglecting the others' (Matt. 23:23). Amazingly God lets us decide how to use 90% of our income and only claims 10% as a sign of our gratitude for his providential provision. This is where some people take much leeway with the 10% figure. The 10% is a start. In agrarian society, it was sometimes much more since it was meant to be the first fruits of your harvest. Before you took crops to feed your family, you had to set aside the crops for the temple. This could mean that you could starve during a bad harvest. Contemporary church probably tithes at a "pay-as-you" go model by submitting a monthly check or hoard until year end when your expenses are already accounted for.

People steal from *themselves* through hoarding or meanness when they deny themselves legitimate pleasures or necessities; when they waste their resources irresponsibly for example, by spending without saving;

when they idly waste their time; and when they foolishly stand as an unrestricted guarantor for a friend in some enterprise. Some steal from *others* by snatching a purse, robbing a bank, insider trading, making an improper tax return, inflating an expenses claim, burglary and kidnapping. But we may well steal less obviously, for example, from the IRS by making a dishonest tax return; from our employer by claiming dishonest sick days, pilfering company supplies, inflating our expense account, or using the work phone for personal calls. We steal from God in a variety of ways including not intervening when inconvenient or to suffer possible consequences. We rationalize. We sin. (James 4:17) 'Anyone, then, who knows the good he ought to do and doesn't do it, sins.' It is the equivalent of washing your hands of a situation. How many people want to deal with the consequences of or an association with failure? What if your expertise or involvement can help a transaction and you choose not to for one reason or another. How often have you heard of people who tell you "I will accumulate or create a lot of wealth, then give it away when I am old" or "I will contribute, mentor or give back when I retire". Is this arrogance and does it have a place in the Kingdom? This thinking can infect both the investor and the entrepreneur. This philosophy misses on five important factors: This philosophy is not supported by the Bible. The Bible has numerous parables on tithing in times of famine or feast. This kind of thinking also assumes that one will live a long life and that hard work or long hours, alone, will bring about economic success. Moreover, greed for wealth becomes relative and insatiable. Most of all, by adhering to this philosophy, one is missing potential fellowship with others which is can be of mutual blessing.

While we should be on the lookout for possible risks to any investment, we know that there is a mystery to why some investments are clean, respectable, and run ethically but for one or another reason, it ends up failing and not making a mark in the marketplace. Divine providence "shows up" beyond the spreadsheets in the marketplace. Divine providence means good and bad ideas alike can die via bankruptcy, malfeasance, in-fighting, and even under a flood of cascading macroeconomic factors. These factors may include oil shock, sovereign indebtedness, global recession, tight credit markets, poor consumer confidence, or political unrest. It means that even if people fight hard, double-down, pray a lot, and come up with creative financing, businesses will still go bankrupt. Some people, such as strategy guru Seth Godin, think that it is worse to muddle along than to fail! [2] Maybe this is a new and refreshing way of thinking. When a company muddles along for months or years before eventually failing, what good can come of it? For the people involved, it wastes time, money, brain power, labor, collective energy, and possibly scars them from collaborating on future endeavors. Of course, there are relationship costs. We often cite the work life and personal life balance when successful CEO's speak of the costs of rising to the top. But there is cost to all parties involved. The fact is that starting and running an organization, regardless of sector, is incredibly risky. According to the U.S. Small Business Administration, more than 50% of all small businesses started in the U.S. fail within the first three years. Behind that statistic are entire networks of people who have paid a financial and personal price.

Failures suffer some fatal flaws, whether internal or external. Without money, all companies will fail but money is rarely the only reason. If a company runs out of cash or access to cash then it will go bankrupt and close down. For small businesses, perhaps they did not manage working capital well or did not anticipate slow or non-paying customers. Maybe a bakery did not anticipate needing a new commercial oven that requires a six figure outlay. Not all failures are caused by dire events. Some failures are caused by unexpected growth which tasks the company's capacity. Managers can forecast incorrectly. Or a business owner did not cultivate key commercial banking relationships before the business needed a loan. Maybe a business owner assumed that the current partners have the capacity to lend or invest more if necessary. Commercial banks will tell you fairly early whether they will underwrite you a loan. This too is a judgment call and about managing risks. Some banks do not like certain industries but will still go through the process to maintain a good reputation in the neighborhood. Once the commercial banks turn businesses down, word gets out in the community. If banks do not lend then there are non-traditional lenders who will charge higher interest rates, fees, and other onerous terms. We are not talking about loan sharks though we are sure people do turn to them. For larger businesses, the fundraising process for larger entities is time consuming. It can take up to 12 months from beginning to end if successful. Entrepreneurs with shorter cash reserves often failed to take this into account. Companies may be reticent to raise funds because of a lack of progress. Without any growth or new initiative to fund, prospective investors will not find it worthwhile or attractive to invest. We see that failure can lead to a bigger calling as was the case of Joseph in the Bible. (Genesis 37-50) Joseph's journey includes attempted fratricide, enslavement, and imprisonment on false charges before he is put in charge of Pharaoh's palace. Joseph's main goal was not survival but to glorify God and as a result he never lost hope and garnered wisdom and understanding. Also, with Job, one can see that our circumstances are a reminder of our relationship of dependence on Him alone. These are hard things to explore or fathom but we are comforted to know we are in His plan. Divine providence means that just as God loved Jacob and hated Esau some ventures will thrive while others do not.

Individual Rights

The eighth commandment assumes that our neighbor is made in the image of God and as such has intrinsic value and worth. Love to our neighbor requires us to hold sacred their person (the sixth commandment) and their marriage (the seventh commandment), but also their property and their due. Theft however it manifests itself, always injures others. It was blind jealousy mixed with a competitive spirit and a lust for more that drove Satan's rebellion against God and resulted in the Fall; it led to Cain killing Abel; and Rebekah and Jacob to steal the birthright from Esau (Ge.4:4; 27). Overlooking the Greek-speaking widows in the Jerusalem church breed disquiet, and no small degree of hurt among the people (Acts 6).

It isn't hard to see that the second table of the law is concerned with the love of neighbor as someone made in the image of God and benefiting from His common grace. Just as it is a human right not to be murdered so it is a human right to own property, make money, buy goods, and make investments. John Frame says, 'We should not sharply separate property rights from human rights. To steal someone's property is to take his inheritance and to assault his dignity and freedom.' [3] Keeping the eighth commandment is a fundamental expression of my love of neighbor. In his exposition of the eighth commandment Martin Luther writes:

> Next to your own persons and your wife, your worldly goods stand closest to you, and God means them to be secured to you, and therefore commands that no one shall take away or lessen any part of his neighbor's possessions...Now this is a common vice...For...stealing signifies not only emptying chests and pockets, but also taking advantage of others at market, warehouses, wine and beer shops, workshops, in short, wherever people transact business and give money for goods and labor.'

Love of neighbor requires us to hold sacred his person, his property and his due. Luther says we break this commandment whenever we 'take advantage of our neighbor in any sort of dealing that results in loss to him.' [4]

It is easy to work out the broad applications of this principle. Time, taxes, savings, service, money and goods are possessions belonging to someone somewhere, whether an individual, a corporation or the state. We steal time from our *employer* when we start late and finish early, when we extend lunchtimes and inflate expense claims, when we waste time or abuse time in the workplace. We steal from the *state* when we withhold legitimate taxation. We steal from a *customer* when we don't give value for money. The Scriptures condemn false weights and measures (Deut.25:13-15; Amos 8:5), which in modern terms applies to overpricing goods and services. We steal from a *lender* when debts are not paid at the agreed time we rob the person owed of the use of money to which they are morally entitled. The apostle Paul says, 'Owe no one anything but to love one another,' (Rom.13:8). It is stealing when we fail to pay *employees* the agreed salary in a timely fashion. In Leviticus 19:13 it says, "You shall not oppress your neighbor nor rob him. The wages of a hired man are not to remain with you all night until morning." If the people you owe are living hand to mouth, and you pay them in cash or in goods and you delay that payment overnight you are taking advantage of them and that could be critical in their case. You are to pay them in a timely fashion. We steal from potential *investors* if we raise money from people under false pretences or without communicating the risks involved or the hidden costs entailed.

For a Christian to engage in dishonest trading or to be responsible for defrauding an employee, employer or customer, is to threaten the integrity of our witness and the credibility of the gospel. Paul writes to Titus in Crete: 'Slaves are to be submissive to their own masters in everything; they are to be well-pleasing, not argumentative, *not pilfering*, but showing all good faith, so that in everything they may adorn the doctrine of God our Savior' (Titus 2:9-10 ESV). For a Christian to impoverish another Christian is not only to make life miserable for them and their family but it is to tear the unity and diminish the testimony of the church. The kingdom is affected if a Christian is caught in a financial scandal; and the church suffers if workers are not rewarded appropriately and they are inhibited from tithing to the work of God. Communities suffer when resources are mishandled or taken away.

People live in communities for a variety of reasons, including having the support of the resources of family members. This extends to their financial capital and wisdom especially in the areas of conducting commerce. In olden times, family businesses were an extension of a clan's prominence so it was natural to pool resources to start and operate them. A family's presence in the marketplace and civic affairs enhanced a family's standing. As society moved away from family-based enterprises, family members had to compete with other business owners based on better ideas and execution rather than by blood ties. For our purposes, when we refer to the investor, we typically mean one that invests in private companies. Investment can be in the form of direct cash infusion for some equity ownership, revenue share, or a loan with collateral or unsecured loan, or even a loan that converts into equity ownership. When we refer to entrepreneurs, it will mean the owner of a small business in a community or one that has a regional or national presence. Investor categories can range from friends and family, angels, venture capital funds and private equity firms, and occasionally hedge funds. We will focus primarily on the friends and family stage. This stage is the next step after self-financing. Angels are individuals who are able to write large checks and make quick decisions. Venture capitalists, or institutional investors, are legal entities that pool funds for the purpose of investing. The friends and family stage is viewed as the most unsophisticated and riskiest type of financing since it is seed capital or very early stage of a company. Angels, in general, can provide advice in additional to funds. Venture capitalists are expected to bring an entire network and industry experience. Typically, friends and family financing amounts range from a few thousand up to mid-six figures. Any amounts higher than that would mostly involve third parties, such as angels and institutional investors.

Friends and family money is usually easiest to secure because of proximity and the relationship. You live near family or have access to them. Family gatherings are a wonderful place to present your newest venture idea. It is a given that family members, whether by blood or by marriage, are already acquainted or intimate with each other. Whereas most investors need to have good historical performance, or a "track record" in order for entrepreneurs to seek them out, friends and family members who actively invest or are asked to invest, do not need such bona fides. They just need to have money or access to money. While an outside investor needs to produce good investment returns so that he or she can report back to the limited partners as well as market this performance attract new investors for future funds, the bar or rate of return is very subjective for friends and family. Expected rates of return may be unreasonably low due to familial obligation. In the marketplace, competition for financial and intellectual capital, in its purest form, is the process of pursuing an agreement between a willing investor and willing investee. Small businesses, especially the neighborhood ones with little vision or ability to scale, are incredibly risky. Small businesses, with one or a handful of locations, are easier to verify than larger businesses but the caliber of people who want to work for such businesses may be lacking. Small businesses probably suffer from a lack of access to capital, a sufficient pool of talented employees, high employee turnover, succession plan, and may be more susceptible to theft, crime, or other factors such as tax treatment and regulation. Institutions typically do not like to invest in small businesses because they are looking for big returns and that would involve larger ventures.

Furthermore, small businesses may not have legal structures for large groups of investors. This makes sense because most small companies view the limited liability corp. as easiest to establish. A LLC does not accommodate new investors easily. Few people would invest in a small business. Most small businesses probably run on credit more so that traditional investment dollars. Institutions shy away from family businesses because of a myriad of reasons. Again, smaller businesses are riskier because they take lots of time and energy to monitor and exit strategies are not great. For example, try and think of a realistic and financially rewarding exit strategy for a pizzeria or delicatessen or coffee shop. With larger transactions, an entrepreneur will offer up a percentage of ownership in the company in return for investment dollars to help fuel the growth of his venture. This agreement, usually written in the form of a term sheet, should reflect the value of the company's individual traits (e.g., sales, product(s), service(s), size, management team experience, the market it serves, competition, geography, etc.) relative to marketplace realities, including other offers, if any. If an entrepreneur has multiple term sheets from prospective investors, she must work to get the best investment offer in terms of dollar amount, company's valuation, working arrangement, use of proceeds, and other conditions that would benefit her and her venture. Investors want to invest in a business at the lowest price point (valuation) to get a higher ownership percentage and to position it for a better financial return. On the flip side, the entrepreneurs want the most investment dollars with the highest possible valuation so they can keep a larger possible percentage of ownership. There are other factors such as the investor's expertise and management philosophy – active or passive- and its network's multiplying effect. Whether the investor is an individual or an institution, this is usually the operating principle. For an entrepreneur, her business will require additional rounds of financing to realize its projections and achieve an exit, IPO, sale, i.e., or sustainable operating status. Behind the commandment lies the Bible view of property: namely, that ownership is stewardship, for one day we will be called upon to answer for how we managed the resources he put into our possession. At its most basic, stealing is a failure to accept God's provision for us, or it is a failure to trust God for his future care. The eighth commandment is a call to trust in the providence of God and on His kind provision for us in all our need.

WORK ETHIC, ROLES, AND RESPONSIBILITIES

To some people work is meaningless (a tedious consequence of the Fall), a necessary evil (facilitating our leisure activities), or simply a useful sphere of witness (often the received Christian view). According to Scripture work is a blessing not a curse, it is the Creation and not the Fall that makes work significant; and God the worker has made his image-bearers workers too. Work is an honorable thing and the commission to work is a creation mandate. Although the Fall introduces the element of hardship and toil into work, nonetheless it remains necessary and beneficial. Work is intrinsically good before the Fall. Even with the fall, there is goodness in all that God has put forth. The legal sector protects, advocates, and facilitates resolutions and justice. The education sector provides instruction, learning, and empowering citizens. The finance sector creates wealth and investment opportunities for institutions and individuals. The arts sector inspires while creating tangible goods that enrich the lives of ordinary citizens. Even in this fallen world, God has given us these sectors and the entire marketplace so that we can live out our Genesis mandate.

Tied into this mandate to create and participate in the global marketplace is this concept of Missio Dei, or God's mission. His mission is for us to be in the world, serving, doing, and living out our fellowship with Him in a unique way. Work ethic is more pronounced when someone understands that their work is important and relevant to God rather than being a weigh station to the New Jerusalem. If Christians understand that work is inherently good because it was given to us from God, this may produce a sea change in productivity and joy of humanity. Without this proper foundation in a fallen world, mankind would lean toward sloth or distraction from the work we have been given.

The apostle Paul warns against idleness: 'If anyone is not willing to work, let him not eat. For we hear that some among you walk in idleness, not busy at work, but busybodies. Now such persons we command and encourage in the Lord Jesus Christ to do their work quietly and to earn their own living' (2 Thess. 3:10-12; see also 1 Thes.2:9 ESV). The NT juxtaposes work and theft, 'Let the thief no longer steal, but rather let him labor, doing honest work with his own hands, so that he may have something to share with anyone in need' (Eph.4:28). Work produces reward which, among other things, provides the opportunity to do good to those in need. Interestingly, Jesus likened the kingdom of heaven to that situation where a master entrusts his servants with a portion of his wealth represented by talents. (Mathew 25:14-30 ESV) The master gives five, three, and one talent, respectively, to three servants. We can glean several glints of wisdom from this parable. One is that the master expected his servants, of differing gifts, to do their best to bring about a return. Second is the bad attitude of the third servant. Was he risk-adverse, as some have said, or was he downright belligerent in burying the one talent in the ground? He was a grumbler. He did not think his master should be rewarded for not toiling alongside his servants. Thirdly, the third servant could have consulted with the other smarter and better performing servants who turned doubled their "portfolios". It is interesting to note how even Jesus uses a parable to remind us of our responsibilities regardless of whether the talents are purely about financial matters or allude to spiritual matters. It does point to having an excellent work ethic and doing things unto the Lord.

An entrepreneur's work ethic can be measured in several ways. The most straight forward manner is the actual time spent shepherding the organization and carrying out appropriate activities. Is the entrepreneur fulfilling fiduciary responsibilities or out padding the T&E account? Is the business a place to create wealth by providing a service or is it a place to socialize? Another way to measure an entrepreneur's work ethic is to have some "skin in the game" or their own capital. This is where ownership of property, as pointed out earlier, is valuable. To have some personal assets or savings gives the entrepreneur flexibility in choosing prospective financing sources. Business owners only seek outside capital when they lack enough funds, the business does not generate sufficient funds (i.e., losing money), or they want to sue other people's money and not their own. We know of some entrepreneurs who have taken out loans on their homes or second mortgages or put up other assets for financing. The glamorous image of the caffeine-fueled all-nighters is not work ethic. Furthermore, work ethic is not just how hard an entrepreneur works but what they are working on or not working on. Are they trying to grow sales when they should be working on training employees to handle new customers? Are they working on operations and cutting expenses when revenue growth is the only way to be financially profitable? Working harder could be problematic if they have the wrong plan. To mitigate any of the latter, an investor needs to part of formulating an appropriate strategy. This is where good communication and having a common set of expectations is helpful. The entrepreneur must be mindful of her responsibilities to the investors, and not just financial ones.

As we discussed earlier, the investor's work ethic depends on his or her investment philosophy. Even with small businesses, some investors are prone to manage by being present and providing counsel, solicited or not. Investors in small businesses can protect their investments by staying close to the operators. But for all investors, they should have some philosophy to guard their time. They need to decide early on whether they are active managers who want and can play a major advisory role? Or are they more passive and manage when needed or only on bigger decisions? In larger companies, where there are several institutions involved, there usually is one lead investor. A lead investor usually means the one who has put in the most money in a transaction and speaks as the leader of an entire investment group when dealing with management or outsiders. Given their large ownership percentage and expertise, lead investors usually have a seat on the board of the company, do most of the work, and coordinate and manage communications with the entrepreneur.

So how can investors work smarter? Working smarter for investors may involve a system of combining key practices. According to a study done by consultancy McKinsey [5] on top performing exits (sales or IPO's) by private equity firms, there are 5 key factors that helped produce better financial returns: 1. Expertise, 2. A value creation plan created with management, 3. Monitoring and honing the value creation plan, 4. Devoting hours of time with management during first 100 days, and 5. Quick management removal if necessary. These findings would confirm that work ethic alone does not bring about superior results. By showing up with a plan that the management and board understands and is aligned with can help to bring about better performance and be a differentiator. This can be helpful to investors as well as entrepreneurs. A solid work ethic is assumed for those rare breed of entrepreneurs as well as those who are on the investing side, so seeking differentiators is important. Having a criteria before seeking capital or investing capital would certainly fall under working smarter, improving chances of success, and mitigating problems. No matter what role we play or the outcomes which are in His hands, we are to live out Jesus commandment to Peter (John 21:15-25) to "feed my sheep". In seeking financial returns, we sometimes see people as means to profit and not as people to nurture and care for. This is not to say we coddle people but to value them and make sure they fit in the plan. Certainly, how do Christians squeeze our inefficiencies and expenses from potential investments while mitigating costs to society? The world of investing does not lack for flawed personalities, outsized egos, embellishments or shenanigans, but needs wisdom.

Areas Requiring Discernment

The purpose of this paper is to address the gray areas, the areas especially relating to capital investment, and in particular the friends and family model. Some of us may know horror stories of the friends and families of an entrepreneur who have been inconvenienced or impoverished due to their support of a start up venture that went wrong. Sometimes there is a history of failed enterprises but this information is not passed on to the potential investors. On occasion we have seen people take out a bigger mortgage in order to facilitate a purchase of equipment or property needed to advance the building up of a business. The one raising the money for this capital outlay has not taken into account either the loss of earned interest on deposited money or the accrual of interest on the mortgaged money. This failure has led to a loss is real terms – though the loan is repaid the potential gain from investment is lost and the cost of remortgaging is also lost. There is the obvious opportunity cost to all parties involved and it is more glaring if the investment capital is lost or not fully repaid. This sin is in line with the parable of the talents where the last servant, whose heart, was not joyfully aligned with the well-being of his very demanding master, buried his lone talent. One has to wonder if burying the talent was an act of defiance to deny his master additional wealth or of stupidity because he did not consult the two other servants who were more talented and found better investment opportunities.

So in order to get the best return, as an investor, or to get best investment terms, as an entrepreneur, what are the rules of engagement? If we are dealing with friends or family members, should the transaction be done informally? Can terms be discussed at the dinner table or a lawyer's office? Is it done by a handshake and oral agreement? Regardless of the role they play, the adrenaline of starting a venture, the possibility of doing something that will be financially rewarding can sometimes induce people to cut corners to speed the process. Most investors and entrepreneurs try to keep things "simple" to dispense with or minimize costs. Simple should not mean cheap or sloppy. But the first expenses they try to reduce upfront are legal or tax advisory. These are expenses they should incur to minimize future misunderstandings and problems for the business let alone in dealing with the investors. So what are the ground rules that should be observed? Simple documentation will introduce facts and establish legal precedence should there be a disagreement based on difference of opinion or faltering memories. Operating agreements, loan agreements, roles, responsibilities, economic terms, investment duration, and possible exit strategies can be spelled out in a simple word document or other low-cost legal stationary. Other good practices involve a quick due diligence check list, including contracts, copies of incorporation papers, credit, drug, and back ground checks, loan agreements, investment agreements, investor lists, etc. An organized file with all the legal paperwork in it makes for good business practice. This step may be difficult for some people who are prone to dump things into a shoebox but it is prudent. A well-managed business can manage future growth and opportunities as well as problems. Having the paperwork organized will help with any investing due diligence or underwriting process and give the perception of a competent manager.

How do you prudently conduct due diligence on family members? It may be embarrassing and uncomfortable. We may know of family secrets or overlook small indiscretions or legal matters. But if we know our cousin cheats on her taxes, how will they behave as a business partner? Will they cheat you in some manner we have already discussed? For any individual investor, a simple background check should be performed to uncover personal issues such as jail, arrests, habits, previous litigation, aliases, etc. Family members may take umbrage so it might help to have outside investors push for that rather than a family member. We are not sure of the empirical evidence but anecdotally background checks for friends and family would be rare. For investors from the angel stage and up, there is more due diligence performed. In one example, before American Apparel became public through a reverse merger, how many people may have known much about its founder or had any responsibility to care about his lifestyle. But given recent allegations, his continued leadership has impacted the value of the company and its investors. The founder is the majority shareholder. Once a fashion retailing high flier --- with its sexually charged advertisements a strategic celebration of its founder's vision --- it is now viewed as a speculative investment given the several lawsuits alleging his sexual assaults of former employees. These lawsuits are taking up precious time and money while American Apparel's brand has suffered and its stock has plummeted to around $1. ($1.00 as of May 20) It is a cautionary tale of how investors should include prudent legal conditions to mitigate such problems. Employment contracts can include a clause whereby such behavior should automatically be grounds for removal of the founder. But if the founder has control and is integral to the company's fortunes, then that is more complicated. The other way to completely avoid such problems is by not investing in such a person or corporate vision regardless of the potential financial return. However, if such a scenario does occur, how does an investor bring about something redemptive in the process? Is it even possible? What shall Christians do?

Other situations may not be as explosive or tawdry and fall under the radar but could be considered questionable in light of Question 141. Would you consider the following behavior moderation in affection concerning worldly goods? For example, some entrepreneurs, after taking investor funds, can wasteful in their spending and incredibly consumption minded. They spent not for strategic purposes but for appearances sake to "keep up with the Jones". This consumption was exemplified in the Internet 1.0 phase of the mid-to late-1990's by the ubiquitous and expensive Herman Miller furniture. These Internet companies spent money like it grew on trees without producing any revenue! So what happened to most of the companies when the marketplace started to correctly value these new ventures? These companies went out of business in the same spectacular manner as they were launched. The one-two punch of the Internet bubble being burst and 9/11 resulted in those memorable auctions of the same Herman Miller furniture for pennies on the dollar. After such a traumatic economic upheaval exacerbated by 9/11, most people surmised that such irrational exuberance would not happen again.

So what have we witnessed more recently? The easy credit policy throughout the global economy again produced a bubble, exemplified best by the growth of the hedge fund sector. The desire for investment professionals to run their own funds and enrich themselves was a great growth driver. Most hedge funds charge a minimum of 2% of assets under management and a percentage of the appreciation. These key financial incentives, along with the low investment cost of starting your own hedge fund, caused a proliferation of hedge funds to such a degree that in 2007, there were more hedge funds than mutual funds in 2007. It was estimated to be over 13,000 hedge funds managing about $2.68 Trillion in assets in 2007.[6] Of course with track records being all the same, most set up offices in prime real estate locations with impressive works of art and threw wonderful conferences or parties to entice prospective investors or referral sources. A 2006 hedge fund conference in the UK hired The Who to play and entertain. This was the largess we experienced before the great recession. So what did all that money spent do for their track records or sustainability? Many folded in the great financial crisis that began in 2007. There are still more than 6,900 hedge funds operating [7] and most still charge clients 2% of the funds under management. Both examples were part of the easy money and perhaps lax investor mentality that contributed to a bubble and binge consumption. Ventures burn through precious resources given to them to grow the business when spent on ancillary items. So robbing God is not just outright theft, but also poorly managed resources. One certainly cannot run a successful business on a shoe string but there is a lot of maneuvering room between excessive consumption and monastic frugality. To hedge against such behavior, investors do their best to put in strict guidelines to mitigate going into distinctly different business from that described in the offering memorandum.

What is our responsibility when we see a bad business situation developing? What if we are working for a business that is making poor spending decisions? What if we are on the outside, as an investor? Do we step in early? Maybe we could have avoided all this by turning down a bad idea. What are we to do when listening to a bad idea or investment opportunity? Do we listen intently, ask smart questions, mull it over a few weeks, stop taking their calls, and move on? Or do we share our input in firm and constructive tones and tell the entrepreneur that the opportunity is terrible and they should quit? Is that too bold or arrogant? With anyone, it may be easy to be honest because we may never see them again. With relatives, it is trickier. We may damage a relationship if we are curt or dismissive. We may damage a relationship even if we are diplomatic and thoughtful. If we merely say no or pass on investing are we fulfilling our duty under the eighth commandment? Is this sufficient? If our family member's venture fails and we did not warn them or actively intervene, we will bear the consequences if the person's well-being is hurt by the business's failure. If the business is successful, the relative may not let us live it down by for not investing or by rejecting the idea as not worthy. Even without the complication of family relationships, investing in or starting a business is extremely difficult and risky.

The pitfalls and problems of investing or starting businesses should not and does not deter people from doing so. Glory be to God that we are in His economy. This is quite unique. In some eastern religions and cultures, there are hard caste or class systems where such freedom and creativity is forbidden and enforced. In some cultures, it is unseemly to be upwardly mobile. As Christians, we are reminded that even with the Fall, we have a responsibility in God's economy. Ultimately, we may understand that in God's economy, we are called to participate and be good managers of His resources. In doing so, we are in a position to use our gifts to perhaps create wealth, employ and bless people, and to create new products and services to bring about human flourishing thereby pleasing Him.

Notes

1. Niall Ferguson, *Civilization: the West and the Rest*, (2011, Allen Lane)

2. Seth Godin, *The Dip*, (2007, Penguin)

3. John M. Frame, *The Doctrine of the Christian Life*, New Jersey: P&R, 2008, 798

4. Martin Luther, *The Large Catechism* (Philadelphia: Fortress, 1959), 39

5. Joachim Heel and Conor Kehoe, *The McKinsey Quarterly*, 2005 Number 1

6. Q3 2007 Hedge Fund.net (HFN) Hedge Fund Administrator Study (www.hedgefund.net)

7. David Pauly, Hedge Funds Succumbing to Mutual Funds' Mediocrity, (Bloomberg.com, October 17, 2010)

EFFECTS OF IGNORING GOD'S COUNSEL

AN ANALYSIS OF 2007-2008 FINANCIAL CRISIS

PHILIP CLEMENTS

PHILIP CLEMENTS

Phil Clements is the managing director of the Center for Christian Business Ethics Today, LLC. Phil has been a leader in the business community for over thirty years. In 2003, Jack Templeton, a fellow board member of the National Bible Association, challenged Phil with a question of the role of faith in commerce. Phil's research affirmed the foundational importance of the principles of our Christian faith and the quality of business commerce. That research confirmed the changes he has experienced during his business career as the world moves away from these Christian principles.

Phil founded the Center to meet this concern that is articulated in Judges 2:10–11.

From September 2001 to October 2004 Phil held the position of Executive Vice President of Standard & Poor's Corporate Value Consulting ("CVC") division. He led the transition of CVC to S&P, after S&P acquired CVC from PricewaterhouseCoopers LLP (PwC). Prior to joining Standard & Poor's, Phil was the Global Leader of the CVC practice of PwC. During FY'99 and FY'00, Global CVC grew to a fully integrated global service unit. Prior to becoming Global Leader for CVC at the formation of PwC, Phil ran the Coopers & Lybrand's Corporate Finance Practice for the U.S. This practice included CVC, investment banking, transaction structuring, due diligence and bankruptcy turnaround services.

From 1989 to 2000, Phil served on the U.S. boards of Coopers & Lybrand and Pricewaterhouse Coopers and the global board of PwC. Phil was a member of the Finance Committees of both firms. The board experience included the board approvals of the merger of C&L and PW to form PwC and the oversight of the transition to PwC operations globally. Finance committee work included the capital structure of the firms and financial reporting. Although both firms were private, they had substantial numbers of partners for whom financial results were very relevant.

Community service plays an important role in Phil's life. At Grace Bible Chapel, a non-denominational evangelical church, Phil has been the High School Sunday School teacher for the past thirteen years, an Elder, and part of the touring praise and worship team, PowerSurge. Phil was Chairman of the Board of Trustees of the National Bible Association. Seattle University School of Law Board of Visitors, International Leadership Board of Advisors, and HOPE Bible Mission board are others boards that Phil has served or is serving on.

Phil has three daughters and lives with his wife in Chester, New Jersey. He has a passion for the water, which drives his two favorite pastimes—sailing and sea-plane piloting.

The recurring questions for the Credit Crisis of 2007-2008 is, "What is going on in the financial markets?" Subordinate questions are, "How did we get here?" and "What does this crisis mean to the future?" This paper was originally prepared for general distribution and was posted on CFO Magazine website, being the most downloaded paper through the end of 2008. The paper explores how the business and financial activities leading up to the financial crisis violated the clear counsel of God as found in the Bible.

The paper is included in this text for two reasons. The first reason is to answer the claim that the financial crisis was brought on by individuals and businesses that were stealing. While stealing and greed played a role, many other factors underlay the crisis. The second reason is to illustrate further the valuable role of the Bible's principles for understanding how business needs to operate. Using the Bible, this paper articulates many basic financial principles for commerce. The Bible provides similar guiding principles for businesses today as they wrestle with business practices and issues. The advantage biblical principles is their timelessness, as well as their God-given essentialness to how God's world operates. A business or community cannot violate biblical principles with impunity.

I. HOW DID WE GET HERE?

A. What is truth?

As a preamble we need to address the question, "What is truth?" Without a clear understanding of what has happened and what the implications are of these events, it is difficult to formulate actions for the future. In this paper Bible passages are referenced for examples of the financial principles and issues seen today. The Bible is being used to show that these financial principles and issues are not new. [1]

In Mark 11:27-33 we find the following exchange between Jesus and a group of Jewish leaders:

> They arrived again in Jerusalem, and while Jesus was walking in the temple courts, the chief priests, the teachers of the law and the elders came to him. "By what authority are you doing these things?" they asked. "And who gave you authority to do this?" Jesus replied, "I will ask you one question. Answer me, and I will tell you by what authority I am doing these things. John's baptism--was it from heaven, or from men? Tell me!"

> They discussed it among themselves and said, "If we say, 'From heaven,' he will ask, 'Then why didn't you believe him?' But if we say, 'From men' . . . ." (They feared the people, for everyone held that John really was a prophet). So they answered Jesus, "We don't know." Jesus said, "Neither will I tell you by what authority I am doing these things." [2]

In the search for truth, we see a clear example of what is called "nuanced" analysis. The chief priests consider implications of the question. Note the complexity if they answer one way versus answering in another way. What they do not consider is what is the truth. Their conclusion is not to answer. As we consider the current financial crisis we need to see that many of the comments and analysis will involve this kind of nuanced analysis rather than a search for truth. Often we chock this up to bias, but it is more nuanced than bias. Please understand this lack of willing-ness to search for and accept truth plays a key role in both understand-ing how we got here and what we should do about the financial crisis going forward. The reader is pointed to the discussions around subprime lending and what to do with homeowners who took out subprime loans as an illustration of nuanced thinking rather than a pursuit of truth.

A second passage is John 18:37-38, where Pilate is interviewing Jesus at Jesus' trial just before being sentenced to be crucified:

> "You are a king, then!" said Pilate. Jesus answered, "You are

right in saying I am a king. In fact, for this reason I was born, and for this I came into the world, to testify to the truth. Everyone on the side of truth listens to me." "What is truth?" Pilate asked. With this he went out again to the Jews and said, "I find no basis for a charge against him."

Jesus claims that there is truth. Pilate responds with a rhetorical question as to the essence of truth. Then Pilate asserts a truth – Jesus is innocent of charges. Yet, we all know the story that Pilate goes on to order Jesus' death. For our analysis of the financial crisis, truth does not necessarily lead to actions consistent with the truth. Pilate was expedient in his assessment of what needed to be done, even as in a financial crisis actions taken may be for expediency. This financial crisis arises during the U.S. presidential election. It should not surprise the reader to find that expediency will be the determining standard for action rather than the best fiscal actions, that may have negative implications to various communities.

Therefore, we need to see that wisdom is needed to properly discern truth and the necessary actions. There is a spirit in people that points to a capacity to discern the truth in a matter and address that truth. At the same time, there are spirits in people that deny truth, even when made known to them, and such denial can come at a very high price. Isaiah 6 contains a passage where a spirit of denial is illustrated. Isaiah is told that he is to go to the people of Israel and give them warning of their errors. Yet, Isaiah is also told that they will not hear. Today we need to pray that God's Spirit will aid us as a people to hear and see truth and act upon the truth. [3]

A last point on the pursuit of truth is the role of greed and social dynamics. Greed is another scapegoat. It is easy to say that it is greedy executives, brokers, and investors that caused this crisis. There is some truth to this, but this paper asserts that there are more fundamental principles that were ignored. Just going after the greedy means we will miss the needed reinforcement of fundamental principles. Similarly, there are some social dynamics that contribute to this crisis. It is tempting to blame the crisis on a wayward society, but this would miss the fundamental principles as well.

B. Risk Management

Let's consider the fundamental principles that surround risk and risk management. Risk is the potential that what is expected or desired will not happen, herein called "an event." In addition to the potential that an event will happen, the magnitude of the loss caused by an event is another part of risk. Risk management is about reducing both aspects of risk – reducing the potential that an event will happen and/or reducing the loss caused by an event. Loss transfer, called insurance, is a tool used to reduce the amount of the potential loss if an event occurs. Keep in mind that the reduction of downside has significant value, so risk management has been a valuable business and financial management principle.

There is a lot of talk about financial risk and risk management tools today, but let's look at a few principles concerning risk that are as old as time.

1. Risk of Future Events and Math

Solomon addresses the existence of risk in Ecclesiastes 11:2, "Give portions to seven, yes to eight, for you do not know what disaster may come upon the land." We do not know the future. In Luke 12:15-21 Jesus speaks of a rich man with an abundant harvest who decides to store more for his security.[4] Jesus notes the vagaries of life, in that the rich man may die even that day. While written over a thousand years apart, the risks of the future are highlighted in each passage. Today we have mathematical formulas using portfolio theory and market models that are used to predict the future. Yet the risk remains the same – we do not truly know what the future will hold.

A great example of mathematics failing to predict the future is Long Term Credit. Long Term Credit created highly leveraged models (see below for the principles on leverage, also called debt) based upon the notion that their models fully predicted the effect of market movements. Yet, it seems that these models missed the impact of the Russian credit crisis of 1997. The result was a credit crisis similar to today's crisis. The U.S. government had to bail out Long Term Credit.

2. Diversification

The other principle for risk management Solomon highlights is "do not have all your eggs in one basket." In other words you could say, "Diversify your investments." In business we call it "do not bet the ranch.[5]" The investment community refers to diversity as a modern concept, yet, here is Solomon setting it down about 3,000 years ago. Note that Solomon recommends seven to eight different baskets.[6] This idea of not betting the ranch is critical to understanding Lehman and AIG.

3. Diligence in Risk Management

Proverbs 27:23-24 states, "Be sure you know the condition of your flocks, give careful attention to your herds; for riches do not endure forever, and a crown is not secure for all generations." These verses point out the importance of systematic risk management. When one takes on risks, one must watch them. Great management has the systems to allow the senior executives to monitor the risks within the company. We will see this simple principle contributing big time to the Citibank, Lehman, Merrill Lynch and AIG problems.

The *New York Times* article "Behind the Biggest Insurer's Crisis, A Blind Eye to a Web of Risk: How a Small, Freewheeling Unit Brought A.I.G. to Its Knees" by Gretchen Morgenson[7] does a nice job of showing the lack of senior management oversight of a team that was taking on increasing amounts of risk and the reasons for that oversight failure being profits or the appearance of profits. This notion of leaving the profit producers alone, giving them free reign, has brought down many an otherwise well founded enterprise. Management that fails to administer oversight of even the most profitable units fails in this core risk management duty.

4. Lender Risk Management

There are a number of basic principles of risk management for a lender. A lender's goal is to receive a return of principal (the amount loaned) as well as the payment of interest at the agreed time. Principles to secure loan repayment are a) loan to those who have the capacity to repay and b) loan to those who have the desire to repay. The role of collateral is to reduce the risk of failure to repay by encouraging the desire to repay and by giving the lender an alternative way to collect the principal and interest, i.e., by selling the collateral. Exodus 22:25-27 outlines how to treat a borrower's pledge of a cloak for a loan.[8] The point is that collateral to secure repayment is not a new concept. We will see that much of the credit crisis arises from the failure to follow basic principles for lending.

5. Leverage to Increase Returns

As we approach this topic, the words of Proverbs 23:4, 5 give warning not to labor to be rich, thereby ignoring wisdom, and to keep in mind that somehow riches tend to fly away.

Leverage is a tool used to increase the rate of return on an investment. Leverage is placing debt into the activity. Debt reduces the amount of equity investment. Therefore, the same return or gain generates more return on the equity investment, because the amount of equity invested is less. For example, an investment will pay $100 a year. If $1,000 is paid for this investment the return is 10% ($100/$1,000). If $900 is borrowed and

$100 of equity is used to buy the investment, the return on equity is 100% ($100/$100). For simplicity the interest on the loan has been ignored. In today's world leverage is used in many places, especially in new financial tools, to increase investment returns.

But leverage has a downside – it increases the risk of an investment. In the example above, what happens if the investment value declines by 15%? Where the full price was paid with equity, the equity is worth $850 ($1,000-$150=$850). Where there has been leverage of $900 used, the investment is wiped out and is negative $50 ($100 equity - $150 = -$50). Often the leverage increase and the degree of risk increase is not linear. In other words the risk can go up much faster than the percentage of debt would appear to add. The downside of being wiped out is not the same as losing some equity value, because a wiped out investment does not have the chance to recover if the decline is a market movement rather than intrinsic value change.

These principles apply to companies as well as investments. The concept behind leveraged buy-outs was the same as illustrated above for the investment. If the company hits a down market for a period, the company is wiped out or bankrupt. The more leverage in a company, the less down market it takes to wipe-out the company.

Many of the new financial tools started as risk management tools, but became high leverage tools to increase earnings of those employing them.

6. Role of Government

The last set of principles in risk management is the role of government in protecting the community from risks.[9] The key issue is the balance between the responsibility of the individual or enterprise that is taking on the risk and government protecting that individual from the consequences of the risk. This balance then adds the government's responsibility to protect its citizens at large from risks taken on or created by individuals or entities, often referred to as systemic risks, which can affect the whole economy. The credit crisis has a systemic risk component. In this balancing act, the government has tools it can use: (a) regulation, which is a proactive approach to risk management by constraining risks that can be created or assumed, and (b) allowing the burden of risks assumed to impact the assuming individual or enterprise to various degrees. Needless to say since governments are political, regulation is political. Free market language is used to say, that risks and rewards go together and therefore individuals and enterprises should bear the burdens and benefits of their risk taking. Socialistic language says that society is the priority and must be protected from risks, and that rewards belong to the greater community. We will see this balancing act as part of the struggle in how to address the credit crisis.

An added regulation component is pushing social agendas through regulatory agencies and rules. In 1995 the Clinton administration modified the rules under the Community Reinvestment Act of 1977 (CRA) to encourage banks to make loans to lower income individuals who would not otherwise qualify for mortgage loans. Under the CRA, there were requirements for banks operating in certain communities to meet its requirements. This was particularly true for bank mergers. Thus these regulations caused/ encouraged banks not to comply with their otherwise loan risk management criteria and to loan to less credit worthy individuals, creating subprime loans.[10]

C. The Financial Instruments and Innovations

Over the past thirty years a number of financial innovations have been developed. The following is a brief review of these innovations in order to set the stage for how we got here.

1. Securitization
Securitization is a tool for maximizing the value of a cash flow stream by breaking the cash flow into its separate payments and selling these separate payments to different investors. The underlying principle is the interest rate yield curve. As a general rule, the interest rate yield curve shows short-term interest rates that are less than long-term rates. Therefore, a 30-day loan will have a lower interest rate than a 30-year loan. Mortgages in the early 1980s were primarily fixed rate 30-year loans. However, the next mortgage payment was a 30-day loan and the last mortgage payment was a 30-year loan. Yet the interest rate for each payment was the same based upon the 30-year loan interest rate. By slicing the mortgage into a series of payment streams, each stream could be sold to a separate lender, who would give a lower interest for the shorter-term streams. As a result, the financial institution making the fixed rate 30-year mortgage would receive a gain based upon the lower overall interest for the securitized mortgage loan.[11]

As securitization became the industry practice, mortgages were originated with the intention of being sold into pools for securitization. The pools of mortgages were designed to make it efficient to sell off the various cash streams. However, the result was that mortgages went from being owned by the banks that made the mortgage loan to an origination process where there were mortgage writers who never made the loan, but were simply agents for financial companies that provided the funds to assemble the mortgage pools.

Securitization worked well and was expanded to include all kinds of loans and cash streams. A key to making the cash streams securitizable was their predictability of cash receipt. Predictability is an aspect of risk - remember repayment must be timely. Initially, only high quality loans could be securitized. Then more risky, less predictable loans were securitized using various portfolio theory based models.

The ultimate examples are the Collateralized Debt Obligation (CDO) and the Special Investment Vehicle (SIV). These were pools of the unsellable pieces of other securitized loan pools. In short, these were where the risk was. Yet, using portfolio theory models, pieces of a CDO or SIV were treated as high quality investment opportunities. These pools have now been relabeled toxic assets.[12]

A key outcome of a securitization is the separation of the ultimate lender from the borrower. Because the ultimate lender holds a piece of a pool of loans, they do not have direct access to the borrower or the loan's collateral. CDOs and SIVs are the third and fourth iterations of loans. Thus, they are even further removed from the borrower and collateral. This means that evaluating the riskiness of the investment is now more difficult.

2. Mortgages

Adjustable rate, option arm, fixed, balloon, zero down, and the list goes on relative to types of mortgages offered in 2006 and early 2007. What are these mortgages? A mortgage is a loan secured by real estate. Until the 1970's the interest rate was fixed at the start of the mortgage and mortgages were generally paid over 30 years, with shorter terms, such as 15-years, as an option. The monthly mortgage payment covered the interest on the outstanding balance of the loan, the principal, plus some amortization of the principal. The types of mortgages listed above were designed to address the cost of the mortgage to the borrower. The 30-year fixed mortgage was priced based upon a 30-year interest rate, which would usually be higher than the shorter-term interest rate when the mortgage loan was taken out. Adjustable mortgages allowed the borrower to benefit from the lower interest rate of shorter-term money. The lender could give this lower rate because the interest would reset if interest rates changed after the short term. In such a case, the borrower is benefiting from the lower interest rate. However, interest rates change regularly. If interest rates move up, an adjustable rate mortgage could reset at a rate higher than the borrower was currently paying. The short-term interest rates during 2001 to 2005 were historically low,[13] and therefore adjustable rate mortgages appeared particularly attractive. So far, adjustable rate mortgages have been beneficial as a whole for homeowners. This fact may be missed, as the adjustable rate mortgage is now viewed negatively.

As housing prices moved up, their affordability became an issue for buyers. Mortgage loan payments could be reduced by several different features, allowing a buyer to make payments and thus buy the house. Some of the features designed to facilitate buyers' ability to pay were (a) introductory interest rates that were artificially low for a period or (b) interest only with no principal for a period. In many cases the buyer was anticipating either added income, such as from a raise, or an increase in real estate value where the property could be sold for a profit before the interest rates adjusted, generally known as flipping.

Another affordability feature was the reduction or elimination of down payments. Historically, down payments were usually 25% of the purchase price for a residential property. As housing prices climbed, down payments became very large. In developments, the developers began to subsidize the down payment, effectively taking a price cut. Taken to an extreme, the subsidized down payments became zero down needed for the buyer. Since the buyer has put up no monetary collateral, the lender has no collateral above the house. Down payments were a fundamental part of collateral for a mortgage loan. Down payments were incentive for the borrower to pay the loan and added protection to the lender in case of failure to pay.

The final development was the no documentation mortgage. As we have seen, the mortgage terms had been eroding in order to allow buyers to get into properties for which they had little capacity to make mortgage payments. The documentation of the capacity to pay finally went away, with the "no documentation of income and ability to pay" mortgage loans. This meant that the borrower could represent a capacity to pay without proof of such capacity. Lenders" risks increased because they were potentially loaning to individuals who lacked the capacity to repay.

While the capacity to pay the mortgage and the collateral for the mortgage was eroding, the willingness of the borrower to pay was also eroding. Historically, a willingness to pay one's debts was viewed as credit worthiness. With the automation of credit information, credit scores have become the proxy for credit history and willingness of a borrower to pay. Subprime loans are those made to individuals with poor credit histories. This means that subprime borrowers have not demonstrated a willingness to pay their debts.

As lending progressed the riskiness of the mortgage loans accelerated, because of violations of the basic principles noted above. Loans were made without evidence of capacity to repay, with evidence of unwillingness to repay and without collateral support for either willingness or alternatives. In short, these were fundamentally unsound loans. Securitization, Fannie Mae, Freddie Mac, and CRA are all contributors to this state of affairs.

3. Derivatives

Derivatives are a financial tool designed to shift risk from one party to another. For example A borrows from B. B wants added protection from A's potential failure to pay back the loan, i.e., default risk. For a fee, E offers to B to cover A's default risk, effectively guaranteeing A's loan. Proverbs 6:1, 11:15, 20:16, and 27:13 make a number of observations about being a guarantor, generally not showing it to be wise. So the principles of guarantee and risk-bearing are not new and should be treated with a level of prudence and caution.

Derivatives come in a variety of types and forms. The basic idea is the matching of risks. Another example of risk matching is with interest rates. As noted above in the mortgage discussion, interest rates change, so one borrower, D, may have a loan with an adjustable rate and wish to have a fixed rate. Borrower F may have a fixed interest rate and desire an adjustable rate.[14] So D offers to pay F an adjustable rate and F agrees to pay D a fixed rate on the same amount of loan. So far so good, but what if an institution, L, is between F and D? So D offers to pay L an adjustable rate receiving from L a fixed rate and F offers to L a fixed rate and receives an adjustable rate? So far so good, until L fails, then both F and D are out of luck.[15]

Risk transfer is not new; it is generally called insurance. There are many insurance companies that do risk transfer well. Yes, insurance companies do use mathematical models. Lessons from insurance companies and their regulation are useful to this discussion, but beyond this paper (see AIG below).

4. Short Selling

A short seller borrows stock and sells it, anticipating buying it back at a lower price, because the stock has fallen in price. Two types of short selling are notable. The "short against the box" or "covered short sale" are the selling short of securities that you already own. This trade is done in anticipation of downward movement in the stock. There are a number of reasons an investor would not want to sell his stock. The financial result for the investor tends towards a neutral economic effect, which is a positive for the investor if the stock price moves down, since the potential loss is avoided.

The "naked short" is when the seller does not borrow or own the stock, but sells it short. The important market effect of a naked short is that the number of shares in the market can exceed the number of shares issued by the company. Normal short sales and covered short sales involve existing issued shares. Naked shorts expand the number of shares available to buyers. The natural economic effect of increased product with fixed demand is a decline in price.

Add to the naked short concept the concept of "piling on." Piling on occurs when a stock's price is driven down by short sellers aggressively shorting the stock. Piling on is not new. The playground idea of kicking someone when he is down comes to mind. Piling on is a bigger issue today than in the past because of internet and electronic trading. In the past the market involved individuals on the trading floor. While the traders could pursue a movement in the stock, both floor rules and rules similar to requiring short sales to be covered had a dampening effect on the scale of piling on. However, it is fair to say that prior stock market crashes prove that piling on is not the only factor in a stock's price movement.

Today, there is an argument against regulating short selling by asserting that short selling enhances market liquidity. Welcome to a search for truth question. How can short selling provide liquidity? If an owner of stock wants to avoid loss or wants cash, sell the stock. Even more so, how can naked short selling provide liquidity? Naked short selling is a pure speculation activity and absorbs demand for the stock from those who have it and need to sell the stock for liquidity.

5. Speculation

Speculation is investing where one takes on risks, usually higher levels, with the expectation of commensurately higher gains based upon market movements. Investing is distinguished by looking to the underlying investment as the basis for the increase in value creating the gain. While both speculation and investing need the market to move up for gain, investing looks beyond the market to the merit of the investment for the reason for the market movement. Speculation can be based upon both upward movement and downward movement of the market, with downward being a short selling kind of speculation.

Speculation is not new. In times past it was called getting rich quick. Proverbs 23:4, 22:16 warns about trying to get rich quickly. Part of that warning is that the pursuit of riches will causes the pursuer to cut corners, compromise values and often to lose out. What is important to see in this financial crisis is there has been systematic speculative activity where corners were cut, i.e., fundamental principles were ignored, risks were taken and enterprises incurred losses.

6. Investors Pursuit of Higher Returns

We have all heard the adage "if it is too good to be true, then it is not true." This is particularly true for investments where the higher the risk the higher the required reward and vice versa. In a market with ten year U.S. treasuries yielding four percent, an investment offering ten percent does not have an equivalent risk, much less an investment offering fifteen percent. But what about a hedge fund generating thirty five percent in the past quarter, using a guaranteed successful trading strategy? And so it goes. Whenever low risk investments, such as U.S. treasuries, have low yields, the investment community turns to opportunities for higher returns. Proverbs 23:4, 5 would offer caution to those pursuing yield.

As the marketing of investments offering higher yields developed, the investments became more complex. The term "alternative investment strategies" was developed to categorize these investments. Alternative to what? Into these alternative investments went derivative programs, market timing concepts, use of debt to increase yields, and other programs that were to add yield to the investment.[16] The most interesting part of alternative investment strategies is the number of institutions, who are called the smart money, which made or owned these kinds of investments.

On the individual investor side, the money market fund is a place where this converged in 2007 and 2008. Money market funds have been in existence for decades. They are not government guaranteed, or at least not before September 2008. Yet, money market funds were viewed as extremely safe, giving interest on the investment money placed in the fund with a capacity to withdraw the invested money at any time. Money market funds' core principle was a dollar in and a dollar out. In other words, the investor would get back their investment. To do this the money market fund had to value its investments each day, called mark to market, and the value of these investments had to be equal to the amount of the investors' investments. Therefore, the money market funds had to invest in short term very safe investments, often called commercial paper.

What changed in 2007 and 2008 was the application of portfolio theories. As noted above, financial modeling theory suggested, and the math proved, that a certain amount of higher risk and thus higher yield investments could be added to a low risk portfolio and the overall risk in the portfolio would change very little. Bear Stearns and other financial institutions used this theory to add a certain amount of securitized subprime mortgage investments to money market funds they managed. Unfortunately, these investments were indeed truly risky and dropped in value, causing the money market funds mark to market value to be below the investors' investments. The result was a need for the securitized pieces of these money market funds to be repurchased by the managing institutions. This happened in 2007. Yet, the effect of poor investment choices in money market funds continued to worry the market to the point that the U.S. Treasury had to guarantee such funds in September 2008.

7. Liquidity, Values and Accounting

"Cash is king" is a refrain used to discuss various aspects of business and business planning. One component of cash is liquidity. Liquidity relates to the capacity to meet obligations when due. Much of the credit crisis is labeled a liquidity problem.

One principle of operating a company is forecasting liquidity needs and having reserves to meet these needs. Large financial institutions do the forecasting, but also have large liquidity needs. A financial institution would plan on normal levels of deposits and withdrawals or payouts and have an additional measure of reserves. No business can plan or operate its business on abnormal activity. A run on a bank was the idea the deposit holders were withdrawing funds at an abnormally high rate. The bank would plan for normal levels of withdrawals and a normal level of deposits. The bank would have a reserve for a measure of shortages in the amount of deposits as against the withdrawals. The reserves would not be sufficient to cover abnormal withdrawal activity, which is usually accompanied by an abnormal shortage in deposit activity, compounding the problem. Thus a run on a bank creates a liquidity crisis. The liquidity crisis may or may not reflect the fundamentals of the bank's operations. However, when an institution cannot meet its obligations when they come due, the liquidity crisis turns into a bankruptcy.

Valuation and accounting rules contribute to the liquidity crisis and are discussed here. To solve a liquidity need, the institution must sell assets to generate cash. Buyers want to buy based upon market value. Value is the price a willing buyer will pay and willing seller will accept, both having adequate knowledge of relevant facts and neither being under compulsion. Generally this value is what is found in the open market. In stress situations there are a variety of reasons the open market is not working. Therefore, the value of assets is not clear and thus the capacity to sell them may not be available. This is the liquidity crisis that causes financial institutions that are fundamentally sound to become illiquid and thereby bankrupt.

Let's now add the accounting rules. Accounting for financial assets and liabilities has become as complex as the assets and liabilities themselves. Originally, financial statements were based upon costs and were not adjusted for market fluctuations. Increasingly, market changes in values are to be reflected in the financials and the accounting principles have incorporated very complex rules for this process. Financial assets and liabilities are particularly subject to these rules, generally referred to as mark to market. The latest set of these rules came into effect in 2007, so the history of the impact of mark to market accounting is less than clear. The two examples below are too simple to show the proper accounting, but are used to illustrate some of the issues in financial reporting for financial instruments.

For example, let's look at a fee received by B for accepting a default risk on F. The fee has a component of profit, called revenue, and a portion for risk insurance reserves, which should be held on the balance sheet as a liability in case there is a default. So far so good, but what about a year later when the default risk level on F increases because the riskiness of F has increased. The increased risk of default means that a greater reserve is warranted. Should this reserve be booked? If yes, how much and how is it to be determined? Historic cost basis accounting says, no – carry the amount at cost; but proper liability reporting would seem to say yes. Yet, the method for calculating the increased exposure amount is in question. If there is a public market for F default risk, then we should look to the public market pricing for the amount needed to be reserved. But what if the public market was there, then it stops working? Does B have to reserve the full amount of the potential risk, taking a charge against its earnings, or can it use some probability-based method? And does it matter if B has other such default risk instruments that it normally uses mark to market pricing to reserve?

Similarly, if bank A buys an interest in a securitized mortgage pool for $10 million, it would show that as an asset. But the next accounting period, the market for this mortgage pool has dried up. How does bank A mark their investment to market? If there are no buyers, then is it worth zero? In theory, yes, but in reality no. There may be no buyers because the normal markets have stopped functioning. But if one is not sure that the market will return to past functioning levels, then what is the value? Conservatism, an overarching accounting principle, points to the need for documentation and not optimism for financial reporting. As a result of no market, this asset has no market value and an argument for a write-off would seem to be warranted. A write-off would reduce net income, reduce equity and potentially impair the ability of the financial institution to continue to conduct business. Systemic risks develop in that today's financial system has financial institutions inter-connected so that the failure of any one part dries up the market activity for the whole. Thus part of the systemic problem becomes a mark to market problem.

As noted earlier, these examples highlight the issues, but do not give what the actual accounting results could be. There are many other facts that would be considered in the final rendering. The points here are (a) accounting for complex instruments is complex, (b) getting the right answer is difficult in uncertain times, and (c) the accounting rules' effort to reflect changing market activity can lead to unintended results when market activity moves outside of its historic activity levels.

8. Not Covered: Greed

While the human element is a major factor in causing the financial crisis and may underlie the crisis, making it the first cause means we may not under-stand the specifics of what has happened. It is easy to point to the financial institutions, executives, and investors that have made boat loads of money over the past five to ten years. Labeling their takings as based on greed is also easy. But it does not allow us to see the tools used in the market to create the returns and where these tools diverged from basic financial principles.

We also need to see that many engaged in "doing their job." Those selling various financial instruments and mortgages were making a liv-ing, believing that their products were indeed good for their custom-ers. It is unfortunate that subprime loans sold by brokers have become labeled "predatory lending." Similarly, derivatives were taken on or sold by many in the belief that they indeed were good risk manage-ment tools and had real value. Yes, compensation schemes rewarded those employed, but that does not make them evil, bad, greedy, etc.

Similarly, management and board incompetence is not greed. It is incompetence and incompetence is unfortunate, but in the business world generally not criminal. Compensation for incompetent management does become a real problem. Citigroup and Merrill Lynch allowed their CEOs to be fired with enormous severance packages. This would seem to put the greed problem right on the table, but it is really a sign of the incompetence of these companies' boards. Today we have a culture of self interest. Therefore, if one can get a great severance package, why not? If one can get a house for a year with nothing down and no real payments, why not? Yes, they are the same.

A final observation on regulating human behavior would be that it is well known that one cannot legislate morality. Proper behavior comes from the heart of a people. Prudent investing and financial management and business management are not new ideas. Many individuals and companies have operated prudently and for them this storm will pass, all be it with some damage. Teaching and encouraging proper understanding and application of financial principles combined with an understanding of responsibility on both an institutional and a personal level, remains part of the solution.

II. WHERE WE ARE

We now can turn to the events of 2008 to try to understand the events and actions taken or not taken. Keep in mind that 2008 is a perfect storm[17] of financial events creating the financial crisis. An added word of caution, we are outsiders looking in and therefore do not have a full picture of the scope of events, of the scale of events and of the impacts of alternatives. Therefore, the following observations are based upon deductions extracted from published materials, experiences and the above principles.

A. Bear Stearns, Citigroup, and Money Market Fund Guarantees

Bear Sterns was taken over by JPMorgan Chase & Co. (JPMorgan). JPMorgan announced its acquisition of Bear Stearns Companies, Inc. (Bear Stearns) on March 16, 2008. As part of the transaction the U.S. Federal Reserve (Fed)[18] agreed to provide $30 billion of funding for Bear Stearn's less liquid assets. While there are many additional details, the questions to be addressed here are a) why did Bear Stearns need to be acquired by JPMorgan, and b) why did the Fed agree to provide the support in the transaction. It is clear that JPMorgan thought they were getting a good deal.

Bear Stearns suffered from a liquidity crisis and probably an equity crisis, both brought on by a series of business practices that violated the principles noted above. Our focus will be on securitization since it seems to be the central cause of Bear Stearns' demise. Bear Stearns had developed funds to participate in the securitization of mortgages, including subprime mortgages. At this point Bear Stearns believed that they were managing the riskiness of these securities by selling them to others. Bear Stearns managed two highly leveraged funds invested in securitization paper and when the market for this paper declined, these funds were wiped out. Bear Stearns did not intervene, but let the funds fail putting all of the damage on the funds' investors. This started the Bear Stearns liquidity crisis. It is useful to note here that Goldman Sachs had a similar type fund and infused $3 billion to avoid its failure.

Come to find out, Bear Stearns, Citigroup, and others had placed securitized paper in money market funds they managed. These investments quickly were wiped out on a mark to market value basis as required by money market fund rules. The buying back of this paper from these money market funds created some of the write-downs in the fall of 2007 and increased the liquidity issues.

As the market dried up for various portions of the securitized securities, the liquidity and value issues of Bear Stearns continued to grow. With the write downs in the fall of 2007 and resulting illiquidity, the Fed was worried about the financial market system crashing if Bear Stearns was to fail. Remember that bankruptcy can occur because of deficient liquidity, and one company's bankruptcy can cause liquidity problems in others. As a result of having Bear Stearns continue to service its obligations, the problem in the markets would not grow. Thus the placement of Bear Stearns with JPMorgan and the support to JPMorgan for the less liquid assets occurred. Referring to this as a bailout of Bear Stearns would seem to be a misstatement. Bear Stearns no longer exists and the Bear Stearns shareholders suffered losses.

Citigroup is larger than Bear Stearns. Even though it got burned by some of the same issues, it moved quickly to shore up its liquidity by getting additional capital. The cost of this new capital was expensive, but as of this writing, Citigroup is out of the emergency room.

The money market problem continued, however. While the securitized investment pieces had been removed, the credit crisis creates mark to market problems for many companies' commercial paper. If money market funds had to report principle losses to their investors, the money market aspect of our financial system would collapse. Money market funds are a crucial part of the commercial paper market that provides short-term financing for corporations. A collapse in money market funds would result in serious liquidity problems for corporations as a whole, resulting in systemic failure. Therefore, in September 2008, the Fed chose to guarantee money market funds in order to avoid a run on the money markets.[19]

B. Fannie Mae and Freddie Mac

In July, 2008, the Fed agreed to provide rescue funds to Fannie Mae and Freddie Mac in order to address liquidity issues arising from increasing mortgage defaults. On September 7, 2008 the U.S. government[20] assumed control of both entities. Let's review why the Fed did this rather than the Citigroup plan or the Bear Stearns plan.

These two entities buy mortgages and repackage them for investment, in effect providing a guarantee to the buyers of the investments. This worked fine in the early days because Fannie Mae was government owned. Fannie Mae was created in 1938 to help expand home ownership. Freddie Mac was created in 1970 to compete with Fannie Mae. Both do the same thing. Both were private companies after 1968, but had special operating provisions, such as reduced amounts of capital required to support their loan activity. The key aspect of these organizations was that they standardized the mortgage loans. To be bought by these entities a mortgage had to meet certain standards. The lower standards of the subprime loans had to be allowed by these organizations in order to be effective in the market as a whole. Add to this what was noted above about CRA, and the full magnitude of the movement away from prudent financial principles becomes clearer.

As the subprime mortgages and mortgages with adjustable rates began to reset, the default rates rose and these entities had to cover these loans. This created liquidity issues. These two entities support over $5 trillion in mortgage loans. The capital markets could not cover the risks of default that were now imbedded in this loan pool. But the failure of these two entities would not only wipe out their investors, but also be a shock to the holders of the investments sold and would disrupt the real estate market because the mortgage systems supported by Fannie and Freddie would be shut down. "Too big to fail" is a term that seems to apply here.

But we also need to see a sense of moral obligation. These entities were chartered by the U.S. government and given special privileges. The moral obligation notion is not new and the U.S. government did not disabuse the markets from this perception. This does not make the market's perception correct or even a good investment strategy. However, this moral obligation is part of the financial crisis picture.

So the rescue of Fannie and Freddie is different from Bear Stearns and is so for important different reasons.

C. Lehman Brothers

On September 14, 2008 Lehman Brothers filed bankruptcy. It had struggled with liquidity issues arising from the above discussed mortgage and mortgage related investments, plus hedges and investments in real estate. Hedges are a form of derivative. So the derivative problems noted above, including accounting issues, were a strong contributor to Lehman Brothers' crisis. However, commercial real estate positions also seem to be a factor.

Lehman also had another factor – inaction. Merrill Lynch (ML) took a series of actions to head off liquidity issues during the period of fall 2007 until September 2008. Particularly, ML sold a substantial portfolio of illiquid assets at about twenty-two cents on the dollar in July, 2008. Lehman at the time said they did not have the liquidity needs. Unfortunately, Lehman no longer exists.

While it is hard for a non-insider to know all of the decision factors that the Fed weighed in allowing Lehman to fail, some are worth noting here. Inaction is one of them. Capitalism is a concept, based upon individual responsibility for one's actions or inactions. The Bear Stearns and Fannie and Freddie support had been labeled a bailout and inconsistent with capital market principles. So a failure needed to be allowed. The scale of Lehman was clearly not the same as Fannie and Freddie, nor would its impact be felt as much. By September 2008, the Fed had a much clearer picture of where the pieces are and the interconnections so that the risk of Lehman's failure could be better judged than the Bear Stearns' failure. Finally, the market anticipation of Lehman's condition was much longer, giving parties a better opportunity to condition the blow of failure. This last point does not mean that there would be no pain; just that it was not a surprise. So Lehman failed.

D. Merrill Lynch

It is tempting to lump ML with Citigroup. Both had similar subprime issues and the timing of their write-offs in fall, 2007 seemed connected. Both replaced their CEOs when the write-offs began, both took large write-offs, both had to reabsorb large pools of underperforming assets, and both had to raise fresh capital. However, they are very different financial institutions. Citigroup is a bank with other businesses and ML an investment bank with other businesses. Banks have regulators and requirements to maintain certain capital levels to deal with liquidity issues. Think back to the run on the bank issues discussed above and the experiences arising from the crash leading to the Great Depression. ML was basically a free market, capitalistic enterprise.

Why did ML sell to Bank of America on September 14, 2008? Again we need to note the outsider's view is expressed here. John Thain was the new CEO brought in to clean up ML. In July, 2008 he took action to clean out the underperforming assets, now referred to as toxic assets. While many argued that his was a fire sale, perhaps that was indeed what he was addressing. As a result, ML had sufficient liquidity to consider other options. Since the conclusion for ML was a sale, Thain must have seen that continuing as a stand-alone entity was too risky given its portfolio of assets and liabilities, the financial and economic markets and the potential of Fed support. It is likely that ML discussed its situation with the Fed and got a Lehman response – do not look here, use self-help.

The outcomes between Lehman and ML cannot be clearer. Lehman shareholders are wiped out. ML shareholders received a measure of value.

E. AIG

On September 16, 2008, the Fed extended a liquidity facility to AIG, the U.S.'s largest insurer. In the bailout facility, the Fed gets convertible loan terms for about 80% of AIG's equity. How did this happen?[21]

AIG is an insurance company with most of its insurance activities conducted in regulated subsidiaries. These subsidiaries remain financially strong and liquid on the whole. Remember the discussion above on derivatives being like insurance. This is a great example of an insurance company that has strayed from its roots and gotten burned.

A part of the burning has to be attributed to the forcing out of Hank Greenberg by Elliot Spitzer, former attorney general and governor of New York State. Why is this important? It is important because Spitzer began an investigation into the accounting for AIG arguing errors in recording derivatives and other risk products. PricewaterhouseCoopers was the AIG accounting firm issuing audits on the company. In addition AIG was forced to recast its accounting and restate its financial statements. Given the issues in accounting noted above, it is fair to question whether the restatements were more correct than the original financials. But this process led to a change in AIG. In March 15, 2005, Spitzer forced the board to remove Greenberg and put in his number two. The result was a systematic demise of the quality of AIG risk management. Think of the diligence principle for management. Point – managing risk is a key responsibility of senior management and the board must be able to be sure this is done. Greenberg had done this for decades building the best insurance company in the U.S. His successors were unable to manage the company and AIG's shareholders suffered.

AIG strayed from its insurance business at the top company level.

The activity started small as a derivatives desk during the 1990s, selling credit default swaps.   In recent years it took off to where in 2005 this desk produced 17.5% of overall operating income.[22] When the credit crisis hit in 2008, AIG could not control liquidity needs these derivative positions required. Whether Greenberg could have created a different outcome will never be known, but we do know that the new management did not manage this group or the risks that its activities were imbedding within AIG.

The Fed bailout is explained similar to the Bear Stearns situation. AIG is insurance and having the crisis move to insurance would be unacceptable from a systemic perspective. Many have noted that AIG's global reach meant that its failure would impact financial systems around the globe. The speed at which AIG collapsed left fewer options. AIG's core businesses are great, so the collateral value is reasonable for a bridge loan for liquidity. Finally, the Fed forced the shareholders to pay with serious equity to the U.S. for the loan. In short, the Fed got a pretty good deal.

F. Morgan Stanley and Goldman Sachs

Finally we come to Morgan Stanley (MS) and Goldman Sachs. During a single day in September MS stock lost over sixty percent of its value. Why? Short trading. Piling on naked short selling is a speculative way to set value and prices. Does this value impact have any reflection of reality? This is the troubling question. At the time of this writing the SEC is wrestling with whether to curb short selling. What is at stake is the capacity of these and other companies to raise capital in an orderly way.

As of this writing, Warren Buffet has agreed to a $5 billion infusion into Goldman. See here the speed of Goldman's self-help. Yes, it will be expensive, but always remember the Lehman standard for getting self-help wrong.

Whether these two remain independent or find a bank for a home is yet to be determined. However, both have converted themselves to bank holding companies. This puts them under the Fed regulation the same as JPMorgan and Citigroup. Why? They both have the same access to Fed support as banks and this should minimize the short selling capacity to create self fulfilling prophesies.

What is wondered is whether Wall Street as we have known it is gone? But the answer to this question will need to await the outcome of the current crisis.

G. Washington Mutual

On Thursday, September 25, 2008, the Feds seized the assets of Washington Mutual (WaMu), the largest saving and loan in the U.S. These assets were placed with JPMorgan. Think Bear Stearns. A savings and loan is a bank that traditionally specialized in mortgage lending, holding the mortgages it made. WaMu over recent years had undertaken an aggressive expansion plan covering both the West coast and the East. Its demise can be directly attributed to the implosion of the housing market, the mark to market accounting rules, and some measure of subprime lending. In short, it was killed by the real estate part of the credit crisis. Unfortunately for its shareholders, the board acted belatedly in replacing the CEO and taking actions to shore up the enterprise. So the lesson here is diligence both at the board and management level. In that diligence, self-help is a critical factor and knowing the condition of your flock gives one time for a bit of self-help.

Yes, we will hear a bit of fussing over the new CEO's payout package. He is on the job 3 weeks and gets million of dollars, even though he failed. There is some truth here, but was it possible that he could succeed and did he do all that was necessary/possible to create a success? The more important question is what was the payout to the prior CEO, the one that led WaMu into the trouble? Similarly, what is the payout to the board members who were to oversee this enterprise on behalf of the investors?

H. Wachovia

Over the weekend of September 27-28, 2008, Wachovia sold its core banking business to Citigroup with Fed support. Why? Wachovia was caught in the same real estate loan and related credit crisis as WaMu. Wachovia had built itself into one of the largest network bank over the past 20 years and was viewed as a well-managed institution. Of note here is that Citigroup became the new home. Fed support is a backstop rather than bailout, in that Citigroup has to absorb the first $40 billion of losses in the asset pool, thereafter the Fed will cover losses. Think Bear Stearns-type support to JPMorgan.

See here the benefit of getting on to self-help early. Wachovia worked hard at getting a buyer in Wells Fargo, but they did not have enough time to work out a deal. Wells Fargo walked away at the last minute on Sunday night, because they could not get comfortable with some of the risks in the loan pools. Wells Fargo was not willing to bet their ranch. But Wells Fargo had also not kept the Fed in the loop as a fall-back player by saying to the Fed that they could go it alone. Therefore, they could only walk away. Citigroup became the home. Yet, a year ago Citigroup was in such stress that it was canvassing the world for capital and taking write downs, etc. The new CEO of Citigroup clearly did his job in turning around the company so that it could undertake a Wachovia opportunity. Needless to say, whether Citigroup has bitten off more than it can chew or has misassessed the risks will be shown over time.

I. Global Issues

Across the world institutions are suffering similar stresses caused by their real estate, the systemic crisis elements, and individual enterprise ineffectiveness. Governments are struggling to manage some elements of the problem within their own financial institutions. A key element here is the notion that some institutions are becoming "too big to save." When we look at Europe, a pan-global financial institution can exceed the capacity of its home country to bail it out. In the U.S. we have spoken of "too big to fail" in that the U.S. could not let the financial institution fail because of the systemic impact. Now we see institutions of a size that no government(s) may be able to rescue. As we will see below, this is an important message. Self-help becomes a critical management message for players in the world at large.

III. WHERE TO FROM HERE?

There are several observations for the future. But first we should note that required financial disclosure – past performance is no guarantee of future results. This statement is written everywhere; it is a good idea not to ignore it. As Solomon said in Ecclesiastes 11:2 about 3,000 years ago, the future is uncertain. So these observations are just that - observations.

A. Basic Principles of Finance will not Change

A small bit of comfort is that the basic principles of finance as discussed in the first section will not change. Wise individuals and enterprises following these principles will be able to ride out many storms, even perfect storms.

A principle not articulated above, but worthy of note here, is reserves. Less debt is good, but reserves allow the enterprise or individual to truly weather long spells of disruption. Think of Joseph in Egypt some 5,000 years ago. In Genesis 39-50, the well-known story of the dream of seven good years followed by seven bad years is told. Joseph is assigned the task of preparing Egypt for seven years of famine. The key part of this story for this discussion is how long seven years of famine is and how much reserves are required. The story notes that everyone in Egypt knew about the seven good followed by seven bad. Some had some reserves, but few had enough for the full seven years. Economists would argue that Pharaoh's taxes made it impossible, but that is just an excuse. The key point is adequate reserves, especially ones with proper liquidity, are an important part of planning a long term strategy.

B. Deleveraging Leading to a Measure of Economic Slowdown

One of the outcomes of this crisis will be a measure of deleveraging, both of companies and individuals. Deleveraging means paying down debt. Deleveraging will occur because of credit practices of lenders; in other words they will go back to practicing good lending principles. This means less credit will be available in the market to non-credit worthy individuals and companies. The effect will be a decline of consumer activity and thus a decline in the economy.

How deep this slowdown will be remains to be seen. A look at the last real estate financial crisis at the end of the 1980s and early 1990s, points to a moderate level of impact. There will be lots of horror stories for the news and press. But overall it is likely that the economy will roll along with a measure of recession. Why? The global platform of commerce is far more broad based than just the U.S. and its financial activity.

However, we return again to the notion that the borrowers are not driving deleveraging. Thus after the crisis is over, leverage desires will return.

C. Regulation and Unwinding - Years of Work

Clearly there will be an effort for more regulation. Dominique Strauss-Kahn, the managing director of the International Monetary Fund is quoted by the Financial Times as saying, "It's because there were no regulations or controls, or not enough regulations or controls, that this situation was born. We must draw conclusions from what has happened – that is to say regulate, with great precision, financial institutions and markets."[23] However, given the discussion noted above, is regulation really the answer – perhaps Spitzer's actions and the CRA continue to affirm the need for this debate?

We need to see that regulation cannot change essential human weakness. The financial principles that were violated are not new. The proclivity to violate these principles takes a holiday as a crisis winds down but never goes away. When was the last financial crisis? How about the .com crisis of 2000?

We need to see that part of regulation will be the unwinding of the Fed positions and future positions. Yes, there may be more needed. For example there is the $700 billion bad asset fund that the Fed would like congress to set up. This fund and other actions will be coupled with added regulations. However, it will be years before the unwinding of the crisis effects[24] and full implementation of revised capital market activities. In the interim there will be moments of stress, both from the U.S. and from global problems.

This leads to a key observation – the world today is very different from that of the last 50 years. The new world order is global markets. We can regulate the U.S. markets all we want, but there are other markets for trading, investing and speculation. These markets do not have the same standards as the U.S. nor do they wish to have such standards.

D. Caveat Emptor

The warning to investors and enterprises is caveat emptor, buyer beware! While there have been many government bailouts or seeming bailouts in 2008, going forward and going around the world this will not be a good investment plan. The financial markets have always been hostile places, but necessary places to conduct business. Going forward such hostility will not go away. Caution and diligence has been and continues to be the rule for the wise.

E. Inflation - Deflation or "?"

A big question is whether the effect of the crisis and Fed actions are inflationary, deflationary or what? There are serious mixed views on this. Deleveraging means non-inflationary. Yet, the government infusions seem to be inflationary. Yet, if the government infusions are just covering assets, then perhaps they are not inflationary.

Note that deflation has not been associated with this discussion. Japan with its crisis of the 1990s is a key example of deflation and the capacity of a government to fight deflation. However, deflation has some features which go far beyond this credit crisis or the actions taken by the Fed. That there may be limited inflation caused by Fed actions, does not go to deflation. To look at Japan as a basis for deflation assumptions shows a lack of understanding of the differences between the U.S. and Japan. For example, a key difference is demographics and its impact on an economy. The bigger deflation risk to the U.S. is globalization rather than the credit crisis. Globalization means that pricing is based upon the lowest cost producer. Clearly global labor markets are continuing to create downward pressure on U.S. labor prices, i.e., wages. Thus a slowing U.S. economy due to the credit crisis will exacerbate the deflation pressures of globalization.

F. U.S. Debt and the U.S. Global Role

There are many worries coming out of the credit crisis. One of the under-discussed warnings from the crisis is the U.S. debt levels. It was ignoring basic finance principles that brought on the perfect storm of a credit crisis. Can the U.S. debt levels not be seen in this same light? At what point does the deficit spending overwhelm the GDP of the country? At what point do the trade deficits overwhelm the global markets for U.S. currency? At what point do the promises of the government to its people become unfundable? The point is - now is the time to take stock of these issues and the principles being violated and change behavior. This is what has happened to Citigroup, ML, and Goldman. Remember that the capital market standard is self-help and that global finance is a capital market activity. Thus the U.S. needs to begin to address its issues in a self-help fashion.

Failing to heed these warnings on proper financial practices, means that the U.S. role in the global market place will diminish. It is worth noting the number of companies that are adopting a "global company" orientation, claiming to have no home country, particularly not the U.S. As noted above this trend and regulatory trends raise real issues for the character of global commerce going forward. Global commerce character will also influence U.S. commercial practices as well.

G. The World is Still Round and the Sun will Rise Tomorrow

While there is a book about the flat earth and there are flat earth societies, the reality is that the world is still round and functions. In Genesis 8:20-21, it is declared that the world will have its seasons and with them its harvests. It is always tempting to say that this crisis is the defining moment in man's history. While it is a moment, the financial crisis is probably not the defining moment. The seasons and harvests will go on next year and so will many businesses. With some wisdom and God's providence each effort will have some success.

Notes

1. The author also holds that the Bible is the inerrant Word of God. Therefore, the Bible deserves to be treated as a sacred document. A key element of the Word of God is man's fallen nature and man's need for a redeemer/savior. This paper is not about the redemption of mankind. Further, it is often tempting to say that crises, such as this financial crisis, is solely due to the fallen nature of man. The use of Bible passages may cause some readers to think that the author holds to such a view. This would be wrong. Rather there are principles in the world of finance, just like in the world of science, and when those principles are violated, crises may come. The Bible sets forth many of these financial principles. But the Bible is not the source of these principles any more than the Bible is the source of gravity. Rather, these principles are part of God's world and operate within God's world. The fallen nature of man does not change the operation of these financial principles, but fallen man can exploit these principles to man's fallen desires. The exploitation is a separate problem.
2. New International Version (NIV) is used for Biblical text unless otherwise noted.
3. The role of the Holy Spirit in preserving a culture and influencing a society is beyond the scope of this paper. But the reader is encouraged to research and reflect on the Holy Spirit's influence in preserving our communities.
4. Jesus tells the parable to point out the importance of not storing up treasure on earth, when our future is in the after- life. This paper does not explore this point, but the reader is encouraged to fully understand the concept of storing up their treasure in heaven.
5. While do not bet the ranch is used in the context of betting everything, it is applicable in business risks situations, where one does not take on a risk that has the potential to jeopardize the entire enterprise, even if the upside is large.
6. A full discussion of diversification is beyond the scope of this paper.
7. Morgenson, Gretchen, "Behind the Biggest Insurer's Crisis, A Blind Eye to a Web of Risk: How a Small, Freewheeling Unit Brought A.I.G. to Its Knees," The *New York Times*, September 28, 2008, p.1.
8. This passage has a number of provisions addressing lending that are beyond the scope of this paper. Of note are provisions for lending to the poor. It is tempting to extrapolate the provisions in this text to the current situation of the poor in the United States, but discretion should be used. The poor in the United States have

far more opportunities and social support than available to the poor of Moses' day. At the same time, these required treatments are criteria for thoughtful treatment of all individuals.

9. The role and scope of government is a subject of much debate. This debate is beyond the scope of this paper.

10. At this point it should be noted that there is debate as to the magnitude of effect on subprime loans caused by these rule changes. However, in 2005 the Bush administration desired to curb these rules, and that proposal was rejected by the Democrats. Expanded discussions on CRA can be easily found on the internet.

11. Often it is said that innovations such as securitization create or find or unlock value that otherwise did not exist. Generally, this is not true. The banks making 30-year fixed rate mortgages received the profits from the difference between the short term and long term rates, making them stronger. Today, these banks have shifted from lending to a fee business model because of securitization's capacity to skim off these profits upfront. This business model shift contributed to the S&L crisis of the 1980s and to the current problem in many banks today.

12. Please note this is a generalized discussion and exceptions abound.

13. It is argued that the housing bubble was caused in part by Alan Greenspan's, or the Fed's, keeping interest rates artificially low for too long. What is missing in this argument is a full look at the economic environment during the first part of this decade and the fact that the interest rate decision is a judgment call.

14. The reasons why borrowers would desire different types of interest rates are beyond the scope of this paper. However, some reasons involve asset types or anticipations of interest rate movements.

15. Rights of offset and other devises to protect D and F from L's failure are beyond the scope of this paper. For sure, L's failure will require all of the Ds and Fs to expend funds and time to sort out their rights and obligations.

16. Debt to increase yield is not covered here, because the basic principles of borrowing and lending should apply first, then the concept of risk-return comes into play. It should not surprise the reader that both of these sets of principles have been set aside.

17. Perfect storm is a term from the movie by the same name released in 2000 by Warner Bros. The picture is based upon the book *The Perfect Storm* by Sebastian Junger, which was published by Little, Brown and Company, 1997. Depicted is the convergence of natural events off the coast of New England that create a once in a century storm. To a certain extent this notion of convergence of events, each of which individually is manageable, into an unmanageable crisis seems appropriate to the current financial crisis.

18. The U.S. government players in addressing this financial crisis include the Fed, the U.S. treasury, and others. Each of these governmental bodies operates under various legal powers that allow the agency to advance funds and undertake measures of intervention to address emergencies such as this crisis. For the purposes of this paper these will all be called the "Fed."

19. Please note that there were specific limits as to which money market funds were guaranteed. Again not all money market funds are created equal. But a discussion of this is beyond the scope of this paper.

20. The Federal Housing Finance Agency took the action, not the Federal Reserve, and placed both entities under conservatorship.

21. Morgenson, *ibid*, should be reviewed for a more thorough discussion of the events leading up to the bailout.

22. Morgenson, *ibid*.

23. Daneshkhu, Scheherazade, and Bertrand Benoit, "Strauss-Kahn welcomes US plan to 'put out fire,'" *Financial Times*, September 29, 2008, p.3.

24. The S&L crisis lasted for about 4 years, late 1980s to early 1990s and the Swedish crisis lasted about 5 years.

CHURCH LEADERS HELPING THE BUSINESS PERSON KEEP THE EIGHTH COMMANDMENT

SECTION 5: CHURCH LEADERS HELPING THE BUSINESS PERSON KEEP THE EIGHTH COMMANDMENT

PHILIP J. CLEMENTS

The Introduction frames that the Christian worldview holds that God, as Creator, owns everything and gives it to whom He pleases. The individual recipient has responsibility to God for the stewardship, employment and enjoyment of what God has given him. Section 1 covers the theology underlying the commandment not to steal, including that what can be stolen is more than property; stealing includes time, and talent and opportunity. These framing thoughts are not repeated here. Rather the principles here go to the effect on an individual and the individual's community when these basic principles are respected. Section 2 presents the role of property rights as an essential element of human flourishing. Section 3 considers the challenges of social structures and the Eighth Commandment. Social structures necessarily lead to contemplations on the role of government and its actions. All of these principles relate to our conduct of business today. Section 4 explores a series of business situations where stealing occurs that go beyond the normal parameters for the Eighth Commandment. A detailed listing of the topic the Reformers believed to be included in the Eighth Commandment can be found in the Appendix: Chart on the Eighth Commandment and Business Practices.

In John 17:1-26, Jesus in his Pastoral Prayer prays for his people that they would be in the world, but not of the world. The prayer lays before the Church the challenge of helping the Christian maintain his sanctity while he lives life in the world. One of the major contributions of the Reformation was that business was a worthy calling even though it was done in the world. Further, the Reformation found that Jesus' message meant that Christians were not to withdraw from the world in order to live more sanctified lives, but rather to live in the community, doing their business in a sanctified fashion, so that the community had witness of the Gospel.

The Center for Christian Business Ethics Today [1] (Center) believes it is essential for the entire Christian community to participate in understanding business and aid in the development of proper Christian business ethics. The Center's research finds that Christian faith has led toChristian business ethics that have led to the prosperity the world enjoys today. However, because of the church's struggle with whether to accept business, the Center feels called to challenge the Christian community to develop and teach how the church and pastors can better minister to the business person in the congregation.

The two papers in Section 5 address the question of how pastors minister to business people in their understanding and compliance with the Eighth Commandment. David Epstein in "Invest Wisely," undertakes this challenge. Epstein's theme centers on the church's need to (1) train people to invest wisely, (2) exercise church discipline, and (3) teach people to work well. For the pastor, the paper gives both practical lessons on these as well as biblical foundations. "Investing is about blessing and security.... Jesus says, a person's soul is the most valuable asset of all – and to invest your soul in God and His grace, and then to invest yourself in the lives of others is the greatest and wisest of all investments."

Epstein cite's Paul's challenge to the Corinthians for failing to exercise church discipline relative to known error in the members of the church body in support of his view that "the church that does not discipline ungodly members will never be used by God to hold anyone accountable to the eighth commandment or any commandment!" For Epstein discipline includes "the loss of jobs, the forfeiture of ministry, removal from membership, financial restitution, and public (in front of the whole congregation) repentance and restoration." "The question is: Will the church follow the example of Jesus and also exercise discipline, not to destroy people's lives but to restore them?" As to working well, the paper makes this critical point, "One of the greatest ways the church can encourage honesty and integrity in its business people is by teaching them exactly what God expects of them, and how he will empower them in the workplace. ... Marketplace ministry is one of the most difficult challenges the church faces today."

The editor would add to Epstein's message regarding the modern church's challenge with church discipline. Too often the church today suffers from the belief that the congregation members will vote with their feet. Yet, business people know that faithful people are the backbone of any organization. Therefore, integrity in addressing issues should be first and foremost. Christians of integrity will stand with such a church, even as employees of integrity will stand with a business. Too often the Christian message is watered down to appease members of the congregation. Further, overt error, such as violating the Eighth Commandment, is swept under the rug (or just ignored). In business we know that everyone in the organization is aware of what is happening. When error is ignored, the whole organization suffers. The church is no different. Paul cites this in 1 Corinthians, when he challenges the Corinthian church to address those who are practicing sin in their midst. Paul uses the contrast to secular standards, even as has been done in this paragraph, to point out that the church's response is not even at the level of the non-churched. [2]

The editor would also challenge pastors to know the condition of their flocks. In the editor's experience over the past five years of working with smaller businesses, the ones that have failed to pay their bills have overwhelmingly been those vocal about claiming to be Christians. Failing to pay bills on time, especially when one has the funds, is a clear violation of the Eighth Commandment. In several cases the individuals involved were major donors to their churches. The pastors of these churches know of the errors, but refused to intervene. Similar tales span Christendom. As a result, many a Christian will refuse to do business with another Christian, because of this lack of trustworthiness. It is incumbent on the pastors to lead their flocks and correct such errors.

The business community members in the congregation need to be challenged to be disciplined in their business practice. Several of the Section 4 application papers have some good guidance on how to instill a culture of good practice. It starts with training, then oversight, and then accountability. The Church needs not to assume that the members of the congregation know the full depth and breadth of the Eighth Commandment. Specific business fellowship sessions should be used to explore what God expects from the Eighth Commandment and how it applies to the individual's daily practices. Then there needs to be private interactions between the pastor and members of his congregation, when the pastor can explore the depth of application by members of the congregation. The pastor needs to be attentive to the hints in his congregation of those who have gone astray, even as Paul was in being knowledgeable of the Corinthians. When an error is noted, the pastor must be diligent to follow up the report, not presuming wrong, but diligently investigating and then confronting a wrong found. Confrontation can be hard, but it leads to repentance and redemption. Where error exists and the Eighth Commandment has been broken, restitution is to be part of the repentance. The tax collector that Jesus had dinner with was delighted to be Jesus' host, but then realized his errors and promised to restore fourfold. [3] When these practices are done diligently, the congregation is strengthened, because each member feels the diligence in faithful practice of God's commandments.

The second paper in this section, "The Eighth Commandment for Seminaries" by Luder G. Whitlock, Jr., describes the exercise of the stewardship required in the Eighth Commandment. The Eighth Commandment establishes property ownership. With that ownership comes both the benefits and the responsibility of stewardship. For the Christian, we recognize that God is the owner, as Creator, of all elements of creation, including ourselves. Therefore, He gives to us such property and talents as He desires us to have. We, then, are charged with exercising stewardship over these assets for His glory. Whitlock does an excellent job in this paper of applying these principles to the Seminary.

For the pastor of a church, the application is the same. Every elder or deacon in the church should be required to read this paper. Whitlock notes the importance of the basics of maintenance. Then Whitlock's paper raises the bar as to compensation and even the subject matter being taught throughout the church campus. Whitlock would challenge the church's leaders to know and have assurance of high standards of practice in all areas. Why? Because it is God's world that we are engaged in and our church's appearance, function and teaching are all part of our witness to the world. As Jesus prayed, the church is part of the world, that the world may see Him and His Gospel.

Notes

1. The Center for Christian Business Ethics Today, LLC was formed in 2009 to develop material to help the Christian business person operate his business with biblical business principles based on Protestant Christianity. The Center co-hosted the conference that is the source of the papers for this text.
2. I Corinthians 5:1-13.
3. Luke 19:1-10.

INVEST WISELY

DAVID EPSTEIN

DAVID EPSTEIN

Reverend David Epstein has served as the senior pastor of the historic Calvary Baptist Church in New York City since 1997. He is a graduate of Washington Bible College and Capital Bible Seminary with degrees in Biblical Studies. He pursued doctoral studies at The Catholic University of America in Biblical Studies and was a PhD candidate at the University of Maryland in the History of Higher Education and Adult Development. He served as the Director of Athletics, Chairman of Education Ministries, and Assistant Professor of Biblical Studies and History at Washington Bible College from 1978 to 1986. He then pastored the Metropolitan Bible Church in Ottawa, Ontario, one of Canada's leading evangelical churches. In addition to his national and international conference schedule, his popular radio broadcasts The Calvary Hour and Tell It From Calvary are heard by more than 2 million people worldwide. His book, Confessions of a Terrorist: A Biblical Look at 9/11, Islam, and the Church, is scheduled for release in the Fall of 2011.

Long before we started ripping one another off, we were already stealing from God. God confronts us through the prophet Malachi (3:8): "Will a man rob God? Yet you have robbed me…" Long before we used business to steal from each other, we practiced up on God. And of course, with God it is personal, it's not just business!

But it didn't have to be this way. From the very beginning, God did it right. He created everything perfect (including us), and "it was all very good." (Genesis 1:31) But then we blew it! We messed it up big time! We declared war on God, and in our moral rebellion we gave free reign to our pride, selfishness and greed. And of course this moral darkness invaded our families, churches and workplace. That's why there is one thing we can all agree on, believers and unbelievers alike – there is a huge gap between who we are and who we should be – between what the world is and what it should be (including our businesses) – and this gap is what the Bible describes as our lostness, our fallenness. We have fallen and we can't get up! But God, in bringing us under his judgment, which He had every spiritual, legal and moral right to do, chose to offer us mercy. He sent His own son to take our sin and God's wrath upon Himself, thus freeing us to receive God's grace and forgiveness, which results in a total transformation of our life. The Apostle Paul tells us we now have the power and responsibility to "…put off, concerning your former conduct, the old man which grows corrupt according to the deceitful lusts, and be renewed in the spirit of your mind, and that you put on the new man which was created according to God, in righteousness and true holiness…let him who stole, steal no longer, but rather let him labor, working with his hands what is good, that he may have something to give him who has need." (Ephesians 4:22-24, 28) God even transforms the way we do business!

Jeff Van Duzer, who is the Dean and a professor of Business Law and Ethics at Seattle Pacific University, in his book *Why Business Matters to God (And What Still Needs to Be Fixed)* talks about the "messy middle road" in business; how can a business make a profit and still treat people right and put people first? He says, "If we live in a fallen world, how do we live in this messy middle…I wish the church would help us think through principles about how to navigate this messy middle. I try to provide a theology that will help business people understand how their activity can fit into the overall scheme of God's kingdom work." [1]
So what can the church do to help? One way, and it is probably not the way most churches operate, is to hold business people (and everyone else) accountable to obey the eighth commandment – "thou shalt not steal." (Exodus 20:15) What does accountable mean? It means to be" responsible for; to answer for; to be liable for." [2]

But is this accountability even possible? The answer is - yes, no, maybe, and it depends! A recent Barna Survey contends that, "There is very little accountability among Christians in the United States. Only 5 percent of Christian adults indicated that their church does anything to hold them accountable for integrating biblical beliefs and principles into their lives. George Barna concludes: 'With a large majority of Christian churches proclaiming that people should know, trust, and obey all of the behavioral principles taught in the Bible, overlooking a principle as foundational as accountability breeds even more public confusion about scriptural authority and faith-based community, as well as personal behavioral responsibility.'" [3]

So can the church hold business people accountable? It depends on whether the church is willing to:

1) Train people to *invest wisely*
2) Exercise church discipline
3) Teach people to *work well*

INVESTMENT TRAINING

The church needs to present the gospel and the Christian life as an investment opportunity that will totally transform the one who trusts in (invests in) Jesus Christ. Recently I preached a men's conference in the DC area with hundreds of men making a real difference for Christ. I began by saying, "Remember, God has already made a huge investment in us. The bible proclaims, 'For you know the grace of our Lord Jesus Christ, that though He was rich, yet for your sakes He became poor, so that you through His poverty might become rich.' (2 Cor. 8:9) And God wants a good return on His investment. Who does He want? He wants you. How much does He want? He wants it all. God wants your lives, talents, careers, relationships, money, ambition, and your businesses. He wants you to be honest, generous, and caring people. He wants you to be men of integrity. We were the world's men for a long time – the mystery man, the lady's man, the iron man, the Marlboro man and the Bud man – but where are God's men? God wants us to invest in Jesus Christ by trusting the gospel and He also promises us a good return on our investment in Christ: forgiveness, peace, joy, power, meaning, purpose, hope and a future."

Abraham was a businessman who "...by faith obeyed God when he was called to go out to the place which he would afterward receive as an inheritance. And he went out, not knowing where he was going...by faith when he was tested, he offered up Isaac and he who had received the promises offered up his only begotten son, of whom it was said, 'In Isaac your seed shall be called,' accounting that God was able to raise him up, even from the dead, in which he also received him in a figurative sense.' (Heb.11:8, 17-19) Abraham offered God his very best, and therefore God blessed him and made him a blessing. 'Now the Lord had said to Abraham: get out of your country, from your kindred, and from your fathers house, to a land that I will show you. I will make you a great nation; I will

bless you and make your name great; and you shall be a blessing. I will
bless those who bless you, and I will curse him who curses you; and in you
all the families of the earth shall be blessed.'"(Genesis 12:1-3)

There is no caste system in Christianity! That's one reason we had
a reformation, because of the truth of the priesthood of all believers. Every
follower of Jesus Christ is a priest offering God the sacrifices of thanksgiving and service, and leading others into the presence of God – even in
the workplace! Everyone has the privilege of serving God full time. This
service has nothing to do with what you do for a living (as long as it's not a
felony), but everything to do with how much living you do for God. The
full time Christian servant is the man or woman who trusts and obeys God
full time – like Abraham. There are many religious professionals, people
doing so called "spiritual" work with very secular and carnal hearts (consider all the leaders exposed in public scandals with their greed, theft, and
immorality)! And there are many people doing so called "secular" work
with very spiritual and giving hearts.

Abraham obeyed and was blessed. We have the same promise if we
honor God in the way we do business; but if we refuse to follow Jesus and
dishonor God in our work, we will experience the awful justice of a holy
God. We need to invest wisely, and then we need to bring this new biblical world view and value system into our workplace everyday.

This is an approach that I have taken more frequently in my ministry in the years after 9/11, and particularly in the last three years during the
severe economic recession, both in my pulpit ministry and in my speaking
engagements with businessmen. Occasionally, when playing golf someone
will say to me, especially when they find out I'm a pastor of a church in
midtown Manhattan, "I'll bet you see more and more of those wall street
guys coming into your church and getting down on their knees and begging for mercy!" And we do. (Of course, all the government bailouts eased
the pain and suffering big time!)

It's been said that when someone loses their job it's a recession, but
when you lose your job it's a depression! What's interesting is that even
in the worst days of the recession, many of the business/financial big wigs
refused to call the situation a depression – but were more than happy to
call it a catastrophe. Go figure.

When I began preparing to preach a series on Spiritual Investments, I asked one of my board members, a wonderful man and a big time
investment banker, to give me a summary of the investment business. He
said, "It's all about profit, risk and return, and increasing your assets." As I

pondered this, as a pastor preparing to speak to his congregation, it struck me that a "wise investment" will enrich your life today, and secure your life tomorrow.

Investing is about blessing and security. That's why we invest in education, relationships, careers, and our physical and financial health – to enrich ourselves today and to secure ourselves tomorrow. And all of these investments are good and important, but they are not the best and most profitable investment we can make. Jesus says, a person's soul is the most valuable asset of all – and to invest your soul in God and His grace, and then to invest yourself in the lives of others is the greatest and wisest of all investments: "Then Jesus said to His disciples, 'If anyone desires to come after me, let him deny himself, and take up his cross, and follow me. For whoever desires to save his life will lose it, and whoever loses his life for my sake will find it. For what does it profit a man if he gains the whole world, and loses his own soul? Or what will a man give in exchange for his soul?'" (Matthew 16:24-26)

I read an article recently about Ray Romano, whose successful TV show "Everybody Loves Raymond" had finished filming its final episode. He was telling the studio audience how when he flew to Los Angeles from New York to begin filming the show many years earlier, he found a note in his luggage from one of his family members that said, "Ray, what does it profit a man if he gains the whole world and yet loses his own soul." During the question and answer period Ray was asked what he was going to do next now that the show was finished. His response was intriguing, "I'm going to go work on my soul." [4]

We don't think of Jesus as an investment advisor, but actually he is the greatest one of all time. The real question is - are we listening to Him? Are we investing in Him, doing what He says and living like He lived?

I love the story of the ships captain who during a watch in the middle of the night saw the lights of another vessel approaching his. The captain radioed, "Turn your vessel 10 degrees west." The immediate response, "Turn your vessel 10 degrees east." The captain responded, "I am a captain with 35 years experience, turn 10 degrees west." The reply was, "You turn 10 degrees east." The captain responded, "I am piloting a 50 thousand ton frigate! Turn 10 degrees west." The response, "I am a lighthouse! Turn 10 degrees east!" God says to the church, to the business community, to Wall Street, to Madison Avenue, to the human race and to the culture, "You are off course! Change direction! You're making all the wrong investments. Your souls are at risk. Follow the Light – turn 10 degrees east!

Re-evaluate your priorities. Understand what genuine wealth really is. Stop stealing. Start giving back. Pay it forward. Learn to invest wisely – for this life – yes – but also for the life to come.

Jesus said, "I am the light of the world; he who follows me shall not walk in darkness, but shall have the light of life." (John 8:12) He teaches us in the greatest sermon ever preached, which includes some of the greatest investment teaching ever given: "Do not lay up for yourselves treasures on earth, where moth and rust destroy and where thieves break in and steal; but lay up for yourselves treasures in heaven where neither moth nor rust destroys and where thieves do not break in and steal. For where your treasure is, there your heart will be also…no one can serve two masters, for either he will hate the one and love the other, or else he will be loyal to the one and despise the other. You cannot serve God and money… but seek first the kingdom of God and His righteousness and all these things will be added unto you." (Matthew 6:19-21, 24, 33)

One man who learned the hard way that you can't serve God and money was Adolph Coors IV, the business tycoon and head of the Coors Empire. His father, Adolph III, was murdered in a kidnap/ransom attempt when Adolf was a teenager. In his anger and grief and confusion, he immersed himself in business and making money. He says that, "'Every Friday night I calculated my net worth, and if it had increased over the last 7 days I had a good weekend; but if it decreased I had a lousy weekend.' Then a good friend of mine who was very concerned for me said, 'Adolph, do you know what your problem is? You are putting your faith and trust in the things of this world.' And then God began speaking to my heart, 'Adolph, I want to talk to you – I love you – your marriage is in trouble – you don't have the relationship with your boys that you need – your career is your god - and the void in your heart is huge. You need Jesus as the Lord and Savior of your life - put your faith and trust in Him.'" And Adolph Coors IV made the right investment. He now says, "I, Adolph Coors, am a very, very sinful man. I was separated from God, cut off from God's plan with no hope to fill the void except through my Lord and Savior Jesus Christ." [5] God invested His love in him, and he invested his faith in Jesus Christ, and it changed him. "For when we were still without strength, in due time, Christ died for the ungodly…and God demonstrates His own love for us in that while we were still sinners Christ died for us…for if when we were enemies we were reconciled to God through the death of His Son, having been reconciled we shall be saved by His life." (Romans 8:6, 8, 10)

I love the story, probably apocryphal, about the death of Howard Hughes, the eccentric billionaire portrayed so wonderfully by Leonardo DiCaprio in the movie *The Aviator*. Legend has it that after the funeral service a reporter, on seeing the executor of Howard Hughes' will, shouted out, "How much did the old man leave?" And the response was immediate, "He left it all." Paul, in writing to Timothy, told him, "Godliness with contentment is great gain. For we brought nothing into this world and it is certain that we can carry nothing out. And having food and clothing, with these we shall be content; because those who desire to be rich fall into temptation and a snare, and into many foolish and harmful lusts which drown men in destruction and perdition. For the love of money is the root of all kinds of evil, for which some have strayed from the faith in their greediness, and pierced themselves through with many sorrows...command those who are rich in this present age not to be haughty, nor to trust in uncertain riches, but in the living God, who gives us richly all things to enjoy. Let them do good, that they be rich in good works, ready to give , willing to share, storing up for themselves a good foundation for the time to come, that they may lay hold of eternal life." (1 Timothy 6:6-10, 17-19)

I think of all those good and trusting and well intentioned people who invested with Bernie Madoff and Enron, who lost hundreds of millions of dollars, their retirement funds and their life savings. None of their investments were certain; none of them were for sure! None of their investments were fail safe; none of their investments were guaranteed. They didn't have a guarantee of a profit, of a better life now, or a more secure life tomorrow. They were ripped off by a bunch of rich, powerful, greedy men – some of them religious guys in a synagogue on Saturday or a church on Sunday professing their belief in God – who first sold their own souls and then sold out their family, friends and coworkers. There are tapes of some of the Enron traders as they manipulated the power markets, gloating about their cheating and their ripping off of "those poor grandmothers," as they rigged the markets amid widespread blackouts and soaring electricity rates. It reveals a sickening look into the heart and soul of those driven by greed – loving things and using people instead of loving people and using things. These are men motivated by their hero Gordon Gekko, who in the great movie *Wall Street* said, "Greed is good! Greed is right! Greed works! Greed clarifies, cuts through and captures the evolutionary spirit – greed in all its forms. Greed for life, greed for knowledge, greed for love, greed for money is good."

Jesus begs to differ about greed for money. In one of His parables, He responds to two brothers arguing over an inheritance, "Take heed and beware of greed and covetousness, for ones life does not consist in the abundance of the things he possesses." (Luke 12:15) He then spoke a parable to them saying, "The ground of a certain rich man yielded plentifully and he said to himself, 'What shall I do since I have no room to store my crops....I will pull down my barns and build greater, and there I will store all my crops and my goods. And I will say to my soul: Soul, you have many goods laid up for many years; take your ease; eat, drink and be merry.' But God said to him, 'You fool! This night your soul will be required of you; then whose will those things be which you have provided?' So is he who lays up treasure for himself, and is not rich toward God." (Luke 12:16-21) Greed kills!

CHURCH DISCIPLINE

God says that anyone, because of greed, who exploits and abuses those who are vulnerable and less powerful than they will suffer the most horrendous judgment of God. In the book of James, God talks a lot about the rich and the poor and He says clearly that there are only two ways to be rich: God's way and the wrong way. To be rich the wrong way is a death sentence – a riches to rags story – the poverty of riches.

Consider the just punishment that God inflicts upon the ungodly and unjust rich:

1. Because of your idolatry (your love and worship of riches), you will pay the ultimate death tax – your soul! "Come now, you rich, weep and howl for your miseries that are coming upon you. Your riches are corrupted, and your garments are moth eaten." (James 5:1-2)

2. Because of your greed (your hoarding of riches), you will be afflicted by the ultimate flesh eating disease. "Your gold and silver are corroded, and their corrosion will be a witness against you and will eat your flesh like fire. You have heaped up treasure in the last days." (James 5:3)

3. Because of your fraud (your stealing of riches), you will spend eternity in the ultimate slaughter house – hell. "Indeed, the wages of the laborers who mowed your fields, which you kept back by fraud, cry out; and the cries of the reapers have reached the ears of the Lord of Sabaoth. You have lived on the earth in pleasure and luxury. You have fattened your hearts for a day of slaughter. You have condemned, you have murdered the just; he does not resist you." (James 5:4-6)

The vicious cycle is idolatry – greed – fraud – murder - idolatry...and finally, the ultimate judgment of a holy and righteous and vengeful God. And God will judge His own people for our greed, theft, and exploitation – and He will use the church as His instrument!

The Apostle Paul excoriates the church for failing to discipline "so called Christian men and women" who are dishonoring God by their immoral, rebellious lifestyle: "I wrote to you in my Epistle not to keep company with sexually immoral people, yet I certainly did not mean with the sexually immoral people of this world or with the covetous, or extortioners, or idolaters, since then you would need to go out of the world. But now I have written to you not to keep company with anyone named a brother, who is a fornicator, or covetous, or an idolater, or a reviler, or a drunkard, or an extortioner – not even to eat with such a person. For what have I to do with judging those who are outside? Do you not judge those who are inside? But those who are outside, God judges. Therefore, put away from yourselves that wicked person." (1 Corinthians 5:9-13)

The church that does not discipline ungodly members will never be used by God to hold anyone accountable to the eighth commandment or any commandment! In my nearly 40 years in ministry, church discipline has been a major element of my pastoral philosophy and practice, but my churches and I had to grow in our conviction and courage. Church discipline goes totally against the grain of most evangelical ministries because of our fear of litigation, political correctness, friendships and traditions, a lack of awe at the holiness of God, and a culturally induced "live and let live" mentality. But discipline must be practiced if lives are going to be restored, if the church is going to be blessed, and if God is going to be glorified. Over the years we have disciplined church members, staff members, board members, and pastors who have engaged in behavior that has dishonored God and hurt others – including immorality, slander, theft, and willful disrespect and disobedience to biblical authority. Discipline has included the loss of jobs, the forfeiture of ministry, removal from membership, financial restitution, and public (in front of the whole congregation) repentance and restoration. No pain – no gain! Without discipline there can be no accountability. And the motive for discipline must always be to restore – *never* to destroy! In the church, in an effort to restore the individual to God and to others, we offer counseling, mentoring, discipleship, small group support and leadership training. Some have responded well and been restored to God and to each other; others have responded badly and been removed. But when someone is genuinely changed by Jesus and the gospel, even when he or she fails at times, they will respond to loving, just discipline – just like Zacchaeus. He was a chief tax collector. That meant that he was doubly hated by his fellow Jews for being a traitor by collaborating with the Romans, and for being a thief by extorting his own people financially. One day Jesus came to town and said, "'Zacchaeus, come down immediately. I must stay at your house today.' So he came down at once and welcomed him gladly. All the people saw this and began to mutter, 'He has gone to be the guest of a sinner.' But Zacchaeus stood up and said to the Lord, 'Look, Lord! Here and now I give half of my possessions to the poor, and if I have cheated anybody out of anything, I will pay back four times the amount.' Jesus said to him, 'Today salvation has come to this house, because this man, too, is a son of Abraham; for the Son of Man came to seek and to save that which was lost.'" (Luke 19:5-10) Jesus loved him and disciplined him and Zacchaeus responded and trusted Jesus. The question is: Will the church follow the example of Jesus and also exercise discipline, not to destroy people's lives but to restore them? Jesus tells us, "If your brother sins against you, go and tell him his fault between you and him alone. If he hears you, you have gained your brother. But if he will not hear you, take with you one or two more that by the mouth of two or three witnesses every word may be established. And if he refuses to hear them, tell it to the church. But if he refuses even to hear the church, let him be to you like a heathen and a tax collector." (Matthew 18:15-17) But there is hope! .

SECOND CHANCES

One man who learned the value of investing wisely and being lovingly disciplined by God was Mark Ritchie, the author of *God in the Pits – Confessions of a Commodities Trader*. His father died in Afghanistan just before the Soviet invasion in 1979. Mark's dad was a Christian and an engineer helping to modernize the country and serving the poor. In his book, Mark remembers his dad this way, "People wondered why dad wanted to help *those* people. He chose to use his training as a 20th century engineer to build an eye hospital in a 13th century setting. I bought and sold more commodities in one day than his entire district was worth. My friends lived in two of the wealthiest suburbs in Chicago – his friends were the poorest of the poor. My dad's goal: do God's will by serving them. My goal: buy low and sell high. I knew full well that the lover of money carries his god in his wallet, while the poor man carries God in his heart. I've tried God in both places, and no one needed to convince me: God in the heart – what a way to pack the most living into life." [6]

God tells us that people like Mark Ritchie who have invested theirs lives in Jesus Christ want to give back to God and to others – not to steal from them. In the parable of the shrewd manager, Jesus challenges us to "use worldly wealth to gain friends for yourself, so that when it is gone, you will be welcomed into eternal dwellings." (Luke 16:9) We can't take our wealth with us, but we can send it ahead! It's all about giving instead of taking.

The finest man I ever knew, and the most honorable business person that I ever knew was my father, Aaron Epstein. He treated everyone with respect, was generous and fair, and God blessed his business ventures. He had grown up without a father, but he trusted Jesus Christ as a child and as an adult his faith grew. He was a marvelous example of someone who loved God, loved others, and conducted his business with honesty, integrity and a Christ like character. He forgave his father for abandoning him, and that set our entire family free. My dad invested wisely! At the end of his life, suffering with dementia and Parkinson's disease, we would ask him, "Dad, do you know what's happening to you?" And he would say, "Yes, my brain is dying." And we would say, "Are you afraid." And he would say, "No – I'm going to see Jesus." He was a good man and an honest man – God's businessman! What an investment.

Jesus says it's important to build our lives on the solid rock. "Everyone who hears these words of mine, and puts them into practice is like a wise man who built his house upon the rock. The rain came down, the streams rose, and the winds blew and beat against that house; yet it did not fall, because it had its foundations upon the rock. But everyone who hears these words of mine, and does not put them into practice is like a foolish man who built his house on sand. The rain came down, the streams rose, and the winds blew and beat against that house, and it fell with a great crash." (Matthew 7:24-27)

I've had the privilege of speaking to groups of businessmen for the past 12 years, and it is a blessing to see men living for God and pursuing business in an honest manner. While teaching one group in New York City a couple of years ago, I met a very successful Wall Street investment banker named "Bob". He told the group how his entire life and career had been changed dramatically when one of his Wall Street co-workers had become a serious follower of Jesus Christ. One day Bob's friend shared his faith with him and asked, "Bob, on a scale of 1-10, with 1 being near total depravity and 10 being human perfection, where do you put your-self?" Bob thought about it for a moment and responded, "Well I'm not a 1! I'm better than a lot of people – but I'm not a 10 – I'm not perfect – I'm a 7½." His friend responded, "So you're a 7½. What number will you need to be if you're going to be able to stand before God?" And Bob said, "Probably a 10, right?" So his friend asked him, "How are you go-ing to bridge the gap between your 7½ and God's 10?" And Bob said, "I can't - I can't be perfect." And his friend said, "Jesus is a 10 – when you trust Him, He takes your 7 ½ and gives you His 10 – His perfection, His righteousness. He credits it to your account, and in God's eyes, you are a 10 because you stand before God in Jesus Christ by faith." Bob said that he had never heard the gospel shared that way – ever! And he became a fol-lower of Jesus Christ and was transformed.

The greatest thing the church can do to hold business people (and everyone) accountable to the eighth commandment – is to teach the truth about human sin and depravity, God's love and grace, and redemption and transformation in Christ. The Apostle Paul, whose life was transformed as much as any man, tells the Corinthians and us, "If anyone is in Christ, he is a new creation; the old has gone, the new has come!" (2 Corinthians 5:17) And those who invest wisely will work well.

LEARNING TO WORK WELL

Those who have embraced the cross will impact their workplace as employ-ers and employees. One of the greatest ways the church can encourage honesty and integrity in its business people is by teaching them exactly what God expects of them, and how He will empower them in the workplace. In my ministry of nearly forty years, I have utilized just about every tool possible to equip business people for the marketplace – teaching, preaching, small groups, seminars and conferences, networking with marketplace ministries like Priority Associates, and we need them all! Marketplace ministry is one of the most difficult challenges the church faces today. Even those churches who do it well will tell you that they don't do it very well!

Dennis Bakke in his fascinating book *Joy at Work – a CEO's Revolutionary Approach to Fun on the Job* tells us, "My passion is to make work exciting, rewarding, stimulating and enjoyable. Most books on organizational life and work focus on top executives and the strategies they use to guide their organizations to success, which is usually defined by financial results...while economic success is also an important goal...the meaning of success goes far beyond the bottom line...the crucial measure of success is the quality of their work lives...This is a book that celebrates the feeling of fulfillment that can be found in a humane and enlightened work place."
[7] And nothing humanizes and enlightens a workplace more than men and women who have genuinely invested in Jesus Christ and now are investing in others. I began to learn the power of Christ in the workplace almost immediately after becoming a Christian.

I trusted Christ in October of 1970 during my second year at university. By the end of the spring semester six months later, like most other students, I was looking for a summer job. But this job would be special. My first job as a Christian, I was hired by a construction company for big money - $3 an hour! And I was looking forward to having a testimony for Christ!

My first day on the job, within the first hour, I was carting a load of cement along a narrow board - I lost control – and dumped it all over the lawn. I began to get very irritated!

Then my new boss sent me into town with a beat-up, no good pick-up truck to get a huge load of cement blocks. While stacking the blocks, one fell from the top and smashed my finger! Stifling the overpowering urge to use my street language, I started back on the highway with my severely overloaded truck. Almost immediately I began fishtailing violently, with people honking, cursing and hurrying to get out of my way. Then one of the tires blew out, sending me careening out of control into the embankment along the highway. I couldn't wait to get in my new boss's face and tell him just what I thought about his lousy job, his sorry truck, and his stupid judgment! Does any of this sound eerily familiar?

Colossians 3:23-24 says, "And whatever you do, do it heartily, as to the Lord and not to men, knowing that from the Lord you will receive the reward of the inheritance; for you serve the Lord Christ."

Does God really care about my work? And what does it take to please Him? To appreciate this passage in Colossians, we must first appreciate the context, both general and specific. In the general context, God never originally intended our work to be such an ordeal. Adam began his life as a landscaper in a beautiful untroubled setting. "The Lord God planted a garden eastward in Eden...then the Lord God placed the man in the garden to tend and keep it." (Genesis 2:18, 15) What a great job! No co-workers, no attitude problems, no taxes, no human bosses, no paperwork and red-tape – no ulcers! And then Adam and Eve sinned and the consequences were cataclysmic. "*Cursed* is the ground...in *toil* you shall eat of it...thorns and thistles it shall bring forth...in the sweat of your brow you shall eat of it..." (Genesis 3:17-19) The general context is human sin and the ongoing consequences of it!

The specific, immediate context is the book of Colossians. The theme of this profound epistle is powerfully stated in Colossians 1:18, "And He (Jesus Christ) is the *head* of the body, the church, and He is the beginning, the first born from the dead, that in all things He may have the *pre-eminence*."

Therefore in Colossians 3:1-17, we are to put off the "old man" with its sin, and put on the "new man" with its godly life. Paul talks about this new life for *wives* in verse 18, for *husbands* in verse 19, for *children* in verse 20, and for *fathers* in verse 21, and then we come to the new life for *employees* and *employers* in 3:22 through 4:1.

Colossians 4:1 holds Christian employers accountable for the way they treat their employees. Do they treat their workers justly? Do they evaluate them fairly? Are they motivated by power and greed and prejudice – or by God's love and concern for their fellow human beings and fellow believers? The only true boss is the Master in heaven!

And what about the employees? What does God want from them? In this eye opening passage of Scripture there are two essential attitudes for the Christian worker or employee.

First a commitment to *sincere* obedience! "Servants (employees) obey in all things your masters according to the flesh..." (Colossians 3:22a) Paul is telling those of us who spend as much as half our waking lives working for someone else – to obey our bosses in everything pertaining to the work we do (excluding of course, sinful actions).

Obedience has never been easy or natural for most of us! It is a *learned response*. Many of us had the privilege of parents, teachers and coaches who patiently taught us to obey God and man. Unfortunately, that is not as true for this generation. As a child I loved sports and adored my coaches. I followed their directions reverently and enthusiastically; but when I watch many of the young people today, it is amazing to see how many of them ignore their coaches, talk disrespectfully to them, and quit and walk off the field at the slightest offence! Obedience is always tough and it's becoming tougher for lack of training!

Obedience has to be learned. My first day of Marine boot camp, I remember everything was so loud and I was rushing to the *head* (It was an emergency!) and one of my three DI's barked an order to me. I didn't hear him clearly so I said, "What?" Then he said," You slime ball, if you ever say *what* to me again, I'll…" (He then proceeded to use *"certain unrepeatable threats"* to teach me obedience.) And he ended with these words: "The proper response is not *what* – it is, 'What sir!'" And our loving Lord, with a very different attitude, is teaching us to call Him *"Sir"* by the way we *work*!

In Colossians 3:22b, Paul focuses on the *motive* for our obedience. Notice first the wrong motive: "…not with eye-service, as men-pleasers…" That is, not as hypocrites who only obey while the boss is watching, to impress the boss, and to curry the favor of the boss, for personal gain and advantage! This is not Christ like obedience!

In 2 Kings 5:25-27 hypocrisy and personal gain were the attitude and motive of Gehazi, the servant of Elisha. Elisha was used by God to heal Naaman, the commander of the army of Syria, of leprosy; but Elisha, the man of God, would take no payment from Naaman. But Gehazi lied to Naaman and took money and merchandise from him and then he lied to his godly boss, Elisha. And God's judgment struck Gehazi with Naaman's leprosy! Christian employees are not to be hypocrites – men pleasers.

Notice second, the *right motive*: "…but in sincerity of heart, fearing God." Christian employees are not to act deceitfully, hypocritically. We are not to be man-pleasers; rather, we are to behave sincerely, honestly with integrity – fearing God. *God pleasers*!

When I first began working at Washington Bible College, my major duty was as Athletic Director. I was told that my first priority had to be the Intramural Sports Program which was in desperate condition and needed emergency care. The first two weeks on the job that summer, I worked almost non-stop on an exciting, well organized and vastly improved program for the students when they returned for the next academic year. I had soccer and volleyball, and basketball and softball – I even had a men's and women's team in each society, so they could cheer for one another and support one another. I even tried to sneak in co-ed wrestling as an athletic event! But that wasn't too well received by the administration!

Everything was ready – it was dynamic! But I had failed to consider one major fact - one of my superiors (and I had many), was a fanatic about shuffleboard, which is not normally the centerpiece in top 10 sports programs! But he loved it anyway! So the day I presented my program, the fruit of scores of hours of planning and detailed preparations, he browsed it for 2-3 minutes and then made his only comment: "Where's the shuffleboard?"

My first, secret response was to use him for a shuffleboard! Have you ever felt that way about a boss?

My second, secret response was to be a hypocrite and to give him what he wanted and pretend to agree with him about the "strategic importance" of shuffleboard, getting on his good side so I could get my own way later!

But by the time the Lord dealt with my heart, a few minutes later, I knew He wanted me to show my reverence for Christ by sincerely obeying my boss, and trusting God for the wisdom and patience to implement shuffleboard!

God honored that and my ministry was blessed and my boss, one of the godliest men I have ever known, was greatly used in my life to mature me in Christ. "...not with eye-service as men-pleasers, but in sincerity of heart, fearing God." (Colossians 3:22b)

God really cares about my work, and to please Him I must be committed to *sincere* obedience!

We must also have a commitment to *enthusiastic* hard work! "And whatever you do, do it heartily to the Lord, and not to men..." (Colossians 3:23)

Now I have a confession to make that will shock some of you, and bring others to tears – I have not always liked hard work! I, like you, have had to *work* hard, but that doesn't mean I have always loved *hard* work! To show sincere enthusiasm for work which wears me down physically, emotionally, and mentally is not a "natural" response for me – I must *learn* it from the Lord! "For this reason we also, since the day we heard it, do not cease to pray for you, and to ask that you may be filled with the knowledge of His will in all wisdom and spiritual understanding; that you may have a walk worthy of the lord, fully pleasing Him, being fruitful in every good work and increasing in the knowledge of God." (Colossians 1:9-10)

Notice the two great truths the Lord uses to *motivate* us to honesty, generosity, diligence and enthusiasm in our work in Colossians 3.

First, my *reward* as a Christian is secure! "...knowing that from the Lord you *will receive* the reward of the inheritance." (Colossians 3:24a) I am a child of God by grace through faith – and by grace I will receive from my heavenly Father, my inheritance. It is secure!

Peter declares in 1 Peter 1:4 that "we have been born-again to a living hope through the resurrection of Jesus Christ from the dead, to an inheritance *imperishable, undefiled, and unfading, reserved* in heaven for us..." And the greatest part of the inheritance is to fellowship with Christ face to face, to share His glory and to imitate His character! "But we know that when He is revealed, we shall be like Him, for we shall see Him as He is." (I John 3:2)

My parents would occasionally talk to my sisters and me about our family inheritance – and how when the Lord takes them home one day, we will all share in that physical, material inheritance. But like any children who truly love their parents, we always told our parents, very sincerely: "We hope we never even see that inheritance! We would rather be with you, and have you both happy and in good health until you are 100 years old – and then go to heaven together and enjoy the Lord's presence forever!" And that is the essence of our family inheritance in Christ – crowns and glory and rewards, yes – but most important – "to see *Him* face to face" and "to know *Him* even as we are fully known!" And this awesome inheritance is *secure* – and it inspires us to *enthusiasm* in our present work.

Second, "Jesus Christ is Lord!" (Colossian 3:24b) This is the only use of the phrase "the *Lord* Christ" in the Bible! "The *Lord* Christ" – Jesus Christ is Lord! It is *Him* that we serve, even as we work as Christian employees. Such knowledge of Christ can *revolutionize* our working lives!

CONCLUSION

In the modern history of Europe, 1848 was the "*Year of Revolution*." It was also the year that a man who had been greatly influenced by the gospel, but who had eventually rejected it, a man named Karl Marx, published the revolutionary classic, *The Communist Manifesto*.

But Marx died. His vision was never realized – even today his concept of revolution is normally encouraged through the barrel of a gun! And much of communism is already collapsing under the weight of its own spiritual, philosophical and moral bankruptcy.

But the Lord says, a true revolution is still possible in the work-place today – but it will not be a revolution founded on materialism or atheism and a corrupt understanding of history – rather, it will be the revolutionary behavior of those motivated by the *Lordship of Christ* – "For we serve the Lord Christ!"

God really does care about my work! And to please Him, I must be committed to *enthusiastic, hard* work!

We differ in one *insignificant* way – we all work at different jobs! But we are united in one very *significant common purpose* as believers, to be full-time Christian workers, by the *commitments* we make and the *attitudes* we display.

One day, we will all stand before the judgment seat of Christ and give an account of the life we have lived since we trusted Christ – even our life as employers and employees! "And he who does wrong will be repaid for the wrong which he has done, and there is no partiality." (Col. 3:25)

So let's listen to our awesome Lord, "the Head of the Church!" Let's give Him first place in everything – even in the workplace!

So can the church actually hold its business people (and everyone else) accountable to obey the eighth commandment – "thou shalt not steal"? And the answer is "yes" – if and only if – the church is willing:

- To teach the people to make wise investments
- To exercise church discipline
- To teach the people to *work well*

"And whatsoever you do, do it heartily, as to the Lord, and not to men!" (Col. 3:23) Soli Deo Gloria!!

Notes

1. *Christianity Today*, January 2011, pg. 26.
2. *Funk and Wagnalls Encyclopedic College Dictionary* (Funk & Wagnalls, New York, 1968), pg 10.
3. *Church Around the World*, News Bulletin, March 2011, pg. 2.
4. Through an Internet search, you will find many sites that reproduce this story.
5. Radio broadcast, personal testimony by Adolph Coors IV.
6. Mark Ritchie, *God in the Pits – Confessions of a Commodities Trader* (Thomas Nelson Publishers: Nashville, TN, 1989). pg. 264.
7. Dennis W. Bakke, *Joy at Work* (Pearson Venture Group: Seattle, WA, 2005), preface, pg. 13.

The Eighth Commandment for Seminaries

LUDER WHITLOCK

LUDER WHITLOCK

Dr. Luder G. Whitlock, Jr. is a Senior Fellow of the Trinity Forum and served as its executive director from 2003 to early 2008. He currently serves as president of Excelsis, an Orlando-based nonprofit. Earlier in his career he was for many years president of Reformed Theological Seminary.

During his earliest years of ministry in Florida and Tennessee pastorates, Dr. Whitlock traveled widely as a speaker and preacher, was engaged in camp and conference leadership, and accepted multiple responsibilities within his denomination.

Dr. Whitlock joined the faculty of Reformed Theological Seminary (RTS) in 1975 and, at the age of 37, was appointed president, a position he held for 23 years. At the time of his retirement, he had the longest tenure of any active seminary president in the United States. Under his leadership, RTS grew from a small regional school to one of the most innovative as well as one of the ten largest seminaries in North America with multiple campuses in the US as well as gateway extension programs in Asia, South America, and Europe.

For many years Dr. Whitlock served on the executive committee of the Fellowship of Evangelical Seminary Presidents, including eight years as chairman. For eight years he served on the executive committee of the Association of Theological Schools (ATS) in the U.S. and Canada, including a two-year term as president. He was one of only five evangelicals to do so in the history of ATS. His service to higher education also took him to the boards of the National Commission on Higher Education, the Graduate Institute of Applied Linguistics, the International Theological Seminary, the International Leadership University, the International Graduate School of Theology, Covenant College, and Westminster Theological Seminary. In addition, Dr. Whitlock serves on the advisory boards of organizations such as In Trust and the International Institute for Christian Studies.

His years of ministry have been marked by an effort to bring mutual understanding and coop-eration within the worldwide evangelical community, which led him to serve on the boards of the National Association of Evangelicals (NAE), the World Evangelical Fellowship (North America region), Mission America, the Lausanne Committee for World Evangelization, and Greater Europe Mission. He has also participated in several interfaith discussions seeking mutual understanding. He was a leader in establishing the Church Planting Center, which now serves several denominations. He was also co-founder and co-president of the International Reformed Fellowship then later assumed a major role in the establishment of the World Reformed Fellow-ship, also serving as convener for the initial global gathering. He participated in founding the Foundation for Reformation, now Excelsis. He also helped establish the Greater Orlando Leader-ship Foundation, a highly successful model for training emerging leaders in a city.

His interest in research about the church and its future led him to become a member of the Barna Institute board and his pro-life commitments resulted in a board term with CareNet, the larg-est pregnancy resource center in the U.S. He has made his experience and insights available to many similar organizations through participation on advisory boards and assisting informally in other ways.

Dr. Whitlock is well known for his role as executive director of The New Geneva Study Bible and a major revision, published as The Spirit of the Reformation Study Bible. He is the author of The Spiritual Quest and has contributed to more than ten other volumes and over fifteen differ-ent periodicals. He served on the editorial council of Eternity magazine and the advisory board for the English Standard Version of the Bible. He also serves on the editorial advisory board of Leadership

The eighth commandment, prohibiting stealing, makes no sense unless people have the right to private property. Therefore, the pos-session of property is obviously approved by God and those who hold property are accountable to God for its use as stewards. How may indi-viduals acquire property? Various means may be assumed, including produc-tive work, wise decisions, or inheritance.

In each instance, work is required, because even when property is inherited or received as a gift---other than inheritance---someone had to work to acquire it at an earlier date. When a person begins to work, they first provide for the basic necessities of life such as food, shelter, and clothing. After that they do the same for their families as needed. Follow-ing that, they typically desire to improve their living conditions, adding comforts as appropriate. In order to accomplish this, deferred gratification is necessary or everything earned and produced is consumed immediately with no accumulation.

Once a person begins to accumulate money or goods, then they have the possibility of increasing their holdings through careful savings or investing. This also enables them to help others, contributing to the greater good that they come to recognize as a moral responsibility. Frugality or thrift, wisely and beneficially implemented, speeds the process by curtailing the waste of time, energy and resources.

It should be apparent that the right to property justifies a work ethic directed to productivity and stewardship. This commandment indirectly guides us to a positive understanding of work, not only as a means of production and accumulation but also as a life calling and commission from God. The working public does not always perceive work this way, rather often sees it as an unpleasant activity that cannot be avoided. It is an impediment to the enjoyment of life. The ideal is retirement when one can relax, pursue recreational interests, and forget work. As one union magazine explained, "The dignity of work is a medieval concept... hopelessly naïve." Even for some Christians, work is a burden caused by sin and an ongoing expression of God's punishment for Adam's disobedience. It certainly is not construed as a delight or as giving meaning to life. Faith finds its focus in specifically religious activities.

But, as the Bible clearly indicates, work is a creation mandate and therefore good (Gen. 1:28, 2:15). It was God's calling before Adam and Eve sinned. He directed them to make this a better world through their work, building something of enduring usefulness and beauty. Work, for us as it was for them, is intended to give meaning and purpose to life. Therefore, Christians should understand all work as a calling by which God is honored and served.

Work makes human flourishing possible, for the individual and all humankind. Through constructive work and the wise stewardship of what is produced, it is possible to develop a richer, more rewarding and enjoyable life for everyone. This is what God intended by the creation mandate and, redemptively understood, gives meaning and purpose to life. It is essential to the oft mentioned "worldview" concept and culture shaping influences.

The important point here is that those who undermine or resist this understanding of work and its benefits are stealing because they ultimately diminish the possibility of human flourishing for everyone. Stealing, therefore, must be construed as more than the act of robbing a person of property. Stealing may occur in many ways, including taking another person's property or possessions. It also includes failing to pay what is due or fair, manipulating or deceiving others for personal gain, damaging a person's reputation, plagiarizing, usury, etc. Actions that prevent benefits to others may fall into this definition too.

Why would someone steal, disobeying God and incurring certain unpleasant consequences? Why would someone steal from others, triggering a series of responses that reduce the quality of life and good of all? Why would someone steal, knowing it might be reciprocated? Selfishness or a failure to consider the consequences of stealing are a partial answer, to which may be added greed, envy, laziness, etc. Would anyone want to contribute to a culture of prevalent theft?

It should be apparent from the summary above that it is not easy to separate the commandment, "Do not steal," from other closely interrelated Biblical concepts such as work, property, comfort, and human flourishing. These interconnected ideas are essential to and shape cultural formation. That cultural formation, coupled with evangelization, is the task of the church.

THEOLOGICAL EDUCATION

Seminaries are expected to become principal contributors to that cultural and evangelistic task as they train future ministers. Although the intellectual dimension of learning is the principal interest, it does not comprise the whole. Moral, ethical formation is foundational to that task. Sometimes we refer to that as character formation. However, spiritual and character formation have often been neglected, or minimized, by seminaries who assumed that it would naturally occur through participation in the ministry of local congregations or through personal spiritual development.

Unfortunately, what might have been assumed of entering seminary students a hundred years ago can, for various reasons, no longer be assumed. Consequently, seminaries must address these character formation needs more realistically and attempt to make appropriate adjustments to compensate for the changes in society and in the knowledge and character of entering students. In doing so, seminaries should be expected to teach these basic principles of the eighth commandment to their students as well as those of the other nine.

As a matter of fact, seminaries must prepare their graduates to help members of their future congregations understand what God intends for their lives---how life should be different as a consequence of this commandment. The problem is that there are so many things that must be taught at seminaries today that there may be minimal formal instruction about the eighth commandment, apart from the ethics classes and assigned readings. That does not justify ignoring the need and finding appropriate ways to address it at seminaries. Union University has recognized this need and addressed it by saturating the total curriculum with ethical instruction. That certainly helps.

Let me suggest several ways this may be considered in seminaries. A good place to begin is with the hidden curriculum of the seminary---that is, what the institution and its staff actually value and how they behave apart from formal classroom instruction. The hidden curriculum is communicated through the institutional culture of the seminary, a far more formidable influence on students than may ordinarily be thought. Therefore, the character and values of those who teach and work at the seminary carry great influence as they come to expression in daily activities. Students observe the realities of institutional life and tend to be shaped more by them than the cognitive input of the classroom.

As we have noted, this commandment assumes the right to personal property---how it is accumulated, preserved, and furthered for a good outcome. That includes the benefit of seminarians, their churches, and the world. The application of the eighth commandment in the daily life of the institution reflects the degree to which the principles of the commandment are embedded in institutional life. The following paragraphs will illustrate some ways in which this may be accomplished.

THE CAMPUS

The campus is a good place to begin, because the development of a handsome, functional campus is for any seminary typically an evidence of productive work and the Lord's blessing. An attractive well-kept, well-furnished campus reflects accomplishment and good stewardship. It also suggests that the same experience may, or should, be expected for homes, offices, and church facilities as a result of hard work and good stewardship. On the other hand, an unkempt, dirty campus communicates the opposite: neglect, perhaps abuse of property, and reflects on the failed responsibility of those in charge. Administrators and boards quickly learn that deferred maintenance brings the risk of higher costs of repair or replacement, and perhaps permanent damage, wasting seminary money. Seminaries that maintain their campuses well send a message to their students and constituents.

Therefore, seminaries should accept the responsibility to teach their students and staff to value and help care for the campus as they would their own property. Of course, damaging or defacing the campus or its furnishings is a violation of the commandment and should be dealt with seriously. Stealing books or any other seminary property is equally wrong.

On the other hand, extravagant construction or furnishings may communicate worldly pride or wastefulness and the seminary should be careful not to do so. This does not mean that a seminary should eschew aesthetic enhancement. Beauty and opulence are not the same and a seminary is a good place to exemplify this truth.

THE FACULTY

The physical campus is only one concern. An excellent, well-paid faculty and staff testify to an institutional concern for productivity and fairness. It communicates an institutional priority on providing an excellent education for students. This is the principal task of the seminary and its success rises and falls on the quality of faculty and the quality of their instruction.

It also reflects an effort to create a wholesome environment in which faculty and staff can thrive---students also. For this to occur, work conditions must be good and supportive. Work assignments or responsibilities will be clear, in a supportive context. Those who do not meet expectations will be provided the opportunity and support to improve sufficiently. However, those who do not respond adequately will be released so that students and their future ministries will not be deprived of the education that they need and deserve from the seminary. It should be reasonably clear that a failure to provide the education that has been promised to students is essentially stealing from them and the church.

RESOURCES

Of course, it is expected that other institutional resources, in addition to facilities and personnel, should be appropriate to offering a good theological education. Library resources usually appear early on that list and must be adequate to the curricular requirements, keeping up to date with scholarly research and publications. Today technology is essential to that purpose, as it also is throughout the institution that would remain current in facilitating learning and maintaining external relations, including fundraising.

Training and professional development opportunities must be provided to stimulate improvement for faculty and staff in addition to the usual internal learning and self-improvement that would be expected in a healthy institution. A competent development staff and well-executed plan should ensure adequate financial resources. Endowment funds are justified to offset unforeseen financial downturns and to facilitate positive responses to unexpected opportunities. Those funds must be invested wisely or may experience unnecessary loss.

The management of funds is equally important so that all gifts are husbanded wisely. Funds must be spent as designated. The use of funds is a stewardship, necessitating prudence and thrift. The institution should be committed to spend what is needed to function well, not what may be budgeted, especially if it is possible to spend less than what is budgeted. These things should be done consistently and explained to everyone. It not only instructs but engenders trust.

STUDENTS

The seminary bears some responsibility to teach students to accept their personal financial responsibilities and learn from them. Students should expect to pay a fair/comparable tuition and expect a good education in return. There is no reason why they should not be expected to work at least part-time to avoid accumulating (excessive) debt for the same reason. I worked at least 20 hours per week throughout my higher education, pausing to work full-time for an extended period between college and seminary. It enabled my family to get by financially and reinforced a strong work ethic that has stood me well throughout my ministry.

It is hard to believe that some students have been known to naively accumulate debt of up to $100,000 from college and seminary prior to their graduation, imposing a crushing financial burden on their future. This irresponsible debt accumulation has been enabled, if not encouraged, by institutions that may have a greater concern to maintain enrollments than to teach financial responsibility.

On the other hand, there is no doubt that poor and unusually needy students should receive sufficient financial aid, combined with work, to enable them to continue their education. As mentioned above, other students should not expect significant financial aid rather than part-time work. It should be apparent that students who have accumulated heavy college debts should not expect the seminary to subsidize that college debt through substantial aid by the seminary. That would be benefiting the college they attended at the expense of the seminary. It would also be imposing an unnecessary financial burden on the donors to the seminary as well as the seminary itself.

Although it not usually considered to be germane to the standard seminary curriculum, there must be some way to help students learn about money, business, and capitalism so they can understand the people to whom they minister. They should learn about risk/reward, labor, etc. This can probably be incorporated into class instruction without adding extra classes as Union University is attempting to do. It may also be part of orientation, student services, or internships and field experience. If ministers are to understand the world in which their parishioners live and know how to help them develop a healthy Biblical understanding of work, property, and related issues, this is necessary.

To this end, students should commit to lifelong learning in order to add value to their ministries year after year. A failure to keep on learning essentially robs the congregation of the expected benefit of their minister's continued professional growth. Early on, students will learn to give attention to the development of personal libraries, reading books and magazines. Following graduation, they will be encouraged to continue their professional development through courses, conferences, degrees, etc. Other forms of learning will be encouraged too.

Also, students should be taught what plagiarism is early in their seminary experience and be warned to avoid it while in seminary and throughout their ministries.

MINISTERS

If the seminary is successful in accomplishing its responsibilities for shaping the character and understanding of its graduates, then as ministers they will consistently set examples of good work and wise stewardship for their congregations. They will seriously address the importance of providing for their family needs. Careful expenditure of family income should rank high among priorities.

Ministers sometimes deserve the reputation of not understanding anything about business or money. As a banker once told me, he was warned by his superiors about the financial irresponsibility of the three "P's": plumbers, photographers, and preachers. All three proved to be untrustworthy in repaying loans, requiring him to take special care. Fiscal responsibility, with prudent care of family needs, enhances a minister's reputation just as the failure to do so tarnishes it.

Ministers should advance the ministry of their local congregations, their first responsibility after their families. This is what they are called to do and the welfare of the local congregation usually rises and falls with the quality of their leadership. Failure denies their congregations at least some of the blessings that could follow competent ministry.

In addition to the above responsibilities, ministers should educate their congregations regarding the Biblical view of work as a noble Christian calling. All morally acceptable vocations are seen as spiritual callings, not merely those that are specifically religious. In doing so, they dignify the work of all parishioners and illustrate its redemptive benefits. As Calvin put it, "Every individual's line of life, therefore, is, as it were, a post assigned to him by the Lord, that he may not wander about in uncertainty all his days." This also clarifies the means to support and advance the ministry of the church. If no one works and produces, there will be no extra for support of the church as has been the case since the early church was born. It also results in an absence of resources to advance the gospel locally and globally.

Through their teaching and personal example, ministers must demonstrate the approved means for family care and human flourishing by work and good stewardship. They should also be advocates for fair wages for all staff and for a strong work ethic by staff in return.

Although some ministers have been known to pay little attention to finances and have difficulty managing their personal budgets, the church budget is equally a matter of importance that may not be ignored. They must give suitable care to church finances so that the budget is balanced and designated gifts or funds are spent accordingly.

Stewardship becomes a matter of the welfare of the whole congregation as well as its impact on its immediate community. It affects decisions regarding the addition and maintenance of facilities so that the church facility inevitably becomes a testimony to the faith and steward-ship of the congregation. The same can be said for staffing, including the tendency to overstaff, thus wasting funds that might be spent more wisely elsewhere.

CONCLUSION

It is far too easy, in dealing with the eighth commandment, to focus on stealing the wealth of others rather than the implied obligation to create wealth for personal or universal benefit. Recently, a business book entitled The Puritan Gift by Kenneth and William Hopper called attention to the beneficial influence of Christian thinking and behavior on the future of America. Among the characteristics of this Puritan faith were the desire to establish God's reign on earth as in heaven, the subordination of personal interests to the good of all, and the ability to marshal financial, human, and material resources for a single useful purpose:

> It was first brought to the shores of North America in the sev-enteenth century by the migrants who founded the Common-wealth of Massachusetts, a political institution that has survived and prospered for almost four hundred years... In the nine-teenth century, it underlay a series of inland migrations and the building of a network of canals and railroads that opened up, and bound together, almost an entire continent. In the twenti-eth, it generated unimaginable wealth that enabled the citizens of the United States, among other things, to fight two simul-taneous wars, one in the Atlantic and one in the Pacific, and to send a manned spaceship to the moon. (Hopper, Kenneth and William Hopper. The Puritan Gift. New York: I B Tauris & Co., Ltd., 2009. P xxiii, 3.

Reclaiming these great Biblical truths in the seminaries and churches may lead to another era of material and spiritual blessings.

APPENDIX

THE EIGHTH COMMANDMENT: Thou Shall Not Steal

CHART OF DUTIES AND SINS AND THEIR APPLICATION TO BUSINESS*

*The source of these duties and sins is the Westminster Larger Catchesim. Verses are those referred to in the Catechism with some added when appropriate. The duties and sins have been combined where possible to make a single topic.

• Property Rights: Unjust Taking From Another •
• Business Transactions •
• Legal Matters •
• Competition •
• Entity Operating Strategy •

PROPERTY RIGHTS: UNJUST TAKING FROM ANOTHER		
Topic/Activity	Bible Verse	Business Application/Situation

1. Theft - Stealing	Eph 4:28 Ps 62:10	• Taking what is another's without compensation or permission.
		  - One can steal time, talent and treasure.
		• An HR example of stealing time and talent is done by keeping a person on a job with no hope of promotion, but leaving the person believing promotion is possible.
		• The list of theft actions in business is long, but here are a few:
		  - Embezzlement
		  - Using company property for private purposes - construction people for home repairs
		  - Working on personal matters on company time
		  - Leaving and taking clients, customers, IP and staff to one's new company - goodwill stealing
		  - Using software without paying a license
		  - Breaking into data bases for competitive information
		  - Piracy on the high seas and truck stops

1.a. Receiving Stolen Property	Pv 24:24 Ps 50:18	Gray market goods, use of software provided by one who did not pay for it, trading on inside information, using competitive information published without permission.
1.b. Failing to Return Lost or Misplaced Property	Lev 6:2-5 Ex 23:4,5 Lk 19:8	The duty is to return the property, which necessarily includes a reasonable effort to find the owner.

PROPERTY RIGHTS: UNJUST TAKING FROM ANOTHER		
2. Extortion	Matt 23:25 Ezek 22:12	Extortion is the taking of goods or services by coersion. Unfortunately, business transactions can be designed where one side is forced to pay or to provide services to the other's advantage. • A "you scratch my back and I'll scratch yours" can often be extorting or even bribing. • The key to avoiding extortion is maintaining the other party's freedom not to fulfill an agreement or receive adequate compensation for the goods or services. - Premium fees for delivering what would have otherwise been done under a contract. Not included in this are overnight delivery service fees or upfront fees to accommodate a customer's specific request.
3. Usury	Ps 15:5	Forcing high rates of interest for capital that are not warranted by the risk of the financing. • Micro finance has shown that many of the lending practices could be redesigned to eliminate the risks that created the justification for the higher interest rates.
4. Bribery	Job 15:34	Paying or gifting to influence behavior. • Both the receiver and the payor err. • A receiver, because of requiring added payment to do what one is to do. • A payor because the bribe is to get additional benefit. Key challenge in business today is the cultures where bribes are part of "the way things work." The U.S. makes such payments illegal. - Tips and incentive pay can morph into bribes. - "Pay to play" where a company makes donations in order to build relationships so that contracts are won is viewed as a form of bribe. - Bumping fees to get ahead of the line can have the effect of bribery.

PROPERTY RIGHTS: UNJUST TAKING FROM ANOTHER		

5. Vexatious Law-suits	1 Cor 6:6-8 Pv 3:29-30	See also legal dealings.
		• Many times suits are brought to extract funds.
		  - HR example is a suit claiming wrongful dismissal: most settle for avoided litigation costs.
		  - Similarly, accounting firms are sued for fraud and false financials, whether culpable or not.
		  - Or product liability for known hazards, such as hot coffee.

6. Unjust Enclosures and Depopulations	Isa 5:8 Micah 2:2	This is one of the more poorly understood aspects of the Reformation understanding of the Eighth Commandment.
		• In short, it was the fencing of public and tribal lands for private use.
		• In current times, it can be likened to patenting a common process.
		• The concepts behind gleaning apply here. Gleaning is specific to Israel and had important social implications, all of which are understudied today.
		• Depopulation is a large business issue today, but is understudied and under-commented upon. The specific aspects of depopulation and government actions will have long-term effects on businesses and communities. See Gen 1:26-28 for the first commandment, which is about population.
		• Examples
		  - While there is an effort to protect such public intellectual property, much is getting through the system.
		  - Governments have this effect with regulations, which restrict commerce based on meeting market's choices.
		  - Currently fast food is suffering these rules.
		  - The results are burdens on the consumer.

PROPERTY RIGHTS: UNJUST TAKING FROM ANOTHER		
7. Ingrossing Commodities to Enhance the Price	Pv 11:26	Here we go directly to commodity speculation and market manipulation, such as OPEC's control of pricing. The major reason for the Eighth Commandment contrast is that if the world is God's, then we should not hoard or take advantage to our benefit. Instead we should do all we can to use God's resources to be a blessing to God's people. • The modern view of pricing at the point of "what the market will bear" and "maximization of profits" would be generally viewed by the Reformers as inconsistent with the Eighth Commandment. • Modern finance theory can generate a good understanding of the costs of capital that need to be covered with the price for an appropriate pricing strategy. • Using hoarding and other techniques to keep prices up is inconsistent with non-stealing.
8. Other Ways to Withhold Another's Property	Job 20:19 James 5:4 Pv 21:6	This is an interesting catch-all, but the point is keeping what belongs to others, when we can deliver it. • It is inconvenient to stay open so that a person can get his repaired car, but that would be included in this concept. • It is amazing how putting the customer or others first will clarify whether a business is failing here.
9. Unjustly Enriching Ourselves	Job 20:19 James 5:4 Pv 21:6	Unjust is the hard term. Unjust covers all of these provisions. Enriching ourselves is OK, but not if it is unjust - where the other party has been shortchanged or deprived.

BUSINESS TRANSACTIONS		
Topic/Activity	Bible Verse	Business Application/Solution
1. Weights and Measures	"1 Thess 4:6 Pv 11:1 Pv 20:10 Deut 25:13-16 Lev 19:33-36 Mic 6:10, 11 Ex 22:22,23 Zach 7:9,10"	Weights and measures are to be consistent with the representation. The Bible speaks of false weights and measures and also diverse weights and measures. • Variations in pricing of the same product raise a concern. The Reformers discussed this matter, but modern business uses volume pricing to justify variations in pricing. - The burden generally falls on the smaller company - the equivalent of the poor/widow and orphan
2. Removing Landmarks	Deut 19:14 Pv 23:10	Property lines were determined by landmarks. Moving the landmark was a way to increase one's land by taking another's. • Copyright infringement can be similar to moving a landmark
3. Injustice and Unfaithfulness	Amos 8:5 Ps 37:21	While much of this is covered in the specific duties listed herein, the attitude highlighted should not be missed. • Many times business is done with a grudging attitude, leading to actions that cause us to squeeze our conterparties. • Unfaithfulness is a modern trait with the economic concepts of "what the market will bear" and "to the highest bidder." - Unfaithfulness in employment and relationships are highly driven by the willingness to change positions or relationships for more money. - Loyalty is another term useful in the evaluation of unfaithfulness.
3.a. Matters of Trust	Lk 16:10-12	Matters of trust in business are many fold. • Board and management positions, where the company should come before self-interest. • Allowing management to buy a company, then recap substantial gains is a recurring example of breach of trust. • Trading on insider information or back-dating options are breaches of trust. • Using customer information with the customer's competitor is a breach of trust.

BUSINESS TRANSACTIONS		
4. Fraudulent Dealings	1 Thess 4:6	In part this is covered in false weights and measures and faithfulness in contracts and dealings, but it also warrants its own attention. In the complex world, it is possible to mislead a party by either misrepresenting or abstaining from divulging sufficient information. Much of the call for government regulation is to address this matter. • Subprime mortgage lending in 2005 -8 as claimed to be fraudulent because the borrower did not understand the potential adjustments in interest rates.
5. Oppression	Ex 22:24	Larger businesses run the risk of oppressing the smaller businesses whether the smaller is a supplier or a customer. • Liberation theology uses the term oppression against business, when most of the claimed oppression is a normal aspect of business. Profits going to equity, is an example of claimed oppression, but is actually normal business structure. • Examples of oppression could be: - Lease transactions where higher rents are charged for the smaller tenant. - Suppliers being required to supply the lowest price offered to anyone, referred to as "most favored nation" even if there are other circumstances for the lower price. - Longer payment terms required of the smaller supplier or shorter payment terms for the smaller customer, which they have to accept because the need the business. - Lower pay when there are fewer job options.
6. Withholding Property	James 5:4	"Much of this is covered under other aspects listed here, but withholding what is due another is stealing a number of things from the owner: • The enjoyment of that which belongs to him. • The time value of any monetary asset. • The blessing of not having to worry about receiving that which is due."

Legal Matters		
Topic/Activity	Bible Verse	Business Application/Situation
1. Avoiding Vexatious Lawsuits	1 Cor 6:6-8 Pv 3:29-30	This provision is in a list of activities that are designed to extract from another what is not justly due. Even in the 1600's people used the courts to their advantage rather than getting justice. Jesus and Solomon referenced this same use of the courts. Therefore, the standard for bringing suit is a need for justice in a matter. The following are some examples: • Today many class action lawsuits are vexatious. • Intellectual property suits have moved into this arena. • HR suits for dismissal, discrimination, and compensation are often in this category. • Warranty claims and product liability may fall into this category.
2. Suretyship and Guarantees	Pv 6:1-6 Pv 11:15 Pv 17:18 Pv 20:16 Pv 22:26	One of the more modern violations of a simple bit of wisdom is credit default swaps (CDS). A CDS is effectively a guarantee of the debt of another. CDS were a bit part of the 2007-2008 financial crisis. That wisdom of 3,000 years ago was ignored so systematically, is warning that the principles of the Eighth Commandment cannot be assumed.
3. Contract Truth, Faithfulness, and Justice	Ps 15:2,4; Zach 7:4, 10; 8:11-17	Business depends on contracts, their fair negotiation and their fulfillment. As is noted below, lawsuits are not the basis for good contracts. Our word is our bond remains a key Christian principle in contracts. A big problem for breach of contract is in capital structure arrangements. Debts are not paid as agreed, equity does not get its return, and recapitalizations causes risk changes which are not compensated. Jesus tells a number of parables covering these problems.

COMPETITION		
Topic/Activity	Bible Verse	Business Application/Situation
1. Procure, Preserve, Further Wealth of Others	Lev 25:35 Deut 22:1-4 Ex 23:4-5 Gen 47:14,20 Phil 2:4 Mt 22:39	This concept is grounded in the principle that it is God's world and we do our business as His creatures in His world. • Therefore, we are first to aid others in His world to have success, rather than focusing on our success. • We can do this because the God we serve has the power and capacity to bless us as we bless our competitors. • Example - "Miracle on 34th Street" is an example of sending customers to a competitor when the customer is benefited, even if the competitor is benefited.
2. Covetousness	Lk 12;15	The Tenth Commandment covers this in more detail. It is placed here, because coveting a competitor's customers, products, and employees is a big part of modern business strategy. • The result of coveting can be stealing, but also simply impai+D58ring the other's success. • Part of the challenge of modern "free market" theory is when one goes beyond providing a better product and service in the market and begins targeting a competitor. • Examples: - Recruiting away a contented employee of a competitor. - Designing the new "killer app", which is not customer focused.

ENTITY OPERATING STRATEGY		
There are a number of topics that go to how we conduct ourselves. The proper conduct of our activities reduces the temptation to steal. While it is usual to place these in an individual responsibility category, each has an equal application to the business enterprise. Therefore, the topics are listed here and business application explored.		
Topic/Activity	Bible Verse	Business Application/Situation
1. Moderation in Our Judgments and Affections Concerning Goods	1 Tim 6:6-9 Gal 6:14	If all is God's and has been given to us by Him for His purposes, then we should be careful in our stewardship not to convert these resources to our purposes. • The concept of thrift and frugality needs to be balanced by the concept of furthering our estate. As noted below, God made a blessed world for us to enjoy with Him. • Milton Friedman's "main purpose of a company is to maximize shareholder value" is troubling in implementing many of these operating principles. - As we endeavor to maximize shareholder value, we can overreach in our dealings and violate many of the topics covered herein.
1.a. Inordinate Prizing and Affecting Worldly Goods	1 Tim 6:5 Col 3:2 Pv 23:5 Ps 62:10	We are to be content with what God gives us to use for His glory. • Our affections should be heavenward. For the business this means customer focused, being a blessing to the consumer and God's people. • Riches are not trustworthy, but God is and our trust, even as a business, should be in Him. James 4:13-15. • Many modern business and personal strategies are contrary to this topic. • Relying on and desiring worldly goods is stealing the affection that belongs to God. • Like covetousness and envy, it can cause one to steal from another to get "more."

ENTITY OPERATING STRATEGY		
1.b. Distrustful, Distracting Cares and Studies in Getting, Keeping, and Using Them	Matt 6:25, 31, 34 Ecc 5:12 Rom 12:16	Increasing level of goods and business activity come with increasing responsibilities and other burdens. Businesses can be distracted by these factors. But there are a series of specific warnings in this topic: • Distrustful - the warning of trusting in worldly riches rather than the Creator God applies to companies as well as individuals. • Distracting cares - Even companies' need to recognize the God of Creation and trust in Him to aid in preservation. • Studies - The art of business must not miss the fact that all business is done in God's world. One of the lessons of the 2007-2008 financial crisis is that we can over-study certain business facets, and thus be overly trusting in our ability to do business. Further studies can absorb time and effort that can be put to use in a more God-honoring fashion.

1.c. Frugality	Jn 6:12
	Pv 21:20
		Like moderation, frugality aids in avoiding the situation, which can cause stealing.
		• Modern economics discourages frugality. Rather, all conversations are about spending and increasing spending and consumption.
		• The outcome is borrowing and with borrowing the inability to pay and then the default, which is stealing.
		• Frugality in business will limit growth and lavishness.
		  - In modern times, many successful businesses build lavish offices, inside recreational facilities, and acquire jets as business tools.
		  - But these are all overheads and when down turns come the burden on the business can be very distressing.

ENTITY OPERATING STRATEGY		
2. Provident Care and Study to Get, Use and Dispose of Necessary Things	1 Tim 5:8 Pv 27:23-27 Ecc 2:24 1 Tim 6:17-18 Isa 38:1 Mt 11:8	Here is a contrast to above in that there is a "care and study" in these matters. But the key word of contrast is "provident" rather than the above "distrustful, distracting" care. • Provident is the recognition that God is the provider of all. Therefore, the study is of His law on provisions and function of His world. Business is part of His world. Thus the study is how we conduct ourselves, how He blesses that conduct, and how we are to use His blessings to His glory. • The care and study suggest that it is not a natural ability, but something we are to learn. The fall caused man to no longer naturally want to trust in God's provision or systematically give Him glory. Thus even the Christian must learn this discipline.
3. Rendering to Everyone His Due	Lev 6:2-5	The specific Bible verse context is giving to the owner what has been entrusted to another. But the broader context is we have been entrusted many things and justice is that all people be given what is due to them. • Compensation raises the question of merit-based pay. People should be paid what is due. But a better illustration is the parable of the vineyard day laborers. Matt 20:1-16. • Honoring contracts would be more aligned with this topic.
4. Giving and Lending Freely, According to Our Abilities and the Necessities of Others	1 Jn 3:17 Eph 4:28 Gal 610 Lk 6:30,38	We need to see the difference between giving and lending. • Lending has the expectation of repayment, where giving does not • When a person cannot repay, giving is more appropriate than lending. • "According to our abilities" was included to recognize that God provides us with an ability to give. • "The necessity of others" balances our lending/giving according to the needs God brings to us. But we have a duty to see those needs. The parable of the Good Samaritan is a model of this provision. Luke 10:25-37.

ENTITY OPERATING STRATEGY		
4. Giving and Lending (Con.)		• The problem with public companies is that largess is not a part of business basics, but now moves into philanthropy or "giving back" to the community. There is quite a difference between these modern concepts and what this topic suggests. • Example: - AMEX Open program to aid smaller business with a $25 bonus for shopping at the smaller business. One can call this marketing, for it is part of AMEX's community contribution.
5. Our Lawful Business Calling and Diligence in it	1 Cor 7:20 Gen 2:15 Gen 3:19 Eph 4:28 Pv 10:4 Col 3:22-25 Acts 19:14, 24-25 Job 20:19 James 5:4 Pv 21:6	Lawful callings and unlawful callings go to the notion of whether our actions are engaged to justly treat our neighbor. • When erroneous means are used to enrich ourselves, the calling is unlawful. • A lawful calling is consistent with the notion that the time, talent and treasure are used to God's glory, even in our business activities. • Diligence in our activities is a general biblical principle. Diligence is also a basic business principle, so there should be little doubt about its application. • By way of contrast, below there are a number of weak practices that contrast to these requirements. • In modern business, Christians are challenged to limit business activities to those that are God honoring. For example, there are a number of businesses whose core function is to exploit or satisfy human desires, which are inconsistent with the topics herein. The Christian's challenge is how to set the limits. One Christian finds an activity violates frugality, but another finds it a reasonable expression of God's blessing on mankind. How do we decide? Thus the challenge, and God is clear that Christians will have differing views on these things.

ENTITY OPERATING STRATEGY		
6. Procure, Preserve and Further Our Estate	Lev 25:35 Deut 22:1-4 Ex 23:4-5 Gen 47:14,20 Phil 2:4 Mt 22:39	This topic includes part of the topic in Competition. We are to aid others and still aid ourselves. All this is to be to God's glory. We can see the complication of this matter. • Modern man would challenge these two as "oxymoron" because they seem in perfect contrast. • If we see that our actions are to be centered on God, His providence, and His glory, there is sense to these provisions. • The furtherance of our estate in business means that we are to aspire to greater activities in God's world for God's glory. • It is the purpose that differentiates the Christian business person from the general market, because the market emphasizes self-interest and self-aggrandizement, whereas the Christian emphasizes all to God's glory.
7. Activities That Waste Resources		This topic list can be easily confined to individuals, but is provided here with some business applications
7.a. Envying the Prosperity of Others	Ps 73:3 Ps 37:1,7	Some of our internal and external competition is based upon envy as well as coveting. Both are errors and can lead to further errors, including stealing. • Envying is a heart attitude. Jesus warned about heart attitudes in the Sermon on the Mount. • Businesses can create a culture of envy as well as individuals. The result will be similar improper actions.
7.b. Idleness	2 Thess 3:11 Pv 18:9	Wasting the time, talent and energy that God has given us is stealing from God the benefits it could create. • Companies become content with their level of activity and become idle. The concept of a "cash cow" is very close to idleness.
7.c. Prodigality	Pv 21:17 Pv 23:20, 21 Pv 28:19	Lavish expenditures would be an application to business. This is a contrast to being modest and frugal, as discussed above.

ENTITY OPERATING STRATEGY		
7.d. Wasteful Gaming	Pv 21:17 Pv 23:20, 21 Pv 28:19	As with prodigality, it is the abuse of stewardship of resources God has given to us to be used for His glory. • Many would find that gaming and games of chance fall into the wasteful category. • Modern sports have a similar element of expenditure that is inconsistent with frugality. • The challenge of business is addressing business entertainment at games, being in the business of providing gaming. All of which do not create an environment of frugality.
7.e. Other Ways that Prejudice Our Estate	Pv 21:17 Pv 23:20, 21 Pv 28:19	The chairman of Unilever in a private meeting expressed the concept of actions that could prejudice the business's estate, by noting when told of a business risk in an acquisition target, "I was entrusted with this company and when I leave it will be stronger. Therefore, I will not allow such a risk in this company, even if you indicate that it is low risk or manageable." Lehman Brothers wishes it had this kind of chairman. • Too many companies today do not appreciate the risks they are building in to the company with modern business thinking. • In this list of topics there are many practices, which if adopted, will lead to a prejudice against our business estate.
7.f. Defrauding Ourselves of the Due Use and Comfort of the Estate God has Given Us	Ecc 4:8 Ecc 6:2 1 Tim 5:8	God cares for us and our companies. He promises to and does give to us what is necessary for our comfort on the earth. Part of the outcome of God's providence is a life of joy with Him. Our businesses should be places where our people, customers, and suppliers all experience a measure of God's abundance and blessing. • When we fail to adhere to God's requirements in business, we defraud ourselves of this blessing. Failing to be diligent in business can lead to business failure. Failure to honor contracts can lead to business declines. • Business failure means stress for all parties, in short, we will have deprived ourselves of the blessings God would have us enjoy.

THE EIGHTH COMMANDMENT:
Thou Shall Not Steal

BUSINESS EXAMPLES*

*In the text are a series of examples of business application of the principles of the Eighth Commandment.

The cases are alligned with the Confession's topic/answers.

Cases are either Positive (as marked), where theft is not involved; or Negative, where theft is involved.

PROPERTY RIGHTS: UNJUST TAKING FROM ANOTHER		
Topic/Activity	Text Page	Business Application/Situation
1. Theft - Stealing	31 102 31 45 99 99 100 293	• Identity theft. -Intellectual property theft costs • Safety taken and security required. • Positive - King of Tyre and supplying Hiram as skilled crafts man for building the temple and Solomon paying for the resources. • White collar crimes and the cost of theft. • Hayes International - shoplifting thefts • U.S. Chamber of Commerce - 75% of employees steal. • Community Uplift Ministries taken by local individual
1.a. Receiving Stolen Property		
1.b. Failing to Return Lost or Misplaced Property		
2. Extortion	294	• Positive - CoorsTek unwilling to sign contracts that contained inappropriate provisions.
3. Usury		
4. Bribery		
5. Vexatious Law-suits		
6. Unjust Enclosures and Depopulations	31	• Security. Due to security concerns, restrictions on access to businesses is limited, thereby reducing commercial interactions. Arguably not unjust, but see both the taking of freedom and of enclosures reducing access.

PROPERTY RIGHTS: UNJUST TAKING FROM ANOTHER		
7. Ingrossing Commodities to Enhance the Price	322 323	• Movie Informant showing case of price fixing. • Lysine Cartel engaging in price fixing to take advantage of customers.
8. Other Ways to Withhold Another's Property		
9. Unjustly Enriching Ourselves	89	• Ironside and the cobbler, where the quality of work is more important than producing low quality goods. Producing low quality goods is done to unjustly enrich the maker at the customer's expense.

BUSINESS TRANSACTIONS		
Topic/Activity	Text Page	Business Application/Situation
1. Weights and Measures	105	• Rockwell painting showing butcher and customer where both are trying to cheat on the weight.
2. Removing Landmarks		
3. Injustice and Unfaithfulness	414 421	• Fannie Mae and Freddie Mac failure to respect their separate estate, creating a moral obligation on the part of the U.S. government. • IMF and regulation projecting a protection that is not there.
3.a. Matters of Trust	260	• Positive - U.S. Chamber of Commerce: fostering trust in business.

BUSINESS TRANSACTIONS		
4. Fraudulent Dealings	100	• Insurance fraud is $80 billion; 16% is car fraud.
	100, 441	• Enron - April 2001 the 7th largest Fortune company to November $1 share, then bankrupt.
	100, 441	• Bernie Madoff dealing fraudulently with his clients.
	257	• Ananias and Sapphira's stealing from God.
	337	• Worldcom fraudulent numbers due to price pressure.
5. Oppression		
6. Withholding Property		

LEGAL MATTERS		
Topic/Activity	Text Page	Business Application/Situation
1. Avoiding Vexatious Lawsuits		
2. Suretyship and Guarantee		
3. Contract Truth, Faithfulness, and Justice	294	• Positive - CoorsTek unwilling to sign contract with clauses that they could not comply with.

COMPETITION		
Topic/Activity	Text Page	Business Application/Situation
1. Procure, Preserve, Further Wealth of Others	45	• Positive note - King of Tyre helps Solomon build the temple to God; supplying both talented craftsman and resources. While paid for by Solomon, it was consistent with this requirement, because kings are always in competition.
2. Covetousness		

ENTITY OPERATING STRATEGY		
There are a number of topics that go to how we conduct ourselves. The proper conduct of our activities reduces the temptation to steal. While it is usual to place these in an individual responsibility category, each has an equal application to the business enterprise. Therefore, the topics are listed here and business application explored.		
Topic/Activity	Bible Verse	Business Application/Situation
1. Moderation in Our Judgments and Affections Concerning Goods	49 297	• Positive - Unilever chairman who avoided risk to prserve the value of the enterprise. • Positive - CoorsTek company values.
1.a. Inordinate Prizing and Affecting Worldly Goods	335 339	• Positive - Clearfield Wholesale Paper owner prayer for God to provide daily provisions. • Tyco chairman's exploiting of corporate assets for personal pleasure.
1.b. Distrustful, Distracting Cares and Studies in Getting, Keeping, and Using Them	441	• Howard Hughes leaves all his worth at death, showing the waste of accumulation.
1.c. Frugality		
2. Provident Care and Study to Get, Use and Dispose of Necessary Things	245	• Harvard Business School's experience in trying to teach business ethics.
3. Rendering to Everyone His Due	276 295	• Positive - McDonalds example of developing and respecting talented individuals. • Positive - CoorsTek paying suppliers timely.
4. Giving and Lending Freely, According to Our Abilities and the Necessities of Others		

Entity Operating Strategy		
5. Our Lawful Business Calling and Diligence in it	276 414	• Positive - Individual's diligence in his work at McDonalds. • Positive - Citigroup taking action to add capital.
6. Procure, Preserve and Further Our Estate	100 440	• Arthur Anderson bankrupt due to failure to protect its reputation. • Adolph Coors trusting in business rather than God.
7. Activities That Waste Resources		
7.a. Envying the Prosperity of Others		
7.b. Idleness	415	• Lehman Brothers in action in the face of liquidity crisis.
7.c. Prodigality		
7.d. Wasteful Gaming	401 409, 413	• Long Term Credit - math formulas that did not adequately consider the risks of the market place. • Bear Stearns, Citigroup, et.al, using portfolio theory and leverage creating excess market risks.
7.e. Other Ways that Prejudice Our Estate		
7.f. Defrauding Ourselves of the Due Use and Comfort of the Estate God has Given Us	401 401	• Positive - Unilever chairman who avoided risk to preserve the value of the enterprise. • Lehman Brothers, AIG, Citigroup, Merrill Lynch, Bear Stearns all engaging in business practices that put the company at risk.

INDEX

288, 352, 355, 389, 444
Creation: 15-19, 39, 42, 100,
102, 111-113, 126, 143, 189,
205, 235, 269, 270, 312-316,
387, 389, 432, 446
Creator: 16, 28, 42, 50, 91,
102, 111, 159, 201, 222, 243,
280, 285, 315, 429, 432
Curse: 73, 77, 79, 80, 257,
299, 313, 380, 387, 438, 448

D

Decalogue: 14, 35-43, 52, 83,
112, 113, 161, 170, 311
Declaration of Independence:
28, 262
Depravity: 95, 333, 446
Divine: 16, 142, 176, 216-219,
253, 261, 298, 312, 314, 368,
379, 381, 383
Doctrine: 90, 161, 384,

E

Enron: 100, 101, 244, 258, 342,
343, 441
Enterprise: 19, 20, 98, 235-237,
242, 268, 275, 319, 348, 381,
385, 390, 402, 403, 408, 416,
418-420, 422
Equality: 28, 29, 114, 160, 180,
184, 190
Eschatological: 313

F

Fellowship: 16, 75, 313, 381,
387, 431, 451
Flourish,-ing,: 14-22, 50, 89,

111-115, 119-133, 159-162,
172-174, 177, 221, 285, 302,
303, 394, 457, 458, 463
Forbidden: 21, 25, 39, 40, 44,
46, 64, 67, 81, 82, 91, 93-95,
139, 174, 181, 198-200, 203,
205, 226, 230, 325, 358, 366,
378, 394
Frame, John M.: 306, 336,
341, 356, 371, 383, 394
Franklin, Benjamin: 176, 211-
215, 222
Fraud: 99-102, 145, 174, 181,
287, 329-355, 380, 443
Free Market(s): 20, 113, 114,
131-133, 236, 237, 335, 403,
416
Freedom: 20, 30, 31, 59, 127,
129-133, 147, 162, 172, 186-
188, 223-226, 271, 273, 280,
353, 377, 383, 394

G

Generosity: 17, 66, 274, 318,
451
Glorify: 24, 25, 126, 131, 176,
199, 235, 312, 367, 383
Governance: 159, 339-341,
345, 347, 348, 352

H

Holiness: 79, 82, 256, 312, 436,
443
Humanism: 115
Humility: 261, 272, 275
Huntington, Samuel P: 29, 33,
116, 165, 332, 357

SCRIPTURE INDEX